I FOUND THE
KEY TO THE
HEART OF GOD

By the same author:

BEHOLD HIS LOVE
COUNTDOWN TO WORLD DISASTER — HOPE AND PROTECTION
  FOR THE FUTURE
FATHER OF COMFORT (Daily Readings)
FOR JERUSALEM'S SAKE I WILL NOT REST
IF I ONLY LOVE JESUS
IN OUR MIDST — JESUS LOVES AND SUFFERS TODAY
IT SHALL COME TO PASS
MY ALL FOR HIM
NEVER BEFORE IN THE HISTORY OF THE CHURCH
POLLUTION — BUT THERE *IS* AN ANSWER
PRAYING OUR WAY THROUGH LIFE
REALITIES — THE MIRACLES OF GOD EXPERIENCED TODAY
REPENTANCE — THE JOY-FILLED LIFE
RULED BY THE SPIRIT
THE BLESSINGS OF ILLNESS
THE EVE OF PERSECUTION
THOSE WHO LOVE HIM
WELL-SPRING OF JOY (Songs of the Sisters of Mary for
  praying or singing)
WORLD IN REVOLT
YOU WILL NEVER BE THE SAME

By the Sisters of Mary:

THIS IS OUR GOD

I FOUND THE KEY TO THE HEART OF GOD

My Personal Story

Basilea Schlink

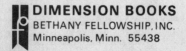

DIMENSION BOOKS
BETHANY FELLOWSHIP, INC.
Minneapolis, Minn. 55438

I FOUND THE KEY TO THE HEART OF GOD
by M. Basilea Schlink

Copyright © Basilea Schlink, 1975
German Edition—1975, Original Title **Wie ich Gott erlebte** . . .
Sein Weg mit mir durch sieben Jahrzehnte

First British edition published in 1975 by Marshall, Morgan &
Scott Publications Ltd., London, under the title, **A Foretaste of
Heaven**.

This English edition published in 1975 by Bethany Fellowship,
Inc., by special arrangement with Marshall, Morgan & Scott
Publications Ltd.

The translation of Part I, originally published under the title
When God Calls, has been completely revised for incorporation
in this book.

ISBN 0-87123-239-1
Library of Congress Catalog Card Number 75-23920

Published by Bethany Fellowship, Inc.
6820 Auto Club Road
Minneapolis, Minnesota 55438

Printed in the United States of America

In deep gratitude to Mother Martyria, who has so faithfully accompanied me throughout the years and without whom I could never have carried out my commission in the Sisterhood of Mary. Only her wholehearted dedication in walking paths of faith with me – especially in acquiring our Land of Canaan – and her continual willingness to make sacrifices, not only in sharing the burden, but in leaving me free for all the other ministries that God has given me has made this possible. May the Lord reward her abundantly.

Contents

Part I

'Almost Always Very Happy'
Childhood and Early Youth in Brunswick, 1904–1920

Gauss Street, Brunswick, was a quiet, residential street with an inviting grove of chestnut trees and a few private homes surrounded by gardens. Yet at times the street was bursting with life. Many children must have been living in the neighbourhood, for a whole band of them, between the ages of eight and twelve, would make explorations through the gardens, although surprisingly enough it was a little girl, and not a boy, that led them . . .

What childhood memories are brought back by the words Number 31, Gauss Street – the house where I lived with my parents and older brother for so many years!

Despite the fact that I was born in Darmstadt (on October 21, 1904), my real home was in Brunswick. My father, a Professor of Engineering, was offered a position at the Technical College in Brunswick when I was eighteen months old, and it was then that we moved into the beloved house on Gauss Street that had a garden, a summer house and a fountain with real goldfish and where I even had my own room. These were my childhood surroundings.

Life in my parents' home was eventful and stimulating, since we participated in the intellectual life of the Technical College, which lay only seven minutes away and where my father – respected by all his students and naturally admired by his little daughter – was Chancellor for many years. My parents followed the affairs of the nation with keen interest, which was intensified by the events of World War I. Thus as a fourteen-year-old I was very conscious of the state of affairs when the German Empire collapsed. This event caused my family to flee from Brunswick, since revolutionary elements tried to take my father hostage.

These experiences, however, did not greatly influence my inner life. The strong ethical convictions of my parents made a far greater impression upon me, as my diary discloses. When I was thirteen I wrote:

L. and B. [two schoolgirl friends] don't think anything about lying, but I do. (January 25, 1918)

Although I received every encouragement in intellectual matters and had God-fearing parents, who prayed with me as a little girl, I grew up without any proper spiritual guidance. In those days my parents rarely attended church and had no contact with believers. They did not yet know Jesus as their personal Saviour. Thus in spite of my many childhood joys, I did not know the greatest joy of all, and could not sing from the depths of my heart, 'I am Jesus' little lamb . . . ' And though I had a cheerful disposition, I was also shy, reserved and fearful. In Scripture classes I heard about Jesus through the Bible stories but my heart was not touched. Thus I had no one to turn to when I was troubled because of a great sorrow my parents were bearing, and often my eyes would be red from crying when I arrived at school in the morning.

Yet, as already mentioned, I was joyful and high-spirited by nature. Despite various upsets in my childhood years I was so filled with the joy of living that I often did not know how to contain all my happiness, and I wrote in my diary:

I am almost always very happy. The world is too heavenly. (January 25, 1918)

Since I could be extremely lively at times, it was an act of grace that I was given a mother who brought me up so wisely, making it plain to me that I must change. Indeed, I took her words to heart, thinking I was the worst child on earth. Repeatedly, I would take stock of my faults such as: 'boisterousness, moodiness, ungraciousness and anger'. But how could this knowledge help me? Likewise as a thirteen-year-old I wrote in my diary:

Oh, I'd like to be good too, but it's so terribly difficult at times. I will try very hard now and earnestly ask God to help me and to show me how to go about it. I just can't do it by myself. I'm so bad. (June 22, 1918)

My mother, like most mothers of that time, naturally wished to have a home-loving daughter who would sit beside her and do needlework. However, I had no desire to sit still. The kitchen was the only place in the whole house that interested me, for I enjoyed trying out new recipes. But most of all I longed to be outside where the children were waiting for their little leader to begin their explorations in the neighbourhood.

Being surrounded by a whole band of children naturally made me even more high-spirited and my father would teasingly call me 'Little Miss Frisky'. My mother had a little scamp instead of a well-behaved daughter. With motherly concern she clearly recognised my liveliness and high-spiritedness and saw where restraint was necessary. In her love she took great pains to set me straight. Thus the development of this side of my disposition was hindered. How I thank God for giving me such a mother, despite the many tears I shed. It was His invisible hand that graciously checked the upward growth of this aspiring little plant, pruning its branches. I thank God for this grace, for it taught me to seek His help at an early age.

Later I felt the restraining hand of God upon me again when I began dancing classes as a fifteen-year-old. Once more I found myself in my element, for dancing and music were my chief delight. As one of the most popular dancers I do not recall ever lacking partners and I enjoyed being in the company of others when we met in various homes. There was one student who meant everything to me at the time and I felt as though I loved him with all my heart. For a year and a half all my thoughts and emotions revolved round him, and my only desire was to know whether he loved me in return. But the Lord, in His bounteous grace, denied me the answer to that question. Once again His hand lay upon me and chastened me, since before the foundation of the world He had chosen me to be His own. With this NO from God my branches were cut down to the stock so that 'the tree would not reach high into the heavens'. Soon my pleasure in dances and other forms of amusement was spoilt, since

15

on each occasion I sensed that the one I cared about did not even seem to be aware of my presence. In my distress I was driven to God. About that time I wrote in my diary:

> What is the point of life? God alone can give consolation in such situations. Without it I could not live with this grief. (July 11, 1922)

The troubles of my childhood and early youth, which at that age I took for real suffering, brought me closer to God. I was taking my first lessons in saying, 'Whatever God does is good. Whatever He does is best for me.' I had met with some of the limitations imposed by this life when we seek to enjoy it to the full. This experience taught me that everything on earth is imperfect – above all, human nature, including my own.

'I think I still have my childhood faith' was an entry in my diary about that time. It was a faith in God, in Christ, without knowing Him as my personal Saviour. However, while I was sixteen, even this faith began to disintegrate. I wrote:

> Of course, I don't believe everything in the Old Testament, e.g. the story of the creation. How can man know how God created the world and other such things? Still, I can't understand how people can become atheists. I could never be an atheist or a materialist. (July 1, 1920)

This last remark stemmed from the good influence of my parents, who were against atheism and materialism. Self-satisfaction and self-sufficiency did not tally with their idealistic way of thinking and this striving to reach a high moral standard was also ingrained in me. I went on to write:

> A person who does not believe in God will not be able to love here on earth. He makes no attempt to achieve perfection or to work on his personality; he only lives for himself and when he dies, it's all over. That is why he tries to make his life on earth as pleasant as possible, regardless of whose feet he treads on. Oh, I'm still so

bad. So envious, jealous, above all so defiant and moody. How awful! I need to improve a lot! I will test myself every day in the small matters until I can control myself and can conquer all that's bad in me so that I may bring sunshine to others. (July 1, 1920)

After I had finished with dancing lessons, a new chapter began in my life – confirmation classes. I had now stumbled into the area of religious controversy. The emphasis on the intellect, the power of judgement and the ability to criticise, which I had inherited from my ancestors, were awakened when I began these classes as a sixteen-year-old. At the time I did not realise how much trouble my intellect would cause me later nor did I suspect what a sinful bondage lies in a strongly critical nature. We had a minister who brought many good and important points to our attention. But despite the fact that he trusted in God, he did not have a personal faith in Jesus as his Saviour. Consequently he taught us a great deal of idealism, challenging us to maintain the moral combat against evil, but his enthusiasm was merely on a human level. At the time I wrote in my diary:

Pastor X said that man can belong to eternity here on earth. We don't have to wait until we die, as some believe. Do I belong to time or eternity? I want to belong to eternity, and I want to work on my personality in order to conquer my Achilles' heel – all my weak points – and become a good and sincere person with God's help. (October 30, 1920)

Pastor X asked, 'What would you do if you knew that you were going to die in twenty-four hours?' One would probably fight with all one's might against one's short-comings and do good, because one would soon be standing before the judgement seat. We should always keep this in mind, for who knows, perhaps we shall be called to our eternal home very soon. Indeed, the will to improve is strong, but the flesh is weak. If only I weren't so terribly moody! (November 27, 1920)

17

Coming to a conclusion, I wrote:

My life cannot continue the way it is. I shall follow the example of the American, Benjamin Franklin, and examine myself every day, making a chart so as to keep track of my improvement. However, first I have to make a list of my faults. At home that would be: ungraciousness, untidiness, unkind remarks, a quick temper – and so many times I've been selfish. (November 27, 1920)

The confirmation classes may well have served to strengthen my ethical strivings, but they also showed me that I was still very far from Christ and had no real contact with God – a new realisation for me.

I am almost convinced that I have made an idol out of X [the boy from the dancing classes]. All my love and thoughts centre round him so that I forget God. I'm not sure, but I don't think I am very close to God, for I do not feel as though Christ is with me when I pray. I am too wrapped up in this world; any close contact with God would be strange to me. I can't quite express it – all I know is that I haven't found the right way yet. When I hear that Christ must come into our hearts, that we should be conscious of Him accompanying us and that we should always be united with Him, it sounds like a foreign language to me. I should like to have such a life too, but where to begin? How does one enter this state? I'm still too wrapped up in earthly things: in love, school, pleasure. I simply cannot understand how great men of God can feel His presence and hear His voice. In my opinion they must sense subconsciously that one thing or another will happen, or that they have to do this or that. Oh, I am searching all the books on this subject, subconsciously looking for something with which I can identify, although what it is I cannot say. All I can say is that I can't find it anywhere. (December 30, 1920)

The knowledge that I was missing something in my religious life was a gift of God, for the truth sets us free.

The confirmation classes brought me closer to the heart of Jesus, although they caused me more doubts. My confirmation instructor found me hopeless. His wife once told my parents that he sometimes came home horrified and said, 'If I had any more difficult ones like little Klara Schlink, I could pack my bags.' I raised so many sceptical questions, most probably in a self-confident and high-spirited manner, that it must have disturbed the class. Finally, he quoted a Bible verse to me, 'The word of the cross is folly to those who are perishing!' With that I was supposed to note that I was bound to perish because of my intellectual attitude! Later, during the confirmation service, he gave me the same Bible verse – this time with the second half as well, 'but to us who are being saved it is the power of God' (1 Corinthians 1:18).

Several years later as a Sister of a Bible college I visited my confirmation instructor. By that time I was serving Jesus and could witness to the power of the word of the cross. He could only exclaim, 'Wonders never cease!'

In my childhood and early youth it was always the same. When my sinful nature sought satisfaction, God sent me a cross so that a part of me had to die. But each time God brought something new to life as a result. During my childhood years I learnt to pray to God for help, because the wise upbringing of my mother made me painfully aware of my shortcomings. Through my great disappointment during the dancing classes I realised in the end that I had made an idol of another person; my thoughts and life revolved round him so much that I forgot God. During my confirmation classes my intellectual attitude and scepticism became a burden to me, because they so grieved my minister, who frequently had to warn me of the danger of being one of the perishing. Painful though this experience was, it was ultimately God who was impeding the growth of my over-accentuated intellect and scepticism, and aiming His blows at my resolute and rational nature to show me my need of a Redeemer. However, in the next year or two I had to suffer increasingly from my strong will and intellectualism before I began to capitulate.

The yearning to draw near to God was born out of these hidden troubles of my childhood and youth, and I had a foretaste of the glory that all affliction brings, for our smallest cross, even the cross of our sins, brings us closer to Jesus.

The Futility of Ethics –
My Encounter with God
Darmstadt, Easter 1921–1923

When I was sixteen and a half, my parents moved back to Darmstadt, my father having accepted a post at the Technical College in his home town. Since my school began four weeks earlier, I arrived in Darmstadt ahead of my parents and stayed with my aunt. If I was high-spirited, bubbling over and full of plans for new escapades as a child, I was even more exuberant and lively as a sixteen-year-old, and often I could not find an outlet for my excess energy. My new field of activity was now my new form where I turned everything upside-down. During gymnastics class, for example, I would teach the other girls the latest dances. In other classes too I was a real problem for my teachers, since I had an answer for everything, and though I was form representative, I had one entry after another beside my name and graduated from the school with a low mark in behaviour. When my parents arrived in Darmstadt, they heard of their daughter's pranks from all sides.

Yet my heart was filled with unanswered questions and a deep longing for God. Of course, I did not let anyone suspect this, and was constantly in opposition to our Scripture teacher, who, as I strongly sensed, did not believe in Jesus. But though my outward appearance was one of self-assurance and confidence, my diary shows that I was inwardly uncertain and seeking answers.

Oh, if only I were still a child and could simply believe everything and be happy! But what can I do if my intellect makes objections and I don't agree in certain matters? No one can give me the answer; I search the books in vain. (May 22, 1921)

I often ask myself if we have a free will at all. In my opinion, no, for God creates people with good or bad, strong or weak characters. Can a person help it if he has bad personality traits and is too weak to resist his sinful inclinations? On the other hand, there are people who find it easy to battle against their weaknesses. I cannot understand this arrangement . . .

Christ died for us, we are told, so that we can conquer sin. But has a person ever conquered sin completely? I am longing to know the answer to these questions, but haven't found it. What is the good of all the beautiful sermons in the world when I doubt the basic principles? I read Schopenhauer on the subject of religion, but I found that he has many strongly atheistic views. Still, these philosophers are most interesting. (May 23, 1921)

That was my innermost state. I yearned for someone to lead me to God, but found no one. Greatly influenced by my brother Edmund, who also studied philosophy later, I read many philosophical works such as those of Schopenhauer, in my pursuit of truth. Yet these certainly did not help me to draw closer to Jesus. I still recall the tours my brother and I made of the bookstores of Darmstadt in quest of books on world views, but I was just as interested in the *belles-lettres*. By the time I was fifteen I had a small collection of art postcards and paid more attention to the history of art and music than to my school subjects. My spirit was hungry and sought nourishment everywhere until I found the fullness of knowledge in Jesus.

But I had not found the Lord yet, and when I was seventeen, I wrote in my diary:

Why can't I enjoy life like others in dancing and superficiality and in having fun? (November 7, 1921)

Christmas time is really splendid, but the inner peace is lacking – I am still searching. Although I no longer act out of conviction, I still hold to the principles which were instilled into me earlier on, and which I don't wish to discard altogether. In my heart I cannot deny the good in man, even though my common sense tells me otherwise. I have a belief in the basic integrity of man. Both believers and atheists act out of conviction, whereas I have nothing. This is the worst possible state. Oh, if only I had some sort of revelation, or could meet someone who would convince me! This uncertainty is terrible! (December 17, 1921)

Why were we born? How can we have a free will when moods come over us which we can do nothing about? Yet if we put on a friendly face when we feel different inwardly, it is nothing but a mask; it is self-deception. Only a higher power can heal us with time. (January 18, 1922)

It was only the incomprehensible grace of God that saw me through these torturous periods of doubts and inner conflict. He let my self-chosen endeavours and my fruitless knowledge come to naught by leading me into new difficulties – as in my childhood and early youth – and thus He kept me from continuing along this pathway.

True to my religion – to strive hard to improve myself – I was determined to overcome my weaknesses. However, the more I strove, the more I realised that I was not advancing.

Everything progresses, only I remain at a standstill. Every day I struggle with myself, and every day I am defeated. Afterwards I see the situation in a new light and can judge the matter more generously and am ashamed at having got upset over trifles. (June 2, 1922)

A certain leading of God brought my frustration to a head. After I finished school in my tenth year at the Lyceum, the next stage was to learn how to keep house. How delighted I was when one of my closest friends from Brunswick came to stay at our home where we could both take lessons from my mother. Then the unforeseeable happened. Much to my distress I developed a dislike for this friend. Living at close quarters with her, I suddenly found her unbearable in her mannerisms and reactions. What should I do? If I showed her my dislike, she would be very hurt, and I wished to spare her. Yet I was too frank by nature to conceal my feelings. In this situation self-control and self-exertion were of no avail. I was faced with my utter helplessness and wrote in my diary:

> The situation cannot remain the way it is. There must be a change – but how? I call R. my best friend and yet I take offence at the most trivial things in everyday life and as a result all understanding ceases and we are no longer in tune with each other. Oh, you miserable creature! If one did not have the hope of a further development in the next world, one could almost seek death out of contempt for the wretchedness of human life. How imperfect and limited are man's will and emotions. But as long as I have the will and as long as my sense of responsibility demands it, I will try to do everything possible to relieve the tension – according to my principle: love must never cease! (June 10, 1922)
>
> In this case self-control is of little use, for I can accomplish nothing by my own will-power. I am at the end of my tether. As a mere human being with an insignificant will, I've reached the point where I can only humble myself before God and accept His grace with thanksgiving. (July 10, 1922)

Even so I had not yet found the way to Jesus. Indeed how can we recognise Him unless He Himself opens our eyes? In the midst of these hardships I made the following entry:

> I believe and trust in God and Christ. However, I am having such troubles, doubts and struggles, and so far no one has been able to lift me out of them. The next thing I shall do is write down my creed, to see exactly what I can believe. I believe in the nobility of man. Ever since I

was intellectually awakened, my innermost feelings and my conscience have told me that this standpoint is the most justifiable one. And I cannot believe the words of Christ, 'No one comes to the Father, but by me!' (July 10, 1922)

Then, in August 1922, came the tremendous moment when I could confess, 'Now I have found the firm foundation', that is, Jesus Christ as my personal Saviour. A number of incidents led up to this event. With all my ethical strivings to live in harmony with my friend and with my search for truth by reading books, I had come to the end of my own resources. I began to beseech God that if Jesus really were His Son, the Saviour of the world, who died on the cross for us and became the Way to the Father, He would reveal this to me somehow. And God answered. I was ill and had to lie in bed for several days. Then one night I was permitted to behold Jesus inwardly as the crucified Lord. When I awoke, joy abounded in my heart – 'I know that my Redeemer lives'. I rejoiced to know that Jesus, the crucified Lord, is the Way to the Father, that He had redeemed me and I could follow Him. What amazing grace!

I did not confide my secret to a soul. Nor was I sure of the next step now that I had found Jesus, for I did not know any other believers. However, God Himself guided me. My parents, who took an interest in all intellectual and religious matters, had a number of biographies and books by people of different religions in their collection of books. They also possessed, without my knowing it, the autobiography of Jung-Stilling.* While I was sick – on the day after that memorable night when I found Jesus – my mother brought me this book. I read it eagerly, almost devouring it. Now I could write in my diary:

Oh, I am so happy and thankful that I have found my Saviour and that He lives within me. Now my heart will

* Johann Heinrich Jung-Stilling (1740–1817), famous eye doctor and professor in Marburg and Heidelberg, Christian hymnist and author, whose memoirs were very popular.

conquer all the torments of my intellect. I know that my Saviour dwells in me and that His love will grow and grow in me. Oh, if only I too could be pure love one day! How I long to sing and compose songs about love, for what could be greater than Christian love? (September 2, 1922)

Now I understand that everything depends on grace – a concept that I could never make head or tail of. Before my confirmation I was certainly on the wrong track when I still made daily entries in a book to see how far I had improved. How little I was able to accomplish by my own efforts! If I had had any idea of the meaning of 'Christ for us', life would not have been such a drudgery, and I should have been happy at the end of the day for having been forgiven for Christ's sake, and have asked for new strength and love. Where love prevails, weaknesses naturally retreat. Of course, we still have to work on ourselves, read God's Word and pray, for then this attempt to put the theory of sanctification into practice will have God's blessing, even though we shan't experience immediate transformation. Without a prayer life we aren't Christians – but I did not know what a prayer life was before. How much I was missing! I was so alone. Now I have to read a lot so that everything remains alive for me. (October 8, 1922)

Other than that I had no spiritual guidance at all. I felt that I must learn how to pray and grow in love, but who was to point out the right way to me? I knew nothing about claiming the redemptive power of Jesus' blood in faith – and real prayer was quite unknown to me.

The Lord, however, had already prepared the way. Several months earlier when I tried to choose a career for myself, I settled upon nursery school teaching, for then I could work with people. In a magazine I found an advertisement for a Protestant Froebel Academy. This advertisement smiled at me like a greeting from heaven, for did not 'Protestant' mean 'Christian'? At the time I thought so. I had to pass through many disappointments before I realised that not everything that is called 'Christian' necessarily implies belief in Jesus as the Saviour. Nevertheless, God had set my heart on fire for this Protestant academy, for there I was to meet Erika Madauss, who was to found the Evangelical Sisterhood of Mary with me later. It was she who introduced me to the Girls' Bible Study Group there, which helped me to grow in the Word of God. The course was due to begin at Easter 1923.

During that last half-year in Darmstadt I made my first attempts at walking as 'a new-born babe in Christ' without any proper guidance – though, in fact, I was not without guidance, since Jesus Himself led me.

As usual, during the winter months, I accepted invitations from the student fraternities, since dancing was my delight. But now I could no longer enjoy these dances so freely, for I felt that they drew me away from Jesus and grieved the Holy Spirit. An entry in my diary at that time reads:

So often I am unable to disentangle myself from non-essentials and come to God. (November 11, 1922)
Now I know for sure that I have to go to Kassel. It's either Christ or the world. If I continue to go to dances, my thought world will belong to Satan. Thoughts of dresses, the desire to be beautiful and popular continually whirl in my head. And I cannot pray when I come home at four-thirty in the morning, carried away with the music, the dancing and the simply enchanting atmosphere – even though my fun was harmless. Afterwards I have difficulty in forgetting all the impressions, and God's Word loses its power. My soul is so taken up with other thoughts that it no longer has room for divine, spiritual thoughts. Therefore I shall be glad when I go to Kassel. (December 18, 1922)

This diary entry marked the end of my dancing days. The Lord made this denial very easy for me, for shortly afterwards I left Darmstadt.

Searching for the Way
Froebel Academy, Kassel,
Easter 1923–Autumn 1924

The Protestant Froebel Academy in Kassel consisted of a large house and courtyard with spacious grounds, on the outskirts of the city. With pure, youthful enthusiasm all 120 students would gather in the garden on summer evenings to dance folk dances and to sing the old folk songs and love songs from the *Zupfgeigenhansel* * to the accompaniment of the lute. This was at a time when the youth movement, although on the wane, was exerting its best influence here. A cheerful, friendly, natural, yet well-disciplined atmosphere prevailed among the girls, and I was glad to be accepted into this circle. Indeed, what eighteen-year-old would not have been happy to live together with so many others of the same age in a house, studying and singing and having fun in such an atmosphere of camaraderie?

Great emphasis was placed upon this good atmosphere by the staff, who considered it their duty to train these young people – the future teachers of the German youth – to be loving, responsible and willing to serve. We were encouraged to take an active interest in the national crises of the time, rather than be overinvolved in our secluded boarding school life. It was an unforgettable moment on November 9, 1923, when we heard of Hitler's first and unsuccessful revolutionary attempt. We could sense the impending upheaval for our nation. As the shades of inflation drew over us, we endeavoured to share our devalued pocket money with each other, for that money also had to buy our daily ration of bread. This was all part of our training, for our teachers set great value on such high ideals.

They were untiring in their efforts to instil in us a sense of duty, prudence and consideration for others. But did they not wish to lead their students to our Saviour, Jesus Christ, as I had assumed upon reading the advertisement for the

* A German youth movement songbook, compiled at the beginning of the century.

Protestant Froebel Academy? For the fine directress with her high moral standards and for the minister who gave religious instruction, Jesus was an ideal figure, rather than the crucified Lord and Saviour. Thus I did not find the spiritual nourishment for which I yearned so much, although I did receive an excellent and invaluable training in ethics. God let me wait some more years before leading me to a Bible college where I found my heart's desire: a Christian fellowship where I could hear about Jesus and be shown the path of discipleship.

Yet during my time at the Froebel Academy God gave me everything that was necessary for my spiritual development. Through our good training He gave me growing insight into my heart, and little by little He convicted me of my sins. God had a definite goal in mind. He did not intend me only 'to rejoice for a while in his light', enjoying the classes and recreation, the conversations and celebrations. He took care to bring me into a group where I could not make friends as easily as I had been accustomed to doing. In this educational system the 120 boarders were divided into family units, each unit having a teacher for 'mother' and living by itself on one floor. After several weeks had passed by, it was discussed which of the boarders should be nominated for election as 'senior' in the new term. The mother and the senior of our family called me to them and said that they could not permit me to be a candidate for this office, although I was qualified for it Such a position would not be good for me, they told me, since I was overconfident and too aware of my intelligence. This news was a blow to me, for the office of senior would have been a great pleasure for me. As senior one held a responsible position, taking part in organising the life of the college, and in helping and caring for the other members of one's 'family'. This blow was painful for yet another reason. The verdict 'overconfident' was completely new to me. After this disclosure I wrote in my diary:

The candidates for senior were announced, and I was

not to be one. All at once everything collapsed. Then I heard why – because I am overconfident and too aware of my intelligence . . . Now I know that I lack the highest virtue of all – humility. Every day I shall ask for humility and much love. I thank God for letting this happen. He can help me. Indeed, I must be grateful to God for this great gain, for coming to know myself better. And if God has brought me into this situation, He will also give me the strength to get over it. (August 13, 1923)

In His great love the Lord showed me my weak point, letting me sense for the first time that nothing stands in His way so much as a self-confident and proud nature, and that humility is the most precious thing in His sight. So often I had been the centre of attention; up to that point I had taken my popularity for granted, since I felt that it was part of my life. Now, during those weeks, I realised for the first time that this had an evil, sinful root – pride and the desire for recognition – since God, in His goodness, denied me the popularity and respect that I was accustomed to receiving.

I wonder what God's intention is for me when He lets me go through such suffering and shows me my greatest weakness without sparing me. More and more I am aware that my ambition and pride are not gratified. I rely too much on the recognition of others, as I well and truly learnt a few days ago . . .

When we envy another person, we can fight this attitude with the weapon of love. But what do we do when the problem is more general – such as the desire for recognition? Again, we must show much love to others, but most of all ask Jesus continually to help us to fight this evil streak. I must really take it to heart that if I wish to be a true child of God I must first humble myself. That is the whole point and probably why I was put in this situation. O Lord, help me! (August 27, 1923)

Truly, it was by the grace of God that I was humbled and corrected. Our troubles and the frustration of our wishes are worth their weight in gold, because they bring us an immeasurable wealth of blessing. By denying me the love and attention of others, God gave me something far more precious in return – a genuine realisation of my sin. As a result I was driven to Jesus, whom I met in a completely new way. He did not let me perish in my proud, egoistic nature, but aimed a blow at it. I gave God my consent and submitted to this chastening, determined to humble myself, as I repeatedly wrote in my diary. Yet I still received no instructions or guidance in following the Lord. But what grace that God Himself took care of my soul! He showed me now that the most important thing was to let others tell me the truth and then take the next step, by doing that which I had failed to do, rather than retire into myself. In this case it meant humbling myself beneath this reproof and serving others in love whenever I had the opportunity. From then on I did this to the best of my ability. After a number of weeks the mother and the senior of our family told me that they had decided I could be nominated for the post of senior after all, since I had not been offended and had been so willing to submit to others and to serve them.

Having come through this experience, I was elected by the boarders in a later term to be chief senior and thus representative of the entire student body. This office revealed new weaknesses in my character, showing me that I was in great danger of letting such leadership, organising and activities fully preoccupy me just as dancing had formerly done. Soon I sensed that my life must change in this respect. And I wrote in my diary:

As the chief senior at the academy, I am so taken up with worries about peoples' lives and other matters that I don't feel like a child of God. Instead of being so affected by such things, I should be abiding in God, taking care of everything in His strength. Because I have not been doing so, I have often become overinvolved, making calculations and trying to work everything out with my limited understanding. All this preoccupies me so much that I can no longer find the way to God. Oh, I beg God to change my life in this respect. I yearn to live in Him alone so that I can be a vessel of His blessing. But how can I be a blessing when I make spirited remarks, which are frequently impetuous, and witticisms about people and things? (Whitsun 1924)

The Lord increased my longing to be freed from being overinvolved in activities, and through my friendship with Erika Madauss He led me to spiritual sources. Erika took me with her to Hoexter, to the large Whitsun conference of the Girls' Bible Study Groups in 1924 – a very special experience for me. Hundreds of dedicated Christian high school girls from all over Germany came to this conference to hear a message about the living Christ, who was calling young people to wholehearted discipleship. This was the message that I had been longing to hear all that time. The Spirit of God was moving in this conference and set my heart on fire to become Jesus' disciple, to become wholly dependent upon Him and independent of people and the things of this world.

That August I could spend a short holiday with my mother in a Christian retreat centre (my parents had been converted the previous year during an evangelistic crusade). There the Lord spoke to me graciously, and gradually I began to see my office as chief senior in His light. In my diary I noted:

I have definitely decided to serve the Lord with all my life and to dedicate myself completely to Him. Therefore, I long for the day when I can leave the Froebel Academy, for although the existence of God is acknowledged there, Christ is little more than a moral teacher. (August 31, 1924)

With all my heart I longed to abide completely in God according to the example of Sadhu Sundar Singh, whose biography I had bought on the way to Hoexter. Yet what powerful elements in my personality still stood in the way of leading such a life! This the Lord disclosed to me little by little.

Give me some of Your infinite love, for often I am so unfeeling and abrupt, with not a glimmer of human sympathy stirring in me. At times I can be so cold and unloving towards others. I know how terribly small and bad I am, but I am trusting in Your grace. In my self-confidence I am always finding fault with others, although I know that they all have been entrusted with a different 'talent' and may have put theirs to better use than I have mine, which outwardly appears so very ethical. Oh, forgive me the sharpness of my critical thoughts. I am still so ambitious and pleased with myself, living in the world and seeking the things of this world, and valuing the opinions of men so highly, being dependent upon people instead of upon You.

O my Saviour, make me wholly Yours. Show me all my sins without sparing me. Let Your light and truth penetrate me and help me to believe in Your grace and power so that I may become more like You. Let my wicked self be dethroned at last and grant that Your love may emanate from me so that others will recognise me as Your disciple. (September 25, 1924)

As a nineteen and twenty-year-old, I had but a glimpse into the innermost recesses of my soul. Yet the Lord revealed more to me after I had finished my education in Kassel in 1924 and began my studies with great expectations that October in Berlin at the Women's College for Social Welfare Training in the Home Mission. I learnt of the college through Erika, who intended to become a Christian social worker. There one could receive a two-year course to train as a social worker and religious instructor – a continuation of my education at the Froebel Academy. Yet my reasons for going to this social welfare training college were not a desire for further education, let alone a career as a social worker. To this very day I can remember how it came about. Erika and I were polishing our shoes together when she told me that after finishing her education at the Froebel Academy she planned to go to Berlin, where one could prepare for the Lord's service and then receive a Christian job. That hit home.

With these same expectations I had gone to the Protestant Froebel Academy in Kassel, without finding my heart's desire; but now, according to Erika, this college in Berlin with its branch in religion was the very answer. Thrilled, I said, 'That's the place for me!' and my parents gave their permission. While I was on holiday, before leaving for Berlin, I wrote a few lines, which expressed my inner state at the time:

O God, I thank You that I can love You so much now. Preserve this inner life, but take away my self-esteem. All that I have comes from You and all the good in me can only be attributed to You, Lord Jesus. That I know very well. I thank You for Your immeasurable love and it is my fervent plea that You come to others too who do not know You yet. This I pray now that I have seen Your glory. Help me not to be unfaithful to You any more, but to fight determinedly against my lukewarmness so that I shall never let You go. Abiding in You is the all-important thing, for then one is strong and can make progress. Help my unbelief! Help me when I suffer intellectual doubts. Help me to overcome my love for the world and the desire for marriage. Let me be wholly Yours so that I may reflect Your nature and win others for Your kingdom, and so that You can bless my work. Lord, I thank You for Your infinite love. Grant that I may grow in You and bring You fruit. Amen.

The book by Countess Waldersee has taught me much. Now I see how faithless I was. I hadn't taken Christ and His cause seriously enough. Now I have examined myself thoroughly to trace the cause of my mistakes and I have pinpointed them. I won't give up the struggle, for according to the Sermon on the Mount God expects much of His children if they wish to inherit the kingdom of heaven. I know very well that I am lost if, in spite of all my knowledge, I bear so little resemblance to Jesus. And so I will wrestle in prayer that I may abide only in Jesus and never forsake Him. I have promised myself that for the rest of my life I shall spend half an hour every day with God before I get up in order to begin the day with Him. (September 1924)

My Wings Are Clipped
Women's College for Social Welfare Training in the Home Mission, 1924–1925

In October 1924, after celebrating my twentieth birthday, I arrived in metropolitan Berlin. What effect did this big city have on me? It brought to light all my hidden longings for the world. After a few days I wrote:

Now I've arrived in the metropolis! At first I was struck with such a desire for the world, for excitement and pleasure that I should have loved to plunge into the life of the city.

At the earliest opportunity Erika and I climbed aboard the open-roofed double-decker buses to make tours of the city, for we were very keen to gain as many impressions as possible of the sights of Berlin, such as the avenue 'Unter den Linden', the cathedral and the old museum with its valuable works of art. Attracted by the sights, we made a different excursion through the city every day. This was all in keeping with the aims of the college, whose hostel was located in the west end. The college especially fostered a broadminded outlook on the world. One was supposed to be able to analyse the intellectual, social and artistic trends of the times, to attend lectures, to visit the theatre and to go to concerts, and at the same time to be well-grounded in the Bible and in Christ. Full of enthusiasm, I plunged into all that was offered in the classes, as well as into intellectual and cultural activities.

If God, in His grace, had not set up definite limits in every respect that year and clipped my wings, who knows whether I might not have found complete satisfaction in these experiences and in a particularly precious friendship. As in all the earlier chapters of my life it was God's NO, the cross that He sent into my life, that was my deliverance. In each case the cross was a bridge that led me into a new and previously unknown land of His love and brought me His nearness and the revelation of His glory. Thus in retrospect there is nothing in my life that I can praise more highly than the crosses that the Lord sent me in every period of my life – each time in a new and different form. Either He denied me the desires of my heart, or He took away that which I treasured and valued above all else at the time, the loss of which almost broke my heart. But in each case such distress gave birth to new life and an undreamt-of blessedness in Jesus. Whenever He took, He gave, in accordance with His word, 'Whoever loses his life will gain it'.

I arrived in Berlin, unconsciously seeking to 'gain my life' in those first weeks. Without realising that something was amiss, I wished to satisfy the longings of my soul and intellect. Soon I discovered, however, that this openness and love for the world and my keen interest in intellectual affairs did not bring me joy and enrichment as I had expected, but rather distress. The desire to marry – a natural inclination in itself – began to get the better of me, and through the intellectual approach in the lectures, especially through the textual criticism, I once more had doubts about my faith and fell into a state of inner conflict as a result. After those first few weeks I wrote:

I have a terrible struggle to resist intellectual doubts and worldly desires. O Jesus Christ, help me and my unbelief! Time and again I tell myself that this is my thorn in the flesh. You must give everyone a thorn to bear, according to his character, so that he can strive to win the Kingdom of God and never lapse into self-satisfaction, which is spiritual death . . . And then reference is made to so many other Bible passages, and these too are supposed to be unauthentic. That hurts deep down inside, for my faith is everything to me. I will not let Jesus be taken away from me, but my faith cannot be very strong if it suffers under these gnawing intellectual doubts. Thus I beseech You, Lord, give me books to read where I can sense Your Spirit at work, for in You alone can we find true redemption and peace. Help me to conquer my doubts, for You are greater than our limited human understanding. (November 9, 1924)

How disappointed I was that the classes caused me such inner conflict. Here too, in the Women's College for Social Welfare Training I had failed to find my heart's desire. I had come to Berlin with the wrong expectations, hoping to find a type of Bible college that would help me to grow in the Word of God, lead me further along Jesus' pathway and thus equip me for Christian service. Instead I found myself in a college for social welfare that only had a branch in religious instruction for parish workers. Later on I was most grateful for all the stimuli I received in studying social and theological matters and the humanities, for they widened my outlook. I am especially grateful for the teaching of Mrs Elisabeth Nietzsche, who later became the directress of the college. However, at the time all I felt was that I was not in the right place for my spiritual development. Unlike most of the other girls, I did not come from a Christian background and thus as a young Christian my thirst for true, spiritual life and the working of the Holy Spirit in the classes was greater than theirs. Moreover, I still lacked the inner maturity to understand properly the other things that were offered to us, and consequently my doubts were able to gain such a hold over me.

Soon I became very unhappy. The big city suddenly lost its charm. It was a trial for me to have to pore over my books and to harass myself with these intellectual doubts that sought to crush me and to rob me of my faith and of Jesus. The little room, which had so delighted me at first and which I had made my little palace, now seemed like a prison. There was not a single garden, shrub or tree in sight. How different this hostel was from the Froebel Academy in Kassel where for educational purposes there was an active community life in the form of a family system and where the boarders were encouraged to share each other's joys and sorrows.

Although life was pleasant in Berlin with a good Christian atmosphere under the leadership of the honoured directress, Countess von der Schulenburg, we lived more like university students. Apart from sharing a floor together, we lived independently, and I felt lonely as a result. In addition, I no longer had a field of activity as in Kassel where as chief senior I organised activities, worked with people, helped them and was loved and respected by them in return. Here in the social welfare training college I was one of the youngest; no one took much notice of me and I was left to myself. Thus, I concentrated all my affection and attention on a particular friendship at that time. This friendship was like an island in the stormy seas for me. It was my refuge. The mutual affection and understanding was my joy.

But once again God, in His wisdom, said NO. First He placed many doubts in my way so as to put an end to my enjoyment of the intellectual life, which He knew would prove to be a snare to me because of my intellectual attitude. And then He prevented me from losing myself in a soulish love by letting me suffer an even greater disappointment than I did in my classes, where so much emphasis was placed on the intellect. My friend, a girl who had shared all my joys and sorrows, suddenly formed another friendship. This disappointment was very humiliating and made me jealous. I felt wounded and darkness crept into my soul.

In my little room I shed many tears over my troubles. All desire to make excursions in Berlin had long since ceased. My wings were clipped. I let them hang low. In addition, I had no one with whom I could share my troubles and inner conflict. The heavens seemed tightly closed; indeed, Jesus seemed dead. And I did not know what my next step was, for with my studies at this college I had launched on to a path that I had never intended to take. In my diary I poured out my heart to God and He answered me in His bountiful mercy. He answered me so wisely, as only a loving Father can, as a Father who knows His child and lovingly seeks to correct him. He showed me how to untie this knot of confusion, of sorrow and tears. He showed me the solution, the true solution for every problem, as I discovered throughout my life and later for the Sisterhood of Mary. He pointed out to me that my sin was the root of my great distress. Because my love for Jesus was still so small, my world collapsed at this loss of human love and friendship. I became unhappy as a result and darkness filled my soul. In addition, it was my pride and jealousy that caused me such trouble now that someone else was preferred to me. This I suddenly realised.

Forgive me for being so small, envious and proud, and for letting something like this make me sad. No matter what the cost, make me fit for Your kingdom. Let me weep about other things . . . I know that it is not yet possible for me to love only in spirit. I am not yet capable of that, for it makes too much difference to me whether or not she returns my affection. Cleanse me. O Jesus, impart Your divine love to me. (January 25, 1925)

Several weeks later:

Quite different things make me sad now . . . I deplore myself. Now I see how very, very small and human I was, how very attached I was to others, and how much this hinders God's working. (March 28, 1925)

This knowledge of my sin was a blessing, for it brought me to repentance, which is a never-ending, hidden source of new life. Even today I am filled with awe and wonder that the Spirit of God granted me this realisation; otherwise, poison would have accumulated in my heart – bitterness or tension. The recognition of our sin (an insight we should derive from every hardship) and repentance set us free and make us happy. Then we can no longer accuse God of laying burdens on us, of taking away all our happiness, or of frustrating our plans, nor can we accuse others who disappoint us. We can only accuse ourselves and thank God that through these troubles He seeks to free us from our fetters and to draw us into His fellowship.

After those months of 'wandering through the wilderness' I went on holiday at Easter with my parents. During this time a new and deeper love for Christ was granted to me and I could renounce my intellectual desire to plunge into all the cultural activities.

So much has changed, because God has given me clarity about many things and because ardent love for Christ has been kindled in me. Now I have no other desire but to serve and glorify Him. I can see very well how small and human I was, and how beneficial and necessary this disappointment was for me. Now that that time is over, Christ is especially close to me, and His presence is so strong. Now I clearly realise how much my heart clung to people and things, how dependent I was on the praise of others, and how all this hindered God's work in me. Now I know that it is Satan who tries to persuade us that we must be educated and interested in intellectual matters. But when we see how very much this hinders the Spirit of God, then we know that it is not the will of God. Considering that so many souls are waiting to be shown the way to Him we should bring them Him alone. The main point is not that we can share people's interests, but rather that God's Spirit shines forth from us with such power that everyone begins to see that we have something special, something divine. My sole desire is to serve Christ. I long for the day when I shall be entirely dependent upon Him, living for Him alone, and I pray that He may enrol me completely in His service, purify me through suffering and draw me closer to Him. But whether I am to become a deaconess or lead some sort of enclosed life, I do not know yet. (April 8, 1925)

O Lord Jesus, once more I am resolved to spend my life

for You alone, to live to glorify You, and to consciously renounce all earthly things. O Lord Jesus, grant me strength so that I shall no longer be attached to clothes, food and living conditions. Grant that I may be content with the bare necessities. Above all, help me and set me free from my desire for recognition. Render me immune to all that would foster my self-love and need for attention. Let me seek only Your honour. Oh, give me strength for the time ahead in Berlin . . . Even if I have to suffer there as I did before Easter, I'll gladly do so – if only I can come closer to You and be cleansed as a result. Please forgive me for grumbling about suffering. Lord Jesus Christ, I love You more than anything in the world. Make me completely free, completely humble and fit to live and work for Your honour. (April 16, 1925)

Dear Lord Jesus Christ, You know my soul and know that I cannot sufficiently express my ardent love for You. Your goodness and greatness are infinite. No one could ever praise You enough. Lord Jesus Christ, if only I could demonstrate my overflowing gratitude to You! Oh, let me suffer, let me be despised, if it should please You, and if I might be cleansed and able to glorify You all the more. Lord Jesus, use me as Your instrument so that I may bring You glory. Let me proclaim Your almighty love and power, and bring souls to You and make them happy . . . I do not know whether I can bear it yet, but I long to suffer for Your sake. Let Your love flow deep into my heart and abide there so that it stands the test in suffering. Oh, if only I have You, I will gladly endure everything. (May 1, 1925)

The cross that weighed so heavily upon me during those winter months brought me immeasurable glory and bliss in the love for Jesus. It brought me a heart full of adoration and new dedication. When we accept our cross willingly from the hands of the heavenly Father in the knowledge that He sends us the cross out of love in order to purify us, we shall be more closely knit to Jesus, and a stream of blessing will be poured over us, as I experienced. The Father further demonstrated His love to me by leading me to an educational institution, a Bible college, where the longings of my heart would finally be satisfied after all those years. There Jesus was preached in the power of the Holy Spirit, as the risen Lord, who lives and works today, performing miracles.

One day in May 1925 a fellow student happened to show me a picture postcard, saying, 'This is a Bible college not far from here. I shall be going to visit a friend of mine who is studying there.' At the words, 'Bible college', my heart leapt and my old yearnings were reawakened. Perhaps this was the place I had searched for so long, a place where I could be trained for the Lord's service. Accordingly, I set out one day to view this Bible college for myself and to hear what was taught and proclaimed there. Out in the country in a hollow near Bad Freienwalde I found several buildings nestled against the woods and bordered by meadows on the other sides. Set apart in the tranquillity of nature, it seemed like paradise to me after Berlin.

As I approached the main building, I could hear the strains of organ music and singing coming from various houses. I could sense the presence of God in this valley. Here were people who knew that they were called to serve Jesus with their whole life – many had received a vocation to serve on the foreign mission field. The friend of my fellow student in Berlin showed me through the house and brought me to a large, bright classroom where the spiritual founder and leader of the college, Jeanne Wasserzug, was lecturing. I was carried away as she spoke. This was life and spirit! This was not the Christ of the past, but the living Christ, who loves, judges and performs miracles today, who sets hearts on fire today and calls people to enter His service. In the presence of His reality all intellectual doubts had to disappear. He was truly there – Jesus Christ alive today! After this class I was overflowing with joy. At last I had found the object of my quest. I took a few steps into the woods and lay down in the grass, my heart almost bursting for sheer joy at having such a wonderful Lord. If I had a thousand lives, I should have liked to give them all to Jesus out of love for Him. In that hour I surrendered my life to Him once and for all, dedicating myself completely to His service.

My heart sang as I returned to Berlin; I had made up my mind. In autumn I would discontinue my studies in Berlin and go to Malche Bible College.

When I told my parents of my plans at Whitsun, my father, understandably enough, considered my decision irrational, feeling that I should first complete my education in Berlin and take my examination as a social worker and parish worker. My mother, however, sensing how much this step meant to me spiritually, spoke on my behalf. And the day came when my father, who had been adamant until then, suddenly asked from behind his newspaper, as we were sitting on the terrace, 'What are the fees for that place?' The ice had been broken, and moved by God, my father gave his consent.

What a joyful return that was to my small room in Berlin! No longer did it seem like a prison cell, for now the door had swung open and soon I could fly out to the land of my heart's desire – to Bible college. Life, not theory, was what I sought. My whole desire was that this year at Bible college would help me to come to know Jesus more intimately and teach me about His nature so that I could follow His example. While working with a church youth group in Berlin, I discovered the importance of a living testimony and wrote in my diary:

Now that I am leading a youth group, I clearly realise that Bible studies [by that I meant theory] are not the way to share Christ with girls who do not yet have a personal relationship with Jesus. One can only reach them if one is on fire for Jesus with every fibre of one's being and radiating His love – and not if one is as bad as I am. First of all, one must renounce everything else bit by bit and rely completely on Christ and draw apart with Him in

42

solitude, prayer and renunciation. One must be knit to Christ, bearing His love inside so that being firmly rooted in Him and radiating His love, one does not lose Him in everyday activities. Help me, Lord, that I may become childlike, humble and lowly, for only then can I be enrolled in Your holy service. Forgive me all my trespasses. (May 16, 1925)

In July and August 1925 I fulfilled the field work requirements of the college in Berlin by working at the welfare office in Darmstadt. My job entailed accompanying groups of children to holiday camps and on the return journeys I would read the biographies of Mathilda Wrede, George Müller, Finney and others – books that made me yearn all the more to be surrendered wholly to Jesus and to sacrifice everything to Him. Sometimes the greatness and glory of Jesus overwhelmed me.

Lord Jesus, how great and wonderful You are! How can we ever express all our gratitude! O Lord Jesus, to think that You have been with me so often and visited me with Your glory and that You have granted me the great and holy joy of abiding fully in You! How great You are! Sometimes it is too wonderful for me to comprehend! It is almost too much glory for us sinners to bear! Oh, I'm so bad. Lord Jesus, prepare me now as You wish to have me for eternity. Yet so many millions do not know You; they are living in spiritual darkness. What unspeakable sorrow! But You know why You have ordained life on earth this way and why so few people know You. Lord Jesus, send us Your help. Awaken people like Finney and George Müller so that our nation may turn to You, and Your kingdom will be greatly increased. Call people to work for Your kingdom.

My Lord Jesus, I really long to thank You once more with all my heart for Your amazing grace in granting me the privilege of being Your child. My joy at this overwhelming act of grace and this glorious privilege, and my love for You are sometimes so great that I feel as though

I shall burst. All I can do is praise You. Yet I have often been so cold towards You for long periods of time. Forgive me, Lord. But now let my life be aflame with love for You alone. And when I do not abide fully in You, lead me along paths of lowliness until I am free of all worldly, human interests and belong to You alone. Grant me the grace to glorify Your name wherever You place me. Oh, that I may reflect Your countenance one day so that even non-Christians would know that it was only Your doing, Lord Jesus. Take my life, Lord. I long to live for You. Use me. I surrender myself to You with all that I am and have. Bless my beginning at Bible college. Grant that I may be clothed with Your love and humility . . . (July 25, 1925)

On September 23, 1925, almost twenty-one, I arrived at Malche Bible College.

Overflowing Life Discovered
Malche Bible College,
Autumn 1925–Summer 1926

The cheerful atmosphere and fellowship that I had experienced at the Froebel Academy on a human level I now found at Malche Bible College on a spiritual level. Once again we were split into groups and I lived with some other Sisters (we addressed each other as 'Sister'). They put us 'young ones' together, for, unlike the Froebel Academy, the Bible college did not only consist of young people – the average age in my course of sixty Sisters was thirty to forty years, and I was one of the youngest.

Instead of driving through the noisy streets of Berlin in search of life, one retired to the tranquil woods after receiving so much spiritual stimulation during the classes. Indeed, when Miss Wasserzug finished her lectures, I usually found it hard to remain in my chair and would hurry to the woods – running, skipping, singing for joy, my heart full with all that I had heard about the greatness and glory of Jesus and His marvellous purposes concerning the whole world. Or else I would have times of sharing with the friends whom God in His love had given me that year. How grateful I was for the oneness in Christ and mutual understanding that God granted us. Altogether it was a blissful year, bringing me my heart's desire, for Jesus had become greater to me – more real and more precious.

The majesty of God is so wonderful and awe-inspiring that it constantly fills my thoughts. I am so overwhelmed by the omnipotent greatness and love of my Saviour, who daily grants me deeper insight into the riches of this treasure house. He has set my heart on fire. Every day I am privileged to experience more of His presence and to behold more of His glory. And to think that this Lord is my Saviour and God! Every time I think about it, I burst out in rejoicing and long to dedicate my whole life anew. O to be found in You so that I may attain the first resurrection! Grant that I may press on towards this goal without making any detours!

O my Lord and my God, I scarcely know how to bear the greatness of Your glory, now that Romans 6:8 has been disclosed to me. O God, how great You are! I can only stand in worship before You and rejoice that I am Yours, that my old self has been crucified and buried with You and that it is no longer my ego that lives, usurping Your rightful place, but rather You in me! Teach me to reckon with You at all times, and with Your power by which You created the heavens, the earth and the waters, and subdue them. O Lord Jesus, let me show my gratitude for such a wonderful Lord, by spending myself completely for You. Let me only strive to attain the goal that lies ahead. To be a pillar for You – let this be my sole aim. (April 1926)

However, Jesus could only be magnified in my eyes in

so far as I let the Word of God speak to me, for Jesus can only be revealed to us to the extent that we let His Word convict us and bring us to the end of ourselves so that we lie at His feet as sinners. That was my experience in Berlin and in Kassel. Whenever there is recognition of sin, whenever there is contrition and repentance, new life breaks forth and God grants us a deeper knowledge of Himself, which He imparts to those who have come to love Him in receiving His forgiveness. The more resolutely I took up the battle of faith against my sin in total dedication to Jesus, the more I was confronted with my sinful state. But in the same measure I came to know Jesus in His redemptive power, which creates new people and transforms them from glory to glory. During this year at Bible college I experienced this as never before through the power of the Word of God, which I met here for the first time in my life. In a new way I learnt that Jesus lives, Jesus answers prayer, and Jesus brings deliverance, and that whoever claims the promises of God in faith will experience their fulfilment. On the day I arrived at Malche Bible College I wrote down a specific request to the Lord. I made, so to speak, an agreement with Him.

Lord Jesus, I am writing this down now so that on the day when You have accomplished it, I can openly declare Your miracle and thus give You special thanks and praise. Then others will also learn to believe that with God nothing is impossible.

Today I still long so much for honour, I am so pleased with myself, so rooted in my nature. I am pleased when others often ask for my opinion, when I am made to feel I am needed, when people know that I am clever, talented and popular. I am glad when I am friends with everyone, when I can share with others what is in my heart, when I can shine. But Lord Jesus, You were a servant of all. Today I surrender all desire to be great; I renounce all pleasure I take in being important. Every time You lead me along the path of lowliness, where I am unnoticed and unpopular, I shall not be sad or ever think of how I could change the situation so that others will see the good in me [by that I meant my talents and intelligence].

Lord Jesus, I want to come to You every time with this request: help me to accept willingly this path of humility from You and to follow it gladly, since we must reach the point where our sole joy is to have You and to be recognised by You. Give me the strength to endure when my heart is often filled with pain. Help me to struggle through in prayer until I reach You and then let me rejoice in humiliations. Jesus, from this day on I want to follow this path in truth – when people don't know me here, when they may even consider me merely childlike and when perhaps I do not play any role. Help me to follow You. I shall begin today so that when I leave Bible college later, I can write underneath this entry that You were able to set me free, in spite of this sinful trait of mine which is so ingrained in me, and that You help everyone who places himself in Your hands. Make me lowly and humble this year. (September 23, 1925)

God graciously answered this prayer. That year a definite beginning was made, although the Lord was to continue with His process of purification, working on this feature of my character at a deeper level during the course of my life. Thus in June 1926 I recorded:

My Lord and my God, I want to thank You with all my heart. Lord, how great You are ! And how wonderful that today I can write here that You have indeed heard the prayer I made at the beginning of the course, and answered it – just as I asked – by the end of my year here. At the time I wrote in faith: 'At the end of the course I shall be able to write down to Your glory that You have accomplished it.' And today, a few weeks before the end of term, I can testify that You have made a beginning and that You keep Your promises. You have taken away my pleasure in being able to shine, for through the working of Your Spirit I felt a bitter sting whenever I received praise or recognition from others. It no longer makes me

47

purely happy to be praised, but rather sad and fearful. I know that You will continue to wean me from this desire for recognition through many difficult leadings. And since the good feeling that comes from being praised does not please You, it is no longer pleasing to me. O Lord, that You have wrought this in my soul is far greater than any other real miracle. Help me never to take pleasure in the things that do not please You. Teach me this more and more.

A special blessing was that in her classes Miss Wasserzug taught us about the redeeming power of Jesus' blood. Now I could claim the blood of Jesus so as to achieve victory in my struggle against sin. Previously I had known little of this.

The nine months sped by quickly. Having suffered from spiritual drought so long, I rejoiced in this time of refreshment and drank in deeply the living waters, drawing at the fount to my heart's content. After the previous disappointments in Kassel and Berlin, I was scarcely able to comprehend that I had found my heart's desire and thus I saw everything at Bible college with radiant eyes.

However, there was one problem that perturbed me during my course at Malche Bible College, which was not solved then, despite the many other blessings that year brought me. Indeed, it was many years before I found the answer to this question, but when I did, it unlocked the door to a wonderful treasure house. My problem concerned world-renunciation or world-affirmation; it was part of the question of law or freedom. As a committed Christian how far is one permitted or obliged to engage in cultural activities? I would reason with myself: If I wish to live solely for Jesus and His kingdom, I am like a soldier going to war. He no longer has time for various pursuits as in days of peace, even though these pursuits are permissible in themselves. Instead, he must devote himself completely to warfare, since the fate of his nation is at stake. But in the battle between the kingdom of darkness and the kingdom of light even more is at stake. It is a matter of eternal life and death, of snatching souls from the clutches of hell. Consequently, should one not feel more than obliged to lay aside all else, get one's priorities right and live exclusively for the Kingdom of God? Even so I was not convinced. There was another side to the argument. Why did God so lovingly create the beauty of nature and grant us the arts and so many other things? If we turn our backs on all this like ascetics, then there must be something unnatural about our lives, because we are denying and rejecting the very things that God has created out of love. I was unable to reconcile these two conflicting points of view.

In my distress I went to a highly respected teacher, who was tolerant and broadminded in her outlook, and I shared my problem with her. Referring to the people Tersteegen describes in his book, *Leben heiliger Seelen*, I asked her whether these people, who were ascetics to my way of thinking, were right after all, since they lived wholly in God, reflecting Jesus' image and possessing great authority. Perhaps she saw a personal danger for me; at any rate, she strongly advised me against such a way of life, explaining that this was mysticism, which she felt could be a pitfall. She told me that wherever the Lord led me I should enjoy complete freedom like a child, but always remain fully committed to Jesus. That was precisely my problem! How this theory was to work out in practice she did not say. For instance, what should I do now? Should I pray, or should I take time to visit the art gallery, pursue intellectual interests, have discussions and seek company?

By heeding this warning not to follow the example of the lives portrayed in Tersteegen's book, I suffered a great spiritual loss. In view of these questions I made the following entry:

O Jesus, I lay before You once more my last ten weeks here, dedicating them to You completely. Help me not to spend a single hour in doing something that is not according to Your will. My sole desire is to be utterly dependent upon You so as to be wholly at Your disposal. Have You not placed me, Your child, in the midst of life in this world? You know how receptive my mind and soul are to all that You have created, to people, the fine arts, psychology and questions about life, and You know that we have to have both feet on the ground. Continue to show me every hour, every minute of my life, whether I ought to get involved when, for example, other people introduce me to such matters, or whether I should draw apart in order to seek You, study the Word, and attend to Your business. Legalism will never solve this problem, but You are Spirit and Life. Give me Your Holy Spirit so that I can decide from case to case what to do. Lord, grant that I may follow Your leadings alone. Prevent me from making any detours on the way, for my sole aim is that You will be everything to me, that I shall reflect Your image and live exclusively for You. Help me not to be occupied with the world – neither emotionally nor intellectually. Let me always see Your truth in this world, but keep me from becoming a legalist. (April 22, 1926)

Love for Jesus was the only answer – a truth I did not realise at the time, since this love was still so little alive in me.

Consequently, after my Bible course had ended, this problem followed me in my new job. My unanswered question would still cause me many difficult hours – though at first the joyful expectation of entering the Lord's service and working for His kingdom prevailed. The words of Miss Wasserzug were burning in my heart, 'There is no greater honour than to be called into God's service.'

During my first holidays from Malche Bible College in 1925, when I went home for Christmas, the preacher from the City Mission in Darmstadt visited my parents. Upon hearing that I was training at Malche Bible College, he suddenly asked if I should like to start the youth work in the Darmstadt City Mission after I finished my course. My parents and I felt that this was God's leading and the board of the Bible college agreed to send me as a Sister of their college to this ministry, which was to commence in August 1926. I was then twenty-one years old.

However, before beginning my job, I found myself in severe inner conflict. It was the same matter that had greatly perturbed me at Bible college as a result of my education in Berlin, and now it flared up again as I spent some weeks at a Christian retreat centre where the importance of the *Gemeine*, 'the body of true believers', was taught. According to this teaching the *Gemeine* is comprised of the elect, those who are truly regenerate and for whom total self-denial is imperative. In the Bible studies, which were powerful and richly blessed in themselves, it was repeatedly emphasised that everything in the world was merely imperfection and suffering, and that one must go through life with sorrow in one's heart.

But within me I could always hear the words of my teacher, Miss Wasserzug, who, in contrast to this grave teaching, would tell us in her natural, joyful manner about the love of God and how He delights in making His children happy and granting them good gifts. Of course, this did not exclude the fact that He has to lead us along paths of chastening, which we so need. What she meant was that God cares for us as a loving Father. But in this retreat centre it was continually stressed that God leads us only along pathways where we have to die to self. Christians who thought differently were considered not to have advanced spiritually. Though they were converted, they were not 're-generate'. Moreover, this group of Christians held to the principle that women were not permitted to proclaim the Word of God, not even to other women and to young people; they maintained that no blessing could come of such a ministry. An adherent of this teaching, a high school teacher, talked with me earnestly and appealed to my conscience not to accept my new job for this reason. In a state of great inner conflict I then wrote in my diary:

My Lord and my God, You see my agony; You see my bewilderment at all the different paths followed by Your children – each maintaining that his alone is right. Lord, I am indeed willing to renounce everything if only You show me clearly that this *is* Your way. Give me a sign, some sort of answer, for I do not know what to do. Oh, I would rather that You ruin all my plans than let me be disobedient and set out on a path that is not Yours. Lord, consider my tears and hear my pleas. You see how troubled I am by that which Mr X always says. Show me what is right. Please tell me. Don't let me get caught up in anything narrow. Don't let me fall into legalism again. But, on the other hand, don't let me become so broad-minded that I pay less attention to the one thing that is needful. Give me discernment when I hear such statements as, 'Those who are born again are the elect. No amount of searching and wrestling can help the others.' Here it is further said that a woman who speaks in the congregation loses much grace and glory, because she is acting against the will of God and therefore lacks one of the traits of true children of God. Does that imply then that Miss Wasserzug, who is not entirely of the same opinion, does not belong to the body of true believers?

O Lord, they are all Your children. It is not our position to judge who is born again and who is not yet. Whether a person is one of the chosen or not cannot depend on how far he accepts this particular teaching concerning the body of true believers as the counsel of God. Rather, it can only depend upon the fullness of the Spirit, the degree of devotion and of love for Christ. Then everything else will spring quite naturally from this basis – fruitfulness, the right relationship to the world and to all other things. The main point is always how much my life, thoughts and actions are governed by the Spirit, by love and devotion to Christ. I feel it is bordering on legalism to compartmentalise people into the born again, the converted, the spiritually alive ... (July 16, 1926)

Amid the confusion of these different teachings I had a foretaste of the distress that I was later to help to alleviate as part of my lifework – the distress of the disunity among God's children, the strife, the quarrelling and opinionated-ness. In the hour of trial God had given me a glimpse of the solution. Love for Christ would give the right attitude to the world and all else of its own accord; it would bring forth genuine fruit and form the one true basis for unity. But first God had to prepare me by leading me along many paths of chastening before I learnt from experience that love for Jesus is the only practical solution to the tensions and divisions in the Body of Christ. Before beginning to work in the Lord's service, I struggled through in prayer until I received the assurance that I was acting rightly.

I thank You for giving me the certainty after all, that when one is fully dedicated, there is no need for legalism. Provided one adheres to the guiding principles in Scripture, one has complete freedom in the Spirit – and that includes women also. (July 25, 1926)

My Battle: World-denial or World-affirmation
Youth Work in Darmstadt, Summer 1926–Summer 1928

In August 1926 I was publicly installed as the new youth worker during a worship service at the City Mission. At the very outset the preacher informed me that he would give me free rein in my ministry, and he generously kept his word as long as I was there. His main concern was that I call girls together to form a new youth group. We enjoyed a good, harmonious relationship in this joint ministry, in so far as it could be called joint, seeing that I was left to myself in all the external and spiritual arrangements and bore the responsibility of counselling alone. Apart from that I was young and inexperienced.

Shortly before, a tent mission had been held in Darmstadt and several girls, daughters of members of the City Mission, were converted. I visited them, prayed with them and tried to help them in their many problems. With these girls I then began a youth group, which soon increased to about forty girls, half of whom were older than I was. But despite this good beginning I was most unhappy. I had set myself too high a goal. At the age of twenty-two I was under the impression that fettered souls could experience a swift and extensive release and transformation by faith in Jesus. I was convinced that within a very short time the redemptive power of Jesus would be demonstrated in everyday situations – in victory, joy and dedication. But none of this was evident from my counselling talks with the girls. It was a grief for me to realise that in many cases the members of the Body of Christ are the opposite of what they ought to be, since Jesus' redemption is not visible in their lives – a fact that made Nietzsche's criticism understandable: 'These Christians must show me they are redeemed, before I'll believe in their Redeemer.'

In spite of the counselling sessions I had with the girls over a period of time when I prayed with them about their needs and bondages I found that they not only fell back into sin, but that they even refused to follow Jesus in certain matters, although they were believers. It was a frustrating struggle with these girls, and I felt almost crushed. I loved them dearly, and their troubles and trials became my own. I simply could not understand why they did not experience release and thus the work became an unbearable burden for me.

My parents, sensing that I was working too intensely, tried to win me back to an easier way of life. Consequently, I faced a battle on both sides with no one to help me spiritually. Time and again I came to the conclusion that I was too young and ill-equipped for this work and that the power of Satan and all the misery on earth were too great. Darkness engulfed my soul. The joy that had seized me at Bible college disappeared in the face of all these problems. Time and again my diary contained such passages as the following:

L. is on the verge of despair. H. didn't come. She has no courage. She has no hope. You simply aren't helping her. Oh, please show her why. Let her see where she has gone wrong. K. is at the end of her faith again. At the meeting with the girls yesterday, I was again unable to speak the way I had intended, because there was such a spirit of opposition. Mrs B. is almost hysterical because of her hardships and struggles – unable to find any peace, unable to believe that You took her husband away out of love ... O Lord, where are You? Have mercy upon them. You love them. Lord, help! You are Mercy! Please send help for Your name's sake, for You are omnipotent ... Give me faith for them. You must help me in the youth work tomorrow. Spiritually I am under such pressure, in such darkness and so far away from You that I can't possibly deliver a message. But in You we have everything. Lord Jesus, I will not complain or despair. You are my Strength and my Joy; You accomplish Your purposes gloriously. I trust You! O Lord, if You humble me, You will exalt me. I thank You. Oh, don't let the others suffer any harm. Help me so that they can still be blessed. Amen. (November 1, 1926)

Lord, why have You forsaken me? I can't continue to live like this. Lord, I'm too young. Oh, if only I didn't have to give talks and to counsel, when I am so poor in myself. Often I think it would be better to perform the simplest chores if only I can glorify You. O Lord, and yet it is by Your grace alone that I am enrolled in Your service, and therefore, I will serve You gladly. (November 28, 1926)

Why was it so dark in my soul? Apart from the reasons mentioned above – my youthful inexperience and lack of knowledge – there was another reason, a personal one, which had to do with my sin. Although I was in no way emotionally attached to any of the girls under my charge, I loved their souls in that I was determined to extricate them from their troubles and bondages. Accordingly, I spent my last ounce of strength in this ministry. Nothing was too much for me; no burden they brought me was too heavy. In Darmstadt I had my own room with a private entrance so that I could receive the girls, who came to me at all times with their problems. They were at home in my room where we had our many counselling sessions and prayer battles. I loved my girls in all their weaknesses, and they loved me. With every fibre of my being I lived for this group of girls entrusted to my care. An aunt who visited us said that at first I was silent and unresponsive. But when she asked me about my work, I suddenly became a different person, because I talked so enthusiastically about my girls. However, my love for them was not purified. I loved their souls on a human level. In addition, many of the pleas for help in my diary at that time sounded like accusations against God, as if He were not helping His children.

Why can't people believe? Why is life so terrible? And now L. too has such doubts and is rebelling against You. Oh, soon I shall no longer be able to bear it all. It is so terribly difficult. O Lord, my God, I've reached the end of my tether. Give me faith and new strength so as to subdue the voice of despair, that keeps on asking WHY in view of these struggling, seeking souls. You simply aren't helping them or manifesting Yourself to them! (April 5, 1927)

I think my heart will break if I have to stand by and watch these people go through such agonies: J., Mrs W., L. and so many others. They want to believe, they want to be victorious and yet they cannot. Why this to and fro in their lives and dispositions and temperaments? O Lord, I will not ask why; I will trust You, because You are truly righteous and holy. But there must be a solution, even though we probably shan't be able to understand it until we are in heaven. (May 26, 1927)

Indeed, there was a solution, but different from the one I thought. I felt that I had to struggle for a deeper faith. Certainly this struggle was necessary and right, as well as a good training for me so that later I could build up and lead an entire organisation – the Sisterhood of Mary – along pathways of faith. In His great wisdom God taught me to keep faith even at that early stage as I fought seemingly hopeless battles for human souls. Time and again, as my diary indicates, I struggled through until I could have faith in view of my inability for this ministry and in view of the power of the enemy, who held these souls captive.

After seeing the true state of affairs and that the other side is winning, is one then supposed to proclaim Your victory? Yet even if all the others get nowhere, even if I have to continue to live in agony, even if my work should go to ruin, I will believe in You and Your victory, Lord Jesus Christ. I will believe in You as the Lord of life, who is more powerful than sin, as the living Christ, who abides in me. I will believe in You, even if I should no longer be able to understand life and Your dealings with others. (April 5, 1927)

The solution, however, lay elsewhere than in this kind of faith, since the problem was of a more serious nature. Its roots could be found in my own disposition; my sin was the cause. My perspective was wrong and for this reason I had to go through such spiritual night. My heart was filled with more anguish at the plight of these souls than at Jesus' suffering because of them. In other words, I was more taken up with these souls than with Jesus. Instead of grieving in my heart because of the wounds we inflict upon Jesus with our unwillingness, resistance and unfaithfulness, I felt sorry for the girls that they were not experiencing victory and release. I knew little of the heart of Jesus, which is pure love, and consequently, I was not absorbed with His sufferings, nor did I realise that this was precisely where my spiritual life had gone wrong. By letting myself be pulled down into the depths and fluctuations of the human soul, I no longer abode in the peace and joy of Christ and His victory – a connection I had not noticed. The girls' souls were the centre of my attention, just as certain people had previously been.

During my year in Berlin I was engulfed in darkness, because my life revolved more round a friendship than round Jesus Himself. At that time I quickly spotted the reason for my sadness, but now in my youth ministry it was far harder for me to define the cause of my spiritual darkness. Not until many years later did I realise that we can serve the Lord zealously and wrestle in prayer to win souls for Him, but with the people we seek to help rather than Jesus at the centre. God, in His bountiful goodness, must have certainly wished to open my eyes even in those days, but I was not yet responsive. Only later when the Lord led me into even greater battles of prayer and faith for certain souls and I was almost desperate that these souls were not being saved, did He show me the evil root in my heart. I did not trust implicitly in His love, since I harboured a spirit of grumbling against Him. Only when Jesus is the focal point; only when His suffering for human souls, His love and wrestling for them moves our hearts, can we abide in peace, true joy and victorious faith, for then we are centred in Him rather than in people.

During the course of my two years in this work God eased the situation. In His bounteous grace He let me experience a small revival among the girls and gave me an active youth ministry with several different groups. My joy was a small circle of responsible girls who shared the burden and spent many hours in prayer with me. This group had developed into a true fellowship of love that prayed and fought for His kingdom. During our prayer meetings my room resembled an army camp with the girls sitting on the ground; every square inch of floor space was covered. Ardent prayers were directed like rifle shots at many hearts. It was our goal that the whole city be set on fire for Jesus. All this pushed my inner struggles and unsolved problems into the background, and during the second year I wrote in my diary:

My Lord Jesus, how I thank You for showing me the precious side to this ministry. I can only rejoice in the privilege of serving You. This ministry seems to be the most precious thing in my life. (April 3, 1928)

Where is a God like You! Lord, I have found such wealth in You. You have made me so happy that sometimes I feel that it is beyond my comprehension. O 'how inexpressible is the prompting of Your wonderful love!' Unto You I lift my song of praise. 'By the grace of God I am what I am: A bride of the King, betrothed to the Lamb – I blush for joy.' (June 30, 1928)

In retrospect I can recognise the bounteous goodness of God. I was still so young in faith and very young for this work, but He never allowed me to be tempted beyond my strength. He showed me His love by blessing my ministry, thus greatly encouraging my faith. On the other hand, the Lord continued to work in me. Time and again He attended to the sores and sick spots of my nature – my doubts and protests because of the failings of people for whose souls I wrestled in prayer – and showed me that something was amiss in me. Not until later, in the Sisterhood of Mary, did I truly grasp the solution that I was seeking at the age of twenty-two when I wrote, 'There must be a solution.' The solution lay in the comprehension of Jesus' sufferings and the concerns of His heart.

At the time I did not find the answer to my other major problem either: world affirmation or world-denial. On the one hand, I was afraid of losing my full dedication to Jesus, but, on the other hand, I was afraid of becoming legalistic. In vain I searched for someone to advise and guide me. In my ministry I was very much on my own, even though for a while I had a blessed prayer fellowship with the deaconess in charge of the women's work in the Darmstadt City Mission. We understood each other well in the matters pertaining to the Kingdom of God, but my problems were not hers, since she was not placed in the midst of the cultural and intellectual life as I was. Thus time and again I struggled with these problems by myself.

Not only was I so alone spiritually in my ministry in Darmstadt, with no one to accompany me, but I experienced much distress in yet another matter at the time. Erika Madauss, who had brought me closer to Christ during our days at the Froebel Academy, and with whom I had always remained in close contact, despite the fact that we were led in different directions at times, came to be spiritually separated from me as well. She was so taken up with art and cultural life then that Jesus no longer had first priority in her life. That was a painful experience for me.

Yet I could not overlook the fact that Erika had a clear, natural, unbiased perception of that which was genuine or false, also in regard to me. When we were together or corresponded, she would question my 'greenhouse' piety. Her words were not without effect, but even though I had to admit that she was right in many respects and tried in love to understand her, her way of life did not seem to be right to me either. But where was I to find the right way? My diary mirrors my distress.

> I just don't know what to do. How utterly miserable I am! Lord, what is the way out of this maze? Is Erika's faith something entirely different, or is it merely another form? Sometimes I am so at one with her and understand her fully when she says that a Christian's place is in the midst of life with all its variety, whereas at other times her way seems so foreign, so different to me, that I feel we cannot tread the same path. Still I don't want to criticise. As for me I hardly dare to use this freedom, but perhaps this is Erika's leading . . . (December 21, 1926)

In the midst of this conflict I made a vital discovery. Up till then I felt that the resolute type of devotion, as I had mainly experienced it – pietistic and with more of an emphasis placed on one-sidedness – was ideal. In my ministry, however, I found that many believers who adhered to this type of piety, sadly enough often produced lifeless sermons and prayers.

A little experience gave me a clue to the right direction. I shall never forget the time I visited a seriously ill woman whose Christian life was rather free – as I could tell at first glance. Yet she made Jesus more real to me than the sermons and prayers that I had recently heard. One small remark of hers revealed her utter abandonment to God, her dedication to His will and her humility. In her I encountered the living Christ, the One whom I longed to live for – and bear witness to. This woman gave me a copy of Dürer's woodcuts of the Passion and again it was quite remarkable: through these pictures, that is, through a work of art, Jesus spoke to me with a directness that I had so missed in the sermons and prayers in the Christian fellowship I attended. Shortly afterwards I noted in my diary:

According to Pastor X everything here on earth must be shunned, since it is under a curse, and therefore, we must go through life with sorrow in our hearts. To have an experience with God we must be absolutely one-sided. Christ can be found only in the Word and as 'Christ in us'. But that amounts to renunciation of all life – a depressing thought.

One treats life as if it did not exist and thus one is unrealistic. Yet if I seek God in the full variety of life and participate in everything as a Christian, I fear that I shall be divided in my devotion to Christ. All the really fruitful men and women of God reached this state by living a life of holy resolution, i.e. Paul and all the 'holy souls' Tersteegen writes so much about. Or were there others?

Lord Jesus, help me to understand Your gospel, for I am unable to. It seems so contradictory to me. On the one hand, it stresses total dedication to the point of legalistic self-denial; on the other hand, it proclaims tremendous freedom . . . Grant me the right form and free me from the law. You know how legalistic I am. I almost have a guilty conscience when I do something that is not directly related to Your service. If once in a while I read art books or purely literary works, I'm afraid that I'm not making the best use of time in this short life for You and Your cause. Oh, what is the way? (January 4, 1927)

As is evident from my diary, this question was a real cross for me.

This question is probably the cross of my life. (January 20, 1927)

When in my struggle I had come to the conclusion that it was possible to have an encounter with God in all the variety of life, I rejoiced:

Lord, I thank You for revealing Yourself to me in people, nature and the fine arts. I thank You that I can live for You and at the same time rejoice in all these things with a clear conscience, since they only increase my love for You . . . I thank You for having freed me from the law. (January 6, 1927)

Yet, a few weeks later, I felt I was not on the right track after all and wrote:

I always have the feeling that I am not devoting all my energy to the Lord's service, and that I am not accomplishing enough. Everything seems so futile and empty. O Lord, at all costs I want to spend my life completely for You and Your cause and to be on fire with Your love. Oh, preserve me from ever becoming a half-hearted worker for the Kingdom of God, a spiritually half-dead Christian from whom no streams of living water flow. (January 26, 1927)

Thus I was tossed to and fro. I harassed myself with this question but found no solution. As I now realise, God had a purpose to this suffering. He did not wish me to discover the answer theoretically but rather through personal experience, since I was to found and lead a Sisterhood. I had to follow these paths for the sake of the girls who would one day join the Sisterhood, so as not to lead them into a legalistic, world-denying type of Christianity that would turn them into spiritual cripples or self-righteous pharisees, nor to leave them in a lukewarm, worldly type of Christianity that lacked the salt and power of full dedication. Only from personal experience could I point out the right way to my spiritual daughters: as a child of the heavenly Father to accept His good gifts gladly and naturally, enjoying them with thanksgiving whenever He grants them, and at the same time as a bride of Jesus to accompany Him in love along the pathway of the cross, the pathway of self-abandonment and self-renunciation under the guidance of the Holy Spirit.

Furthermore, I was to call others through various writings to the path of true discipleship, which is not legalistic asceticism. And this message, which I was later commissioned to pass on in my literature, contained the answer to the very question that had so harassed me at that time. Love was the answer. Not a general sort of love, but a personal love for Jesus, for the Father, for the Triune God. However, during my youth ministry in Darmstadt I had not yet fully comprehended the solution.

The pathway of discipleship where love for Jesus is the sole incentive and which is free from lifeless, legalistic narrowness was not shown to me through one particular form of devotion, whether it be that of the *Gemeinschaftsbewegung*,* the Protestant Church or any other group. During my ministries in the following years the Lord brought me into touch with a variety of Christian groups. In the course of time I worked in various fellowships and organisations where I had to come to terms with many different Christian views. Through these experiences God gradually gave me the right understanding of that which His Word says about the law and the gospel.

During my youth ministry I underwent much inner con-

* The *Gemeinschaftsbewegung* is a movement in Germany that was formed at the end of the nineteenth century as a reaction to the secularization of the industrial era and to the liberalization of theology. It was stimulated by the evangelical outlook which partly came from America and England. In the *Gemeinschaftsbewegung* the emphasis is placed on personal sanctification. *Gemeinschaftskreise* are the individual groups within the movement.

flict as I was faced with one of the problems of pietistic circles. To this very day I can recall my first Christmas celebration at the City Mission as a Sister of the Bible college. In a large, plain, somewhat dark hall about four hundred people – members of the City Mission and their families – sat round long tables, drinking coffee and eating cake. Poems were recited; choirs sang. I found everything too human – too human and too loud. Coffee and cake seemed to be so important. My heart was filled with sorrow. Where was the presence of Jesus? In my diary I wrote:

> O Lord, I don't think I can work here any longer. I'm out of place here . . . Everything is so empty and yet so obtrusive – the prayers and the talks. (December 28, 1926)

How enthusiastic I had been at Malche Bible College, whose spiritual background was the *Gemeinschaftsbewegung*, but here I was greatly disappointed. It seemed to bear little resemblance to that which the fathers of the revival had intended. Certainly in many pietistic groups this is not the case; however, God probably granted me this experience so as to teach me to look beyond the spiritual characteristics and outward forms in search of the true centre. And that can only be Jesus. I came to learn that the fact that we have been converted does not imply that we are following the path of true discipleship. On the contrary, I discovered that as evangelical believers we often use the statement, 'I've been saved', as a cushion to rest on or even as a shield to protect ourselves from further penetration by the light of truth and from God's judgement. Consequently, the danger of hypocrisy and pharisaism is great. Assuming that one's life is in order, one proudly looks down on others, sometimes even being reluctant to take communion with 'mere churchgoers', who also attend lectures and concerts, i.e. those who still 'belong to the world'. One fails to realise that some of these churchgoers are more pleasing to God, since they are like the publican who prayed, 'God, be merciful to me, a sinner.' On the other hand, I was aware of the great indifference that frequently rules in church groups that are 'open to the world' and lacking activity and zeal for the work of the Kingdom of God, which is often great in pietistic circles.

One thing was evident to me then – later I was to recognise it even more. In every type of Christianity there are nominal members as well as genuine disciples of Jesus. But what is the secret of true discipleship? The Lord showed me the answer with increasing clarity through His Word, which He illustrated in His guidance for my life. It is a humble and contrite heart that regards itself a sinner before God and man, that acknowledges its sins and accepts reproof. Such a heart cannot but love Jesus with all its strength (Luke 7:37–50) and this love brings true freedom, answering all questions and solving all problems. However, at that time I had not yet found the key.

Next the Lord led me in the opposite direction, placing me in the midst of a type of Christianity that is open to the world. Once more He brought me to the Women's College for Social Welfare Training in Berlin. This time I did not go there full of enthusiasm as I had done four years ago, but rather in obedience to God, following a pathway where my wishes and desires would be thwarted.

Why the return to Berlin? This move had to do with all my struggles and conflicts. My parents felt that I was devoting myself too exclusively to counselling and was no longer open to anything else. They considered it absolutely necessary that I leave this work. Accordingly, they consulted a number of leading Christian men who visited us and they also wrote to the board of Malche Bible College. From all sides, including authoritative Christians, I received the same advice: I must leave such a narrow field of work and come to grips with the world once more so as not to become a legalist and a spiritual cripple. I was strongly advised to complete my education at the Women's College for Social Welfare Training and to concern myself with social and intellectual problems. The thought of returning to Berlin was bitter, but I knew that it was the Lord's will.

Why This Detour?
Return to the Women's College
for Social Welfare Training, Berlin, 1928

Once again it was autumn when I returned to Berlin. Four years had elapsed and I was now twenty-four. Again I was given a small single room in the hostel facing the other side of the building with a view of the courtyard. But this time everything was so different. The metropolis did not entice me as it had at my first arrival. Abiding in Jesus in an entirely new dimension, I very much sensed the darkness of the big city. Not only living within these walls but also being in this atmosphere tormented me. For the first time I noticed what sort of girls were standing in the doorways near our hostel. I could sense the dark goings-on and the misery of sin lurking behind the façades of these large, stately Berlin apartment houses. As a result of my counselling work the anguish of sin bore into my heart.

This time I would sit in my room with all the problems of a student who had interrupted his studies four years earlier and now had to follow a new curriculum, sometimes studying under new teachers. Since there were so many new laws to learn by heart, I had to catch up on almost the whole first year's course. My diary expresses my inner feelings:

Laws, laws and more laws to drum into my head . . . Horrors! Oh, this dreadful city! The atmosphere is almost stifling me. These brick walls! This city! Dead in all its life. Soulless in all its activities. This is what faces me wherever I go . . . and to think I have to live here for a year! I often clutch my head and ask myself, 'Why did you do it? In order to acquire a greater understanding about social concerns? In order to be better equipped to give advice in practical cases?' Whenever I am tempted to blame my stupidity for having taken this step, I overcome this temptation by telling myself that an inner compulsion, which is equally present in me, was my reason for coming. It was in obedience that I came. O Lord, help

me! With all my soul I long to be in Your service!
(October 17, 1928)

Indeed, I could not rationally explain why I was back in the college that I had previously left by my own decision. But I was certain that God had a plan, which, even if I did not understand it yet, He would disclose to me in due time.

Saying farewell to my girls in Darmstadt that August was a moving experience and when I thought of my youth work there, I felt very homesick, for my heart's desire was to serve in the Kingdom of God with a ministry to human souls. However, for years God denied me the fulfilment of this wish. He saw the dangers of such a ministry for me, even if I was not aware of them at that point. I was full of zeal for Jesus' dominion, but without realising it, I became more involved in my ministry, in wrestling for souls, than in devoting myself to Him who sought to be my only love. In those days I did not yet know that the spiritual can be mixed with the emotional, love for Jesus with love for one's ministry.

But God is a jealous God. He wanted to be loved with an undivided love and to be loved only for His own sake. Accordingly, He began to purify my soul, no longer giving it the satisfaction of a ministry to people, for this desire of mine was soulish, although it appeared to be spiritual. He led me into desolate and empty places, where for many years my heart had no cause to which it could devote itself. But the glory that crowns every pathway of the cross is so wonderful that today I would gladly pass through even wider expanses of spiritual desert in order to attain it. The pathways of the cross led me into the secret of bridal love for Jesus, the secret of 'Christ in us', which brings us heaven on earth, since it brings us Jesus Himself.

At the time the whys and wherefores of this path to Berlin and later 'desert roads' were hidden from me; I was firmly convinced that once my year in Berlin was over I would be given a ministry in the Kingdom of God again. The inner compulsion and obedience were a sufficient answer for me at the moment. Soon I was fully participating in all my classes, and even enjoying the intellectual and theological material. Unlike my first year in Berlin, nothing, not even biblical criticism, caused me doubts. With another Christian student I arranged Bible discussion sessions for our course. In addition, I attended lectures, concerts, and visited museums, since I had come to Berlin for the second year in order to penetrate all the contemporary intellectual and social matters – apart from that, the history of art had always interested me. And yet, as I noted in my diary:

I constantly yearn to be free again for Your cause and Your kingdom. Although there is much here that is beautiful and stimulating, it is a life wrapped up in itself. The prayer, 'Thy kingdom come', spurs me on. (February 11, 1929)

However, this urge to spend myself for His kingdom was to go through a process of purification; that was the purpose of this year in Berlin. Firstly, the Lord gave me no opportunity to work in His ministry, and secondly, people with whom I lived offered me helpful criticism, which He used to show me that something was amiss in my personality and attitude. The Lord arranged it so that from various quarters I was repeatedly told the same thing.

Today L. told me again that I was lacking vitality. She says I'm too tense, too serious. I can't be childlike, relaxed, natural and happy-go-lucky. I depress other people. (April 20, 1929)

Most unhappy about this state of affairs, I wrote:

It can't continue the way it is. I don't want to inhibit and depress others. How awful! It's probably all the distress I met in my youth ministry that has made me so serious.

Indeed, as I recalled my childhood and early youth when I had been extremely happy, I realised that I must have changed considerably. The more serious side of my nature had the upper hand, since I was now involved in so many struggles. And in those days I still fought my battles very legalistically. If Christ is the fulfilment of the law (Romans 10:4), we shall not be spared the phase of legalism. The hardships of those years had left their mark on me and the more serious traits of my personality were increasingly brought to the fore. This caused me much distress.

Darkness surrounds me. O Lord, show me Your way. What is right? I really don't know. My goal – was it wrong? Why is everything so unspeakably confusing and complicated? Lord, it is You speaking to me when from all sides I am told in no uncertain terms that I am so tense and always under such pressure that others feel as though they are frivolous in my presence. They say that I am constantly weighed down by a great sense of responsibility, but how can it be otherwise? If only I were not continually faced with the deep distress of others, the utter misery of the human race! But how can I ignore all this and live for my own enjoyment and the natural development of my personality? H. actually strengthened my convictions when she said that full dedication in the work of the Kingdom of God involves the sacrifice of the natural man in one way or another. There are enough people who develop the beauty of the natural man. Shouldn't I then be able to offer mine up to Christ? Only, I don't wish to depress others . . . (April 22, 1929)

After those weeks I came to the conclusion that I must serve Jesus and spend myself entirely for Him.

Let me be a true child of Yours. I believe that You will ease all the depressive tension in my life . . . (April 28, 1929)

Thus, my second period in Berlin showed me that something was wrong with my serious, tense, legalistic type of Christianity. That was the wonderful grace of God, for 'the truth will set you free'. Only by submitting to God's judgement, shall we find the true solution to our problems and come to know Jesus and comprehend His love. What a wise leading of God to remove me from my ministry in Darmstadt where people no doubt considered me to be especially devout in my manner! Humanly speaking, however, my return to the Women's College for Social Welfare Training was meaningless, seeing that I never became a social worker. But a teacher at Bible college had often said, 'The Lord is more concerned about you personally, about your soul becoming Christlike and reaching its supreme destination than about your work.' And my soul would have been harmed; it would have grown like a plant in a greenhouse as Erika Madauss told me while I was working in Darmstadt. 'If you go on like this, you will soon become a saint, but everyone will be afraid of you because of your piety!' She probably meant to say that I was not very childlike, natural and happy – the signs of true love and humility.

This phase was not easy for me. Like a butterfly I yearned to emerge from the chrysalis, but lacking the wings of love, I could not yet fly into freedom. God, however, had already prepared everything. He was to lead me along further paths of chastening to this goal.

The Refining Fire
Teaching at Malche Bible College,
Autumn 1929–Autumn 1930

When the year in Berlin was over, I did not return to the youth ministry as I had expected, since the board of Malche Bible College asked me to join the teaching staff after I had passed my examinations as a social worker and parish worker.

To return to the Bible college where I had spent such a happy year was an attractive prospect, although teaching was not really my inclination and at heart I still yearned for a youth group that I could spiritually guide and lead on in the Word of God. Moreover, I had only a hazy idea of what was involved in a teaching job at Bible college, but when I was asked to serve there, I knew that I ought to accept this offer.

Thus, in October 1929, I arrived at the Bible college for a second time after four years. Little did I realise how great the difference would be between being a student and being a teacher.

I lived in the same house, but this time not together with some young people as I had during my first stay when I had such rich fellowship with them. Instead, I had a small room to myself, which literally became a prison cell – just like my first room in Berlin.

What did my life consist of now? I held classes in the missionary teachers' course, as well as in the Bible training course and in the advanced course for parish workers, teaching German, psychology and church history among other things. Since I did not have any other contact with the students and did not live with them, I had only two alternatives after I finished classes – either to return to my room or to take a lonely walk. My place should have been with the other teachers, but I did not fit in there either, for as a twenty-five-year-old I was actually closer in age to the students. In the next room I could often hear the hum of conversation when some of the staff who had known each other for a long time gathered together. However, since they did not know me, they never invited me to join them – no doubt my reserved manner also made it rather hard for them. Some may delight in being alone, but for me this continual solitude was a heavy burden.

Yet loneliness was not the real reason why my second stay at Bible college was so different and hard for me. Now I was older and more mature. Four years ago my joy at being at Bible college was partly due to my youthful enthusiasm, which had naturally abated. Apart from that I did not associate with the young people as much as I had during my training; owing to my teaching responsibilities I had more to do with the members of the staff, all of whom were older.

The older we grow, however, the more set we become in

our ways. Once again I was aware of the same thing that had disquieted me while working in Darmstadt. As older Christians we very quickly assume a certain type of religiosity, a certain pious tone, which can be oppressive. This is often an indication that we still have things in our hearts that we have not overcome or solved and that we try to cover up with such mannerisms. To find these symptoms here as well was hard for me. But was it not my own reflection that I now saw in others? After gaining a little more spiritual experience, I discovered that I was becoming subject to the same malady.

It was a special act of grace that God had relentlessly shown me my nature in Berlin, equally so that He now confronted me at Bible college with the danger of pious stagnation. Again it was the grace of God that here, where I had nothing to satisfy my longing to work actively and creatively in the Kingdom of God, my soulish desires withered. In Berlin at least I had the variety of life, the intellectual stimulation and the company of other students – but here I had no opportunity to minister personally to human souls and almost no opportunity for fellowship.

They [my colleagues] are quite different from me. They don't have much sense of humour, are never exuberant or enthusiastic. This teaching routine! – When I am dying to get things going and try my hand at something new! I should like to live with people and take care of all their needs – not merely their intellectual ones . . . (November 8, 1929)

The Bible college, which had previously been a source of joy to me, now lay like 'a heavy weight upon me' as I noted in my diary. In addition – but it may well have been my imagination – I felt that the other teachers withdrew from me. Probably they noticed that our spiritual characteristics, at least to outward appearances, were very different.

Thus I sat like a small bird in a cage. But this was not my only problem. For my class preparation I had to read various psychology books, including Cordier's *Jugendkunde*, which psychologically interprets the experiences that great Christian men and women of all times have had with God as human and emotional. As a result I suffered much inner conflict.

However, these troubles were all insignificant when compared with yet another problem that almost brought me to the edge of despair. God began to drive the wedge. After that year in Berlin He had denied me the youth work that I longed for and led me into the 'wilderness' – where I felt buried alive – so that the soul and the spiritual man might 'wither'. But first and foremost He dealt with that part of my nature which had already caused me so much trouble during my youth work in Darmstadt – a false zeal for human souls. This time it concerned Erika Madauss. She had strayed farther and farther from Jesus and her many doubts had brought her into deep distress. My heart almost broke. Although I could accept the will of God readily when He sent suffering into my own life, I found it hard to consent to His will when it affected those who were dear to me. I came into such turmoil because of their troubles that every time I had to struggle through until I could believe in the love of God again. The fact that I had difficulty in withstanding these temptations revealed their root – grumbling against God's leadings. This the Word of God showed me all too clearly. In view of these struggles I wrote:

Oh, why is it so hard for me to believe in the love of God? In everything that affects me personally – whether it be the loss of my job in Darmstadt or the fact that I have a lonely, unsatisfying occupation now – I know that this is the only way blessing can come. And though I may be very sad, I never despair, because I can see the hand of God in all this, and because I do want to follow the path He ordains for me, even if it should lead only through death. But here it is a matter of eternal destiny, for if people do not press on to attain the goal of glory, their eternal fate is sealed. In addition, they have to undergo much suffering in this lifetime, since they are so torn. I simply cannot stand by and watch that happen. O Lord, when will You answer my prayers? Why do You save so few people? The thought torments me . . . Lord Jesus Christ, demonstrate Your might and teach me to believe in Your love. Forgive me. Amen. (November 16, 1929)

Never before had I experienced such deep spiritual night. The Word of God did not speak to me. Prayer in the power of faith was beyond me. There was no one in whom I could confide. God no longer seemed to answer. Never before had He appeared so distant and so dead. Day after day I sat in my room; tears were my bread and my thoughts were filled with temptations. I was in deep anguish, because someone who was dear to me had drifted so far away from God.

It is incomprehensible to me how the Lord brought me through this situation. It was as though Jesus was asking me, 'Will you still stay by Me? Will you live for Me alone? Am I enough for you even when I seem to be dead, even when I do not give you inner consolation or loving proofs of My presence? Will you still be content even if I do not grant you a satisfying ministry in My vineyard, even if I do not seem to hear your prayers for dear ones when they are engulfed in darkness, even if I do not answer your questions about the Christian's place in the world?'

If the Lord had not helped me as He did during that first hard year in Berlin, probably my response would have been sadder still. But in my affliction Jesus mercifully let me recognise my sin. And a penitent sinner, lying at the feet of Jesus, cannot lose Him, since the Saviour and the sinner are inseparable. Thus during these periods of intense struggle I wrote:

It becomes increasingly evident to me that my Christian life is utterly powerless. Otherwise I could not be in such despair at the very time I am supposed to be keeping faith for someone. Lord, I pray that You will grant me faith . . . (November 4, 1929)
I don't know, but my life seems so poor spiritually and so fruitless. What does my Christian life actually consist of?

Perhaps I am too preoccupied with myself and my misery . . . Help me to renounce with the utmost resolution all feelings of self-pity and this agonising question WHY. Such a question should no longer exist in my life, seeing that I know of the love of God. (November 7, 1929)

You know that I have failed to keep faith during the past weeks. Lord, I am determined to use the weapon of prayer and every other weapon given to us in the Word of God so as to fight against this unbelief, which is nothing but grumbling against You . . . (November 25, 1929)

Why is my faith so dead that I speak to God as if He ought not to allow all this misery? 'My thoughts are not your thoughts.' When will I comprehend this and humble myself accordingly? Each time it is such a struggle before I can submit. (January 25, 1930)

How different my diary entries suddenly read after the Lord brought about a turning point!

The scales have fallen from my eyes. Now I can behold Your glory again. I am overflowing with joy for what You have done for Erika. Now I see all my unbelief, bitterness and even defiance towards You, my spiritual lifelessness, my slackness in prayer, my unlovingness when I neglected the others here because of my own problems. I can only weep in shame over this winter . . . (May 19, 1930)

Lord, I thank You for passing such judgement upon me and for showing me at the same time that prayer is the way to new life. Pray, pray, pray – that is what I want to do. And I know You will grant me the spirit of prayer anew. Oh, if only I had turned to You more often! (June 12, 1930)

In His loving-kindness God took His child by the hand as He led him through this vale of darkness. He heard my pleas that ascended to Him in times of deepest affliction:

I pray that every dark and fearful hour of death in the innermost recesses of the soul will give rise to love – love that bears all things, hopes all things, endures all things in thanksgiving that You have always brought me through such times in the past. (December 4, 1929)

I have but one desire in life, and that is to be loving. This is my deep longing and heartfelt plea to God. Fill me with love, love and more love so that I can respond with love wherever You have placed me, even if others are hostile towards me. (December 16, 1929)

The Lord answered all these prayers literally. No doubt He pays special attention to prayers that are raised in the midst of deepest night with a faith that hopes against hope – prayers that arise from a God-smitten heart that no longer has strength of its own to believe.

Humanly speaking, my soul seemed to be burnt out in the furnace of affliction. Not a spark of faith, joy or love remained in me. I had come to an end of myself. God wished to expose my true nature so that I might finally see myself as a wretched, but pardoned sinner – pardoned by Him who showers His riches upon the poor and has mercy upon the afflicted.

The year at Bible college drew to a close, bringing with it a visible answer to prayer. Erika, for whose soul I had wrestled, found her way back to Jesus. My heart was brimming over with joy, exultation and thanksgiving to God, but at the same time I was filled with shame because of my unbelief. The end of the school year also marked the end of my time of teaching at Bible college – and that was a release for me. Yet where would my path take me next?

The head of the advanced course at Bible college, Dr Traeder – later Mrs Wasserzug of the Beatenberg Bible College – had previously been an active leader in the Women's Division of the German Student Christian Movement. After I had been teaching at Malche Bible College for a few months both she and Miss Jeanne Wasserzug felt that I should work as a spiritual counsellor for women students, since there was a lack of dedicated Christian workers in this field. The idea was that I should work especially with foreign students. However, in order to carry out this type of ministry properly, I needed a university education. That seemed impossible, since I had left school three years before I could take the examinations that were necessary for studying at university. But in Berlin, at the Ministry of Education, one could take an aptitude test, provided that one had high recommendations from well-known people about one's ability.

It was not a matter of course for me to receive such recommendations, to be admitted to the examinations and actually to pass them. Yet God wished me to follow this path. Professor Luchtenberg of Darmstadt, later Minister of Education in Rhineland-Westphalia, one of whose seminars on psychology I had attended during my youth work in Darmstadt, gave me the necessary recommendation that admitted me to the aptitude test. After the written examination it seemed doubtful whether I could pass; then came the oral examination. At the Ministry of Education on the avenue 'Unter den Linden' I had to sit alone at a long table and face a row of professors and other high-ranking officials in the Ministry of Education, who tested my intelligence and aptitude in a whole range of subjects. And by the grace of God I passed the examination. Now the way was clear for me to go to university, with psychology as my major subject and philosophy and history of art as minor subjects. However, my studies were only meant to be a bridge in order for me to bring the gospel to university students.

The Beginning of a New Ministry
At University,
Berlin, Autumn 1930–Autumn 1931

A year after leaving the Women's College for Social Welfare Training I was back in Berlin – for the third time now. As a university student, I felt even more lost in the big city than I had at college. Everything turned out contrary to my expectations. To pursue my own studies and at the same time build up an entirely new ministry among foreign students in this city was impossible owing to the time factor; the distances were so great that it often took half a day to make a single visit. After spending several weeks in this manner and after organising two public meetings for foreign students, I realised that under such conditions it would be impossible to finish my studies in the normal space of time. Accordingly, I decided to first complete my studies in preparation for the planned ministry. A few weeks later the Berlin branch of the Women's Division of the German Student Christian Movement (DCSB) asked me to work with them and I agreed to do so, because it seemed to be possible in addition to my studies and because I was hungry for fellowship with dedicated Christian students.

My studies weighed upon me like a cross. Certainly I took an interest in intellectual matters. Even as a young girl when my mother taught me how to keep house and later during my youth work in Darmstadt, I took courses in psychology, philosophy and history of art, but I never had the inclination to spend many hours sitting over books. When I was a child, half an hour of reading would suffice and I would be up and about again. I was anything but a bookworm. Yet now for weeks, months and years I had nothing else to do but pore over books – books about psychology, philosophy, history of art and above all about theology, since I studied mainly theology in the first year.

In my major subject, which was psychology, I attended the lectures of the brilliant founder of a new school, Professor Spranger, who among others had examined me during the aptitude test, and whose generous treatment of psychological questions from the scientific aspect opened up many new perspectives for me. Through their lively presentation of theological matters, Professor Deissman and, in particular, Professor Luetgert, under whom I took a seminar, taught me to enjoy theology. When questions concerning textual criticism were raised, they could no longer cause me any difficulty personally, although it distressed me to see how such criticism made other young students doubt their faith. Usually it was extremely difficult to help them.

While I was in Berlin, I would frequently spend Sundays with Erika, who had returned from England the previous year and who now had a position as a social worker in Hamburg. Once more we had true spiritual fellowship, which was a great gift of God for me. The fact that we had again found complete oneness in the Lord was significant, because later we were to tread the same path and found the Sisterhood of Mary together in obedience to a call of God.

Unfulfilled under 'Cheap Grace'
University and Travelling Lectures,
Hamburg, Autumn 1931–Autumn 1935

Beginning with my second year in autumn 1931, I studied in Hamburg, living with Erika and her family. For both of us this marked a new phase in our spiritual lives. In the course of my life, there had been several crossroads when I made decisions in obedience to a clear inner compulsion – for example, when I interrupted my education at the Women's College for Social Welfare Training to enter Malche Bible College and later when I gave up my ministry in Darmstadt to complete my social welfare training in Berlin. This inner compulsion played a special role in the question of marriage. Should I or should I not marry? Much though I was attracted to marriage by the desire to have children, it was nevertheless clear to me that I had to go the way of celibacy according to God's vocation and leading for my life. Every time the question of marriage arose, I knew that I must say no, because I was being called to dedicate my life exclusively to Jesus and His service.

Likewise while I was studying in Hamburg, it was an inner compulsion that led me to begin a common life with Erika; we shared all our possessions and kept a common purse. During this period I received another proposal for marriage – this time from a minister who asked me with great sincerity. But even though the idea of serving in a congregation as a minister's wife appealed to me, I knew beyond doubt that I had to decline because of the inner assurance of a divine plan. God intended Erika and me to found and build up together a ministry in His kingdom.

Indeed, this divine plan was to be fulfilled later, but how little prepared we were at the time. To be sure, we read many theological works, especially those of Luther and Karl Barth, as well as histories of Christian missions, and in contrast to my year of teaching at Bible college, I was happy. But was I really 'happy in Jesus'? On a human level I was happy. My life somehow seemed to be transformed. The two previous years had been lonely ones, filled with trials and temptations and various problems, whereas now I found myself in a warm nest. No longer did I live alone in student lodgings, but with a family who cared for me lovingly. After suffering a year in the brick desert of Berlin, I was very grateful for the change. Here, in a residential area of Hamburg, were many trees, gardens and parks. Not far away was the Alster, a broad river which ran into the sea. Hamburg was truly a lovely city and won my heart immediately. The small university, which was surrounded by lawns, was situated near the 'Dammtor' and within walking distance. How relieved I was that I no longer had to take the underground railway to university! I felt that I had emerged from the unnatural existence of the past years and settled down to a more natural way of life. Body and soul rejoiced in the light and sun.

While I was teaching at Malche Bible College and while I was studying in Berlin, books were more or less my only companions, whereas here, in Hamburg, I had fellowship with Erika, who shared all my sorrows and joys as well as my interests, and I was at home in her family. Together we made art tours that were necessary for my studies, going to Holland, France and Italy, and during these travels we discovered the wealth that lies in all the gifts of art and nature.

No longer did I have to study alone in my room, for

Erika, who had always been interested in art and psychology, even shared my studies with me. Late in the afternoon, after Erika had finished her day's work at the welfare office, we would either meet in the university where she attended some of the lectures with me or else on the banks of the beautiful Alster. On those marvellous summer days many yachts would skim along the surface of the water – a cheerful picture – with the old, venerable towers of the Hanseatic city rising in the background.

It was easy to study in Hamburg, especially during the last summer before taking my Ph.D. examination, when Erika helped me by testing me on the material, as well as by typing my thesis. This was a treatise on the psychoreligious theme, 'The Significance of the Conviction of Sin in the Religious Conflict of Female Adolescents', based on four hundred letters, which I had received from the girls in my youth work in Darmstadt. In 1933 I presented this thesis to the well-known psychologist, Professor Stern. In contrast to Spranger, Stern's psychology was empirical, and it was his lectures that had inspired me to do my psychological research on the empirical basis. However, owing to the political upheaval in 1933 I could not complete my doctorate under him, but had to change professors. To my deepest regret, and the regret of many other students, Professor Stern, as well as my highly respected and distinguished teachers, Professor Cassirer (philosophy) and Professor Panofsky (history of art) under whom I took most of my courses, were compelled to relinquish their positions that year, since they were Jews. Consequently, I was examined by new teachers and it was not a matter of course that I passed with good grades.

Despite the fact that God, in His loving-kindness, made my studies as easy and as pleasant as possible, at heart I still yearned for a real ministry like the youth work I had in Darmstadt, for my studies left me basically unsatisfied. Certainly I was soon more involved in the work of the Women's Division of the German Student Christian Movement (DCSB), becoming president of the branch in Hamburg, later regional and then national president – but to my distress, the Word of God did not find much fertile ground among the students. It was choked by the thorns of the many intellectual and theological discussions. Moreover, my work from 1933 to 1935 took place during the time of National Socialism when every Christian student group was split in two: those adhering to the Confessing Church and those adhering to the 'German Christians'. Wherever one went, this was usually the main topic of discussion, and there was a sharp clash of opinion.

I myself was a registered member of the Confessing Church, and it was in this spirit that I led the DCSB. What battles ensued as a result at that time! I still recall the stormy night session in Hanover in February 1934 when the question was discussed as to whether or not as a student Christian movement we should comply with the demand to introduce the Aryan paragraph. I succeeded in persuading the group to reject this move. That meant that Hebrew Christian students would continue to be accepted into our circles, but it also meant that we had to reckon with the possibility of the entire organisation being dissolved. As national president I wrote a letter to all member branches of the DCSB on January 16, 1934. After mentioning the board's rejection of the Aryan paragraph, I went on to say:

. . . In many universities we are now faced with serious decisions because of the prohibition of double membership. It is a question of remaining in the DCSB or of switching over to the ANST (General National Socialist Student Organisation). For some this has already caused much fear and trembling, especially in those places where the ANST is hostile towards the DCSB, since one's chances in the examinations could be ruined and one's future career jeopardised. It is inevitable that such thoughts will occur to us, once we face the situation. However, as Christians, we must combat this reality with the reality of Christ, before whom the facts of this situation will dwindle into nothing. People and things are nothing before His might and majesty. They are subject to the Lord who created heaven and earth; they are mere instruments to accomplish His purposes for His own, according to His commands. Therefore, I entreat you, 'Ponder anew what the Almighty can do!'

It is vital that we now desire to bear witness to Christ and that we consider ourselves bound to uphold His cause, especially when our profession of faith can bring us harm. We are living in a highly significant time, since it is a time of decision. Let us not allow this time to pass by without giving our testimony when God calls us to do so. Let our declaration be, 'Christ is my Lord. I belong to Him in life and death.'

May the Lord find the DCSB alert in these critical days so that His promise might be fulfilled for them, 'The spirit of glory and of God rests upon you.'

Let us now close ranks and uphold one another so that no one leaves the movement out of weakness. Let us be one in professing Christ our Lord, and let us courageously believe Him, for His is the kingdom and the power!

Although I had not rested until the DCSB had rejected the Aryan paragraph, and although I myself was in full agreement with the spiritual principles of the Confessing Church, I did not consider it right that Christian student fellowships as a whole should join the Confessing Church, since the student fellowships were supposed to be evangelistic. If fellowships of the DCSB were incorporated in the Confessing Church, seeking students who were ignorant of this conflict would be refused admittance, since they did not possess a 'red card' (the membership card of the Confessing Church). Consequently, they would miss an opportunity to hear God's Word and to come to Christ. Many were unable to comprehend my attitude in this matter and thus I had not only 'German Christian' students against me, but also students from the Confessing Church, for the latter demanded that the DCSB as a whole join the Confessing

Church. In the midst of this controversy I stood by sadly, for my deepest concern – to bring students closer to Jesus – was almost always frustrated by such theological discussions, which were often not carried on in the right spirit. Even in the Bible studies my fellow students usually reacted only intellectually.

From 1933 until completing my doctorate in 1934 I was national president of the DCSB, whereas from 1934 on I was national president as well as travelling secretary of the movement, and regularly visited the DCSB branches in the various university towns.

Grateful though I am for all the inspiration, insight, correction and fellowship that I received during this time, I look back on those days with sadness, for I feel that I did not give my best to the university students and the graduates. I myself sensed that my ministry had little power. It lacked the authority that would have reached the hearts of the students, and I was conscious that I was mainly to blame that I found this ministry so trying and unsatisfying. It could not merely have been the intellectual attitude of the students nor the theological arguments, caused by the historical events of the times, that were responsible for this fact. The cause must have lain deeper.

At the time the reason was not clear to me, but I can now see it in retrospect. During those years in Hamburg I had no cross to bear! Since God had given me a new and deeper fellowship with Erika, I no longer stood alone. All that would have otherwise weighed me down – political concerns, troubles in the DCSB, or in my studies – she bore with me. In addition, we had rich times of sharing. Even matters that had caused me many pangs of conscience in the past such as the question of world-affirmation or world-denial had faded into the background, although a true solution had not yet been found.

However, the real reason why my ministry lacked power was that during those years when life was pleasant for me I had become conformed to the world and lukewarm in my love for Jesus without realising it. I was no longer challenged by His words, 'If any man would come after me, let him deny himself and take up his cross.' The truth was that I shirked the cross. During my many travels for the DCSB, when I had to suffer various discomforts, especially because of my rheumatism, I sometimes complained about the strenuous work and did it reluctantly. Small wonder, then, that my ministry did not bring forth fruit.

The way Erika and I spent our Sundays was typical of our spiritual life at the time. All week long we looked forward to Sunday when we would make an excursion out to Wedel, a small village near Hamburg-Blankenese. There we had a wonderful view of the Elbe as we wandered over the dikes for an hour, wending our way through lonely pastures where many herds of cattle were grazing. To be sure, we always made an early start in order to reach Wedel in time for church – for the Word of God was important to us – but the main emphasis of our Sundays was the enjoyment of the beautiful countryside. In the wide pastures we could relax and Erika could paint her lovely water-colours. Usually we read spiritual books, such as the works of Martin Luther and Karl Barth, but Jesus was actually in the background. Our main purpose was not to spend Sundays in quietness, meeting Jesus anew in prayer. We were more concerned with theological knowledge.

Our workdays were similar. 'Morning watches' and evening devotions had their fixed times, and we were faithful to them, as we were to church services and the weekly Bible studies. But where was the resolution and perseverance in the battle of faith against sin? Where was the sacrificial spirit and genuine zeal for Jesus and His kingdom? Where was the wrestling in prayer for human souls? Where was the spirit of adoration, the awe and wonder at the magnitude of the love of God? My life was a piece of bourgeois Christianity, even though the students considered me an uncompromising Christian, who insisted upon one-sided discipleship. Despite all the riches I gained from the fellowship with Erika and the stimulating intellectual life during those years, I was poor. Because I rarely wept over my sins, my soul could not rejoice in Jesus, my Redeemer. Consequently, I was unable, in the power of the Holy Spirit, to bring the students the message of the glory of Jesus as our Redeemer and King and the call to love Him.

If those years only let me stray from the true purpose of my life, why was it that God led me to university? I frequently asked myself that during the hard times following 1935. Today I realise that the period in Hamburg was serving to a highly significant end according to the wisdom and goodness of God. Through my studies my keen psychological attitude towards life and thus towards all religious experiences was strengthened. In myself and in others I learnt to discern that which was not purely spiritual but rather influenced by the soul and personality. Thus I became very sceptical of much of the 'Christian life'. This was the wise leading of God, for later I was to experience the tremendous grace of bridal love for Jesus and to introduce my spiritual daughters to this secret. I was also to bring this message of bridal love, of 'first love' for Jesus to many others through my books.

In this bridal love for Jesus one must be quick to discern whether there are any soulish elements or even repressed drives present. Through years of studying psychology and psycho-analysis I was well aware of this danger and had become even more alert in this respect, after having realised at an early stage that all soulish Christianity, whether in its inflexibility or over-enthusiasm, can usually be traced back to repression. Bridal love, in contrast, is soundly rooted in the truth. It lies in the personal conviction of sin, in contrition and repentance, which is a change of heart and an amendment of one's ways. True bridal love is, therefore, the outcome of the experience of forgiveness, as we can see from the love the sinner expresses for Jesus (Luke 7).

Only as the Holy Spirit disclosed my sins and brought them into the light, did I receive the gift of first love for Jesus. The contrition that was granted to me then brought me into a closer relationship with the Lord and kindled me with a deeper love for Him. In Jesus I found all that I sought

– fulfilment and blessedness for my life. Jesus inclined Himself to me as the Bridegroom, revealing His heart of love, just as He had come to me as the crucified Lord, Redeemer and Saviour when I was seventeen years old. The sign that this love for Him was genuine and imparted by His Spirit was that God granted me more love for my cross and more grace to overcome than I had ever experienced. From then on no sacrifice would have been too great for me, since 'the love of Christ constraineth us'. Now I could say, 'For Jesus' sake I do not account my life of any value nor as precious to myself.'

One can only lead others or pass on a message, such as the message of bridal love for Jesus, if one has thought the matter through and undergone the suffering involved – as in my case with the conflict between world-affirmation and world-denial. Then one can guarantee that the way is right. Only if one has intimately faced the dangers and knows every aspect of the path is one in a position to lead others along this path and to warn them of the pitfalls. Thus I was privileged to see that my spiritual daughters, who followed this path, did not fall into emotionalism, lose themselves in spiritual fantasy or become inhibited. Instead they became free and natural people, happy and joyful, since nothing can make a person happier than loving Jesus.

However, the years in Hamburg were significant for me in yet another respect. In reading the works of Luther and Barth, Erika and I comprehended anew the gift of living under justification by faith. After I had been disappointed by people who relied on their conversion, Luther was a new discovery for me. As a reaction against the legalistic and contrived striving for sanctification in which I had been caught up and which had such a dampening effect upon others, I welcomed this teaching, though I was now in danger of emphasising justification by grace alone, of separating grace from faith, which inspired by love, brings forth fruit. Thus I was in danger of living by 'cheap grace'. However, for the time being we rejoiced anew in the fact that we were 'justified by grace' and that sinners of all people – the 'godless and condemned' – are pardoned and justified. We drank in this teaching to our heart's content.

Our studies of the works of Martin Luther and Karl Barth were also significant later for leading the Sisterhood of Mary, since these books gave us new insight about the necessity of daily repentance. Until then I had mainly heard about the doctrines of conversion, regeneration and sanctification and they were the basis for my spiritual life. But even though the Lord in His grace always led me into situations where I experienced that only new conviction of sin and repentance open the door to deeper knowledge of God and closer fellowship with Him, I still had no theological grounding for such divine guidance. However, this was now shown to Erika and me as we read these works together. We made the vital discovery that the experience of salvation – sinners, who have fallen short of the glory of God, are justified by grace – is not confined to a single hour during the actual conversion (as generally thought in pietistic circles), rather it should be a permanent state of the life of a Christian. Every day the Christian sins against God and man, and, therefore, every day the Christian stands under judgement because of his wrongdoings. But at the same time he stands under grace. In other words, he is convicted of sin ever anew through God's judgement, and by faith in Jesus he receives forgiveness. Only if a person lives in a state of daily repentance, will he be protected from pharisaism and hypocrisy – the two main sins of believers. Indeed, Jesus refers to this malady of religious people time and again.

The seeds that had been sown in those years in Hamburg put forth shoots later when this theory, which we had accepted mainly with the intellect, was put into practice as we followed difficult leadings under the judgement of God. Now we had to acknowledge ourselves as sinners before God and man in everyday life. Painful though it was to see ourselves as sinners, we discovered that the sinner's place at the feet of Jesus becomes the place of those who, filled with gratitude for the forgiveness of their sins, cannot but love Him. This personal leading of God was an act of grace in view of the Sisterhood of Mary, which would be called to lead and proclaim a life of bridal love for Jesus. Thus the sound basis that sinners are justified by faith alone was of the utmost importance so that souls would not climb up into mystical worlds and lose the ground of reality from under their feet, devoting themselves to an imaginary piety and holiness. For this reason, Erika, later known as Mother Martyria, fed her spiritual daughters on the wholesome diet of the Letter to the Romans as the basis for their spiritual lives.

Although those years in Hamburg were not fully dedicated to the Lord, they were filled with His preparatory dealings with me. But now the time was coming when Jesus would lead me into a deeper and more exclusive committal to Him than I could ever have imagined during my years of legalistic striving for sanctification. At the same time He would deliver me from the bonds of legalism and introduce me to the naturalness of God's children, which stems from love for Jesus. But in order to do so, God had to bring my humanly pleasant years in Hamburg to an end and to lead me into new depths, along new 'desert roads', which were to be in direct preparation for the Sisterhood of Mary.

All in Vain?
Bible Courses in the Steinberg House,
Darmstadt, 1935–1938

At the end of my time in Hamburg, God laid a new commission in my heart. I had the unmistakable assurance for it, even though the details were not clear at first. It seemed to me as though the Lord wished to erect a 'house on a hill', a place where the great deeds that He performs today as of old would be proclaimed to His glory, so that His name would be magnified and people would be called to Him.

In 1935, at the age of thirty-one, I moved back to my parents' home in Darmstadt – this time with Erika. The next step had been shown to me. We were to begin three-month and half-year Bible courses for young women, above all, for future wives of ministers. At a time when the current trends were in opposition to Holy Scripture, these courses were intended to lead young women deeper into the Word of God before they began to train for a career or serve in a congregation as a minister's wife.

In order to be certain that I was not following a self-chosen path, I asked for a confirmation, since, humanly speaking, this path seemed to be shrouded in darkness. Even though I was so sure of this God-given commission, I was prepared to return it to Him. If the board of Malche Bible College should ask me to serve there, I was willing to give up the ministry that Erika and I intended to begin in Darmstadt. In earlier years the principal had frequently mentioned that she would be glad to have me on the staff after I had finished my studies, and thus it was highly probable that she would now ask me to come and teach. I prayed that God would direct the heart of Miss Wasserzug, the principal. Her decision would be His decision at this crossroads; it would be a sign to me of the will of God.

In February 1935 I set out to visit the Bible college, but God took the situation into His hands and I was not invited to teach. Half a year later the invitation came, but by then the die had already been cast. Erika had moved to Darmstadt with me; during a time of widespread unemployment she had relinquished her position as a social worker in Hamburg with her guarantee for a pension in order to serve Jesus. And I had resigned from my office as national president of the DCSB, although they wished the work to remain in my hands and asked me to stay. There was no turning back now.

The move from Hamburg to Darmstadt was like Abraham's move from Ur, but in miniature. It was a venture in faith. We set out in obedience to a commission of God, not knowing if, or how, the entrusted commission would materialise. Nor did we know how it would be financed. Yet since this commission was from God, I was utterly convinced that it would be carried out. Thus when the Bible college asked me to serve there, I wrote to the board, 'I believe that God intends to do a great and significant work in Darmstadt, and, therefore, I feel obliged to remain here.'

But nothing seemed to come of this commission! In the winter of 1935–6 Erika and I lovingly prepared the attic apartment in my parents' home, the Steinberg House, for the students who were to come and live there; we made a kitchen and dining room in the cellar, spending no small sum of money on these alterations. During that first year Erika and I lived in cramped quarters one floor beneath the attic apartment in the room where we held Bible studies for women in Darmstadt, since we wished to reserve the upper storey for the coming students. My parents had warmly welcomed us and provided us with furniture and bedclothes.

However, the beds remained empty and the rooms silent. After publishing a brochure about the Bible courses, we waited week after week for applications – but they did not come. And the few girls who did apply withdrew shortly before the course was due to begin. What a disappointment! During those first years the words, 'in vain', seemed to be stamped on all our preparations. In vain had the rooms been furnished. In vain had Erika spent all her savings from her social welfare work in Hamburg on the interior decoration of the rooms. In vain had she given up her government job. It had all been in vain.

Now came the voice of temptation. Had I been mistaken, as others tried to tell me, in thinking that this was a divine call, a God-given commission? Was I walking in disobedience to Him? How joyfully we had moved into the Steinberg House, 26 Hoelderlin Drive! But soon that friendly, one-family house, with its large garden, in a lovely residential district close to the woods, no longer smiled at us so kindly. What painful recollections we have of the walks through the woods when we discussed our situation! To this day it cuts us to the heart whenever we see one of those benches where, engulfed in darkness, we sat in tears and conferred about our frustrated plans, wondering what the next step would be.

A great consolation along this dark pathway – in contrast to the dark times in my youth – was that now I had someone with whom I could share the burden. Together Erika and I recognised more and more clearly the voice of God speaking to us through the circumstances. Although we began these Bible courses at an unfavourable time – in the era of National Socialism – when girls had almost no opportunity to attend such a Bible course owing to Government and Labour Office regulations, we clearly realised that it was God alone who was saying NO in this situation. He showed us unmistakably that He could not yet use us for such a ministry. All we could do was to humble ourselves and say, 'Lord, Your ways are holy!' Time and again God helped us on a step further, for instance, by granting us the opportunity to hold regular Bible studies in the Steinberg House for thirty to forty women.

A few months later, at the request of a teacher, I took over a Girls' Bible Study Group that had been officially dissolved in 1933 owing to the political situation. I began the ministry with a sad heart, for nothing had come of the Bible courses, which we thought were our real ministry. Little did we realise that this Girls' Bible Study Group (MBK) was a seed that would grow from year to year and one day blossom into the Sisterhood of Mary. Indeed, the hour of birth for the MBK work at the Steinberg House marked the beginning of God's hidden plan for the Sisterhood of Mary, as is evident from the verse that I chose after much prayer for the first Bible study with six girls between the ages of fourteen and eighteen. 'Repent, for the kingdom of heaven is at hand' (Matthew 3:2). This verse has faithfully accompanied us throughout the years in the Sisterhood of Mary. It was the theme of the dedication service of the Herald Chapel and has become the watchword of our Land of Canaan and all the Canaan Friends.

How could we have realised the significance of this first unpretentious Bible study group for girls? All we could see was that our plans lay in ruins; the continual reproaches of others that such self-chosen paths were bound to lead to a fiasco was another way of God saying NO to us.

But in the darkness of that first year God let a star of promise shine upon us. It was a verse of Scripture that He had given Erika at a critical moment.

> For still the vision awaits its time; it hastens to the end – it will not lie. If it seem slow, wait for it; it will surely come, it will not delay (Habakkuk 2:3).

Over the years we steadfastly claimed this verse in faith. Indeed, we had no other choice but to follow the pathway of faith. With no fixed income we had to ask the heavenly Father in faith to supply all our material needs, and in view of our inner commission we also had to walk by faith. For months on end the rented attic apartment stood empty before our eyes, and when the Bible courses failed to materialise, the furniture that had been given for that purpose was no longer available – and without it there was no possibility of accepting students later on.

Those first years after the move from Hamburg were fraught with trials and temptations. We had to go through a long, dark tunnel and we thought we should never see the light again. But in our hearts a new and different light appeared. Now we were to experience in real life the spiritual truth of the doctrine that we had intellectually accepted in Hamburg – the justification of sinners. The NO from God, the contempt and disgrace, the many difficulties in living together with others, all helped us to abandon our intellectual acknowledgement of sin and to see ourselves as sinners that deserve reproaches in everyday life. Thus we had cause to weep over our sins, but likewise to accept Jesus' sacrifice and forgiveness – and as pardoned sinners to accept true justification with thanksgiving.

God had in mind the Sisterhood of Mary, which was to be founded and built up on contrition and repentance. The movement of repentance was to begin in the MBK during the revival years, 1944–5, and then continue day by day, year by year as God repeatedly granted conviction of sin in our Sisterhood. Only in this way could new life be born and love for Jesus kindled. Since we were to be the founders, it was inevitable that judgement and an ever new experience of contrition and repentance would be the pattern of our lives in the years preceding the foundation of the Sisterhood of Mary. During this period Jesus began to grant us repentance, and after the first difficult year I wrote to Erika for her birthday in 1936:

'Who is a God like thee, pardoning iniquity!' (Micah 7:18). We can praise and glorify God for many things, but no exultation on earth can or will surpass the exultation over God's gift of the forgiveness of sins. The song of rejoicing, 'Bless the Lord, O my soul', resounds not only here on earth, but also throughout the heavenly spheres today, for there is joy in heaven over one sinner who repents. And if the anthems of praise for all God's goodness to us in this life cease one day, another song will be raised by the heavenly throng above – the song of the Lamb who has borne our sins.

Does this song of thanksgiving resound in our hearts – 'Who is a God like thee, pardoning iniquity' – or do our prayers lack this note of praise? If so, how can we then join in singing the song of the Lamb at the throne?

Erika, at the beginning of last year, we scarcely knew the song of jubilation expressed in this verse of Scripture. But do you remember when we first found Christ? You will recall your confirmation classes and the time in Kassel and I my time at Bible college. Among my favourite songs then were, 'O the joy of being redeemed' and 'There is a fount where holy blood for wretched sinners flows . . . When I was sunk in sin and woe, for me the blood of Jesus flowed, so I'll rejoice until I die and praise the crimson tide . . .'

Yet all those years, while I was studying and waiting and you were involved in social work, our hearts were so laden with the things of this world that the song of the

Lamb died away, and our hearts no longer knew this exultation, 'Who is a God like thee, pardoning iniquity!' We had resigned ourselves to the fact that we were not victorious over certain sinful traits in our characters. We were no longer so grieved about these bonds as we were before – and consequently we no longer had a daily encounter with the Redeemer and could no longer rejoice over His forgiveness and His power to deliver us from our sins. We strayed farther and farther along this path, without realising that it was leading us away from Christ.

But Erika, God in His grace sought us so that our hearts could once again sing the song of praise to the Lamb and so that we could be with Him on His great day. By the grace of God we became strongly aware of our sin and bondage in the past year – during our work in winter but especially last summer with X. One thing we both learnt was that we cannot forgive, be merciful, suffer injustice or react with meekness. In our present state we shall not be able to take our place with the overcomers one day, for without holiness no one will see the Lord. O Erika, to think that God gave us the recognition of our sin this past year! What could have been greater!

What other verse could we have received for your birthday than this verse of thanksgiving, 'Who is a God like thee, pardoning iniquity'? What could have been more fitting, especially in view of the lost years?

Erika, now we can begin our ministry. Previously, we weren't really able to do so, for unless one's heart is filled with this song of jubilation, one cannot pass on the good news of the forgiveness of sin. One can only do so and have the power and authorisation to carry out such a ministry if one's heart rejoices. 'His blood has washed all my sins away,' and if with shining eyes one points to the Lamb – the Lamb who has accomplished the greatest and most wonderful deed. The old year brought us the knowledge of our specific bondages and the forgiveness of God. The new year, let us solemnly resolve, Erika, shall be devoted to fervent struggles and wrestling in prayer so that we may overcome our sins, for, 'if the Son makes you free, you will be free indeed.'

If in the years before that we had been lukewarm in our struggle against sin, since we did not stand under chastening, which would have brought our sins to light, the unmasking had come this past year. Once again our hearts rejoiced and sang of the redemption – and this song of the Lamb, the song of love for Jesus, was to be the song of the Sisterhood of Mary. Even today I cannot fully comprehend the Lord's grace in rescuing me from the lukewarmness of my time in Hamburg, and filling me once more with the jubilation of a truly pardoned sinner.

As in my childhood and youth, it was the cross that was my deliverance. Without the cross and without chastening in my life I should have been the most wretched Christian on earth: self-righteous, self-satisfied, lifeless and in addition, proud – and either legalistic or worldly. But what blessings of God I received along pathways of the cross! These hardships made me the happiest person imaginable. The cross always gave me a two-fold perspective. It brought me not only a glimpse into the abyss of my heart and my sin, but also a glimpse into God's heart of love and mercy, letting me behold the crucified Lord, whom I had 'pierced'. This glimpse kindled me with a love that grew stronger with each new cross and that paved the way for the mystery of the Holy Trinity to be unfolded to me in later years.

One day the Sisterhood of Mary would also follow the path of ever-new conviction under God's judgement as in our times of 'fellowship in the light' (1 John 1:7). Indeed, this would have to be the spiritual basis, since it was the way God had led us, the future founders of the Sisterhood.

At the end of that first sad year (autumn 1935–autumn 1936) an urgent request came from Malche Bible College. My revered teacher, Miss Jeanne Wasserzug, lay on her deathbed and asked me to step in for her and to teach some of her classes. Since I still did not have a definite ministry in Darmstadt then, and Erika was in a position to take over the MBK and the Women's Bible Study Groups, we decided that I should go for three months. During that period my beloved teacher died and I was requested to stay on in view of the momentarily difficult situation. Thus I continued to hold lectures until summer.

Erika remained alone in Darmstadt – a strange city to her, where she knew hardly a soul. She had no money, for from the very outset we felt clearly led not to accept any support from our parents as long as we were certain that God had called us to Darmstadt. By means of occasional tutoring Erika managed to tide over this period. Unknown to anyone, she was living in real poverty, though she did have the basic essentials of life.

It was a time of dying and thus a time of grace, a time of repentance and of bearing fruit. How could we have begun the Lord's work as we were when we came from Hamburg – proud and unbroken? Through chastening and suffering God led us on to the paths that we were later to tread voluntarily out of love for Him in the Sisterhood of Mary – the way of faith and poverty, the 'way of the Lamb'. But first we had to follow these paths, undergoing the suffering involved, before we could call the Sisters of Mary to go the same way.

One year, then a second, passed by in this manner. Now we had an inkling of what it meant to keep faith, to be poor. During the winter as I helped out in Malche Bible College, I possessed little more than a skirt and a pullover. Like poor people we were dependent upon the gifts of others. In the previous years we had saved the money that would otherwise have been spent on clothing in order to finance our future independent ministry. My father kindly offered to give us the attic apartment without charging any rent and to help us in other ways. But we felt we ought to decline this offer, since God, through His calling for our lives, was leading us along this path of the cross to teach us to follow Him and persevere in faith. Only in this way was God glorified in the end for having brought us through and having led us along the right path. At the same time poverty was an effective cure for our pride.

One thing in any event did grow during this dark period, and that was the small MBK, which soon developed into several groups. Yet as far as we were concerned, this was not the commission originally entrusted to us. Consequently, in July 1937, at the end of the course at Malche Bible College, where I had been helping out, we were still not sure where our path would take us in the future. It seemed as though it would lead us away from Darmstadt and as though God's commission for us there would never materialise, because that summer the Bible college had asked Erika as well to come and teach there on a permanent basis. Although I still had the unshakable conviction that our real ministry was in Darmstadt, we agreed to comply, feeling that God intended to lead us on a detour. Then I received a significant letter from the Bible college, which made it clear to me that we could not go there. I withdrew our consent – though not before waging a hard battle of prayer to discover the will of God.

Thus we remained in Darmstadt. We had no income – often we had less than five marks between us. But above all we were not yet working at our real task. Certainly, the MBK ministry had continued to expand, but only for the women's weekly Bible studies in Darmstadt and the occasional lecture that I was requested to give out of town, for example, in a ladies' group, did we receive a small honorarium. It was extremely humiliating for me to have to wait for an occasional request to minister, but I never doubted that this was precisely the right way. I knew that the main point was to bear it out of love for Jesus. After the first nine months in Darmstadt I wrote in our working diary:

May the future be as God wills in regard to our ministry. That the ministry will materialise· we know. But what detours and blows are necessary! Christ must be glorified in every situation! May God help us to do so. (June 29, 1936)

In the summer of 1938, some future wives of ministers

came to us for a Bible course – the first and last one. There were only three girls living with us and one day-student, and before the end of the course one of the girls had to leave, because her wedding day was put forward and so it was not really a Bible course after all.

When the course was over, all our hopes crumbled. A second course failed to materialise. God continued to chasten us by humbling us more deeply as He led us further along the pathway of hardship and poverty. We felt His holy hand upon us, disciplining us out of love as He led us along a desert road for many years. We humbled ourselves beneath His hand, realising with greater perception our insistence upon being right and our rebelliousness towards others. But as He led us along these dark pathways of chastening, we came to see His infinite love all the more – and that made our faith grow as our diary entries in 1937 and 1938 indicate. On October 21, 1937, Erika wrote:

> Even though we must grope in faith, His love is behind all these leadings concerning the commission. It is His love that is leading us through the dark vale. Above it a bright light is shining – He has not taken the commission away from us. What a wonderful act of grace! Even though we cannot see the commission with our physical eyes, He has let us see it clearly with the eyes of faith.

Beneath this entry I wrote:

> He will do it. His word is true and unfailing.

Since to all outward appearances we did not have a full-time occupation, Erika received an offer for a travelling lectureship with the Leipzig Missionary Society. Once more the ministry threatened to end. On November 16, 1937, I wrote:

> Lord, have mercy upon us. The way is very dark. I believe Your promise in Habakkuk 2:3 for our ministry that is to begin at Easter.

On January 21, 1938, I wrote:

Humanly speaking, it is as black as night. But why does God continue to postpone our ministry? He must have a purpose in this. Oh, I simply have to believe it. Free us from our insistence upon being right and our bitterness towards X. Do not let these sins stand in the way of Your ministry. You know that this is our one great concern, our one great plea.

On April 2, 1938, when only three registrations arrived for the course for future wives of ministers:

Once more we face a task – time-consuming, expensive and requiring all our effort – and yet it neither thrives, nor does it die. In actual fact we have no real ministry (particularly in my case, since I do not have an extensive youth ministry as Erika has) and the humiliation is great. But behind it all is the hand of God. That we can sense. We can only be grateful that if You humble us, You will exalt us!

During those first three years (1935–8) God led us with great wisdom. Though we did not realise it at the time, we were privileged to tread in the footsteps of Jesus along the pathway of poverty, humiliation and lowliness, along the path of faith engulfed in darkness and surrounded by impossibilities – what tremendous grace! In His love God Himself led us on to these paths. With trembling but grateful hearts we followed Him, for we knew that His love was guiding us and that paths of lowliness were good for proud sinners. On these paths Jesus drew close to us and since they were 'His ways', they became precious to us. Later these same paths would be characteristic for the Sisterhood of Mary.

In September 1938 we reached our lowest point. After the somewhat unsuccessful Bible course for prospective wives of ministers in the summer, no new registrations arrived, as already mentioned. Again we stood before a huge nothing – but this time it seemed final. We were about to strike tents in Darmstadt. The rent for the attic apartment had to be paid and there was not a single glimmer of hope. In October 1938 we were down to our last penny.

During those days the Leipzig Missionary Society invited Erika again to serve as a travelling lecturer, and in view of the hopeless situation at the time, we asked ourselves whether this might not be God's leading. He no longer seemed to be confirming our joint ministry in Darmstadt. We faced the end of our commission. If we accepted this proposal and Erika went to Leipzig, we should be separated and thus all hopes of a joint ministry would be buried for good. But God intended to bring the Sisterhood of Mary into existence and thus He held His hand over the ministry in Darmstadt, although He let us sacrifice this calling in spirit – just as Abraham had offered up Isaac.

It was most strange. As God demanded this sacrifice of us, He also inspired us with the faith that our 'Isaac' – our commission in Darmstadt – would be rescued from death and come into being after all. The Spirit of God helped us both to remain unshakable in our faith, to cling steadfastly to the verse of Scripture that had continued to be our weapon in the battle of faith all those years.

For still the vision awaits its time; it hastens to the end – it will not lie. If it seem slow, wait for it; it will surely come, it will not delay (Habakkuk 2:3).

We went into town to procure a suitcase for Erika's ministry in Leipzig, and with that we sacrificed our common life and joint commission. But upon our return home, we found a note in the letterbox. Only a few words were written on it. 'Don't leave Darmstadt. A circle of friends will support the youth ministry.'

For us it was an intervention of God. What was the story behind it? The leading minister of the local deaconess house, who had always had a soft spot in his heart for youth work, had been watching the growth of the MBK with interest. When he heard of the renewed request the Leipzig Missionary Society had sent to Erika, he moved swiftly. Together with the Rev. Wolf, the minister of St Paul's (most of our girls lived in this parish), he arranged for steps to be taken. A circle of friends at St Paul's committed themselves to support the MBK work from then on by providing a small monthly stipend, since a year earlier, in 1937, the MBK had been formally affiliated with this church owing to the political conditions of the times. Thus God bound us anew to Darmstadt.

The work that I had begun in 1936 with six girls had grown in two years under Erika's leadership to a membership of a hundred high school girls. God had given His confirmation to this ministry and let it flourish despite the unfavourable conditions under the National Socialist regime, which was actively opposed to all Christian youth work. When someone suggested to us in those days that the commission God had shown us for the Steinberg House might develop from the MBK, it seemed utterly incredible to us. But God's plan was far more wonderful than we had ever imagined. He had called the MBK into existence, since it would later give rise to the Sisterhood of Mary. At the time we were not permitted to see this plan, since we had not yet undergone all the preparations ordained by God for our future ministry.

With the youth work Erika had received a ministry from God. Despite the fact that I had begun this work and had longed for such a youth ministry for years now, since I so enjoyed working with young people, I had the clear conviction that it was not my task to share the leadership of these youth groups. In the autumn of 1938, after our first and last Bible course for future wives of ministers, I had no ministry. The MBK continued to grow, but I knew that this was Erika's commission and not mine. My attitude must have seemed rather strange, but I was firm despite Erika's solicitude and her pleas to lead the Bible studies with her. A year later it was evident what stood behind this inner compulsion, but for the time being I had no field of activity. I continued to wait until I was invited to give a lecture or hold a retreat for a ladies' group or was called to stand in as a substitute speaker.

My birthday in the autumn of 1938 was filled with tears and humiliation. It was a beautiful autumn day and in the morning Erika and I took a walk to Eberstadt, a residential suburb of Darmstadt. We went to pay a visit concerning an occasional opportunity to minister. It was very humiliating. Once again the answer was NO. After this disappointment we sat down on a bench with a direct view of the place where our Mother House now stands, but the future was hidden from our eyes, and I shed bitter tears, not knowing what fruit these tears would yield. In the afternoon some relatives who came to pay a birthday visit told me that all my ways since my youth work in Darmstadt had been self-chosen and egoistic. God's 'alleged call' to begin the Bible courses and all my talk about His 'guidance' were nothing but a 'tempting of God'. Had I not learnt my lesson now that I was confronted with the collapse of all my plans and undertakings? Was I not finally ready to repent? A few months later as I looked back on that half year, I wrote in our working diary:

But Lord, You know that I only sought to obey You. You know that every time I was faced with a decision, I sought Your will alone and accepted all Your leadings. And so one day You will demonstrate before all the world that we have been following Your guidance. (March 2, 1939)

The next weeks led me deeper into the vale of humiliation. Although I was now in my mid-thirties, had completed my studies at vocational colleges and at university and had held positions of responsibility, I had no other choice in the present situation but to hire myself out for housework and gardening at an hourly wage. At the time I wrote:

I feel despised and my hands are tied, but I know that I stand under Your grace and that I am in Your school – and that is more important than all activities and happiness.

The Lord had to prune my soulish desires – my creative impulse, my longing to be actively involved in His service –

a process that continued for many years. Ever since I left my youth work in Darmstadt as a twenty-two-year-old, the Lord had not fulfilled my desire for a similar ministry. This chastening was so necessary that He took me into His hand for almost twenty years, up to the founding of the Sisterhood of Mary. God wished to purify the inclinations of my soul in order that my activities and involvement in His project, the Sisterhood of Mary, would be done out of love for Him and not for my personal satisfaction under the cloak of piety.

It was painful to see how my 'strange' ways caused my father such distress, and in response to his urging to seek a job that would be fitting for a person with my academic training, I wrote a letter of application, but felt unable to post it. Once again I was acting according to an inner compulsion, for I knew that when the time was ripe, God Himself would intervene, and until then I had to remain in Darmstadt.

A few weeks later, in the midst of this distressing situation, the Missionary Society for Moslems in Wiesbaden suddenly asked me to take over their travelling lectureship. With a trembling heart I went to the interview. Thankful though I was to receive a ministry now, I was faced again with the spectre that had loomed before me eighteen months earlier – the possible doom of the commission that God had been showing me since 1935 for the Steinberg House.

During this interview I discovered how wonderful the thoughts and plans of God are. The missionary society, which had a strict rule that its co-workers had to live in the mission centre, made an exception in my case. God had turned their hearts. The director felt that God was at work in the Steinberg House through the Bible studies that Erika and I had begun together, and that therefore it would not be right to remove me immediately. He said that I could remain in Darmstadt to begin with and undertake the travelling lectures from there. At Easter 1939 I began this ministry, which was to last for seven years, and all the time I was permitted to have my headquarters in Darmstadt.

God at Work
Travelling Lectureship for the
Missionary Society for Moslems, 1939–1945

What was the situation now at the beginning of this new phase? The planned Bible courses for the prospective wives of ministers, which failed to materialise, seemed to have been transformed for good into Erika's MBK work and my travelling lectureship on behalf of the Missionary Society for Moslems. Yet from both these roots grew a tree – the Sisterhood of Mary. How wonderful are the ways of God! When I was inwardly restrained from leading the MBK together with Erika, I knew nothing of God's hidden plan. He was reserving me for the ministry in Wiesbaden, the acceptance of which would ultimately lead to the founding of the Sisterhood of Mary. At the time the purpose of God's leading was not yet visible. Since I was now employed by the Missionary Society for Moslems and Erika was fully occupied with the MBK work, there seemed to be no hope left for our actual ministry. Thus after accepting the position in the missionary society, I wrote the following in complete faith as my last entry in our working diary:

'My thoughts are not your thoughts.' God's thoughts are higher and more wonderful than ours – and He will accomplish His purposes gloriously.

My travelling ministry took me to the missionary society's circle of friends, to church groups and fellowships where I was asked to give missionary talks and, above all, Bible study courses. Owing to my physical weakness and the wartime conditions, I did not find travelling easy. I still recall the cold winters of 1940 and 1941 when there was a serious coal shortage. Shivering day and night, unable to sleep, I travelled in weather of minus 20° to 40° F for four weeks in East Prussia. During the blackout I often had to make my way alone through the city streets at night – I, who had always been fearful by nature. During my long-distance travels, for instance, between Hamburg and Munich or between Basle-Loerrach and Rhineland/Westphalia, almost suffocating in the over-crowded trains, I often heard the enemy bombers roaring above us. In my letters to Erika I described the situation:

Bielefeld, May 23, 1943

... After an hour and a half of sleep, we were awakened by the air-raid warning. The anti-aircraft guns were shooting violently and we went into the cellar. Although the raid was on another town, the doors rattled in their frames as the bombs fell. When we went back upstairs at 3 a.m., I simply couldn't fall asleep again. I was filled with fear and terror as I thought of the plight of the people in the town that had been hit. That night I didn't sleep a wink ...

June 18, 1944

I have safely arrived after having experienced the wonderful protection of the angels. I am immersed in Jesus Himself, in His peace and joy. When I left Bielefeld this morning, the sirens were wailing. It was at the height of the alarm. And the train was crammed. But you cannot imagine how secure I now feel during all these travels – perfectly happy as a child of His. I can really feel the love of Jesus, who seeks to sweeten the hardships of the journeys I undertake for His sake. My heart is full of thanksgiving.

Two small words made everything easy for me during those hard times – 'For You!' During my lectures I could speak about the power of the blood of Jesus, about His victory, about His coming again and His glory. With love for Jesus spurring me on, I could now perform my ministry in a completely different attitude from that when I was travelling for the DCSB. My main themes were 'God's Plan of Salvation' (which covered the second coming of Jesus, God's plan of salvation for Israel and the City of God), 'Heaven and Hell', 'The Blessings of Suffering' and 'How to Overcome'.

That which I now proclaimed was completely different

from the talks I gave as a twenty-two-year-old during my first youth work in Darmstadt. In those days as I worked among the young people, I myself was still so young and not yet proven in anything; the contents of my talks had not yet been fought through and spiritually digested. Consequently, my words could not be a genuine testimony. Now, in contrast, I could stand up for my convictions, since they had been tried and proven along pathways of chastening. In particular, it was the call to go the way of the Lamb out of love for Jesus that was constantly put to the test through God's working in me during those years.

From 1939 to 1944, that is, up to the time of revival in the MBK, the Lord allowed us to pass on some of the fruit of the last four difficult years and at the same time He gave us further preparation for the great hour of revival and the birth of the Sisterhood of Mary. In the years from 1936 to 1940 Gommel's *Lebendiges Wasser* and Bonhoeffer's *Nachfolge (The Cost of Discipleship)* were a help to me. Both of these books, so different from each other, gave me new incentive in the hard struggles that Erika and I had to undergo at that time. In the face of accusations and unjust demands we now had to learn to tread the path of the Lamb, taking the words of the Sermon on the Mount as binding: 'From him who takes away your cloak do not withhold your coat as well; love your enemies, do good to those who hate you.'

Even during my first youth ministry in Darmstadt (1926–8) my insistence upon justice, my difficulty in bearing wrongs committed against myself or others had been a real problem for me. The cry for deliverance constantly arose from my heart. How I longed to experience the power of Jesus' sacrifice in this particular sphere! At that time I wrote in my diary:

Oh, I could almost hate X! How annoying, how aggravating she is! For Your sake, Lord Jesus, I want to humble myself before X. (September 30, 1928)
I find it so hard to give up my rights for the sake of love.

I can only do it when I pronounce the name of Jesus, for then something melts in my heart. I am also helped by the verse, 'Overcome evil with good.' (October 7, 1928)

Indeed, I could sense how hard I found it to love when I had obviously been treated unjustly – and the thought agonised me. Yet it was a wonderful act of grace that even at that early stage God brought a person into my life who was an almost unbearable burden for me. Thus the plea to be full of love, which was my prayer request during my second year in the youth ministry in Darmstadt (1927–8), became the prayer of my life.

Grant me love, love which is not irritable or resentful, which bears all things, hopes all things, believes all things, endures all things. (October 21, 1927)

Now, ten years later, the Lord took me into His school again in a special way – this time together with Erika – in order to teach me this lesson. All those years my constant prayer was that He would truly grant me His love. That took a long time with a disposition such as mine. It took many years of hammer blows from one particular quarter. My heart would cry out because of all the injustices I experienced, but God did not desist. It was evidently part of His plan that arrows should be shot continually at this hard spot in my heart until it was 'riddled with holes'. Then my heart could overflow with contrition and repentance over my inability to forgive and love, and He could fill me with His love. My 'old self' writhed. But the blood of the Lamb, which I learnt to claim a great deal, demonstrated its power, melting the hardness in my heart bit by bit and gradually filling me with a merciful attitude towards the sin of the other person. In this way God taught me to go the way of the Lamb, no longer to justify myself but rather to suffer and endure in patience and to bear unjust reproaches. That alone is Jesus' pathway as I discovered.

Behind this situation too was the wise leading of God.

Later it was especially the message of perfect love that I was to proclaim in my books. But how could I write about this if God had not taught me under chastening and suffering to claim this love in faith according to the verse, 'Walk in love, as Christ loved us' (Ephesians 5:2)? Time and again His Word had clearly shown me that in situations where we are called to love our enemy, our human love reaches its limit and we come to the end of our resources. But God was gracious, and after spending many years in His school, I could testify from personal experience that when we are daily brought lower and our self-righteousness comes to naught, He opens the gates of His righteousness for us, and we are 'in Christ' and 'He in us'. In this way Jesus' words in John 17:26 are truly fulfilled, 'I made known to them thy name, and I will make it known, that the love with which thou hast loved me may be in them, and I in them.'

The struggle in faith to attain true love and the battle against my other sins gave rise to biblical lectures on the theme of 'How to Overcome'. Since the talks were based on experience, they spoke to the hearts of those who were faced with the same problems and inner conflicts. Upon the initiative of a minister the lectures were taken down in shorthand, typed and duplicated, and without my knowledge, hundreds of copies were distributed. I was filled with thanksgiving that the Lord had opened the doors for His Word, but little did I realise at the time that this was the very first beginning of my future writing ministry, which was to be one of my main tasks. Letters dating back to this period testify how much I yearned to overcome in my personal life, especially in areas where victory seemed almost impossible. Grief over my lukewarmness in the battle against sin (Hebrews 12:4) now spurred me on.

In March 1942 as I was in Karlsruhe for a speaking engagement, I wrote the following in a letter:

Watchwords for hours of temptation in seemingly hopeless struggles against sin.

In dark hours when I am tempted to say that all my struggles have been in vain, I shall tell myself:

1. It is my own fault that my chains are so tight, because I did not truly repent of my sins for such a long time and because I did not fight the battle of faith against my sin, which would have led to victory. Consequently, my chains became tighter, and now I must wait, in all humility, until God frees me. But I will keep up the struggle until the victory comes. No matter how long I have to wait – even if my struggle is ten times in vain – I will persevere until I am free.

2. God wants to train me in faith and teach me to believe as He taught the sisters of Lazarus at his death. He delays in sending His aid so that I may learn to have faith before seeing any results. And if I learn to keep faith, I shall see the glory of God. That was the outcome of the story of Lazarus and it will also be the outcome of my struggle.

3. God postpones His aid, letting me feel my chains and weakness so as to make me truly humble. Then He will receive the honour in the end and I shall praise Him alone.

Therefore, I want to learn humility in this inner conflict. And when the chains refuse to loosen, I will not rebel or grow discouraged, but rather persist humbly – like the Syrophoenician woman. I will beg and beg again, even when Jesus repeatedly seems to turn me away too and does not help.

Only those who have overcome and been made humble can take part in the first resurrection. And if I become humble and patient, it will have been these trials and temptations – especially if they lasted long – that brought me eternal fruit, victory and transformation into the image of Jesus. And perhaps it will have been these very trials and temptations that brought me to maturity and let me partake of the first resurrection.

4. Therefore, I give thanks for the exposure of my sin and

for my trials and temptations, for here in particular I shall be able to experience the victory and glory of Jesus as surely as Jesus sets us completely free. I give thanks that these trials and temptations are cleansing me of a number of sins that are revealed in the process, thus making me an overcomer who will one day inherit the crown – for without holiness no one will see the Lord. He who overcomes will inherit all things.

In the post-war period, beginning with 1946, it was once more possible to print Christian literature, and since there was such a great demand for copies of the lecture, 'How to Overcome', which had arisen from the above-mentioned struggles, we decided to have it printed. How wonderful are the ways of God! Amid chastening and suffering I fought my battles in faith in the power of Jesus' blood in the situations where God had placed me and God used my testimony to help many others in their temptations as we learnt time and again from letters and conversations. The significance of these leadings, however, was that God had in mind the Sisterhood of Mary and its commission. To accompany Jesus on His path out of love for Him, and thus to go the way of the Lamb, the way of patient, enduring love, the way of lowliness – that was to be the calling of the Sisterhood of Mary.

In yet another area the hand of God reached out to me more and more during those years, redirecting the course of my everyday life. I sensed that God wanted to take possession of my life in an entirely different way than previously, with every hour dedicated to Him and every penny placed at His disposal. It was as though Jesus were entreating, 'Give Me more of your time for prayer, for reading the Word. Give Me more room in your life, more of your gifts and possessions!' With this challenge God also granted me the gift of a deep love for Him, for He never gives the first without the second. Love is always exclusive. It yearns to give everything to the beloved. But whenever we put this love into practice in everyday life, it clashes with other things, which of necessity must yield or disappear – things on which we had previously spent our time, money or interest.

When I drew these conclusions for my life, it was at first hard for Erika to understand. Basically she was one with me, but when it came to putting one thing or another into practice, she raised rational objections. She asked whether this was not self-effort, which would stand in the way of grace. By nature Erika had never been inclined to follow another person's leadings, unless she herself was inwardly convinced that it was the right way. This complicated the issue somewhat.

Once again there was doubt about our joint ministry, which we still bore in our hearts as a God-given commission. In the present state of affairs we could not work together in the Lord's service and build up and carry out a joint ministry. Yet in my heart I definitely knew that I must follow my conscience and obey this call of Jesus, even if it meant separation, even if it meant the painful sacrifice of our joint ministry. Inwardly we battled the matter through as indicated by some of my letters in 1942–3 during my travelling ministry. In reply to Erika's objections I wrote at the time:

Bad Oeynhausen, December 13, 1942

. . . You write in such a depressed manner, because you cannot share my views. The point is not that one is no longer permitted to do anything that is not directly concerned with the ministry, but rather that from within one is so driven to prayer and Bible reading and to making visits out of a desire to win souls for His kingdom that there is little time left for personal interests. If a minister's wife, for instance, takes the time to read all the latest Christian novels, it is a sign that her spiritual life is not in order. If she truly longed for souls to be saved, she would be busy day and night in the congregation. If in our hearts we seek first the Kingdom of God and accept the other things only in so far as God chooses to grant them to us, that is not being legalistic. It is a question of whether love for Jesus and for human souls spurs us on.

Out of this love for souls, Blumhardt fasted in obedience, since Jesus had shown him to do so. That was not legalism. Otherwise, all Christian discipleship would be legalistic, for in true discipleship we renounce and part with things in obedience to Jesus. Does not Jesus say, 'Whoever of you does not renounce all that he has cannot be my disciple'? Likewise it is not legalistic when I abstain out of love for the souls of alcoholics. Let us earnestly pray that this love for Jesus and His kingdom and for human souls will motivate us. Then everything will take care of itself and we shall know what and what not to do.

Two days later I wrote:

You feel that my wish to place all areas of our lives completely under the dominion of Jesus is exaggerated – but, actually, it is biblical. Moreover, what you feel is law is not law at all. If I love Jesus, I have the desire to surrender myself fully to Him so that He may have control over everything. I long to serve Him with all that I am and have, and to place everything at His disposal.

Do you not feel that I had reason to be sad at the results of our tithing? That we have given too little money for the Kingdom of God is an indication to me that something in our love for Jesus and His kingdom must have been amiss and that we lacked the ardour to give Him everything. It is like being suddenly reminded that for a long time one has not given anything nice to a person one used to love very much and overwhelm with presents. Then one is forced to draw the conclusion, 'You probably do not love him as much as before.'

Everything that you regard as law is to me an opportunity for showing Jesus love and dedication, which can be expressed only in the practical issues of life. One cannot say, 'I want to belong fully to Jesus and be detached from the world,' and then as soon as one particular point is mentioned, one backs out, calling it legalism and suddenly no longer feeling so committed as to surrender this particular thing to Jesus, to let go and give it away. What is your concept of total committal to Jesus? It cannot take place in a vacuum, but only if all areas of our lives are completely dedicated to Jesus, placed at His disposal and under His dominion. It occurs in so far as He takes them more fully into His hands and under His control (our money and time, etc.) so that we serve Him alone in everything. Love is total dedication. Love surrenders itself and all that it has to Jesus, retaining nothing for self.

In contrast, it is law when you reckon that one thing or another is indispensable, that we need to be cultured and to take time for this. Love does not do that. If we love Jesus wholeheartedly, first seeking Him and His kingdom, God will grant us all that we need in the way of a cultural life. Love leaves it completely to Jesus, trusting Him. Otherwise, we are not on the right track. Under the pretence of not wanting to become legalistic, we fall short of the full devotion of love to Jesus. This is one of Satan's wiles. He is determined to keep us from making a total dedication to Jesus, which would bring us a fruitful life, abounding with joy. So let us pray for the spirit of repentance in this matter and God will grant it to us. It is clear to me that I cannot turn back. Otherwise, it would be disobedience towards God and what He said to me. I must obey Him. If we are to continue together, Erika, you must come my way. Actually, I do not see why this would not be possible, especially since it concerns the eternal salvation of the soul . . .

Let us discuss everything in the light of Scripture, and it will convict us if we pray much about this question and begin to 'lose our lives' in the respects that God indicates to us. We cannot be taking the matter seriously if we continue to wait for a revival and a working of the Spirit without heeding the prompting of the Spirit in practical issues and responding where He is already moving in our lives now. We have to begin somewhere and be prepared to 'lose our lives' . . .

114

The thoughts expressed in these letters came from an inner compulsion such as I had experienced at other times in my life. And the Spirit of God, who wished to prepare us both for a joint ministry, gradually made us one in this matter too – a unity which was all the more wonderful, since it did not come about through a natural understanding, but rather through His working. The call of God to a total committal, which was so significant for me at the time, was later to be of the utmost importance for the spiritual life of the Sisterhood of Mary and for my personal life in particular.

During those years there seemed to be yet another important factor in God's plans for the founding of the Sisterhood of Mary. No doubt this was one of the main reasons why He gave me the travelling ministry. He willed to bring us into contact with people who would be of significance in the years leading up to the establishment of the Sisterhood of Mary. At the same time it was an answer to prayer. Since 1939 it was our earnest prayer every day that He would send people into our lives who could lead us on spiritually, and through my extensive travelling we came into touch with Christians who became a great blessing to us.

Moreover, my travelling ministry during those seven years introduced me to many different church groups and Christian fellowships – doubtless all part of God's plan for the Sisterhood's future commission to live for unity within the Body of Christ. He opened many doors and soon I was not only speaking to the missionary society's circle of friends, but also receiving requests to hold Bible courses for other groups throughout the country. With great generosity the missionary society left me free to plan my itinerary so that I could accept all the invitations. It must have been God's plan that I came to see the diversity in the body of believers through my encounters with many different types of Christian fellowships and learn to love and respect each one for what it was. I was to learn to see Jesus in every denomination or fellowship where people believe in Him and love Him. Also I was to take to heart the sufferings of Jesus because of His torn Body, although I was little prepared for this at the time.

One of my speaking engagements led me to Beerfelden, a small town in the Oden Forest where the minister's wife introduced me to her 'best pray-ers', the pillars of the congregation, who lived in a nearby village. There, in a home Bible study group, I became acquainted with the gifts of the Spirit as described in 1 Corinthians 12 and 14, and which were being used in a sound, biblical manner. I was also blessed through the uncompromising discipleship of the leader of a fellowship in Kassel, who was a true prayer warrior and a good spiritual counsellor.

Of all the encounters during my travels God must have especially planned the encounter with the future spiritual Father of the Sisterhood of Mary – Paul Riedinger of Ansbach, District Superintendent of the Methodist Church. This is how it happened. During the winter of 1942–3 I had to hold a Bible course for a church in Hof-Saale where I spoke on the topic of 'Heaven and Hell'. Among the listeners was a minister with whom I had a short but significant encounter before his train left. We discovered that we shared the same thoughts on this particular subject.

Shortly after that, this minister invited me to a small circle of friends, which met a few months later in a Bavarian parsonage. Most of them were clergy who originally came from the Oxford Movement and who did not shirk from humbling themselves and from confessing their sins in exact terms. But that was not all. When Erika and I came to visit this group, we were deeply moved as our future spiritual Father, Pastor Riedinger, whom we met there for the first time, knelt down and began to worship the Father, Son and Holy Spirit. We had come to people who lived in the spirit of adoration and we could sense the presence of the Holy Spirit. He had given this circle of believers new songs of adoration, which we all sang together in great joy. Here the call to a priestly way of life was proclaimed – to follow Jesus, the Lamb of God, not growing indignant at the difficult personality of one's neighbour, but bearing and overcoming it in a spirit of repentance for one's own sin. This was the same path along which God had led us.

I was then requested to hold Bible courses in various church groups in this district and thus we became even more closely connected with these Christian brothers and sisters the following year. This was especially the case in July 1944 when the fellowship met again. Those were unforgettable days! Early every morning at six we left the Affaltertal parsonage to go to the parsonage in Egloffstein, filled with thanksgiving for the encounter with these Christians, since we were so hungry for fellowship in a deeper life with Christ. Owing to the political pressure of the time the meetings were held in a room that did not look out on to the street. Only with great difficulty could the journey be made. A further hazard was the bombing, which took place almost continuously. It was there on the evening of July 20, 1944, that we heard the radio announcement of the attempt to assassinate Hitler. Thus not only our intercession, but also our prayers of adoration were integrally bound up with the desperate state of our nation, the plight of the Jews and God's plan of salvation for them.

During this politically sinister period God held His hand protectingly over my travelling ministry. Informers were frequently present at my lectures, but nevertheless I felt constrained to speak of God's plan of salvation concerning the election of the Jews and their leading position and commission to all nations in the millennium kingdom. Twice I was reported to the secret police and was interrogated for hours because of my challenge to follow Jesus, since in their opinion there was only 'one true Fuehrer'. But oddly enough I was not called to account for my lectures about God's eternal plan for the Jews. And they let me go.

Each one of the Bible courses that I held on my travels I naturally held also in the MBK in Darmstadt. Even though I did not lead these MBK groups, my whole love belonged to them. Thus these girls heard the challenge to go the way of the Lamb, to follow the path of discipleship out of love for Jesus. They learnt that the way to overcome is to hate and renounce sin, and they heard the message of Jesus' second coming and God's plan of salvation for Israel. After each speaking tour, these classes were a deep joy for me, since through them I had a greater share in the work of the MBK. I knew and loved each girl and was familiar with her spiritual condition as if she had been entrusted to me. Indeed, later many of these young people would be entrusted to my care when they became my spiritual daughters in the Sisterhood of Mary, but I had no inkling of this at the time.

During my travelling lectureship the work of the MBK steadily grew. In addition to the groups for high school girls, there were groups for children – including one for boys – as well as groups for housewives, college girls and career women. Through these Bible studies approximately 150 people heard the Word of God weekly. It was an act of grace that the Lord held His hand over the youth ministry during the era of National Socialism. Erika was already on the black list, because she taught the young people not only the New Testament, but also the Old, which had been entirely rejected by the regime. She also taught them to profess their faith openly. As a result there was a certain amount of conflict in the groups and some even left. However, most of the girls forwent positions in the *Bund Deutscher Mädchen* (a political organisation for girls during the Third Reich), because they did not wish to give up their membership in the MBK.

During my time of travelling I was permitted to taste some of the fruit of those long years of chastening when my real ministry in Darmstadt still seemed to stand under God's NO. My longing for a satisfying counselling ministry in a regular and established group had been stilled and I could accept my travelling lectureship, which was not my natural inclination, as coming from God and could do it with joy, abiding in His will. In His incomprehensible love God had freed me from the desire to have children as well as from the longing for human love. To the glory of Jesus' name I can testify that I have learnt to find complete satisfaction in Him. At that time I wrote the following in my Bible as my testimony: 'God is the greatest, the fairest, the best; God is a firm rock; He is the sweetest, the most noble treasure of all.'

Love for Jesus now constrained me to voluntarily choose poverty with Him, to voluntarily follow pathways of lowliness and to walk dark avenues of faith so that God would be glorified. He answered the prayers I made during the darkest times at Bible college in 1929 when I implored Him to lead me into a relationship of love to Him, whatever the cost. In this love for Him I found that the whole world was mine, since it belongs to Him. How different it was from my years in Hamburg! Love for Jesus showed me the way. In view of the goods and possessions of this world I learnt to 'have as though I had not'. With that all false scruples about sacrificing one thing or another were swept aside. Love for Jesus now drove me, for example, to spend as much time as possible on Sundays with Him alone, to seek Him and His Word, to commune with Him in prayer or to sing of Him.

At the same time I could enjoy God's gifts in nature, art and cultural matters whenever He granted them to me in His fatherly love. Jesus had made one of my favourite verses come true: 'So if the Son makes you free, you will be free indeed' (John 8:36). He not only releases us from sinful bonds, but also makes us completely free for Himself and thus happy, natural and childlike. And He does so more and more. My problem concerning freedom or legalism, total committal or openness to the world, spontaneity or one-sidedness, which had been causing me such distress since I was twenty-two years old, was now solved. The key was love for Jesus, which bound me entirely to His heart and taught me, in unity with Him, to use everything in the world in the right way.

God Comes When All Is Dark
Air-raid on Darmstadt,
Revival in the MBK,
The Founding of the Sisterhood of Mary,
1944–1947

Judgement came upon Darmstadt on the night of September 11–12, 1944, when God let fire rain upon our city. In eighteen minutes it was almost completely demolished by an air-raid. The city became a sea of flames, a mass of rubble. Only the houses in the outlying districts remained standing. The next morning thousands lay buried beneath an expanse of ruins, and the survivors, most of whom were completely bombed out, were evacuated into homes throughout the countryside within a radius of sixty miles.

At the time I was in Wiesbaden where I was holding a Bible course. When I heard of the events of that night, I was most alarmed, but I could not go back to Darmstadt immediately, because I felt obliged to finish my assignment in Wiesbaden. Erika endured the night alone in Darmstadt. The next morning as she searched the burning city for the girls of her Bible Study Groups, the horrors of death stared her in the face wherever she went. She found charred corpses lying in front of the bombed-out houses. The people seemed to have been swept away and there was a deathly hush about the city. Although most of the girls had miraculously escaped death, they had fled from their burning homes and left the city with their parents. Only a handful of girls had remained. The ministry of the MBK seemed to lie in ruins.

But to our surprise, five days after the air-raid, on the first Sunday after this terrifying night, a whole band of girls came to see us in the afternoon. Most of them had cycled a long way from the Oden Forest and the Bergstrasse, not heeding the attacks from low-flying aircraft, which were growing increasingly frequent. New faces appeared at our house every day. One after another the girls came to see if we were still alive. Faced with many problems, they now longed to pray with Erika. In previous years these young people never would have made such sacrifices to attend a Bible study or a prayer meeting! Never before would they have given up a precious free Sunday for this purpose. The night of death contained the hour of birth. Death brought life. The seed of the Word that had been sown over the years now put forth shoots and our Bible studies took on an altogether new character. It was like being one big family; we were closely knit together in a deep fellowship of love in Christ.

In His grace God had let the Steinberg House stand, though badly damaged, whereas some of the neighbouring houses had been flattened to the ground. Since most of the train services had been discontinued and more and more cities destroyed, my travelling ministry came to a complete halt. Thus I remained at home the greater part of the time. This was significant, because it meant that I was living in Darmstadt as the revival among the young people began.

For years we had been praying for a revival and now the moment had come when God granted it. The night of judgement had become a night of grace for many of the girls in our groups. Faced with death and terrified by the thought of the eternal judgement of God, pious, self-righteous girls learnt to weep over their sins and repent. As a result, many came to confession for the first time. This night had brought the hour of renewal. With the experience of Jesus' forgiveness the joyous song of the redeemed broke out during our Bible studies. 'O the joy of being redeemed, Lord, through Thy precious blood'. This hymn resounded in our midst ever anew. A spirit of overflowing joy had gripped these young people, although outwardly they had little reason to be happy. Through the increasing air attacks more and more towns were set ablaze, death taking thousands as its toll. The misery assumed unheard-of proportions and everyone lived in constant peril. Most of the girls had lost their homes together with all that had made their lives pleasant and rich, and in some cases they were even separated from their parents.

One name was the source of their joy – the name of Jesus. As never before His name had begun to shine in their midst. Had they not known Him before? Certainly. Very well indeed. During the era of National Socialism they had sometimes even jeopardised their education and declined positions and honours for the sake of His name. But until then the name of Jesus had not caused their hearts to sing, because they had not yet recognised themselves as sinners nor wept in repentance over their sins and made amends as they now did. If there is joy in heaven over one sinner who repents, why should there not be joy on earth? In previous years how often Erika and I had looked with sadness upon the large, flourishing groups, which others considered to stand under the blessing of God, and thought in our hearts, 'They have the name of being alive and are dead'. But now new life had broken out with the spirit of repentance and joy, the spirit of love for one another and the spirit of prayer.

Repentance had arisen from conviction of personal sin, but above all, it was sparked off by the realisation of our serious sin, as Christians, towards our nation. More and more painfully we saw that we had utterly failed in the hour of trial. We had not devoted ourselves to God in prayer and fervent entreaty, humbled before the holiness of God when His judgement fell upon our nation. We had not interceded for our brothers and sisters, who entered eternity by the thousand each night. Seldom, if ever, were we at hand to show what help we could when the 'apple of God's eye', the Jews, were so cruelly maltreated.

Yet outwardly we seemed so religious. Every morning we read God's Word; every week we attended the Bible study and participated in intercession for the war. Now the scales fell from our eyes and we could scarcely comprehend our blindness. Struck by the seriousness of our sin, we were driven by the thought to make amends by standing in the breach for our people from then on (Ezekiel 22:30) and devoting ourselves to prayer.

One Sunday in February 1945 we were gathered together

for the youth Bible study in the Steinberg House in a small room called the 'blue room' – the badly damaged roof had not yet been repaired, but here the rain did not seep through as quickly as in the rooms upstairs. I spoke to the girls about our priestly commission of prayer and adoration as well as about our failure to recognise this commission, let alone perform it. I related how the heathen people of Nineveh repented in sackcloth and ashes when only threatened by God's judgement (Jonah 3). Yet as Christians we had not repented under the judgement of God. All those years we had remained proud and unmoved, although judgement should begin with the household of God.

Suddenly, in the middle of this Bible study, a shower of repentance rained down upon everyone present. Girls who had never prayed aloud in front of others spontaneously began to pray. Genuine tears were shed because of all our sin, because of all that we had failed to do. Before, it was individuals that had come to repentance – and mainly for their personal sins – but now repentance had taken hold of the young people as a whole. We were filled with grief over our lukewarmness, our spiritual death, our failure to fulfil our priestly ministry of prayer for the sin and distress of our nation. Out of this repentance God granted us a new prayer life of intercession and of adoration for the Triune God.

Erika and I could now witness how our young people underwent the same experiences that the Lord had granted us in the past years. Whenever there is conviction of sin and repentance, new life breaks out. We were overjoyed. Our prayers all those years for a revival among the young people had been wonderfully answered.

Our fervent plea was that God would now keep us and them in the grace of repentance and God saw to it that through wholesome judgement repentance and thus love for Jesus never ceased in our midst. To this very day in the Sisterhood of Mary we have passed through many a time of chastening and divine judgement. In this way God has kept us on the path of daily contrition and repentance and has never let the song of exultation over His redemption die out in our hearts. On the contrary, our love for Him has increased, for God has graciously shown us in our daily lives, now far more than in the beginning, how much our nature is infested with sin and how deeply lovelessness, self-will, ambition, disobedience and greed are rooted in our hearts. In order to help us to recognise our sins, He has also given us the sisterly ministry of admonishing each other in our times of fellowship in the light. This helps us to humble ourselves more specifically beneath our sin, confessing it to God and when necessary asking others for forgiveness.

In March 1945 we took some of the girls to Falkengesaess in the Oden Forest for a retreat that had been planned a long time in advance. Our heavenly Father had arranged these days in His loving-kindness, 'preparing a table before us in the presence of our enemies'. The danger of attack from low-flying aircraft had grown to such an extent that one scarcely dared to go out on the streets. The American troops were just outside the city limits of Darmstadt. Any day they could take the city according to common opinion. Those who had been politically involved fled the cities in large numbers. Everything was in a state of high tension. One and all were entirely taken up with the frightening events of the present situation, and rightly so.

But although we were affected by the events and our lives were imperilled, we were like children, happily and peacefully abiding in the Father's heart. Inwardly we were filled with the deep love of Jesus and all the blessings that He had granted us in the MBK during the past months.

Despite the hazardous situation, God laid upon Erika's heart and mine that we should risk going to Falkengesaess with fifteen of the girls for some days of quiet and preparation for our priestly ministry of prayer. There it was possible for us to stay in the small home of friends where we could be together without attracting attention at this time of political pressure.

I had already gone on ahead to hold a Bible course in the near-by parish of Beerfelden. Thus up to the last moment Erika had to face the decision alone of whether or not to undertake the journey. She probably would not have risked it in this time of extreme peril if the Lord had not clearly promised her in prayer that they would have the protection of angels and that she would be able to return the girls to their parents before the Americans took over the city. She was particularly concerned about this last point, since there was a very real danger that, while we were away, the demarcation line might be drawn between Darmstadt and the Oden Forest, thus preventing her from bringing the girls back to their parents. Humanly speaking, we could not understand that this retreat was a commission from God. We simply acted in obedience to an inner compulsion, as had so often been the case before when God intended to perform something significant.

Indeed, something significant for the future Sisterhood of Mary was to happen during those days – a continuation of the memorable hour of revival in the 'blue room' of the Steinberg House. Accordingly, the Lord led this small group of young people, under such impossible conditions, to a quiet place where they could come apart with Him.

Between Erbach and Hetzbach their train was shelled and the protection of the angels became a reality. Screaming and moaning passengers rushed out of the train while the enemy aircraft still circled above and shot down those who tried to escape. But in that moment of dread and death the girls had a deep sense of security and not one of them was harmed. Thus the assurance of their leader was wonderfully confirmed. Above in Beerfelden I could hear the fierce shooting and knew that it was aimed at their train. For over an hour I headed in that direction, crawling more than walking, for the low-flying aircraft were still circling over the area. After what seemed like ages I met Erika and the girls, who were all safe and sound. After an extremely hazardous walk we finally found ourselves sitting in the small house in Falkengesaess where we were warmly received. Our hearts were filled with thanksgiving to God.

Day and night enemy bombers roared above our heads. Yet in the face of such danger God was laying further foundations for the future Sisterhood of Mary, although this was hidden from our eyes. We spoke about our priestly ministry in the light of 1 Peter 2:9, 'You are a chosen race, a royal priesthood . . . ', and sought to define this ministry by considering the example of the Old Testament priesthood. Before the priests began their service in the sanctuary, they had to remove their clothes and wash them, since they could have nothing impure on them. During those days we wished to be prepared anew for the priestly ministry of prayer and worship and thus we too had to first undergo a cleansing process if our prayers were not to be superficial and powerless. The hearts of the girls were kindled with this longing.

One afternoon, as we came together again, the Spirit of God led us quite naturally – one after the other – to kneel down and confess our sin in so far as it did not belong to private confession. This hour, in which we sensed the Spirit of God resting upon us as the Spirit of truth who brings hidden things into the light, bore seed for later times. It was, so to speak, our first time of fellowship in the light for the Sisterhood of Mary, which was yet to be born.

Greater than the danger from the enemy aircraft above us, greater than the fear of some of the girls was that which God had kindled in our hearts through His Spirit and His Word – repentance, love and adoration. Our young people experienced even greater inner joy than they had known during the previous months, since they now tasted more of the love for Jesus which is granted to pardoned sinners. It was as though Jesus were in our midst as the Bridegroom, wooing for personal, bridal love. In those days we had no idea that there would be a Sisterhood of Mary where a ring would be worn as a symbol of bridal love.

Before I left for my ministry in Beerfelden, a soldier had delivered a letter to me from a minister friend of ours, for at that time there was no postal service. The letter contained a meditation on the Passion, since it was Lent, and I was deeply moved to read it. How my heart yearned to paint a picture for the girls of Jesus as the Man of Sorrows, forsaken and lonely on His path of suffering, waiting for our loving companionship. I felt as though Jesus the Bridegroom were standing before us and addressing us with the irresistible plea, 'Who will share My path, the path of lowliness, of poverty, of obedience and disgrace?' In that hour many silently gave their consent out of love, 'Where You go, I will go too.' Some renewed their pledge to Jesus later, on the day they entered the Sisterhood of Mary, for out of love for Him they desired to share His path and to follow Him in truth.

On the last day in Falkengesaess I held a Bible study for the girls about the City of God, during which the Spirit of God filled us with overwhelming joy in expectation of that day when we shall enter the heavenly Jerusalem and behold His countenance. This glimpse of the City of God created in us a deep longing that Jesus might prepare us for the goal of glory, the Marriage Supper of the Lamb, no matter what the cost.

After four days we departed for home, having had a taste of heaven's glory, which not even the horrors of war could take away. In Hetzbach, upon our arrival at the railway station, we learnt that the trains had ceased to run four days earlier. We had taken the last train from Darmstadt. Consequently, we had no other choice now but to go by foot. After the experiences of the past few days we felt as though we were being borne along and when, after walking for seven hours, we did grow weary, a lorry picked us up. Disbanded troops and refugees streamed towards us and when we inquired about Darmstadt, they shouted back, 'You'll never get into Darmstadt. It's already occupied by the Americans!' But quite unperturbed, we continued to sing one hymn after another into the night on the home journey so as to greet the soldiers and refugees with the love of God. At two a.m. we finally arrived in Darmstadt. It had not yet been taken by the American troops and we were able to return the girls to their parents, just as the Lord had assured Erika in prayer before the retreat in Falkengesaess. A German general had deterred the Americans another day; otherwise, it would not have been possible for us to return home. And that afternoon the Americans marched in.

The National Socialist regime had come to an end. All the restrictions imposed on Christian organisations were removed and thus the MBK, which contained the seed of the Sisterhood of Mary, could develop freely and the revival that had begun could grow unhindered.

The first thing that Erika and I did in the attic apartment of the Steinberg House was to rebuild a wall that had fallen in during the bombing. For years this small apartment had waited in vain for Bible students. Now the large room was suddenly brought to life by many young people. It was not just a few Bible students but rather forty to fifty high school girls and university students who came to spend an entire day with us once a week. Since the occupying forces had instituted a curfew that was only lifted for an hour in the morning and an hour in the evening, the girls would arrive in the morning and leave in the evening.

Singing, thanksgiving and adoration filled these rooms in response to Jesus' loving forgiveness for every new sin that was brought into the light. All that we now experienced was like a miracle of the grace of God before our eyes after the long years of following dark pathways of faith, suffering and prayer for the sake of our original commission, which seemed as though it would never be fulfilled. The attic apartment became a home for all the young people. Even in those days we had a form of community life, which became more defined and comprehensive later in the Sisterhood of Mary.

Since the colleges and schools were still closed that year, nothing prevented our meetings from taking place on a weekday; we met once a week for a whole day. Many of the young people had to cycle long distances in order to reach Darmstadt – often thirty miles – and some of them would stay overnight and join us for the meals. In the aftermath of the war food was scarce and we would all share what little we had. Yet if the lunch break on such days lasted more than ten minutes, the girls were almost indignant at the waste of time; they were so eager to hear the proclamation of the Word, especially concerning the principles of priestly service, and to humble themselves before God and have times of worship, intercession and singing that they were anxious not to lose a single minute.

Our greatest joy was that the Lord Jesus granted our young people the spirit of adoration. This had been our specific prayer for them ever since we had met Pastor Riedinger and others in the Egloffstein circle. Since the last summer of the war we had thought that one of these brothers in the Lord ought to come to the MBK to introduce us to the realm of adoration. However, the circumstances of the war frustrated this intention – a factor no doubt planned by God, since He willed to lay first the proper foundation for adoration through repentance. Later too the spirit of adoration was granted to us ever anew on this basis alone. The judgement over our city taught us to walk along the path of daily repentance; this gives birth to love for Jesus, which in turn gives rise to adoration.

The Lord had blessed us abundantly, as the Apostle Paul expressed it, ' . . . so that you are not lacking in any spiritual gift' (1 Corinthians 1:7). God had bestowed upon us not only the gift of adoration, but also other gifts of the Spirit mentioned in 1 Corinthians 14, such as the gift of prophecy, the gift of speaking in tongues and the gift of healing. Thankful though we were for the gifts, because they are 'for the common good' (1 Corinthians 12:7), they have never been the decisive factor in our spiritual life. The source of our spiritual life is love for Jesus, which comes from repentance. This was our deep personal experience as a result of long struggles. Moreover, it was the kind providence of God that He led Erika and me in earlier years to revival groups where we became acquainted with the charismatic gifts and that He taught us to take the biblical attitude towards them. Thus amid all the joy and the somewhat strong emphasis that our young people placed upon the gifts at first, we felt it was important to teach them to see the proper place of the gifts as defined in the Bible. God kept us from making our spiritual foundation the 'baptism in the Spirit', which had never played any role in our fellowship. Instead love for Jesus, which flows from repentance and leads to uncompromising discipleship, was always our basis for new spiritual life.

Next to the proclamation of the Word, prayer stood at the centre of our meetings now. The hours spent in intercession simply had no end. Love for Jesus constrained us to pray for individuals and our nation as a whole, which was in dire need at that time. In contrast to the obligatory intercession that we had had in the MBK prayer meetings, we now learnt to wrestle in prayer in view of acute problems: for the refugees; the women, who often had to suffer at the hands of occupying troops for the grave sin of our nation; the deported; the imprisoned; the many who were starving; those who had been deposed because of the political collapse, such as the Nuremberg prisoners who now stood laden with serious guilt as they awaited eternity.

The Evil One was roused to anger, for with our prayers we were invading his territory. He was enraged at the new life and mobilised all his forces to persecute us, almost seeking our very lives. As his instruments he used people who spread false rumours. Indeed, 'Pilate and Herod became friends' in order to proceed against us. God in His wisdom had begun to fulfil the request that I had written prayerfully in my diary as a twenty-year-old.

Lord Jesus Christ, if only I could demonstrate my overflowing gratitude to You! Oh, let me suffer, let me be despised, if it should please You, and if I might be cleansed and able to glorify You all the more . . . I do not know whether I can bear it yet, but I long to suffer for Your sake. Let Your love flow deep into my heart and abide there so that it stands the test in suffering. Oh, if only I have You, I will gladly endure everything. (May 1, 1925)

First Erika faced Satan's barrage. Some of the girls'

parents were horrified at the recent events, because their children had become 'too pious' and were following other courses than those their parents desired. Erika and I were assailed by accusations. From all sides we received letters, warnings, threats. Our names, which until then had been respected in Christian circles that knew us, were now under disgrace. People withdrew from us, declaring that we were 'fanatics', 'sectarians', 'Roman Catholics', 'Pentecostals' and 'extremists' and that we were always talking about repentance. Each criticised us on a different point. Waves of contempt and even hatred rolled over us. In the end they surged from everywhere in Germany, from the church groups and the fellowships within the *Gemeinschaftsbewegung* where I had delivered lectures during my travelling ministry. Despite the fact that there was still no postal service, the Evil One caused the news of the revival in the MBK to spread like wildfire throughout the land. Much to my sorrow even the Bible college withdrew from me and for a while forbade its Sisters to correspond with me.

Since the revival had brought us many blessings – our young people had found spiritual life and love for Jesus – we now had to pay the price. Erika was abruptly dismissed from her position as youth leader of the MBK, which was affiliated with St Paul's. She had a most distressing talk with the senior minister during which he laid down stipulations that she felt unable to fulfil in good conscience. I shall never forget the evening when, filled with grief, she told me about the breach with St Paul's. For years now, in a harmonious relationship with the minister, Erika had held Bible study classes for the MBK at St Paul's and I too had a share in this work. That evening as we prayed for a word from the Lord in view of all the disgrace, we received the verse, 'Thou hast maintained my just cause; thou hast sat on the throne giving righteous judgement' (Psalm 9:4).

Several months later the missionary society made certain stipulations for me, asking me not to mention particular subjects in my lectures any more, and since I could not comply with them in good conscience, I resigned from this ministry. Yet ultimately God was at work in all this. According to His will I was soon to be fully involved in the building up of the Sisterhood of Mary. Although in our present situation we no longer had any income, we were not disconcerted, since we had already faced so many uncertainties in the past and God had always intervened at the right moment.

Our girls on their part encountered similar difficulties – some in their own homes. God was immediately submitting them to the test. Yet had we not dedicated ourselves to follow our Lord Jesus? His was a path of manifold suffering, a path of disgrace. So far this characteristic of Jesus' pathway had been lacking in our lives. Although we had experienced many personal humiliations, we had never suffered persecution and contempt for His name's sake – a fact that had always disturbed us. Thus we had no other desire but to follow this path along which God was now leading us.

'Rejoice in so far as you share Christ's sufferings' (1 Peter 4:13). This verse, which I often received in prayer at that time, was especially fulfilled during my last speaking tours for the missionary society. Until the time of the revival I had received a certain amount of recognition and esteem during my travelling ministry. I was invited to speak to many church groups and fellowships and my lectures were well-attended. But now my travels lay under the lash of contempt. News of the revival had gone ahead of me and I was thought to have gone astray and to be spreading heresy. Meetings that had already been arranged were cancelled. The reasons given were very humiliating. A letter that I wrote to Erika at the time (July 4, 1946) indicates the situation:

Here in M I had to go through a fire of purification. The verse I received in prayer for this period was fulfilled, 'Rejoice in so far as you share Christ's sufferings, that you may also rejoice and be glad when his glory is revealed'. Thus in all my grief I was richly consoled by my Lord and can only give thanks. The nucleus of both the young people and the women social workers of the Home Mission – the actual prayer fellowship – was in total opposition. Everywhere they spoke against my proclamation. They did not come to the prayer meetings beforehand and seldom attended the lectures. When they did come, they brought such a spirit of opposition with them and the atmosphere was so charged that I could hardly speak. Fewer and fewer people came to the evening meetings – something that I have never experienced before. I am like an outcast. One of the loyal ones fought on behalf of the message entrusted to me, but she is suffering much inner conflict as a result. After all, the others are believers and they reject my message. Thus I had a difficult time with her also. Among other things, she thought that my words about judgement and repentance were not in accordance with the gospel. The Bible School in X is mainly responsible for the fact that people who were hungry for this message two years ago, because it helped them, and who distributed copies of my lectures as valuable are now so antagonistic towards me.

My travelling days are more or less over. My reputation is gone. The ministers here have spread the word that I belong to the Pentecostal movement or to some sort of high church.

That which the Lord impressed upon my heart has come true. Now I am forsaken and stand alone outside the camp, despised, scorned, ridiculed by everyone, with no lodging and no commission. But to be entirely one with Jesus in His disgrace and anguish – this is what brings me deep joy.

The fewer the people that came to the evening meetings, the more joyfully I delivered the message. I saw Jesus and nothing else, and proclaimed His glory. During the counselling sessions I noticed that some were convicted and made solemn commitments to the Lord. Tomorrow morning, two or three of the women students from the Bible school wish to come and tell me what their reservations are. I need much love and humility.

. . . The main point is that I do not grow weary when there are often opponents at home and everywhere else now – and this is only the beginning. Yet did we not choose the thorns of Jesus . . . ?

At that time in Darmstadt so many people were working against us that it seemed as though the young people would no longer be able to meet in our home, but in a remarkable way the Lord sent us friends in our greatest plight – friends who could strengthen us and intercede on our behalf. Best of all was Pastor Riedinger. He had a heart full of love and understanding and was entirely in agreement with our spiritual leadings. Considering that we had known him since 1943 when we met in Egloffstein, it was a special leading of God that he paid us his first visit at this point.

And this is how it happened. In August 1945, Erika and I were on our way to Nuremberg in a coal truck – there was not yet any public transport. Our purpose was to visit a minister with whom I had been in touch since our meeting in Hof and Egloffstein, for we wished to seek his advice and to discuss with him all the matters that had been on our hearts since the beginning of the revival. But shortly before we arrived at our destination, American soldiers removed us from the lorry that had picked us up in Nuremberg and took us under custody to the Erlangen prison with several other people, because they thought that something was missing from our papers.

It must have been God who placed these American soldiers as 'angels with fiery swords' in our path, for as we could see in retrospect, we were to meet our future spiritual Father, District Superintendent Riedinger, on this journey. The following day we were released from prison, but ordered to take a direct route back to Darmstadt. Then God gave us the idea to try to contact Pastor Riedinger in Ansbach, since Ansbach lay practically on our way. The plan proved to be successful and we were able to stay with him for a week. God knit us together in a close bond of fellowship in Christ. Pastor Riedinger showed much understanding for our spiritual leading, when we discussed all the problems and questions with him. We left with a rich blessing.

And then in November 1945 Pastor Riedinger came to visit us in Darmstadt. It seemed as though he and our young people had always belonged together. From the very first moment they opened their hearts wide to him and his message in their great spiritual hunger and eagerness. He shared with us the wealth of his proclamation and spoke to us about the calling to priestly service, about loving the members of the Body of Christ in all branches and denominations, about bridal love for Jesus, and the heavenly world. No one could speak as he could of the City of God and of the priestly service of worship in the sanctuary of God with its sacred laws. From then on he visited us frequently and soon we were calling him 'our Father Riedinger'. His visits were red-letter days for us. As he spoke, the presence of God seemed to fill the room.

On his first visit he mentioned in passing during a Bible study that in all ages there have been brotherhoods of communal life. When he said this, it was as though he were telling us something that we had known for a long time. For months we had been feeling the urge to begin such a life where we could live together permanently in the spirit of poverty, of prayer and of bridal love for Jesus. The girls were inwardly kept from applying to deaconess houses or Bible colleges, though some of them, who knew that they were called to the Lord's service, had sent for brochures. Here too it was evident that an inner compulsion had guided the girls. Without realising it, they were waiting for the Sisterhood of Mary, which God had already planned for them in His heart.

When Father Riedinger, Erika and I first shared our thoughts and plans about beginning such a communal life, the Lord gave us the verse: He is 'wonderful in counsel, [and] excellent in wisdom and effectual working' (Isaiah 28:29 *The Amplified Bible*). As we spent much time in prayer to learn God's will concerning the details, His plans for the spiritual development and commission of our Sisterhood became quite clear to me.

The work of the MBK was to give rise to the Sisterhood of Mary. Even before my travelling lectureship this development was in its early stages and God's commission had slowly begun to take shape. Thus it was inevitable that the Sisterhood of Mary would be guided according to the same spiritual laws the Lord had shown Erika and me for our lives during the long years before its foundation.

Before me I could visualise the future Sisterhood of Mary – a community life based on daily contrition and repentance in the light of God; a fellowship of love rooted in bridal love for Jesus; a type of discipleship involving complete dependence upon God along pathways of faith; a life of prayer, of adoration and of sacrifice. This was the pathway the Lord had shown me for my life and which He had taught me to follow during many long years of spiritual struggles and hardships. Now I was to lead my spiritual daughters along the same path, aware of the pitfalls along the way, yet declaring with the utmost certainty, 'This is the way! Turn neither to the right nor to the left!'

During the winter of 1946–7 we had earnestly sought the Lord concerning the proper development of the spiritual life and commission of the Sisterhood according to the guidelines He had shown us, for we knew we had to be loyal to them. But now the way also had to be cleared externally for the founding of the Sisterhood and we were faced with immovable obstacles. In those days a licence was required to found a sisterhood and when I went to the government offices in Wiesbaden in late January 1947, I received a flat refusal. That evening when I came home, Erika and I experienced another of those occasions that had been so familiar to us in the past eleven years. All our hopes were dashed. Once again we had to sacrifice our 'Isaac' – God's promise that He had a special ministry for us in Darmstadt. Night crept into our souls, but as we prayed, we received the verse, 'Fight the good fight of the faith' (1 Timothy 6:12). That brought us back to life and strengthened us to persevere in the prayer of faith even when there was no further hope.

Next morning God suddenly inspired me with the thought to go to the American information centre in Darmstadt and inquire whether there might be another way to obtain a licence. In the opinion of others it was a futile undertaking, since I had already been to the only place that was authorised to issue licences and had been refused.

Nevertheless I was reckoning with the fact that we have a God who works miracles. With this confidence I set out for the *Amerika Haus*. The woman to whom I spoke sent me to the Municipal Youth Council of Darmstadt and that very day I was able to have an interview with the official in charge. It turned out that he knew my father; his son had studied under him and was very grateful that my father had helped him in a particular matter. Thus his heart was moved to help us and he suggested an unexpected possibility – we could have the Sisterhood of Mary licensed under the category of a youth club. He mentioned that the committee that considered such petitions met only four times a year, but was due to meet the following week. I could scarcely believe this wonderful leading of God and hurried home, eager to share the news with Erika. Without any delay we handed in the necessary documents.

On February 4, 1947, one of our young people came to us, joyfully waving a newspaper. What news did it contain?

The Municipal Youth Council met in the City Hall last Friday. The following organisations received licences: Schlaraffia Tarimundus Club, The Arheilgen Social and Paddle Club, The Sisterhood of Mary . . .

God often chooses to use strange ways to accomplish His purposes. Years later we discovered by chance that this permit was not valid – but by then the Sisterhood was so large that the authorities could not do otherwise but grant the correct licence. In view of all the mountainous difficulties that stood in the way of the founding of our Sisterhood, the Lord had given me this verse, 'The mountains melt like wax before the Lord, before the Lord of all the earth' (Psalm 97:5). True to His word, He had caused this huge mountain to melt and the other ones were melting too. Parents who had forbidden their daughters to enter this newly established Sisterhood, which seemed to provide no security, now gave their permission.

A further obstacle, which also seemed insurmountable at first, was that of gaining permission from the Housing Authorities, for in the early postwar years it was obligatory to have a permit of residence. There were strict regulations about moving from one town to another and the Housing Authorities had the right to assign all living quarters – and in those days they did not give permits for such purposes as ours.

Seven Sisters wanted to come, but where would they sleep? Erika had already given up her bedroom, which was also her study, and turned it into a multi-purpose room – dining room, parlour and classroom. I had moved into a small storeroom so that three Sisters could sleep in my room. But where were the other four to sleep? We prayed and believed that God would intervene within the next seven days, for the Sisters were due to arrive in a week. A day or two later a neighbour came to ask whether the student who was renting a room in my parents' house could move into her house for the next term – so that he could study together with her lodger in preparation for the examinations. Since he would not be paying rent, we could feel free to use the room as we pleased during this period. Our hearts rejoiced over this unexpected aid from God, which made the beginning of our community life possible.

Thus our founding ceremony could take place on March 30, 1947, and our spiritual Father, Pastor Riedinger, joined us for the occasion. God had given him the name for our Sisterhood – 'The Sisterhood of Mary' – after the mother of Jesus; it was to be symbolic of the pathways of faith and loving dedication to the will of God, which Mary followed as the first disciple of Jesus.

The unity of love that was demonstrated at the founding

138

ceremony of our Sisterhood was significant for us. The minister of our parish – the successor of the minister who had dismissed Erika – gave the address; Darmstadt's youth minister as well as the Methodist minister and the Roman Catholic priest from the neighbouring parish gave a word of greeting. My parents, who had lovingly received the young Sisterhood into their home, were also present – filled with joy.

And where was the ceremony held? In the very rooms that had remained empty for years, waiting for the students of the 'Steinberg Bible Courses', the rooms where the vacant beds had stared at us for so long, telling us that all our paths had been in vain. Now the room was filled, not only with the seven Sisters dressed in white (it was a year later that we received our proper habits), but also with a large number of the young people from the revival, many of whom felt that they too had a call to join the Sisterhood of Mary.

In 1935 we had imagined that the 'Steinberg Bible Courses' were the purpose of God's leadings. But this was far too small for God. He had something greater in mind! He desired to form a group of people who would surrender their whole life and follow paths of faith – as He had taught us to walk them – so that His name would be magnified. He desired to give us spiritual daughters who, out of love for Jesus alone, would accompany Him on His way of sacrificial love, His way of the cross, which bore the stamp of poverty, disgrace, lowliness and obedience. On the founding day we could only worship God for what He had done. Now, after twelve years, we could see the visible results of our faith. The long, dark pathways had led to a wonderful goal: we were privileged to found and lead the Sisterhood of Mary as a work of God for His glory. In deep humility we could only say, 'This is the Lord's doing, and it is a miracle before our eyes. We are not worthy of all His mercy and faithfulness!'

Part II

In Jesus' Footsteps
Inner Conflicts – Disgrace – Poverty – Weakness – Humiliation
1947–1951

Mother of the Sisterhood of Mary – But Who?

It was 1947, during the first year of the Sisterhood of Mary. One evening as I sat together with our young Sisters, sharing with them about our communal life, one Sister asked spontaneously, 'Oh! please may we call you "Mother"? – since you are our spiritual Mother!', and all the others joined in. Mother of the Sisterhood of Mary? For twelve years the Lord had led me through suffering and disappointments in preparation for this task. He wanted to entrust me with this commission – in all its joys as well as its responsibilities and burdens – for the second half of my life. Yet it seemed as though it was not to be.

A few months earlier, before the foundation of the Sisterhood of Mary, a minister was sitting in the same seat as this young Sister. This brother in the Lord, who had been in close fellowship with us for several years already, shared with me what God had shown him about the new Sisterhood. A Mother would be in charge, but that was to be someone else. My ministry would mainly consist of visiting various Christian groups and holding lectures. Together with the Sisterhood an ecumenical Bible college, open to all Christians, was to be established in the Steinberg House – and I would be teaching there. The Sisterhood was to merge with another Christian organisation.

This announcement was like a stab in my heart, since the consequences would be serious and painful for me. I was not to be Mother. I was not to have an active part in the leadership and development of the Sisterhood of Mary. Yet had not the Sisterhood grown out of the MBK that Mother Martyria and I had led? Had not the Lord already given me clear inner guidance about the course the Sisterhood of Mary should take, which I laid before this minister and his friends some months earlier? Despite various phases of inner conflict, the Lord had unfolded His purposes to me with increasing clarity. Contrary to the spiritual insight of these brothers I had become more and more convinced that God's intention was neither an ecumenical Bible college, nor a merger with another Christian organisation. He wanted the Sisterhood of Mary to be a new off-shoot on the tree of the Church with its own God-given commission.

I did not yet know in detail what the commission would be, but I was certain that the basis and source for everything in the Sisterhood of Mary would be a communal life with fellowship in the light of God and a never-ending flow of repentance. Love for Jesus would be the incentive and impulse of our lives, leading us to forgive and love one another and to accompany Jesus on the way of the cross, of poverty and lowliness. This was the sort of life I visualised for the Sisterhood. I knew that such love has authority when it is put into practice; this alone would be the source of power for every commission that God would give us later. Indeed, the future commission of Canaan – to represent a kingdom of love, as a foreshadowing of the kingdom of heaven – was hidden in this inner impression. I sensed that the Sisterhood of Mary was conceived in the heart of God according to His divine purposes, and that it was not a project that had arisen out of human needs and desires.

These friends, however, did not understand the burden on my heart – but this was part of God's plan. He brought this situation into my life so that the full measure of inner conflict and surrender of the will would be laid into the spiritual foundations of the Sisterhood of Mary. Along the ways of faith that God led me, I discovered that the actual suffering for me never arose from the seemingly insurmountable difficulties, but from the inner conflict. Whenever I had the absolute certainty that God had given me a commission, the hardest part was not keeping faith in view of the overwhelming obstacles, but rather undergoing the trials and temptations. And these now began in full force.

As the Sisterhood was in its initial stages, letters would often arrive from friends, telling us what God had shown them about the Sisterhood. 'The Sisters should not seek the security of a private Mother House for training, but should die to their personal longings and join other existing Sisterhoods instead, serving in charitable works'. 'You are not to be something new, something that has never existed before, but . . . ' Yet these proposals contradicted the very fundamentals of that which the Lord had shown me so clearly.

The letters went back and forth. Private talks took place as well as discussions at meetings. The thickets grew more and more impenetrable. For Jesus' sake I truly desired to die to my opinions, outlooks and everything else that seemed important to me, but on the other hand, I was under an obligation to the Lord and could not give up the commission He had entrusted to me. As a disciple of Jesus, I had committed myself to go the way of the Lamb, but did the way of the Lamb really entail giving up this God-given commission, for which I had received the inner assurance? Would following the way of the Lamb not lead to the destruction of all that had come to life like a blossoming branch after many long years of waiting and believing? Was I supposed to hold tight or to let go? Was I supposed to resist or to submit to the guidance of the others?

I was in deep anguish that the Sisterhood was not to be led the way God had indicated to me. If I was to hold lectures and Bible courses throughout the land, and the spiritual life of the Sisterhood of Mary was to be conducted along other guidelines, the Sisterhood would lose the commission originally intended by God. God had promised that He would entrust us with a ministry at the Steinberg House and that I was to be the spiritual Mother. For twelve dark, meaningless years He let me wait for the fulfilment of this promise.

A battle was raging in my heart. Should I have insisted that God had given me the inspiration? Had not this commission been entrusted to us in 1935? Should I have explained that Mother Martyria and I had built it up with the MBK? Moreover, the revival did not come as a result of the preaching of these Christian brothers, as we had expected, but as a result of the bombing of our town, shortly before the planned mission. New life broke out in our youth groups at a time when all communication with the brothers had been broken, and during the first year we tended this young shoot on our own.

Certainly I could have expressed myself this way to the brothers, but God restrained me. I knew that I could only be Mother of the Sisterhood of Mary, if God also gave a confirmation through these brothers, who were close to us, that He Himself had appointed me. I struggled through in prayer until I could believe that if the Lord had imparted to me His plan for the Sisterhood of Mary, and if I was to carry it out, He Himself would contend for me. Thus I committed everything to God, and all that He had appeared to give me I returned, laying it in His hands.

> I follow now close in His footsteps
> The path that He trod here below;
> I only desire what He gives me,
> And only His way I will go.*

At the time this act of committal cost me a great deal, but looking back, I can see now that the enthusiasm of a revival cannot be a foundation for a far-reaching ministry. In His kingdom God lays the foundations according to the type of building He plans to erect. Only if God has been able to use trials and temptations to dig deeply, and only if suffering and sacrifices have been laid into the foundations, can a work of God stand firm. The greater the agony, the more solid the foundations. Every commitment the founder makes to the various sufferings God has brought into his life is significant for future generations and the further development of the ministry and commission. Thus founding times are usually times of extreme suffering, and in our

* *O None Can Be Loved like Jesus* (Songs of Love for Jesus), No. 32.

case too God brought one hardship after another for us to lay into the foundations.

In those years, however, I did not yet see God's purposes. When the Lord showed me that at the founding ceremony I should let myself be installed in the office the brothers had assigned to me and not as Mother of the Sisterhood of Mary, it was a painful experience. It was more bitter than all the previous disappointments I had to face during the twelve years when I seemed to be waiting in vain for the fulfilment of the promise. A ray of hope shone in my life with the founding of the Sisterhood of Mary. Perhaps the Lord's time had come to fulfil the promise, 'For still the vision awaits its time . . . wait for it; it will surely come' (Habakkuk 2:3). Now this ray of hope vanished. Yet it was the grace of God that after twelve years of chastening my heart had become more flexible so that it could submit to the will of God in this difficult leading without breaking or rebelling.

In 1947 at the foundation of the Sisterhood of Mary the Lord entrusted me with the leadership of the Sisterhood, but only temporarily; the person who was to become Mother was not yet free to assume her post owing to other commitments. Thus during this first year I was to lead the Sisters as 'Dr Schlink' together with Mother Martyria, then still known as 'Miss Madauss', who was installed as 'Novice Mistress'.

For about six to eight months I lived in this uncertainty. I was the leader and therefore the spiritual Mother of the first Sisters who came to live with us in the Steinberg House in 1947 – and yet I was not. Every day I returned the leadership to God, fully consenting to His will, sacrificing the desires of my heart ever anew. I had no idea that the Lord was leading me this way purposely, so that I might forsake the things I cherished. Then there would be room in my heart for a deeper and more fervent love for Him, our beloved Lord. He longed to take possession of my heart completely. It is the secret of Jesus' love that when He takes something that we have been looking forward to all our

147

lives, He has something far greater to give in return, which will increase our joy all the more: He wants to give us Himself. And only His love can make us truly joyful. At that time I was not so conscious of this spiritual truth, but later I was to experience it more fully.

Finally God intervened. The brothers' plans concerning the leadership of the Sisterhood failed to materialise and in 1948 the Lord returned my sacrifice. He Himself confirmed my calling to be Mother, since from that time onwards the brothers regarded me as Mother of the Sisterhood as a matter of course. The Sisters had no idea of all that had taken place, and after the first year under my spiritual leadership it was natural for them to look upon me as their spiritual Mother. Without any long and involved discussions I was invested by Father Riedinger as Mother of the Sisterhood of Mary in 1948 when Mother Martyria and the first Sisters and I received our habits. As Father Riedinger blessed me, he gave me the name 'Mother Basilea'.

Like a child I accepted this name as a gift of God with the joy that I had often felt in singing the song, 'I'm a child of the King, in Jesus, my Saviour, a child of the King'. This name expressed the promise of the Lord that we have been redeemed by His blood to become kings and priests (Revelation 1:5f. AV and 1 Peter 2:9). Indeed, the names we receive as Sisters of Mary are meant to express our calling and to be a constant challenge to us and an aim of faith for our spiritual lives. Biblical callings had always been great and holy and precious to me, especially the calling to the royal priesthood. I had always realised that this vocation could only be fulfilled by following Jesus' footsteps along the path of lowliness and self-denial. Yet at that time I could not imagine how much grief, disgrace and hostility this name would bring me. I would be accused of wanting to be a queen in my pride, thus taking the glory from God.

In the year 1947 when God ever anew asked me to say, 'Yes, Father', and to surrender my will totally to Him, I spent a week in a Christian retreat centre. During those days Jesus drew close to me, overwhelming me with His love, filling me with deep bliss (John 14:23). For the first time in my life I understood the testimony of those who could say in deepest suffering that they were completely absorbed and set aflame with this overwhelming, sweet love of Jesus. A verse from the Psalms came true for me, 'Thou givest them drink from the river of thy delights' (Psalm 36:8). In the midst of my distress I could scarcely comprehend the bliss of His love. My heart rejoiced, 'No one is so worthy of our love as Jesus, none can compare with Him . . .' By giving Jesus the desires of my heart and surrendering my rights, I had made a marvellous discovery. Whoever loses his life and that which makes life worthwhile for him, whoever surrenders it freely will find life – Jesus Himself – and taste His love, which brings us wondrous joy.

But Jesus yearned for me to understand more fully the depths of His heart; He longed to draw me into a closer fellowship with Him. God wants us to grow in the knowledge of Himself so that our love for Him will increase and abound. When we accept Jesus as our Saviour and Bridegroom, it is as though we have entered a wonderful new land, and the further we penetrate it, the greater the splendours and treasures we discover. Words cannot express what Jesus is truly like. The whole fullness of the Deity dwells in Him. All the beauty of heaven and earth can be found in Him. He is the King of kings, great in power and majesty. The entire universe is subject to Him. He is the crowning glory of all creation and at the same time He is the Lamb of God, who bears the sins of the world. During the course of the years His divine heart and the heart of God the Father were to open up to me more and more and become a source of deepest joy.

And where does God reveal His heart? According to Scripture only along Jesus' pathway, for that is the only place where He can be found. 'He who has my commandments and keeps them, he it is who loves me . . . and I will love him and manifest myself to him' (John 14:21). And what are His commandments? To follow Him along His path of poverty, trials, disgrace and lowliness, to surrender our will, and commit ourselves to the cross. The Lord was calling me to follow this path – and there I found Him.

The Servant Is Not above His Master

'As we follow the way of the cross, You reveal Your heart to us . . . ' are some lines taken from a hymn that we often sang later. But as we follow Jesus, we are taken along stony pathways step by step. From that time onwards I was to encounter more and more disgrace and receive many bruises and wounds on the way. Almost twenty years in the Lord's service lay behind me (1926–45). As leader of the youth work in a city mission, teacher at a Bible college, President of the Women's Division of the German Student Christian Movement, and as lecturer for a missionary society, making speaking tours throughout the country and holding Bible courses in many churches and fellowships, I had always been respected and enjoyed a certain amount of recognition in Christian circles. It was part of my life. But in those years I did not realise how little that was to be taken for granted.

The hostility aroused after the revival of our young people in 1944–5 increased steadily after the founding of the Sisterhood of Mary. I experienced what it meant to be a 'controversial personality'. A shadow was cast upon my name and I became a byword of reproach. On all sides I was faced with opponents – and this suffering never left me. The Lord took away my good reputation so that I might not obscure His glory. He made me contemptible in the sight of others so that I might not become falsely attached to them, but give the Lord my foremost love. He answered my prayer and accepted my dedication to follow Him along the pathway of disgrace and humiliation.

Disgrace became an integral part of my life. Often I would sit in my small room in the attic apartment of the Steinberg House and read my post. Certain letters were like a sword piercing my heart. For example, one of the leaders of the *Gemeinschaftsbewegung* tried to prove to me that we were demonic, because we had received the gifts of the Spirit. Scarcely able to remain on my chair, I knelt down at my bedside and laid the letter before the Lord with tears in my eyes. Another time a leading theologian wrote, vehemently accusing me of disgracing the Protestant Church, because he thought we intended to become Roman Catholic. He added that our way of life would cause a church schism. Yet a church schism was the last thing we desired – the fellowship of love was our aim.

The rumours spread; friends left us and took sides with our adversaries. Speaking engagements were cancelled repeatedly, because people were warned about us. But no one ever came to test our ministry before spreading these warnings. A student at my former Bible college informed me that I was the topic of discussion at a conference, where I was declared a blemish for the entire organisation, because we had received the charismatic gifts. People were advised to withdraw from me.

At a large conference of the *Gemeinschaftsbewegung* the speaker warned the gathering about us, declaring that at the Steinberg House people rolled on the floor, screaming loudly. My father, who happened to be present at that conference, asked the speaker afterwards how he came to make such false statements. It turned out that these incidents had occurred in a different region, in another fellowship, which had no connection with us. The speaker withdrew his statements in my father's presence, but the many participants at the conference, who heard the false rumour, took it for the truth. When they went home, they passed it on to their churches and fellowship groups, and warned people about us everywhere. Later, so we were informed, Christians were told to burn my books, because I was said to 'have the devil' and everything I had written was supposedly 'demonic'. People were discouraged, even forbidden, to set foot on our grounds.

A prominent preacher had been circulating a pamphlet with forty accusations against us. At the request of a third party I was asked to have a talk with this preacher who then put me through a cross-examination. He was obviously embarrassed when I had to point out the fallacy of his claims, for the items listed were completely untrue. Nevertheless, he continued to spread his libel. A member of our ladies' group returned very upset from a ministers' wives' convention for the State of Hesse. She was received with marked coolness because of her association with us, for they presumed we had 'left the Church'. In actual fact, however, our young Sisters acted as parish workers, teaching the children at Sunday School and leading church youth groups, because we felt we should serve within the Church.

My little room became a place of tears. But I experienced the fulfilment of the Scripture verse I received from the Lord when I moved into this room, 'I, I am he that comforts you' (Isaiah 51:12). How gracious of God to give us this pledge in this situation! On all sides we had to face a great deal of mistrust and even outright hostility – not only because of the charismatic gifts, but because the effects of the revival were feared. People were worried that our spiritually alive young people might break the norm and not follow a usual way of life. Accusations and even threatening letters came from parents who were opposed to their children's wholehearted discipleship. They were upset, because their daughters, instead of marrying, wanted to follow the Lord's call to enter a new Sisterhood, which had no visible means of security. In addition, other Christian organisations that had hoped our young people would join them grew distant towards us because of their disappointment.

What was the cause of this rejection, this hostility? As far as the charismatic gifts were concerned, it was especially hard to grasp, since by no means did they play a key role in our fellowship. During the revival in the MBK the Holy Spirit created something new and different, which also became the spiritual foundation of the Sisterhood of Mary. He granted a deeper relationship of love to Jesus, which comes from an ever-increasing flow of contrition and repentance – the source of all spiritual life in the Lord. As Martin Luther once said, a Christian's life should consist of a daily experience of contrition and repentance, and that was the predominant feature of our youth groups and later of the Sisterhood of Mary.

Another reason for the widespread rejection was our 'ecumenical' outlook, although we were only ecumenical in the sense that we wished to have fellowship with brothers from other Christian groups, denominations and branches of Christianity, in the love of Christ, according to His last request, 'that they may all be one'. But the *Gemeinschafts-kreise* in particular, with their anti-Catholic attitude, felt we were making a serious error. We had no intention, however, of conforming to Catholicism. It was love for Jesus that was my motive for seeking fellowship, since I had learnt that 'the closer we are to the heart of God the closer we are to each other'. As far as we were concerned, the cross of Jesus was the only meeting place for brothers and sisters in Christ, the love of God the only basis for true unity. But how were we to clear these misconceptions when in spite of our requests for a brotherly talk, all doors for communication remained closed?

God evidently intended to lead me along Jesus' pathway and teach me to suffer injustice and disgrace in patience. It was God who was at work here; people were only His instruments. Yet it was an act of grace that He did lead me along this path; Jesus' way of the cross became a reality in my own life, for 'the servant is not above his master'. Sometimes I was reminded of my years at university. On one occasion I had to lead a Bible study on 2 Timothy 3:12, 'All who desire to live a godly life in Christ Jesus will be persecuted.' I was at a loss as to what to say. I could only ask myself, 'Does this verse really apply to me, seeing that I know nothing of persecution, disgrace or rejection?' But then the Lord let me taste this kind of suffering – and in abundance. He even used those who had been very close to me, and that was the most painful experience of all.

Disgrace is humiliating, but only through humiliations can we become more humble and really learn to follow the

153

Lamb, who did not return insult for insult, but showed love and forgiveness. Along this path the Lord intended to teach me love that is long-suffering and forgiving, love that blesses its enemies. His aim was to make me more loving and more humble in order to draw me closer to His heart. God wanted to entrust me with a commission, but first I had to be broken. By leading me this way, God was actually answering the prayer of my life.

May Your name shine forth gloriously! Let me live with this aim in mind, burning myself out for this one purpose. Extinguish me completely so that Your glory can shine forth mightily . . .

By treading the pathway of disgrace, I received yet another gift. By losing the recognition and respect of others, I gained something far more precious in return: I came to know Him more intimately and to share in the 'fellowship of his sufferings' (Philippians 3:10 AV). That which many men of God had testified to became true for me: only those who go through suffering can understand the sufferings of Jesus. After 1948 as I followed the way of suffering, a treasure house was opened for me, to which I had no access before – the sufferings of Jesus. I came to know and love Jesus more and more as the Man of Sorrows. During that time I wrote in my diary:

O Jesus, meditating on Your Passion is blessedness, for in doing so we dwell upon the greatest wonder of the Godhead. Greater than the omnipotence of God, who created the universe, greater than the wisdom of His thoughts and plans in all eternity, greater than His understanding, which is unsearchable, is His act of redemption. God takes upon Himself human flesh. God surrenders Himself into the hands of mankind whom He created – into the hands of sinners. God allows Himself to be mutilated and lacerated like an animal. Like a sacrificial victim the Godhead suffers death. Every thought and word of God, every creation of His hand is holy, but holiest of all

154

is Christ's Passion. Here God reveals His nature completely, permitting us to gaze into His heart, which is perfect love. 'O Love, how strong Thou art to save! Thou beddest Him within the grave Whose word the mountains rendeth!'

I had written further:

As the Man of Sorrows You have granted me a completely new love for You, my Bridegroom. Your suffering for the sake of the world and the souls of men has finally begun to touch my heart of stone. You have set my cold heart aflame with the ardent desire to share Your sufferings . . .

In the midst of all the grief that I encountered along the path of disgrace, I discovered that Jesus' words are yea and amen. 'Blessed are you when men . . . utter all kinds of evil against you falsely on my account . . . your reward is great in heaven' (Matthew 5:11f.). But this promise is not merely reserved for the life to come; fulfilment begins in this lifetime. Jesus' love is so great that He cannot wait until the next world to shower His gifts upon those who have borne their cross after Him and suffered for His name's sake. Here on earth He gives them a hundredfold in return for having 'lost' their lives and forsaken their dearest possessions, as I personally discovered. I received a hundredfold in return for the brothers and sisters that I lost. In the years to come the Lord gave me so many new brothers and sisters – believers throughout the world with whom we are united in Jesus – that I could no longer keep count of them. The joy of the Lord and the love of Christ welled up in my heart. He gave me life in all its fullness, granting me knowledge of Himself and the fellowship of His sufferings.

But His love went even further, watching over us like a royal guard. The libel and slander that were intended to destroy our ministry did not succeed in doing so. There were strange incidents. Men who had met together for this purpose suddenly became at variance with each other, while others changed their opinions quite inexplicably during the meeting. It was as though Jesus, the loving Protector, was watching over His commission, preventing the unfavourable resolutions from being passed. Once again I discovered the truth of Jesus' words, 'He who loses his life for my sake will find it' (Matthew 10:39). In this case 'life' to me meant having a good reputation and not being continually subject to defamation. Even when I was young, I would become very upset when someone had to suffer injustice. Whenever I discovered any falsehoods, I would get to the bottom of the matter, even at the cost of my popularity. Later Mother Martyria would often say, laughingly, that I was a born lawyer. Suffering injustice really meant 'losing' my life, because it went against my nature, and now I received countless opportunities to give up my rights and my good reputation. The Lord brought me into such situations intentionally so that I might follow His example. 'He did not revile in return; when he suffered, he did not threaten; but he trusted to him who judges justly' (1 Peter 2:23). By taking me along this path, Jesus made more room in my heart for Himself and His divine life.

How I had sought for this 'divine life' earlier, this deeper, more intimate relationship with Jesus, which alone is true life and fulfilment, without being able to find it! Then at last I found blessedness – at the only place where it can be found – on the way of the cross, which at that time was strewn with the sharp stones of disgrace.

Treasure in the Cross of Illness

During the winter of 1947-8 there was still a drastic shortage of food supplies in post-war Germany. Consequently, I developed a serious stomach disorder. Feeling very weak physically and hardly able to stand upright, I would force myself to go through the day. Sickness was the new phase along the Lord's pathway. It was painful when others outside our family of Sisters repeatedly criticised me for looking so ill. Barely able to collect my thoughts, let alone hold the lectures for the Sisters, I found it humiliating not being able to perform my ministry as I wished to. But the hardest part was that I could scarcely pray owing to my weakened condition. The sickness would not depart, and the burden of this cross weighed heavily upon me, causing me much inner distress.

Then the Lord reminded me of the treasure that is hidden in every cross and showed me the key to it – the prayer, 'Yes, Father'. But I discovered that we can only say these words wholeheartedly if we firmly believe that God in His love has something precious hidden in the cross. We cannot declare, 'God is Love', like an empty formula of faith. Far more is involved when we believe in the love of God. We must firmly expect that when God takes something from us – whether it be health or strength – He will give us something greater in return in His fatherly goodness, something that will make us even happier. This is love's way. It became clear to me that if God gave me this small but painful cross, I had to trust implicitly that He had a gift for me hidden in it, since love always grants gifts and makes others happy. And God is the very source and essence of love.

I wanted to learn to cling in faith to His promise of love. In this difficult situation I began to put my faith into action by saying, 'Yes, Father', with complete trust in His power to intervene. And there was a wonderful transformation! I received not just one but two great treasures! First He gave me a certain amount of independence from my physical condition so that weakness and ill health could not restrict me. At the time I did not realise what significance this gift of the Lord would have for the rest of my life. For the first time, as an act of His amazing grace, He let me see the Holy Spirit triumph over the flesh, over fatigue and physical ailments. To my astonishment I discovered that more can be accomplished when a person is in ill health than when he is well, since God's 'power is made perfect in weakness'. After I said, 'Yes, Father', trusting in His loving care, I was able to stay up later at night to pray, and to carry out my ministry during the day, in spite of my frail condition.

This weakness seemed to be part of God's loving plan, because from that time on sickness and frailty were more or less life companions for me. The greater part of my books was written during such a state of weakness and exhaustion. When, in obedience to God, I wrote down passages, often during the night, frequently overtired, unable to think properly, I was doubtful of the results. Yet when I read the text over later, I could see with thanksgiving and amazement that the Spirit of God had been at work.

The same applied to my journeys, my speaking engagements, the times spent with my daughters and all my daily tasks: God answered my fervent plea that no one would notice my physical weakness. Indeed, I was even considered to be vivacious and a picture of health. Often I received new strength from Him at the last moment, just as I began my talk – and other times I did not. When I held a meeting – in India or America, for example – and people thanked me afterwards, mentioning how much the message had meant to them, I could only silently praise God for what He had done. He had been at work, although I had not realised it.

Ever since those first years I have been able to pray very early in the morning, although it was often late before I went to bed. Time and again I marvelled at what the Lord can do: when we are weak and ill, His divine energy imparts strength to us so that we are able to accomplish more than if we were strong and healthy. Naturally, I respect doctors as a gift of God, according to the words of Scripture, and I am especially grateful to our family doctor for all his assistance. Yet I have also experienced that in various illnesses when neither medical treatment nor medicine could heal me, the Lord would suddenly restore my health when His time had come. Again there are other ailments He has let me bear all my life without taking them away, in order to demonstrate His strength in my weakness.

There was yet another treasure hidden in the cross of illness, as I discovered. When I awoke about four o'clock in the morning, I would have an inner compulsion to rise and pray. Inwardly I would behold the most beautiful countenance of all, the countenance of Jesus. One song after another would flow from my pen. Like the Psalmist, I longed to drink in the loveliness of His holy countenance to my heart's content. Later my spiritual daughters asked me if I had ever seen Jesus, since His beauty and the splendour of His countenance are a recurring theme in my songs and writings. I replied that I felt moved to express my adoration this way, because I had beheld Him in my heart. There are times when we 'see without actually seeing'.

The morning that I first had this experience I found a note slipped under my door. A Sister had written down what she had received in prayer. It was as if she had seen an angel give me a brush to paint the most glorious countenance of all – the countenance of Jesus. On the same morning another Sister wrote a Bible verse with artistic lettering and laid it on my desk. 'I shall be fully satisfied, when I awake to find myself beholding Your form and having sweet communion with You' (Psalm 17:15b *The Amplified Bible*). Neither Sister knew what had taken place early that morning.

As I bore the cross of sickness, the Lord took away my strength, my capabilities and healthy appearance, so as to manifest His power and glory. He made me weak and incompetent, because He only reveals Himself to the poor and weak (1 Corinthians 1). I could scarcely take in the bliss and joy when Jesus drew so close to me, letting me partake of His love, glory and beauty as a foretaste of heaven. If illness and suffering had brought me such a blessing, how could I refrain from praising my cross?

A Chapel Built by Faith

Never shall I forget the fourth of May 1949! As I was in my room praying, God suddenly gave me the inner conviction that I should build a chapel for the Lord Jesus, so

159

that He would receive more adoration. This divine commission set my heart aflame and evoked in me the response, 'Yes, I will do everything possible for the Lord to have a place where He will receive the praise and love of fervent hearts, and where anthems will rise to heaven, proclaiming the greatness of God before the visible and invisible world.' He Himself would inspire the songs and music. He would be glorified as the Lamb of God enthroned on high; the King of glory, power and majesty; the Father, the Almighty, the Omnipotent and Holy One. In this chapel countless numbers of people would experience the presence of God and His holiness. There they would be kindled to love and worship Him.

Although I was set on fire and overjoyed at the prospect of building a place of worship for Jesus, the anxious question arose within me, 'How can I possibly build a chapel for the Lord? How will this plan materialise?' We had neither the money nor the land. Yet in His bountiful goodness the Lord strengthened me for this commission when, a few months later, I was able to pray the matter through as I spent several days apart with Him. He greatly encouraged me by giving me the following Bible verses in prayer.

Take heed now, for the Lord has chosen you to build a house for the sanctuary; be strong, and do it.
1 Chronicles 28:10
And let them make me a sanctuary, that I may dwell in their midst.
Exodus 25:8

How I needed this encouragement! Even though Mother Martyria was in complete agreement with me, I soon discovered that many friends and even some of my daughters did not understand this commission of building God a chapel, and our 'ministry unto God' through praise and worship. The majority of people, including some of our closest friends, expected us, as Sisters, to devote ourselves exclusively to nursing and charitable works. This commission to build a chapel was new to me as well, but the lack of understanding I encountered was the first of many painful

160

experiences. Each time I received a new commission from the Lord, it was the same. Christians are in favour of building hospitals and old people's homes and of sending Sisters to work there. (Indeed this form of service is necessary and we too began it on a small scale later on Canaan.) Yet people often fail to appreciate the need of rendering praise and adoration to God, and even the need of proclaiming His Word and giving spiritual counsel. We discovered this when, in addition to our ministry of prayer, the Lord gave us more and more ministries in these areas.

Consequently, only a few friends supported our ministries with their donations. When we began building on a garden plot, given to us as a present, we only had thirty marks and little hope of receiving funds from elsewhere. According to our inner guidance I felt constrained not to publicise our needs or to ask for donations or support in any way. The ministries, nonetheless, were carried out according to the spiritual law that God always provides for the ministries He gives. He does so, although He frequently leads one along dark avenues of faith, where one must reckon with His assistance alone, since there are no human resources to draw from. Often we had to wait a long time before His help came, but that was the Lord's plan so as to make us humble and to demonstrate that everything was accomplished by Him and not by human efforts, so that He alone – and not man – would receive the glory.

The Lord had placed the main responsibility of the Sisterhood upon my shoulders. During these hard months while the Mother House Chapel was being built, I discovered in particular what that involved. It was clear to me that every commission and insight received from God must be confirmed by another party. And Mother Martyria stood faithfully at my side. I never took a single step unless I had her agreement so that we could forge ahead together. Yet the ultimate responsibility rested on me, since God had given me the inspiration and because our spiritual Father, Pastor Riedinger, had been called to his eternal home earlier that year (1949). During the next two years of building I discovered how painful it was to carry out the commission of the Sisterhood of Mary as a woman without the help and advice of a spiritual Father. We were building a Chapel for the Lord and a Mother House without the necessary financial resources, not feeling free to make an appeal and unable to expect help from any quarter – a project that went against all common sense.

The way of faith led along the edge of an abyss, with new crevices constantly opening up before us. Later even friends advised us to stop building; a continuation would be tempting God in their opinion. These inner conflicts were a great strain for me, and under the burden of this responsibility I often cried to the heavenly Father, 'You are the Father of widows and orphans, and You are my Father too . . . ' And God contended for His commission. At every narrow strait He showed me the next step we were to take. He encouraged me by letting us experience many miracles and answers to prayer at the beginning of our construction period in 1950.*

In the summer of 1951 we started to work on the interior when suddenly the heavens closed. Almost no miracles occurred, and we experienced scarcely any answer to prayer. At the time I had a severe brain concussion due to an accident and was confined to bed in another town. There I wrote:

All Your waves are rising over me; tears have been my food day and night. And my soul cries, 'Where is my God?'

I besought the Lord to be gracious to us again and, for His name's sake, to help us pay the bills, which were mounting up considerably. Like the widow in the parable I kept coming to Him with my request. Even so God did not answer. He remained silent.

Up until that point God had kept His promises for the construction in wonderful ways. Thus deep down inside I knew that when He suddenly fell silent, when He did not

* Realities – The Miracles of God Experienced Today.

answer my prayers, when no help came, He was not at fault. When God is silent, there are obstacles preventing Him from acting and granting us the good things He yearns to give us in His love; these obstacles have to be removed before He can intervene. In this situation I perceived that it was His zealous love that sought to purify me and the Sisterhood of everything that did not reflect His image or glorify Him. Accordingly He took me into the fiery furnace of affliction, bringing me under the pressure of financial distress.

The Spirit of God placed my sins in the light of His countenance – sins that I had not yet regretted deeply enough. I could see my life, all my words and actions during the past four years in the Sisterhood of Mary played back to me like a film reel. I could see one or other of the Sisters standing before me and was reminded of various incidents when I had been unloving. Great sorrow filled my heart, and I felt compelled to ask forgiveness. God pointed out to me the times when my work had yielded no fruit, because I had not done it in unity with Him. Further and further the Lord led me into the night of suffering and inner conflict; our financial circumstances worsened week by week and there was no help in sight.

Because of my concussion I was by myself; no one was allowed to visit me. With nothing to divert my attention, I was constantly faced with the dreadfulness of our situation and God's displeasure towards the Sisterhood and myself. I had to drink this cup of suffering to its dregs. The Lord intended to convict me to the very depths of my soul. In the solitude He wanted me to submit to His chastening completely so that I could lie before Him with a broken and contrite heart. A diary entry from that time reads:

All week long hardly any money has come in. The night is very dark. Thousands of marks have to be paid – and more bills are mounting up. Every day we send out many packages of literature, but receive no money in return – only bills, bills and more bills for the building material. And the Lord is silent . . .

163

This time the Lord planned to carry out a thorough process. Months went by with no prospect of help. Our sole comfort was that Mother Martyria and I received the same Bible verse twice when we prayed about the situation – Psalm 25:3, which reads according to Luther, 'Those who wait for Thee shall not be put to shame.' But as God continued to lead us along the paths of chastening, I could only reply, 'I am the guilty one. I am at fault,' for Scripture says, 'Behold, the Lord's hand is not shortened, that it cannot save, or his ear dull, that it cannot hear; but your iniquities have made a separation between you and your God!' (Isaiah 59:1f).

I knew that if God had to judge our Sisterhood to such an extent that He could no longer hear our prayers, His judgement was chiefly directed at me, since He had placed me in charge. It was a deep grief to me when the Lord clearly showed me that I had led the Sisterhood into this distress. In a letter to my daughters I humbled myself for my manner towards them whenever it had been haughty or severe or whenever I had not carried out my ministry to them in proper love and humility. My one fear was that if we incurred debts, God's name would be dishonoured – the most terrible thing that could happen. During those weeks I wept bitterly at the mere thought. Because of our venture in faith many people had been strengthened in their faith in God – the God who answers prayers and performs miracles today. But if we fell into debt, they would be disappointed and no longer able to believe in God's wondrous power.

The Lord chastened and broke me by not answering my prayers. The bills increased monthly, and the fear that they would turn into debts one day also increased month by month. Yet in the midst of my tears I could only thank Him for His graciousness in granting me light and sending judgement. As I wrote, 'You cast me down – only to let me fall into Your loving arms.'

The holiness of God broke into my life as seldom before. My fervent plea was that the Lord would send me back to my spiritual daughters as a changed person, with a broken and contrite heart.

God is Love and He does not allow us to be tempted beyond our strength. As a foretaste of the special blessings this time of judgement would bring, the Holy Triune God suddenly inclined Himself to me for several days during those weeks of sorrow, lavishing His amazing love upon me. All heartache vanished in the indescribable joy. He wanted to make His dwelling place within me (John 14:23) and let me taste the bliss of His love. That was why He first had to cleanse and empty the inner chamber of my heart.

When our financial need developed into a crisis, the hour of deliverance finally dawned and God turned His countenance towards us once more. We were rather ignorant about business affairs, but a friend of ours, a Christian wholesale dealer, showed us the way out of this hopeless situation. In those days instalment plans were new and relatively unknown. Our friend explained to us that when a house is being built, it is normal to make payment on a pre-arranged instalment basis. He even went with one of the Sisters to the various firms, which immediately agreed to do business with us this way. With that the greatest burden was lifted from our shoulders. The Lord was merciful to us and we were able to meet every single payment.

But in spite of this gracious turn God continued to judge us until the end of the summer in order to humble us in the dust before Himself and before man. In September 1951 the Chapel could not be dedicated, as we had informed our friends half a year before, even though the interior of the Chapel was almost finished. In a newsletter, which Mother Martyria sent out on my behalf while I was ill, I felt urged to humble myself and explain that the postponement of the dedication was God's judgement upon us. The letter was headed with a Bible verse, which according to Luther reads, 'I thank You for humbling me and helping me' (Psalm 118:21).

Soon afterwards I moved into our newly built Mother House, still feeling very weak physically. As a penitent sinner I went to each one of my daughters and asked for forgiveness. On September 23, 1951 – the day the Chapel should have been consecrated – all the Sisters gathered round my bed. How often we had spoken of the moment when the Chapel would be finished and the bell would ring for the first time to call the guests to the consecration ceremony! With the bell ringing joyously and our voices uplifted in praise, God would be glorified for His goodness, since He had completed this building in the most marvellous ways without letting us incur any debts. The moment had come. The bell was chiming. The Chapel was built. But there were no guests that day, no consecration, for God's judgement was still upon us. Never before had the ringing of a bell filled me with such sadness. It sounded to me more like the tolling for a funeral. The voices that were to raise their strains of praise to Him on this day remained silent. Only the sound of weeping could be heard. God had to lead us this way because of our sins. And in that hour as God Himself spoke to us through the ringing of the bell, a wave of deep repentance swept across the Sisters as well.

This holy hour of God's judgement proved to be an hour of grace. With the forgiveness of Jesus Christ new life broke out in the Sisterhood. During that summer when God expressed His disapproval I was led along a path of great suffering that brought me to deep contrition and repentance. But I had no idea that God had an even greater blessing in store. A new sun of grace was to rise and shine upon my life as I discovered a few months later.

The Call to Seclusion
1952

His Ways Are Not Our Ways

'The sparrow hath found a nest for herself.' In September 1951 we all moved into the new Mother House, where the Sisters working on the building site had been living provisionally. The upper storey was not quite finished and there was still some interior work to be done, but at last we were reunited as a family. From then on in our communal life we were able to concentrate on the primary commission of our Sisterhood – the ministry of prayer and proclamation. But the Lord had His own plans for laying the foundation of these ministries, which were later to have world-wide significance – plans far beyond my scope of imagination. He intended to give me a special call.

As Mother of the Sisterhood of Mary I was no longer to play an active part in carrying out the ministries that God had given us. He had chosen the opposite for me. He led me into seclusion, into quietness and solitude. His call and His claim upon our love are so powerful that down through the ages people have responded by following paths that they never would have chosen if they had followed their natural inclinations and desires. This was my personal experience. The Lord called me into seclusion – I, who was the typically sociable, active and creative type! During my student days at the Women's College for Social Welfare Training I could scarcely endure being alone in my room for more than an hour or two. I was in my element when I was with people; therefore, nothing and no one other than Jesus Himself could have induced me to lead a life of seclusion.

By calling me to a life of seclusion, the Lord was calling me to a life that was completely foreign to my nature. Yet this way of life was to be the foundation for all our future commissions, which were to be far more extensive than I had ever dreamt. I had often heard of the biblical truth that all great commissions for the Kingdom of God are conceived in solitude, when we are alone with Him. Examples from the Bible demonstrate that solitude and seclusion are the birthplace of new divine life and fruitful ministries for the Lord. I knew that if the Lord calls us to withdraw for some time, to come apart with Him to listen to Him and speak with Him, our ministry for the Kingdom of God will have a special effectiveness. But so far this knowledge had remained more or less theoretical for me. Even though I had always withdrawn for hours of prayer, these times formed only a small part of my life. My common sense had too many arguments against a prolonged absence: I was indispensable to the work; it would be irresponsible in view of my commitments in the Sisterhood, and so on.

The Lord Himself had to break into my life. In the previous years Jesus had already prepared the way, graciously granting me blessed hours of encounter with Him. But then Jesus came to me in the power of His love, which 'passeth all understanding'. It was as if He were wooing me; He desired me for Himself alone, seeking a more intimate fellowship than ever before. As a response, in early January 1952, I voluntarily committed myself to a relatively long period of solitude and seclusion.

I was still suffering from the after-effects of that severe time of God's judgement during the summer of 1951 and was filled with sorrow for having grieved Jesus and my fellow men. Then one evening while I was in prayer, the holiness of God descended upon me once more; this time not in judgement, but in His overwhelming, holy love, which took full possession of me. The Lord came upon me in the power of His holy fire and it was as if I were being consumed with an unquenchable ardour and a divine zeal. What could this experience be? The infilling of the Holy Spirit? No, the experience that I had had in receiving the Holy Spirit and His gifts was different. This time Jesus drew near to me as the Man of Sorrows, our Lord, who baptises with the Holy Spirit *and* with fire as the Bible says. The overwhelming power of His love and suffering came into my life in a way I had never known before.

One of the consequences of this experience was that an even greater love for Jesus took hold of me, blazing like a fire in my heart and constraining me to suffer for Him. In the past years I had prayed earnestly for this fervent love for Jesus that compels us to suffer for Him, since I felt that I lacked this love. In that holy hour a flame of love was kindled in me. I yearned to make sacrifices for Jesus and to have the privilege of suffering for Him. I was also seized with a passionate desire to save souls.

At that time I did not realise that this divine ardour was to be the incentive for everything in my life. So as to prepare me to be a true bride of the Lamb, the Lord wanted to set my heart aflame with love for Him, and as Scripture says, 'Love is strong as death . . . It flashes fire, the very flame of Jehovah. Many waters cannot quench the flame of love, neither can the floods drown it.' (Song of Solomon 8:6f. *The Living Bible*). This ardour was expressed in an inner compulsion to pray. In the first years of seclusion I felt compelled to worship and entreat the Lord for many hours, also at night. And even when my work required intensive mental concentration, the flame of prayer in my heart was not extinguished.

We know from reading the Holy Scriptures that direct encounters with God are a reality. Divine encounters, when God breaks into our lives in a powerful way, are responsible for tremendous turning points in our spiritual lives, and in many instances such events are associated with a new commission from the Lord. I too received a call from God shortly after this divine encounter – a call that was to be highly significant for the commission of the Sisterhood of Mary.

And now it meant following this call and entering seclusion to be alone with Him. It seemed as though Jesus were entreating me, 'Surrender yourself completely to Me.' This event was of deep significance for me. Until then I had been mainly concerned about being active for the Lord, and in this respect my service for Him, rather than He Himself, had absorbed my attention. However, from that time onwards my life was to revolve round Jesus alone. My ministry *for* Jesus was to have priority no longer, even though it did continue, as the fruit of times of prayer. First and foremost I was to minister *unto* Him. That meant spending far more time with Jesus, showing Him my love, and being wholly available for Him. Because of His inexpressible love for us, He deeply yearns for our love in return. Yet, as I came to realise, I had been neglecting His claim upon our love. It was as though the Lord let me gaze into His heart, which is sorely wounded because He is loved so little. He showed me how much He suffers because we always have time for one another, but seldom for Him (Luke 10:41f.). I could almost hear Him lamenting, 'Who has time for Me?' Time and again we find that people, things or our service for Him have grown more important to us than the Lord Himself. Yet no one loves us so much as our Lord, who is waiting for our love in return.

As I wrote to my daughters later:

Listen to your Bridegroom's entreaty, 'I am waiting for you.' What does He expect? Very few are called to lead a life of seclusion, but there is one thing He is clearly asking of each one of you: to give Him all your love . . . Only those who forsake the things that are most precious to them will receive in return the greatest gift of all, which can make us happier than anything else in heaven or on earth – Jesus and His love. This love does not fall into a person's lap by chance, but it comes to everyone who surrenders all he has to Jesus . . . Do not cling to any soulish love, which brings you into bondage. Do not encourage it! It will kill your bridal love or prevent it from blossoming. Jesus does not give us His love if our heart is divided. So let it cost you something to experience this overwhelming, blissful love that Jesus has for you.

During the course of 1952 His pleas and beckoning love grew stronger and stronger.

Is there a soul for whom I can be all,
Who seeketh Me alone, and heedeth but My call?
I ask thee now, am I enough for thee?
Wilt thou in truth leave everything for Me,
For Me alone?

These were the words that resounded within me. Jesus' plea reached the depths of my heart. The revelations of love that He gave me during the following months were so overpowering and filled me with such joy that I could only reply,

My dearest Jesus, how can I refuse?
Lord, I am Thine, to go where Thou dost choose;
For Thee I shall leave all else behind . . .

To respond to His imploring love meant adopting a totally new way of life for the following years. In the winter it meant spending most of the weeks in seclusion away from the Sisters, whereas in the summer there were interruptions owing to journeys the Lord commissioned me to undertake. Yet all in all, a completely different life had begun for me. For the most part it led me into solitude, to be alone with Jesus.

When I made the break in 1952, my heart was in deep anguish, for it meant yielding the Sisterhood of Mary so soon after the Lord had entrusted it to me as the gift He had promised. Since 1935 Mother Martyria and I had waited for the fulfilment of the promise that God had given us; so when the Sisterhood was founded, it was all the more precious to me. This step meant surrendering my beloved spiritual daughters and spending many months apart from them, although I had been looking forward to being with them after my long illness and time away.

My daughters had to make a sacrifice on their part also. As they said later, 'During the two years we spent building, we had often consoled ourselves with the prospect, "When the Chapel and Mother House are finished, then . . . !"' Then they wanted to make up for all they had missed. They looked forward to the festivals that would be celebrated, the fellowship at mealtimes that would no longer be held on the building site amongst piles of old bricks and mounds of earth. The Sisters looked forward to many evenings together and times when I would share more with them about the loving purposes of God and our commission. Indeed, many plans were made for this time, but then they had to be sacrificed.

Since Jesus loves us, He seeks tokens of our love and these are sacrifices. For this reason Jesus challenges us, 'Whoever forsakes . . . for My name's sake.' He looks for sacrifices of love in our lives, and values them highly as the proof and practical expression of our love. This is evident in His gratitude and way of rewarding such sacrifices. His disciples will receive a hundredfold in this lifetime for whatever they gave up for His name's sake, and eternal, divine life in the next world. How few proofs of my love, how few sacrifices had I brought the Lord Jesus up till then! Nevertheless He entreated me to forsake, out of love for Him, the things I held dear and which made life worthwhile to me. Indeed, He asked me to give myself, my all to Him. I could not comprehend His amazing grace.

Then the day came when I was to make the actual sacrifice – October 21, 1952. I had already sealed my dedication for this new way of life some weeks earlier during a time of prayer in a small Upper Bavarian village, and had written a parting letter to my spiritual daughters in order to prepare them. On the twenty-first of October they once more came to me in small groups. Together we sang songs of love and dedication to Jesus and I blessed them. Then the door closed. There was sorrow, grief and tears, but it had to be this way, for the more it costs us to make a sacrifice for Jesus, the more it is worth.

With this act I laid aside the external leadership of the Sisterhood of Mary, but in my new way of life I could still retain the spiritual leadership of the Sisterhood by correspondence with Mother Martyria or by discussions with her in special cases. Occasionally, if I had a spiritual matter to share with my daughters, I would come to the evening meetings, but for many weeks solitude and seclusion were my lot and I was alone in my room with Jesus.

Loneliness is one of the types of suffering that has tormented people of all ages, and I was to discover how hard it is to be alone. It was a dying process and the lights of joy were extinguished. Instead of happy mealtimes with my spiritual daughters when we could share our news and concerns for the Lord's service, I took my meals alone in my small room. In the evenings I could hear my daughters singing joyfully in our Hall of Zion, and my heart ached, for I yearned to join in their fellowship. Sometimes I could hear the sound of voices in the next room as Mother Martyria discussed our various ministries with the Sisters. Certainly I was consulted in writing when there were important issues to decide, but since I was naturally interested in all that happened in our Sisterhood, I sometimes wished to know more. Now I was like an outsider. To a great extent the Lord had removed me from the sphere of outward activity where I could participate in the discussions and give advice.

Since I rarely saw or spoke to anyone for weeks, my room sometimes seemed like a prison – but a prison of His love. We are all acquainted with quiet times when we cannot feel Jesus' presence and have no incentive to pray. How difficult it is to go through a whole day when the emptiness, the loneliness, the spiritual drought are oppressive and we are tempted to break out of our 'cage'. But if we try to escape, we shall forfeit the precious gems that the Lord intends to give us for our spiritual lives in times of solitude when we are alone with Him. Only by going through the desert could Moses encounter God on Mount Sinai.

I remember one day during the first few weeks spent in seclusion when Mother Martyria arrived home after holding a lecture in another town. My first thought was to join her immediately to hear her news. One step through the door and I could have been with her. But then I literally experienced what it involves when Jesus has first priority over us. He was like the master of the household, holding the key to my room in His hand. Gradually I began to comprehend Jesus' sorrow that we, His own, take so little time to be with Him. When an unexpected visitor arrives, we leave what we are doing without further thought, even if we are busy in an important task or enjoying a happy family get-together. But when Jesus comes to visit us, instead of welcoming Him as we should, we turn Him away. Because we feel more drawn to people or tasks, we are more than ready to devote ourselves to them, while Jesus is left as a Beggar of love, wandering from door to door, knocking to see who will receive Him.

> Jesus with love still is seeking
> For hearts that are aflame,
> To make their lives an off'ring
> Inspired by love for Him.
>
> Love that's eternal is waiting
> And pleads with every heart,
> 'O, won't you hear and answer?
> 'Tis pain to dwell apart.'*

As soon as this realisation dawned on me, the enemy resorted to another means of attack. He mocked me, implying that this way would lead me nowhere and that it was senseless to continue. He insinuated that I was acting irresponsibly towards Mother Martyria, although Mother Martyria had actually made it easy for me to obey this leading, always saying with exemplary selflessness, 'When Jesus calls, you must follow Him. I am glad that Jesus receives love in this way.' Even so it was extremely hard for me to lay all the external responsibility on her shoulders. Was I not treating her unfairly? If I did not serve my spiritual daughters as I had done previously, would I not be neglecting them? Could the commission of the Sisterhood of Mary actually be carried out as a result of my call to seclusion? Would not this unusual leading be likely to give rise to misunderstanding and cause more harm than good?

* *O None Can Be Loved like Jesus*, No. 21.

174

In my limited understanding I had always assumed that as Mother of the Sisterhood of Mary I should be carrying out my responsibilities quite differently. I shall never forget the hour when Father Riedinger, the spiritual Father of our Sisterhood, a man filled with the love of God and humility, endowed with the gift of prophecy, called Mother Martyria and me to his deathbed. In that December 1949 we visited him for the last time. As he gave his prophetic blessing, he said that God had appointed me to carry out his commission as well, which he had as the spiritual Father of the Sisterhood. The Lord had shown him on his deathbed that we were not to have another spiritual Father. But I had never imagined that I was to fulfil this commission by withdrawing into solitude. At the time I took it for granted that I could take an active part in the ministry and that would have brought me joy in spite of all the struggles and difficulties involved. Then I discovered that the way lay in the opposite direction, that I had to sacrifice every kind of outward activity.

In the midst of these temptations my four walls sometimes stared at me so cheerlessly. Without meaning to, I began to compare myself with others who had been at university with me, who were also in the prime of life. They held responsible positions. They were in the thick of life. They were listened to and needed. In contrast, if I was invited to speak or if visitors asked to see me, Mother Martyria repeatedly had to excuse me and take my place. In addition, I suffered physically owing to a severe case of rheumatism. But above all, spiritual night and loneliness sought to engulf me at times. When we follow Jesus' call uncompromisingly, we are often faced with the seeming meaninglessness of His guidance for us. Then the Tempter is at our side trying to dissuade us from following this path. He knows that 'death brings forth fruit' and that by dying to self we invade his territory.

Although I repeated this truth to myself time and again, anxiety occasionally crept into my heart. If the Lord were to call me frequently to such long weeks in seclusion – not just for the next few years, but for the rest of my life – could I endure this desert road? Would it not have a harmful effect on my personality, since I had no natural inclination for this type of life and nothing could have been more foreign to me? But such outcomes are only possible if this way of life is self-chosen asceticism – not if we follow Jesus' call out of love for Him. In the latter case we are grafted into Jesus, the very essence of life. When we follow such a call in obedience to God, it will not ruin our lives or cause emotional damage, but rather bring us greater abundance of life and new blessings, which He bestows in His grace.

Mother Martyria and my daughters, who had to sacrifice my presence and help, also experienced that they were blessed as a result. Time and again the Sisters said that because I had gone into seclusion, Jesus had come closer to them in His love, since His words, 'Whoever forsakes will receive', applied equally to them. The love and suffering of Jesus had become more real to them than ever before, and consequently their own vocation to love Jesus with an undivided bridal love had taken on new meaning for them. In a new way they had encountered the holiness, omnipotence and goodness of God the Father and His deep grief over us, His children. The creative power of the Holy Spirit had also taken on new dimensions for them. My daughters said that during the brief times I occasionally spent with them they received many blessings and insights that I could not have passed on to them before.

The Lord had called the Sisterhood of Mary into existence for a specific purpose. By leading me into seclusion, He was preparing me and the whole Sisterhood for a ministry for the end times, for a vast, many-sided commission.

At the time there was no evidence of this. Yet in hours of temptation when my path seemed senseless to me, a little star of promise appeared in the sky – a prophecy given by someone else. 'The more you withdraw, the further the call will resound one day. The commission of the Sisterhood of Mary will be world-wide.' I could scarcely believe it. For the time being it meant holding out in obedience day by day in solitude and seclusion. The spirit of fervent prayer that was imparted to me then would later be naturally channelled into the specific commissions of God.

Alone with Jesus

My calling to go into seclusion did not only include loneliness, trials and temptations and various forms of suffering in the spirit with Jesus. More and more I became aware of the privilege of leading a life away from people, of spending hour after hour in deepest communion with Jesus, of being completely surrendered to Him at all times, of serving Him alone. What a privilege it is to be as close to Jesus as the disciple John was, sharing His innermost joys and griefs! What experience could be more precious than that of drawing close to Jesus' heart? Love surpassing all understanding pours forth from His heart today just as in times past. His heart is so vulnerable, easily grieved by the sins of men – and yet so merciful. We wound Him with our sins, but from these same wounds flow forth salvation, forgiveness and love. Who can fathom the heart of Jesus? His love is infinitely gentle and tender to those who love Him. As it is written in the Word of God, 'I love those who love me' (Proverbs 8:17).

The utter stillness of eternity often rested upon my room while I was in prayer. The presence of God, His holiness and love were almost tangible. And when God drew close and inclined Himself to a sinful soul, His breath could almost be felt. The peace of God was like a flowing stream, and like a veil His tender love would enfold me. At the same time His love was like a blazing fire, kindling me with a fervent love for Him.

How could He not visit us if He loves us so much? Jesus, who is eternal Love, longs to come and dwell with the souls whom He loves, since they are His bride. As He has promised, ' . . . we will come to him and make our home with him'

(John 14:23). He knocks at the door and entreats them, 'Arise, my love, my fair one, and come away' (Song of Solomon 2:10). Yet why does Jesus choose to come at the dead of night when shadows have fallen and the beloved feels as though she is walking through a dark valley? He is drawn to those who love Him; He yearns for His beloved, longing to comfort and restore their souls and to shower His love upon them. This impulse is even present in earthly bridegrooms, who are but a pale reflection of Jesus, our heavenly Bridegroom, who is Love eternal. How much more attentive then must Jesus' love be?

Jesus comes! Indeed, He cannot do otherwise, for it is His very nature. He comes today and tomorrow, and He will also come again in glory as King and Bridegroom to be received by His own who wait for Him longingly.

When He comes, His love fills us with bliss and delight, since it is far greater than any human love we could ever receive. Indeed, what love could be more tender, more pure than the love of Christ? What love could be more ardent than this eternal, immortal flame? Who can describe the might and strength of His love, charged with the infinite power of God when it comes and takes possession of a weak and sinful human soul? What love could be warmer, more sympathetic, or more merciful than His love? Human love is restricted, its capacity and ability to express itself are limited, whereas the love of Christ, which comes from above, is immeasurable. His love is like a never-ending stream, pouring forth from His heart; it is like a blazing fire without beginning or end.

If His love can fill a heart with delight in this life as it is written in the Song of Solomon, how much greater must the rapture and bliss be in heaven? Even during this life-time we taste divine peace when Jesus draws close to us and unites with us (John 17:23). All pain is soothed, all restlessness departs from our innermost being, for Jesus has come. We may rest in His heart and time is like eternity. Deep longing fills us as we ask, 'When shall we be with Him whom our soul loves – united with Him for all eternity?'

The times spent in seclusion brought many blessings and commissions, but none could compare with the privilege of being able to share the innermost concerns of Jesus' heart, which contains the fullness of love and suffering. Nothing could be greater than being loved by Him and loving Him in return. Nothing could be more wonderful than experiencing the fulfilment of His promise to come to us. This unity with Jesus was and still is the source of all our ministries, determining the spiritual life of the Sisterhood of Mary. This abiding in Him, which Jesus mentions in John 15, is the source of all activity and growth in the Kingdom of God. And its significance is eternal, since it is union with God, the Fount of all eternal and divine life.

The Secret of Christmas

During the first months of seclusion, before Christmas 1952, the weeks were long and dark. But occasionally God in His grace would kindle a light. The blessed secret of Christmas – God became man – was unfolded to me in a new way. Suddenly I had a deeper relationship with the Child in the manger, for He became very real to me. Often I was awakened at night and in spite of my weariness I would compose songs about the Child Jesus, under the prompting of the Spirit. For most of us in the Sisterhood the secret of Christmas had been a matter of the intellect up till then – a concept, a thought, a fact, a tradition, but not a living event or a source of divine life. This time God wished to prepare a Christmas for us that would change our hearts and bring a new dimension into our spiritual lives. The songs the Lord had given were part of His plan to awaken a deeper love and adoration for Jesus, the Child in the manger.

In spite of this time of spiritual preparation for Christmas, anxiety arose in my heart. Would it be a repetition of the disappointing Christmas we had celebrated two years ago? At that time, in 1950, God's commission to build a chapel had begun to materialise, and love had set my heart aflame with the desire for God to receive worship. For that Christmas festival I was given in prayer a number of poems and songs of adoration for the Child Jesus. With glowing colours I tried to paint a picture to the Sisters of how the Child Jesus would win our hearts, awaken love in us, fill us with deep joy at His coming and kindle within us the flame of adoration. But when Christmas came, I could scarcely believe it. There was no flame burning in the hearts of my spiritual daughters. The songs had not been practised; there was no depth to the worship; an atmosphere of boredom prevailed. I was filled with sadness. How could we build a chapel if there was no love for Jesus burning in our hearts and no spirit of adoration? Had the Lord not shown me that we were to have a choir of Sisters singing songs of adoration in the power of the Holy Spirit? Heaven would then descend, inspiring many others to join in the worship. Yet at Christmas 1950 there was no sign of this spirit of adoration.

During the Christmas season of the following year, 1951, I even had to disband our Sisterhood Choir temporarily, for the singing, which was lacking fervour, divine life and the spirit of adoration, seemed to me more like an insult to God. Consequently we had no choir for several months. During that time we prayed and earnestly entreated the Lord to remove all the obstacles so that His Spirit could impart new life to our singing and worship. Would Christmas really be different in 1952?

As I came out of seclusion to celebrate Christmas with my spiritual daughters, my heart was filled with eager expectation and love for the Child Jesus. But once again a great heaviness settled upon our Hall of Zion on Christmas Eve and Christmas Day. Yet it was my deep longing that the Child Jesus would receive true worship from us this time and that heaven would come down in our midst. Then, on the Second Day of Christmas, there was a breakthrough – a miracle of the Holy Spirit. Our Hall of Zion was no longer a meeting room, where a talk about the secret of

Christmas was being given, where my daughters would listen quietly and then sing a few carols and songs. It had been transformed into a 'heavenly festival hall'. Just as the shepherds once hastened to kneel down and worship the holy Child in Bethlehem, the Sisters gathered in small groups round the manger, which stood in the centre of the room, and sang to the Child Jesus in fervent love. Till late at night we sang the familiar carols as well as the new songs the Spirit of God had given me for this festival while I was in seclusion.

O Child of peerless beauty,
Whom angels magnify,
You radiate the glory
That comes from God Most High!
O Child, O clearest image
Of God's most tender love,
That sinners dare to praise You,
Whom angels laud above!

Since You to us descended,
No more seems heaven far;
You bring it close for all men,
O radiant Morning Star!
With You love made its entrance,
Among us to abide;
O rapture for all sinners,
Their thirst is satisfied! *

We made up verses on the spur of the moment, singing them to the Child Jesus, praising Him for all He is and brings us – forgiveness of sins and joy, love for one another and thus a foretaste of heaven. Then we would gather round the manger again, full of praise and adoration that God had taken on human flesh and become a little child for our sakes. There was no end to our worship; it was constantly fanned into new life.

The Child Jesus had come alive for us; what had hap-

* *Well-spring of Joy*, No. 27.

pened in Bethlehem long ago became a present-day event. That year we celebrated Christmas, the festival of praise and adoration as never before. Everything was enhanced by the splendour of heaven. Since Christmas was far too short, we went on celebrating until Epiphany. Every evening we came together and worshipped the holy Child even into the small hours of the morning. During these two weeks of Christmas, which I spent with my spiritual daughters, we truly had a foretaste of heaven. How happy we were together – the joy more than compensated for the times we had been apart!

The Child Jesus had turned us into children – happy, natural, self-forgetful and loving. He had begun to set us free from our staidness, pride and sophistication. The seed of true adoration had been planted in our hearts. We could no longer stand round the manger like 'grownups'; we had to kneel before it like children as we brought our worship. The Child Jesus, who is Love eternal, Love incarnate, had called us to love one another and live together in complete reconciliation.

But that was not the end. Love sparks off new life. A vast commission grew out of this divine gift that we received at Christmas 1952. The following Christmas we invited our friends and neighbours to worship with us and while I was in seclusion, the Lord led me to write a very simple nativity play, which we performed in our Mother House Chapel in 1953. We had none of the qualifications for performing or producing religious plays – neither the talent nor the experience. But love for the Child Jesus was the inspiration for this play, which was an answer to the urgent prayer that others too might bring Him love, gratitude and adoration, and begin to live in love and reconciliation.

Towards the end of the nativity play some of the Sisters came to the manger in the chancel of the chapel. Kneeling or standing, they sang songs of adoration. Then one of the members of the congregation came forward to light his candle, and others followed him. As they began to sing songs of worship to the Child Jesus, something wonderful happened. Two families that had been on bad terms with each other were reconciled at the manger. What a victory for the Child Jesus, who is eternal Love! He had come to earth that love might triumph. Jesus proved Himself to be the living Lord, who is alive today and brings about changes in people, enabling them to love. Indeed, whenever Jesus receives love and worship, there are repercussions.

Ever since the mystery of Christmas was disclosed to us anew, it has made an impact on more and more lives. During my time of seclusion before Christmas 1952 when the Child Jesus came so close to me and inspired me to compose songs about Him, I was given the inner assurance that He would begin His triumphal march. And indeed it did begin.

Some years later the repercussions of this Christmas could even be felt in the Nativity Grotto in Bethlehem. When our Sisters began their ministry on the Mount of Olives in Jerusalem, I shared with them my grief that for years at the Nativity Grotto the feeling of ill will existing between the various denominations would erupt on Christmas Eve, of all times, when love and reconciliation should be victorious. Moreover it grieved me for the sake of the Child Jesus that most of the tourists merely rushed through the grotto where He was born – even on this holy night.

My daughters took this plight to heart. They made it their prayer request and aim of faith that every year in the grotto during Christmas many souls would be kindled anew with love for the Child Jesus and bring Him gratitude and praise. Contrary to all human expectations the incredible occurred. Crowds of tourists that normally spent only a few minutes in the grotto, perhaps taking a photograph or two, remained there captivated by the presence of the Child Jesus as our Sisters sang songs of praise and adoration. Soon the grotto was transformed into a holy place of worship. For hours on end songs of praise welled up in the reverent hearts of people from all nations. Christians and non-Christians, including many young people, joined in the worship, and even the Moslem guard forgot his duty. After listening for two hours, he turned to our Sisters and whispered, 'Do you know that what you're doing now has never been allowed before?'

Nevertheless, this scene of worship and adoration has been repeated each Christmas Eve in Bethlehem. Our Sisters not only sang songs of praise in the grotto, but they were also able to spread the Christmas joy in the streets of Bethlehem, which were teeming with pilgrims and tourists, including Jews drawn by the secret of Christmas, and spiritually starved hippies. As our Christmas greetings were passed round, the appreciation could especially be seen in these young people, whose sad faces lit up with a flicker of joy.

God became man; He was born as a child. In many places the secret of the incarnation was rediscovered and passed on. Like rays of light filtering into dark alleys and remote places, the joyous message of Christmas, the singing, the worship and adoration spread. Bethlehem was not the only place. Here in Germany in the centre of our town our Sisters set up a manger with the Child Jesus in one of the main squares. In the midst of the hustle and bustle of Christmas shopping, the sound of singing could be heard, and children joyfully gathered round the Child in the manger, while lost-looking young people watched longingly, and adults joined in the singing and worship. At a market place in Berlin, in a space between stalls with Christmas sales, our Canaan Friends set up a manger and sang songs of worship. Others joined in as their eyes were diverted from the gaudy and crude advertisements; the Child in the manger captivated their attention.

The effects of such worship and adoration were far-reaching. The Child Jesus won hearts everywhere, whether it was in England in the centre of Coventry where a manger was set up, or in the poorest districts of our town, at meetings with Greek Orthodox friends in Thessalonica, in convents in Italy and Jerusalem, at Christmas services in Arizona, USA, or on military radio stations for American troops in Europe. The songs on our Christmas records, our indoor herald boxes (containing tracts and Christmas greetings) placed in shops and waiting rooms, and our Christmas letters that are sent to many different countries – all helped to bring the Child Jesus to many more souls.

The sad of heart became happy and the adults children, for the Child Jesus has all power and might. A bishop, a scientist and former actors, for example, knelt down at the manger to sing their songs of praise to the Child Jesus. And many other guests staying at our retreat house 'Jesus' Joy' once more learnt at the manger to worship God in joyful adoration, as He would have us do.

There seemed to be no end to the blessing we had received that Christmas. The very simple nativity play that we presented in 1953 gave birth to our 'Herald Plays', which have been a means of bringing the message that the Lord had entrusted to us to many thousands of people, during the course of the years. And through these plays many have heard the Lord's call to love and follow Him, and learnt to trust the Father.

Which one of my daughters could have imagined in 1952, when I was separated from them, alone in my room, that the fellowship of love with Jesus during times of seclusion would have far-reaching effects?

The Fellowship of His Sufferings

What was it that made the Apostle Paul willing to give up everything that he had previously regarded as gain? His life as a Pharisee, his privileges as a Hebrew, his reputation amongst his people he counted as refuse in comparison to the privilege of being 'found in him' and of sharing 'his sufferings, becoming like him in his death' (Philippians 3:9f.). Paul's supreme desire, and in his eyes the most precious blessing, was to partake of Jesus' sufferings. How often had I read that passage in Philippians without fully comprehending it!

Paul was not the only one who cherished this desire. The lives of the Early Christians were characterised by this longing to suffer for Jesus' sake. We read that the martyrs of the Early Church were filled with an ardent love that drove them to undergo suffering for Jesus. This same impulse has inspired men of all times and churches as seen in the case of the great missionary and intercessor, John Hyde, who once said that the closer we come to the heart of Jesus, the more we shall partake of His suffering.

Thus we can understand how St Francis of Assisi, who like the Apostle Paul was no theorist, could pray that he might experience in his own body and soul as fully as possible the sufferings Jesus underwent during His Passion. He prayed as one who yearns to share the fate of the beloved, and God granted his desire, leading him into the fellowship of His sufferings. It is said that St Francis' sorrow-laden life reached its fulfilment in the striking resemblance it bore to the life of the Man of Sorrows.

In the previous years as my love for Jesus increased, this desire also increased in my heart – first a gentle yearning but then a growing ardour. Ever since 1952 when Jesus overwhelmed me with the fullness of His love, the biblical truth of the fellowship of His sufferings became a reality in my life. I sensed that suffering, especially the fellowship of His sufferings, yields a great abundance of fruit. Indeed, as Paul testifies, 'We who live are constantly [experiencing] being handed over to death for Jesus' sake ... always carrying about in the body the liability and exposure to the same putting to death that the Lord Jesus suffered, so that the [resurrection] life of Jesus also may be shown forth by and in our bodies' (2 Corinthians 4:11, 10 *The Amplified Bible*).

Paul knew what the fellowship of His sufferings was and prized the suffering he shared with Jesus and underwent for His sake, as many of his letters indicate, particularly 2 Corinthians 6 and 11, where he listed all the types of hardship he had to endure.

If Jesus leads a soul into the fellowship of His sufferings, He may let him partake of His agony in Gethsemane, as well as of His sufferings today when once again He is forsaken in His battle against the powers of darkness. This suffering with Jesus will be quite different from any human sorrow or hardship that may afflict the soul, and far greater, for no grief can compare with the deep anguish of God. Thus it is possible for a person to undergo inner torment, hidden to the eyes of others, to a degree which he would never have met in the normal Christian life, and this suffering has nothing to do with other burdens he may have to bear.

When the prince of death draws near, the soul has a taste of the agony in Gethsemane. The yawning jaws of death threaten to devour the soul when he feels utterly alone and abandoned by God. A person who has frequently enjoyed the deepest and most intimate fellowship with Jesus can be so overcome by the power of death that he cannot find the slightest comfort in the divine and spiritual, and feels as though he had never had a relationship with Jesus at all. It is as though the hand of death grips his heart so that he almost loses all power of feeling or thinking, and is only aware of torment. But deep down inside he is at peace and in all the trials and vexations of everyday life he is able to remain cheerful to all outward appearances. This spiritual suffering does not hinder his daily work nor have an adverse effect on it.

If Jesus leads us into the fellowship of His sufferings, He will often let us partake of His disgrace as well (1 Peter 4:13f.). And as Peter expressly reminds us, we should not be unduly alarmed at such suffering as though it were unusual.

It is possible to have an experience of every stage of the Passion. There is no stretch along His path of sorrows that Jesus would not share with a disciple who has this deep desire, and He will grant this experience according to his capacity to suffer.

In some cases Jesus even longed to impart His wounds to His own. As the Apostle Paul wrote, 'Henceforth let no man trouble me; for I bear on my body the marks of Jesus' (Galatians 6:17). Possibly he was referring to a special moment when he came into contact with God and received the marks of the wounds on his own body and thus was endowed with even greater authority.

Even in the Old Testament there are accounts of painful encounters with God and their consequences. God wrestled with Jacob, touching the hollow of his thigh, and afterwards Jacob limped. Jacob had seen God face to face and his limp was a sign that he was no longer the same man. These divine encounters have tremendous results. Such experiences are granted to the members of His body who are counted worthy to partake of the life and suffering of the Head, which is Jesus. They are a part of Him, for it is written, 'We are members of his body, of his flesh, and of his bones' (Ephesians 5:30 AV).

Encounters with the Godhead bring us into contact with the Lord of Life. Consequently, they do not let us fall into a state of fruitless passivity, depression or spiritual pride. On the contrary, if God, in His grace, leads us into the fellowship of His sufferings, the outcome will be a humble dedication to Him, and a fervent zeal for His commissions and ministries. The soul devotes himself wholeheartedly to the Lord's service – whether it be an active ministry or the sacrificial ministry of prayer – in order that God's commission may be carried out all over the world. Love is his incentive, as it is written, 'The love of Christ constraineth us'. And if love leads to action, its genuineness is proved.

I can only regard it an act of grace that Jesus disclosed to me the secret of the fellowship of His sufferings. No longer was it a matter of the intellect for me; now He let me partake of His sufferings personally and share His pathway. In the previous months there was one song that I would sing over and over again.

Jesus, Jesus, my Beloved,
Lamb of God, now glorified,
Once You chose the cross of suff'ring,
Willingly for us You died.
Let me, Lord, with love now follow
On Your path of pain and death,
Let me feel the grief and anguish
Which You felt at ev'ry step.

This yearning began to be fulfilled in my life, and often when I drew aside for prayer with Jesus, He opened His heart to me and let me taste of His sufferings.

The dark night of Gethsemane engulfed me during the months before I entered seclusion. As I committed myself to a new way of life that seemed meaningless and irrational, I had an inkling of the darkness and struggles of Gethsemane. 'Yes, Father' – this prayer that Jesus uttered in His agony became of great significance for me and my life. My constant plea was:

> Let me bravely stand beside You
> In my own Gethsemane
> When Your presence seems so distant
> In the night of agony.
> Then, when tossed about by conflict
> And assailed by hordes of hell,
> Let me lie before You prostrate,
> Yielded fully to Your will.

Then it meant surrendering myself as a prisoner to Jesus, letting myself be bound to His will when He called me to a way of life removed from any outward activity. This self-surrender was only possible, because Jesus, who let Himself be chained out of pure love for us, came into my life as the Captive, disclosing His sorrows to me.

As I beheld the innocent Lamb of God, who let Himself be dragged before the judges five times, the Spirit of God judged me for my sins to a previously unknown extent. Brought before the holiness of God, I too took the place of the accused and condemned prisoner.

As I followed in Jesus' footsteps along His path of sorrows, the anguish He endured during His Passion cut me to the heart. This experience evoked from me the one and only possible response – tears, sorrow, love and adoration, welling up in a heart that had been stirred to its depths.

That which had begun in 1952 became a far greater reality in my life during Lent 1953. The Holy Spirit filled me with more grief over my sins than ever before as the first fruit of this inner experience. All further periods that I spent in seclusion were characterised by an ever new experience of contrition. Jesus filled my heart with lamentation, by showing me the anguish my sins caused Him, and tears welled up in my heart because of His sufferings. He had answered my prayer, which I had written down in the previous year,

Let me weep with You, Lord Jesus,
In Your night of grief unknown . . .

This experience had a powerful effect on my life, constraining me to do everything possible to bring comfort and joy to Jesus' heart. I felt impelled to make new dedications of love, to make every effort for more souls to be released from the power of sin and Satan, and more souls to be filled with a deeper love for the Triune God. It was only the ever stronger motivating force of this love for Jesus that gave rise to my books and most of my songs.

In previous years during Lent I had also held evening meditations on the Passion for the Sisters, but how different it was in Lent 1953 when I came out of complete seclusion to be with them for an occasional evening meeting. No longer did I give the usual meditations about His Passion, but shared with them about the sufferings of Jesus that had become part of my life, filling my heart with grief and lamentation. I had only one fervent wish for myself and my daughters: to love our Lord more than ever, constantly giving Him fresh tokens of our love, since He underwent such agony for our sakes to deliver us from Satan and hell. And God was gracious, granting me my request. That Lent the hearts of my daughters were open to receive Jesus, the Man of Sorrows.

The delicate veil that lies over the innermost sufferings of a person is only lifted when he shares them with a loved one. By inclining Himself to us in His overwhelming love, Jesus granted us the privilege of drawing closer to His heart. It was a sacred hour full of grace when Jesus disclosed to us the holiest of all, His sufferings. Our hearts were filled with grief over our sins, which had inflicted such pain upon

Jesus. We were so immersed in His sorrows that our hearts were set on fire with love for Him. One yearning alone filled us: to show Jesus our love and gratitude for all that He had done for us. There was no end to the praise and adoration of Jesus in His suffering. As I inwardly beheld Him as the Man of Sorrows, a fervent longing burned within me:

Jesus, all our love must be Yours and Yours alone –
Love and consolation for all Your love outpoured.

All the suffering of being alone in seclusion paled in comparison to the great privilege of sharing the precious secret of Jesus' sufferings with others and of kindling them with love for Him.

The Writing Ministry

I well remember the years before the founding of the Sisterhood of Mary (1939–44) when I had many speaking engagements. After the meetings there would frequently be requests for a written copy of my talk, to which I would reply, 'None of my talks are on paper. I do not have the gift of writing.'

But God had a different plan. As I mentioned before, some of the listeners took down the lectures in shorthand and then had them duplicated and distributed without my knowledge. Not until Mother Martyria and I started receiving orders for more copies, did we realise this, and since we had none, we asked for the texts and started to duplicate them ourselves. Our primitive duplicating methods, however, proved insufficient to meet the demand. Then we explored the possibilities of having the texts printed, since printing restrictions had been removed after the war. For a long time we prayed about whether we should make this venture in faith. The printing costs seemed far beyond our means. Moreover, our poverty had reached its lowest ebb at that point, for it was just after the currency reform when no one had more than his *Kopfgeld* (a small sum of money meted out by the government when the old currency was taken out of circulation).

Nevertheless, we went ahead and had the first three book-lets printed: *Dem Überwinder die Krone*,* *Das königliche Priestertum* (*The Royal Priesthood*) and *Gewissensspiegel* (*The Mirror of Conscience*). The demand exceeded all expectations and the first editions were soon out of print. New editions brought us more large bills, whereas no charges were made for the literature. One of our Sisters suggested that a small offset machine on which we could print the literature inexpensively by ourselves would be the solution. And God answered our prayer. Shortly afterwards we were given the much-needed machine as a present.

Many copies were then printed in one of the small upper rooms in the Mother House in addition to two more book-lets, *Macht des Gebets* and *Hast du Mich lieb?*, but it did not occur to me to write any more. Then during my first winter in seclusion (1952–3) I received a commission from God to testify to Him in writing.

It was amazing that this commission was given to me – I, who had never taken much interest in writing. As far as I was concerned, it was a man's job. Moreover, I was well aware that I had no literary talent, and thus I could only write as the Holy Spirit moved me. The compulsion to write would frequently come over me during seclusion after times of inner suffering with Jesus. Sometimes the prompt-ing of the Spirit was so great that all my former ideas and objections to writing were waved aside. My heart and soul were charged with such zeal that in obedience to the Holy Spirit I could only spend hour after hour writing without pause. Often I would write half the night, without becoming exhausted. I can remember working on a book in 1955 from early in the morning till after midnight without stop-ping, because the inner compulsion was so great.

* If only the German title is listed, the book has not been translated into English.

Although it was the Holy Spirit who inspired me to write, I did not remain uninvolved like an instrument with no free will. Whenever I was commissioned to write a new book, I had to undergo in spirit or experience in real life everything I was to write. Only then would my testimony be genuine. While writing books and pamphlets in seclusion, I had few outward impressions to distract me. Instead, in my soul I beheld Jesus as the Lamb of God, as the King and Bridegroom who will come again, and this image grew more and more radiant during these periods of solitude. It was a privilege to be able to portray Him for others in books and songs.

Certainly there were times when I resisted inwardly, reasoning with myself, 'Now you have written enough'. I was embarrassed at having written so much and I was conscious of the criticism that came from various quarters as a result. In this inner conflict the knowledge that it was the will of God and His commission helped me to obey. I knew that if God had given the inspiration for this ministry, it was right to follow it. Indeed, it was by the grace of God that I was able to write. I became increasingly aware of how wonderful it was to testify to the Father, Son and Holy Spirit, depicting the different aspects of God's character. It was a privilege to portray Him in His holiness and judgement. Yet it was even more wonderful to bear witness to God in His redemptive power, His abundant goodness, love and mercy. Truly, it was a supreme privilege to pass on the call to love Jesus above all else and the call to prepare for His coming.

But with this commission my perseverance in faith and obedience was put to a special test. In order to reach others beyond our circle of friends, we needed openings to bookstores in our country and to publishing houses abroad, but for many years the doors remained firmly closed. As a result of slander and libel, very few bookstores – let alone publishing houses – were prepared to accept my writings. I cannot say how often the enemy tried to convince me that it was pointless continuing to write. And I can only credit it to the divine zeal and motivating power of the Holy Spirit that I did not give up the writing ministry in the face of this seeming meaninglessness. We shall never forget a verse of promise that the Lord gave us for encouragement with regard to the closed doors to publishing houses in the English-speaking world. 'I know the thoughts and plans that I have for you, says the Lord, thoughts and plans for welfare and peace, and not for evil, to give you hope in your final outcome' (Jeremiah 29:11 *The Amplified Bible*).

And God was faithful to His word! When His time came, the bookstores really did open. Moreover, our reading public has increased so much that the Sisters working in Canaan's publishing house have piles of orders to fill all the year long. Our print shop that began very modestly in 1952 has since acquired five printing machines, and even so it is only able to produce a fraction of the books needed. In addition, many publishing houses abroad have opened up for our literature. An American publisher, for instance, wrote that he counted it a real privilege to publish and distribute our books.

In 1952 when I first entered seclusion, it was a step in the dark taken against all common sense. At the time I did not suspect what the Lord had in store. He intended the times of prayer spent in seclusion to be a source of inspiration for many books and other writings. He had a publishing house in mind for us on Canaan that would have a world-wide commission and handle far larger quantities than we ever dreamt, with over a hundred titles and translations in over thirty languages. In 1952 it was completely hidden from my eyes that later many people reading these books would rediscover the love they had at first for Jesus, through contrition and repentance, and commit themselves to discipleship of the cross or comprehend anew the eternal sanctity of the commandments of God. Little did I realise that fifteen years later the Christian faith would be undermined by a theology that denied a personal relationship to God. More than ever Christians would be in need of help and encouragement, of clear directives received by experiencing the

194

presence of God in solitude, far away from discussions.

Thus it was also for the sake of the writing ministry that Jesus called me into seclusion, a way of life that often seemed so meaningless to me in dark moments of inner conflict. God's thoughts are nigher than our thoughts. That which appears meaningless to our fallen human intellect often has the deepest meaning for God and greater results than we could ever imagine.

The Indwelling of Christ

Long before the foundation of the Sisterhood of Mary I had often contemplated the following words of Scripture, which meant a great deal to me.

> The Lord has chosen Zion; he has desired it for his habitation: 'This is my resting place for ever; here I will dwell, for I have desired it' (Psalm 132:13f.).

During the first months of seclusion the Lord granted me the fulfilment of this promise as a special act of grace. This experience was far more comprehensive than that of Jesus' loving presence, which I mentioned earlier. But before I could discover what is actually involved when Jesus comes to make His dwelling within us, according to His promise in John 14:23, I first had to undergo the necessary preparation, since fulfilment does not come overnight.

The indwelling of Jesus! For many years it had been my greatest desire that the Lord would fulfil this promise in my life. But I could sense how far I was from seeing my longing fulfilled. In the Bible Jesus says that He wants to make His dwelling in the hearts of those who love Him, and the proof of our love is that we keep His commandments. Yet in former times I had not taken this admonition of His so literally. Although I was familiar with Jesus' words, I had not considered all of them ultimately binding. Thus I had neglected to fulfil the precondition to carry out God's commands in the power of Jesus' redemption.

But when I was about thirty years old, God's intervention brought me to repentance over my failure to follow Jesus uncompromisingly, and consequently there was a change in my life. Repentance led me to take all of Jesus' commandments as obligatory for myself and I was granted the exclusive love for Jesus again. This love in turn constrained me to take His Word far more seriously than ever before, for if we love a person, we cherish, honour and respect his words, his wishes and claims on us; we consider them holy and binding. A deep longing arose within me: if only the Lord could make His dwelling in me! So often I sensed that I was preoccupied with earthly things and events, people, worries, work, sorrows and problems. The innermost chambers of my heart were already occupied. Although I believed in Jesus, He did not possess all my heart. But now under the compulsion of the Holy Spirit I no longer gave priority to objects and people that had been absorbing my attention so much; I made this break with the utmost resolution.

I well remember one occasion, for instance, some years before the Sisterhood of Mary was founded, when we changed rooms in the Steinberg House. It was necessary to have the workmen in. We had a great deal to sort out and all the cupboards and drawers had to be emptied. All day long there was a bustling to and fro. To this day I remember seeing the danger of letting the move engross me and make me lose the sense of Jesus' presence. Then I besought the Lord to help me to abide in Him constantly through the power of His Spirit. During those days I made a conscious effort to do everything prayerfully, in the sight of Jesus, for I had but one longing – not to lose contact with Him. How grateful I was when He granted my prayer!

Ever since then I have been on my guard, because I yearned for Jesus to make His dwelling in me. I was wary of anything that could preoccupy me, such as my daily tasks. Since I liked to work quickly and accomplish a great deal, every morning I would write down a list of all I planned to complete that day. Usually I plunged into the work energetically, absolutely determined to complete my schedule for the day. But then I renounced this method and reorganised my life. Every morning I brought my list of tasks for the day to God in prayer and then laid it aside.

Instead of thinking of all I planned to accomplish, I kept asking the Holy Spirit to guide me, to show me what to do and what not to do, where to go or stay, whether I should continue with a task or pray longer. I experienced the Holy Spirit's guidance; the deadlines were met and He dealt with every unexpected situation. My constant prayer was that nothing would penetrate my heart, which would upset me or preoccupy me. And God heard my prayer. He enabled me to respond with love, sympathy and compassion for my neighbour and at the same time to abide in Him in peace.

In addition, God awakened in me new love for Jesus and my heart overflowed with praise and adoration as an expression of this love. My innermost feelings and thoughts were taken up with Jesus in His infinite love and beauty as Bridegroom and Lord, the Lamb that was wounded for our sakes and yet full of love even towards His blasphemers. Inwardly I beheld Him in His splendour and majesty as the King who will come again in glory.

It was this love that made me consent to go into seclusion, to break all human ties, to relinquish all personal wishes, desires and activities. And during this time of solitude He could complete all that He had begun in preparation for making His dwelling place within me.

In my first period of seclusion there was a day that I shall never forget. The Lord Jesus fulfilled His promise in Scripture literally by granting me the fullness of His indwelling. It was a holy hour when Jesus was almost tangibly present. Everything seemed to be permeated by the presence of God, who came to make His dwelling here. Then I understood why the previous year as I lay sick in bed for months in another town, He led me through a time of deep humiliation, judging me to the depths of my soul, and moved me to humble myself before my daughters. As it is written, God is the high and lofty One who only dwells with those who are contrite and humble in spirit. Had I not prayed to Him all those years to come and make His dwelling in me? But He was unable to answer my prayer fully, since my heart was still so proud. He had to humiliate me and make me humble. And He must repeat this process time and again, for otherwise He cannot keep His dwelling within us.

During this hour of grace a great blessing was poured out upon me that was to affect my whole life. Later my daughters were amazed at how calm and unperturbed I could remain when I had to face great difficulties and problems involved in the leadership of the Sisterhood. This serenity could only be attributed to the precious gift of God – the indwelling of Jesus. The deep peace the Lord granted me in my innermost heart through His indwelling was a special blessing. Deep down inside I was like a calm sea while outside the storm sometimes raged and the waves rose high. Jesus had made His dwelling place in the very depths of my heart, and He was my Peace. In His wisdom He had already planned a solution for everything, for He was my Helper. My will was merged with His. And when our will is knit to His, the union remains secure even when His will brings us frustrations, obstacles, problems, and suffering.

The indwelling of Jesus brought something else as well, for which I give thanks ever anew. Previously, when I was faced with unsolved problems and had to make many decisions, I was often unsure of His will. Years ago, before the founding of the Sisterhood, although my burden of responsibility was not so great then, I would feel inwardly torn, not knowing what decision to make in a particular situation, what God's will was at that point, or which way to go. Often I could not discern what was right, and when I finally did come to a decision, I would torment myself wondering whether it was right after all. How to know God's will remained a puzzle for me.

At that time I did not yet realise that we cannot know God's will until we really begin to take it seriously. If we wish to recognise His will, we must first surrender our will and give up the desire to rule our own life. Only then can He begin to guide us in all matters. Learning to recognise God's will is a process, a matter of practice, but the first step is to make a resolution. It is worth giving up and relinquishing everything we value in this life so that we may truly love Him above all else. It is worth renouncing our will, opinions and wishes; it is worth surrendering ourselves completely so that only His will, which He has revealed to us in His Word, is binding for us. Then He Himself will come and dwell within us, satisfying our longings, filling us with His love. He brings us all we desire in the way of help, answers and guidance.

This has been my experience ever since I received the precious blessing of the indwelling of Jesus during my time in seclusion, an experience which has deepened in the course of years. It was as if the Lord was guiding me in all matters. However, I had to call upon Him as my Adviser ever anew, beseeching Him earnestly to guide me, since I felt unable to know the right course of action to take in the various situations that arose. And then I felt as though I were being led by the hand and shown what decision to make. It was Jesus who was guiding me so clearly – Jesus who promised to dwell within us. Later it would be confirmed that the decisions in these difficult situations were in accordance with His will.

I also received His guidance in the small, everyday matters. For instance, He would show me that I should not begin a task but do something else instead, and later I would discover that this task had become superfluous, owing to a change in circumstances, and I would be full of gratitude. Or He would show me not to have a talk at that particular moment and later it would turn out that the talk had not been necessary. And vice-versa, He would bid me to call one of my daughters to see me, who, as it happened, had been entreating the Lord to do so, since she needed to speak with me.

If Jesus abides in us according to His promise, and if His

indwelling is a reality in our lives, He guides us, makes all the decisions and takes care of every situation. However, it is essential that we be on our guard and not give in to our own will and opinions, for then we drive Jesus away from our hearts – unless we are sorry and repent immediately. He can only remain in us if we keep His word, that is, if we do His will. If we repent ever anew, if we have a broken and contrite heart, if we bind our wills to His in every situation, then His indwelling will grant us a foretaste of heaven, its peace, joy and blessedness, which I experienced in abundance during my times in seclusion.

Looking back, I can only praise the Lord for His wonderful plan in leading me into seclusion, and thus preparing for me the most precious gift of all – His indwelling.

Journeys for Unity and Reconciliation – Further Results of My Time Apart with the Lord
1953–1955

In Search of Reconciliation

Acts of dedication made to the Lord in times of prayer always materialise, and one day their outward effects will be visible. In the face of all the inner conflicts I had to undergo during seclusion it was comforting and reassuring to know that if our encounters with God are genuine, the fruits of these experiences will also be genuine. During the first Lenten Season I spent in seclusion the love for Jesus as the Man of Sorrows came over me with greater power than ever. This love constrained me to embrace my cross more lovingly than in the past for the sake of His suffering. My desire was to bring joy to Him by dedicating myself to suffering; I yearned to do something that would bring comfort to His heart, for love always seeks to express itself in deeds. And shortly afterwards the Lord showed me the next step.

In the spring of 1953, during the weeks of Lent, my heart was filled with Jesus' present-day sufferings, especially in view of the dissension amongst the members of His Body. This experience was preceded by an incident the previous year. A tent mission had been arranged by a group of Christians and many invitations sent out. But another group had been asked not to attend a special prayer meeting that was held in preparation for the mission. The spirit of fault-finding had led to disunity among those in charge – a most distressing situation. The result was that the outreach meetings were poorly attended and the preaching ineffective. I was filled with grief, especially since I had prayed a great deal for this mission week. Many souls who could have been saved were not, owing to the lack of unity amongst God's children. This experience was a turning point in my life. I prayed that the Lord would grant me the desire to spend myself for the healing of the wounds in the torn Body of Christ.

After the first winter in seclusion had passed by, the Lord shared His grief with me that His last request 'that they may all be one' had not been fulfilled. He reminded me of Christian brothers and sisters who were estranged from us or even antagonistic towards us. Thus after those weeks in seclusion, I went on various 'journeys of reconciliation' in the summer of 1953, as the outcome of my dedication to Jesus, who is our Reconciler. The Lord gave me the longing to do everything possible in order that the breaches between members of His Body might be healed. That meant I had to go to those who were opposed to our Sisterhood and try to remove the barriers between us. During the revival in the MBK and at the beginning of the Sisterhood of Mary many false and even malicious rumours were spread about us. These had a negative influence on various Christian leaders and organisations, with whom we actually felt one in spirit, but who either kept their distance from us or became our adversaries.

In such cases unity amongst Christians is not primarily brought about by theoretical discussions and written dogmas, however necessary these may be, but by following the Word of God, 'I sought for a man among them who should build up the wall and stand in the breach' (Ezekiel 22:30). To apply God's Word in this situation, however, meant giving up my rights and humbling myself when I was treated unjustly. It meant going to the other organisations and leaders, asking them to give me their hand as a token of reconciliation. Jesus showed me how much I lacked this humble love. Otherwise, the thought of these visits would not have weighed me down so greatly. But then the driving force of Jesus' love came over me, and for the sake of His suffering and His last request I prepared to make these humiliating journeys.

Thus I set out, travelling north, south, east and west, usually to visit leaders of Christian fellowships or organisations. The journeys which were all made without a car, were strenuous, and the travelling expenses were not easy to meet in view of our financial state. Did we not have to pray and believe day by day that God would provide us with the basic necessities of life and all we needed to carry out our ministry? But the finances were the least of my troubles. The disappointments and humiliations were far greater.

In one instance I went to visit a large Christian organisation. The Sister who picked me up at the railway station was polite but reserved. In the house the leaders had assembled to receive me, but I did not find any brothers in the Lord. Instead I felt as if I had stepped into a courtroom. Spread out on the table were a few small booklets that I had written, including one entitled, *Die Gebetswaffe* (*The Weapon of Prayer*). Various excerpts from this booklet were read aloud to me, such as, 'PRAYER: to be ready to enter into the fellowship of His sufferings for the sake of the souls for whom we pray.' The gentlemen pointed out to me that such a saying diminished the value of Jesus' sacrificial atonement and that my 'unbiblical' statements would spread heresies. My references to passages in the New Testament were not accepted, although the Bible mentions 'the fellowship of his sufferings' (Philippians 3:10 AV) and Paul declares, 'I endure everything for the sake of the elect, that they also may obtain the salvation which in Christ Jesus goes with eternal glory' (2 Timothy 2:10).

My literature repeatedly came under the attack of such narrow criticism. Single statements would be taken out of context with no consideration given to the rest of my writings and their message as a whole, and I felt unable to explain that I was concerned with the entire biblical proclamation. When I left that organisation, I was bitterly disappointed. I had longed for fellowship and love in our Lord Jesus, but my visit had just the opposite effect.

When I went to another Christian group, my arrival coincided with their general assembly. There I had hoped especially that the bond of love could be tied. The brothers, however, were only willing, provided we conformed to their tradition and joined their organisation. But I was unable to fulfil their expectations, since this group had a different inner guidance and a different commission from the one entrusted to us. Thus instead of fellowship in the Lord there was disharmony. And at another Christian organisation I was not even received.

But in some instances God granted miracles of reconciliation and unity in the love of Christ. New bonds of love were tied with some of the Christian brothers who had been treating us with reservation and in the following years they joined us in our Mother House to praise and worship our Lord Jesus.

Yet the journeys of reconciliation did not come to an end in the summer of 1953. During my period of seclusion in the following winter Jesus drew close to me as the Lord crowned with thorns. I was deeply moved as I thought of how Jesus, the Lamb of God, gazed upon His mockers and blasphemers with merciful love when He was degraded. Jesus, Lord of the Universe, whom all angels serve, Jesus, the King of kings, let the jeering mob press round Him, constantly mocking and heaping insults upon Him. Grief over His humiliation had become part of my life, filling my prayers during the first weeks of the winter of 1953–4.

The Lord granted further journeys of reconciliation the following summer as an outward expression of the inner experiences of this period of strict seclusion. These journeys too came under the lash of contempt. Yet how can the life of a disciple differ from his Master's? The Bible tells us, 'A disciple is not above his master' (Matthew 10:24 AV). If He was slandered and despised, His disciples will encounter the same.

Before I set out on one of the journeys, a new libel was published about the Sisterhood of Mary and my person. Since the book was compiled by one of the district leaders of the *Gemeinschaftskreise*, it found its way to many committed Christians. According to the Lord's plan the book was in circulation in East Germany the very summer I was travelling there. Although I had been invited to speak at various places, the main purpose of my journey was to seek reconciliation. Again I went to various Christian organisations that were against us, for breaches had developed in the Body of Christ. But the libel, which was also sold in Bible bookstores, had done its work in many of the *Gemeinschaftskreise*. As I wrote in my diary at that time:

> It seems as though I have the whole world to stand against. At every meeting the majority of the listeners are prejudiced and critical, full of contempt. The cause is the book containing a 'report' about us. It has been influencing the *Gemeinschaftskreise* in particular – in our land and abroad. It has been turning them against us, against our Sisterhood, which is said to be 'from below' . . .

Even so I had to press on, enduring to the end, although at every meeting it was like speaking to a brick wall and I had to break down the barriers of prejudice and rumours in the hearts of the listeners. The last stop on my journey was at a Bible college. Formerly I had been closely connected with this college and still cherished fond memories of it. But the reception was so frigid that my heart froze. When I was asked to say a few words, I was very conscious of the sharp repudiation of the staff and students. Before I could finish the report requested of me, I was cut short in front of the large audience. Speaking with the leaders of the college afterwards was a painful experience. False rumours about our Sisterhood were circulating in the college, and I was asked to give account for them – but my word was not believed. In deep grief I left the premises. A few years later I received a letter from someone who had been present then. Her conscience had been troubling her and she wrote describing how the students had arranged in advance to treat me with humiliation and contempt during my visit.

About ten years after the publication of this libel several leading brothers of the *Gemeinschaftskreise* officially withdrew the stated charges in my presence. But since they neglected to publish their change of view, and since the apologies did not come from those who had written the libel, many Christian groups continued to reject us on the grounds of this writing.

During this journey of disgrace and humiliation my greatest concern was that the love of Jesus would be victorious in my heart when I met those who slandered our Sisterhood and my person, and caused so much damage to our service for the Lord. When I inwardly beheld Jesus being crowned with thorns, I was deeply moved and my eyes were opened to a spiritual truth. While men were crowning Jesus with thorns, paying Him mock homage, the foundations for His true kingdom, the kingdom of love, were being laid. As Jesus was being mocked and derided by those who hated Him, His love was more evident than ever before and His kingdom of love was being established.

To this day the Kingdom of God, the kingdom of love, is built up when people follow the pathway of Jesus, who was despised and crowned with thorns. The knowledge of this spiritual law gave me the grace to submit to all the rejection during that journey and to bear this grief in the power of

Jesus' love. Was that not the commission of the Sisterhood of Mary: to help to establish the unity of love? As painful as these experiences in East Germany were, in my heart I was convinced that amid all the slander the unity of love was being achieved, although it was hidden from sight. And this was the case – even to a large extent with the above-mentioned Bible college – as I experienced later.

'Repent, for the kingdom of heaven is at hand' – this Scripture verse was to be the motto for our life on Canaan, the land that God wanted to give us for our commission. Canaan, was to be the Lord's domain, a foreshadowing of the kingdom of heaven, which is a realm of love. But how could we reflect this kingdom, unless we had learnt how to love? Figuratively speaking, love is a flower that can only bloom amongst the thorns of suffering, humiliation and disgrace. Love is only genuine if a person can love his enemies as well – a lesson that had to be learnt on this journey and on many other occasions.

There was yet another test to face, which was probably the hardest one of all. In this instance we were not rejected but almost coerced into merging with another Christian organisation. Earlier I related that this organisation had pressed us to adopt their tradition. On a later occasion the leading brothers visited us at our Mother House – an encounter that I shall never forget, since it was so painful. In December 1953 they spoke with Mother Martyria and me, urging us to merge officially with their organisation in obedience to God and for the sake of the unity of love within the body of believers. It would be disobedience to the ordinances in Holy Scripture, if, as women, we sought to carry out our commission without being affiliated with an organisation under masculine leadership. But because of the commission God had entrusted to us we could only remain faithful to our decision and not accept their proposal to be incorporated with their organisation. Consequently, it was implied that as initiator of the Sisterhood of Mary I had refused to submit out of pride, since I was unwilling to sacrifice my commission for the sake of the body of believers as a whole. We were told that the wrath of God would come upon us as a result. From their point of view my decision was completely incomprehensible.

But at the time I clearly knew that I could not take the step expected of me, since then the Sisterhood of Mary and its commissions could not develop the way God had indicated to me. My heart was full of sorrow, for I realised what a division my refusal had caused. Yet in this situation I knew I had to obey God more than people. He strengthened me ever anew by reminding me of the biblical truth that it pleases Him to accomplish His purposes through the poor and weak – and indeed, as women we were conscious of our poverty. In addition, Father Riedinger had blessed me for the leadership of the Sisterhood on his deathbed.

Looking back later, I was deeply moved to see the significance of this decision, which had cost me so much inner conflict at the time. For a young and inexperienced organisation, at the moment it may appear to be a great relief to pass on the responsibility to a board of men, to enter an established tradition, and to have financial security. But if a commission or vocation clearly comes from God, it can only be fulfilled in obedience to Him. In such cases it is not possible to be affiliated with another organisation that has a different leading and commission from God. And the Lord richly rewarded those painful occasions when I had to refuse these proposals for amalgamation. In the years that followed we have been completely independent and free to develop under the Lord's guidance, and He was able to entrust Canaan with the commission that He had planned for it.

Jesus' Last Request

My visit to Rome to have an audience with Pope Pius XII fell between my journeys of reconciliation in Protestant circles.

In August 1952, I received the unexpected, but clear

guidance from the Lord to visit Pope Pius XII with a request for unity of love between the brothers and sisters of the largest branches of Christianity. Inwardly I resisted this commission with all my might, for obtrusiveness went against my very nature. All my life I could not bear to impose upon others, for example, by bringing requests to people in a higher position. While I was National President of the Women's Division of the German Student Christian Movement, I was often amazed at how easily others could approach high dignitaries and start a conversation with them in order to further their cause. No one could have ever induced me to do the same. Yet in August 1952 I was commissioned to ask for an audience with the Pope to share my special concern – and that in the Roman Catholic world where I was completely unknown.

Before Vatican Council II such an undertaking was quite unheard of. At that time the various Christian denominations were not so open for communication as they usually are today. There were still high walls separating Protestants and Roman Catholics. I well remember that Catholic nuns living in the neighbourhood were not allowed to set foot on our grounds according to the rule of their community. Even years later when Catholics from Italy came to visit us, they did not dare enter our chapel. Many evangelical Christians had strong anti-Catholic complexes and were very prejudiced against Catholicism, whereas certain Roman Catholic groups mentioned Protestants in the same breath with Moslems and Communists – as we heard with our own ears.

In those days nothing could have been more pointless than a visit to the Pope; nothing more calculated to arouse hostility and make us even more enemies. Furthermore, circumstances made such a visit almost impossible. As the representative of a Protestant Sisterhood how could I approach the head of the Roman Catholic Church in Jesus' name with this plea for unity of love between brothers and sisters of different branches of Christianity according to His last request, 'that they may all be one'? To me such a course of action seemed like unpardonable presumption. I knew

Childhood years in Brunswick

31 Gauss Street

As a two-year-old

a seven-
r-old

As an eighteen-year-old
at the Froebel Academy
in Kassel

With Erika Madauss
in Kassel

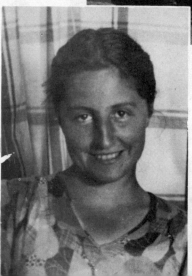

As a student
in Berlin

The parents, Professor and Mrs Schlink,
at the age of ninety

As a travelling lecturer
for the Missionary
Society for Moslems
(at the age of thirty-six)

Left: Darmstadt after its destruction in 1944

Lower left: the Steinberg House – home of the Girls' Bible Study Groups and birthplace of the Sisterhood of Mary

ith
other Martyria
56

196

1959

With Mother Martyria, 1974

Left: the four sections of the Canaan Family:
Sisters of Mary
Sisters of the Crown of Thorns and Sisters of Thorns
Canaan Franciscan Brothers
Canaan Friends

Life and ministry on Canaan

Beth Abraham
Jerusalem

Beit Gaudia Dei
Jerusalem

USA

In New York, 1964

Left: at Mount Sinai, 1963 (beginning of the ministry in other nations)
Lower left: plaque on the Sinai Massif

Small photos: the Sisters who started the ministry in the foreign branches

Great Britain   Italy   Denmark

Greece

Sisters of ten
different
nationalities

1968–1970

Times of fellowship with the spiritual daughters

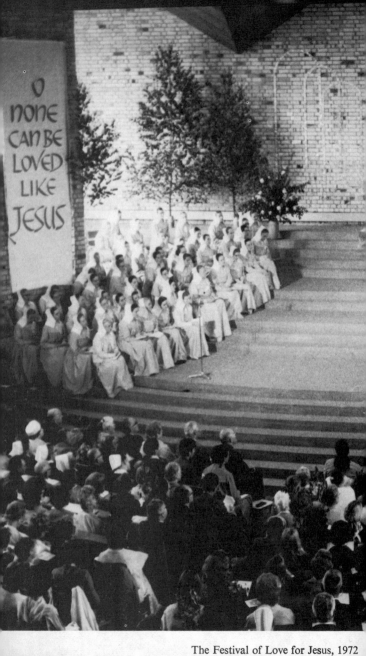

The Festival of Love for Jesus, 1972

Twenty-fifth Anniversary of the Sisterhood of Mary

that as far as the Roman Catholic Church was concerned, there was but one answer: the unity of Christians could only be found within the 'one holy Roman Catholic Church'. How could I explain that I understood the situation differently?

I was advised not to go, and some of my relatives even warned me against it – much to my distress. For the sake of peace and harmony I wished I could have dropped the matter.

In addition, I saw no way of fulfilling this task. If I had a group audience, I could scarcely hope to speak with the Pope personally, but how was I to obtain a private audience? These were only reserved for high dignitaries. Yet a private audience was essential to my purpose. Only if God made the impossible possible, could I take it as His confirmation to speak with Pope Pius XII.

The seeming meaninglessness and external impossibilities of this project tormented me, but even more so, the spiritual suffering. When I approached the matter with my intellect, I felt as frustrated as a caged bird beating its wings against iron bars, unable to escape. There seemed to be no solution. At the same time I felt completely forsaken by God, because He had led me into a state of spiritual drought, which lasted several months. Our fallen intellect needs many blows before it finally dies.

Moreover, I came to taste the bitterness of my spiritual poverty more than ever before. Once after holding a Bible study for my spiritual daughters, I wrote in my diary:

It would have been better to let a stone preach, since my words lack power and vitality. Is there any point in opening my mouth, if nothing I say has an impact on their hearts? I am but a speck of dust, a mere nothing.

And in this state of spiritual poverty was I supposed to bring a message to the Pope that would move his heart? A cry surged up within me, 'I can't do it.' My common sense argued that this quest was futile. How could I, of all people, go to Rome? My heart was not on fire for this commission, and I had neither the faith nor the love to carry it out. One of my diary entries reads as follows:

> . . . Jesus has left me at the mercy of these trials and temptations. I can only walk in obedience, trusting in His love and faithfulness. If I were on the wrong track, He would not let me continue on it; He will not let me go astray.

The only explanation for such severe trials was that the enemy's attacks always correspond to the spiritual significance of a commission. During those lonely weeks of seclusion he made every attempt to draw me away from the path of obedience. He knew that in another ten years when apostasy and revolt against God and His commandments would be widespread, those who love Jesus would be gathered together for the end times. He knew that the suffering entailed in this visit to the Pope would help to pave the way invisibly for the unity of love among God's own.

Suffering for the unity of love? 'Suffering for a cause' – is that biblical? Indeed it is. In Holy Scripture, it is an established fact, as the Apostle Paul says, 'I rejoice in my sufferings for your sake, and in my flesh I complete what is lacking in Christ's afflictions'; 'I will most gladly spend and be spent for your souls'; 'I endure everything for the sake of the elect'; 'I, Paul, a prisoner for Christ Jesus on behalf of you Gentiles'; 'I ask you not to lose heart over what I am suffering for you'.*

Why were these severe inner conflicts essential for this commission concerning the unity of love within the Body of Christ? The reason was that the cause of all dissension lies in the human mind. Everyone clings tenaciously to his own views and opinions. The human mind is the breeding place for all quarrels and faultfinding, all presumptuousness and schisms. The mind of man, corrupt and self-seeking must die so that the divine spirit of love and reconciliation might come to life.

* Colossians 1:24; 2 Corinthians 12:15; 2 Timothy 2:10; Ephesians 3:1; 3:13.

Thus affliction of the mind was an integral part of this commission. I had to die to my preconceived ideas that an audience with the Pope was meaningless and illogical before I could call others to abandon their prejudices and surrender their personal views to God. Only when our fallen intellect has been put to death, can love rise victoriously, and love always seeks ways of being at one with brothers in Christ. Accordingly, my fallen intellect was being purged of all the dross in the fire of temptation. In this way more room was made for the Spirit of God, the spirit of love, so that I could help with the gathering together of those who truly love the Lord. That was God's intention behind all these sufferings.

In the meantime my daughters had written on a small banner the Bible verse that I had received in prayer for that summer, 'Above all taking the shield of faith, with which you can quench all the flaming darts of the evil one' (Ephesians 6:16). One day when I left seclusion for a short while to be with my daughters, they gave me this banner as a strengthening of faith. 'Come, let's sing songs of faith and victory!' I called to them. Filled with the spirit of faith, we all marched through our inner courtyard, inspired by the Bible lesson for the day about the children of Israel who marched seven times round the walls of Jericho. That was the beginning of our 'battles of faith' on Canaan, which later so many people came to appreciate and adopt for their own lives.

The final confirmation for the audience came later when the Lord clearly answered my prayers with respect to three humanly impossible matters. First, I received permission to have a private audience with the Pope, although these were seldom granted. Second, a gift of money came in a wonderful way so that the travelling expenses were covered, and third, although I had no acquaintances in Rome, I received an invitation to stay in a home there. These were the three fleeces that I had laid before the Lord for a confirmation.

Rome, to be exact, the Vatican City, was my destination that May 1953. Almost lost in the crowds of people surging towards St Peter's, I sat on a stone bench facing the Vatican with the Sister who had accompanied me. Together we sang songs of faith and victory aloud in that direction. And although our songs were drowned in the tumult of the crowd, they rose to Him who hears every prayer and crowns every act of faith with victory.

The morning of the audience arrived. My heart was heavy and full of anxiety. But as we sat in the reception room of the Vatican, suddenly all heaviness and fear vanished and I felt as carefree as a child. Half an hour later I could speak in complete freedom to Pope Pius XII, sharing with him the concerns of my heart. In the name of our Lord Jesus I asked that His last request be honoured and that all those who believe in Jesus and love Him join hands across the walls of the denominations. Pope Pius replied that there was unity for believers within the institution of the Roman Catholic Church, but I repeated my urgent request once more. I appealed to him, saying how much Jesus was waiting for bonds of love to be tied between brothers of the Protestant and Roman Catholic Church on a scriptural basis, so that His love could be victorious. The Pope replied with the words, 'Is that really the Saviour's wish?'

Time has demonstrated in the sight of all that Jesus seeks the unity of love among His own. Today in every denomination those who love Jesus, who are truly loyal to the Christian faith and to the commandments of God are being gathered and made one in spirit. In this day and age the foundations of both the Protestant Church and the Roman Catholic Church are beginning to crumble, since the Word of God and His commandments are no longer respected. Standards that have been valid until now are being discarded in the Christian world. The dividing line no longer runs between the denominations, but straight through all churches. Today the true believers from all denominations are coming closer to one another in the love of Jesus. Mutually encouraging each other, they are knit together as an invisible body and being prepared for His coming and the Marriage Feast of the Lamb. All this will become even more evident in the midst of suffering when persecution of

Christians breaks out. On the other hand, the official ecumenical movement has become more and more unbiblical in its development. An anti-Christian spirit has gained ground within it; other religions and even anti-Christian ideologies are being introduced to it. The various official mergers are serving to prepare the way for a universal anti-Christian church.

Had it been worthwhile making this journey to Rome, which had cost me so much? Seeds sown in the dark, in obedience and suffering do not germinate until much later – sometimes years later – but they do germinate. With God nothing is in vain. He has promised that suffering yields fruit. However, at first it did seem as if everything had been in vain. My visit to the Pope became known. A storm of consternation broke out. Many evangelical Christians claimed that we wished to become Roman Catholic – a step we never intended to take. My only concern was that the spiritual unity of love be established. I felt that everyone should continue to serve faithfully in his own denomination and fellowship. But as a result of this visit, the opposition mounted and the division among Protestants increased. Later, however, when the Lord's time had come, new doors for the commission continually opened up in all lands and branches of Christianity so that those who love Him could be strengthened, gathered together and prepared. Dispersed throughout the world, but with their home in the heart of God, the bridal host, the bride of the Lamb, yearns for the unity of love.

During the course of time the Lord gave me ever anew the privilege of writing books and songs that spoke of love for Jesus, that kindled souls to love Him with bridal love and that called people to live a life of reconciliation and love. In addition to the Protestant bookstores, Catholic ones also opened up to us; the books are being read in many convents and thus bonds of love are being tied between those who love Jesus.

But the ministry did not end there, for God opened up branches for us abroad in England, Greece and Italy, in the

Anglican, Greek Orthodox and Roman Catholic Churches respectively. In addition, there is a branch of our Sisterhood in Lutheran Scandinavia and another in America with its wide variety of denominations. Who could have foreseen such a development? When our Sisters stationed abroad write to us about their ministries, one aspect is common to all: their houses have become meeting places for Christians from all churches and religious communities. One of the letters we received from our house on the Mount of Olives, Jerusalem, read, 'During the past few days we have had groups and individual guests from Switzerland, Finland, Denmark and Holland, from Japan and New Zealand – Christians and Hebrew Christians, members of the Salvation Army, Arabian Baptists, Catholic religious and Anglican ministers . . . Often we were quite a mixture, but we were one in the Lord, and many a time we sang and worshipped the Lord Jesus together till late at night.'

When our Sisters return to the Mother House at night after serving at our retreat centre, they can testify to the same miracle each time. At every retreat in the past years a unity of love has been quickly established, despite the very great differences existing between the guests attending the retreat. We have had retreats where almost every well-known denomination was represented. The participants, who all know Jesus as their personal Saviour, have different opinions, views and traditions and have come from all four corners of the earth, but the Holy Spirit moulds them into a marvellous unity as they study the Word of God together. Joining in the prayers, festivals and fellowship at mealtimes, they are one in spirit, for they are gathered round Jesus. Our guests frequently comment that they have a foretaste of heaven and of the Marriage Feast of the Lamb where in the unity of love all will be seated at the table of the Lord. When I hear such remarks, I am often reminded of the visit to Rome – and of all the seeming futility – and can only marvel at the wonderful outcome prepared by the Lord.

In 1953, when I returned from my journey, I experienced something of God's reward. As I was about to move into my little room again, I found a surprise awaiting me. The Sisters had turned the small adjoining room into a chapel. One of the Sisters had made a stained glass window depicting the Holy Trinity – and it was the Holy Trinity that then drew close as I entered seclusion. In my diary I wrote:

> The stillness of eternity was resting upon the chapel. The holiness of God permeated the room, and His presence was almost tangible.

Whereas previously my love was mainly concentrated on Jesus, I was now filled with love for the Holy Trinity, for God the Father, Son and Holy Spirit.

Awed by the holiness of God, I wrote a number of songs in adoration of Him.

> Father and Son enthroned on high,
> With Holy Spirit ever nigh,
> Eternal mystery surrounds God.
> Silence majestic broods over space,
> Cherubim praise the glorious grace
> Of the Three Persons, but One God.*

I was overwhelmed by the love of God. After I had undertaken these journeys for the unity of love amongst His own, He drew close to me as the Triune God – the source and perfection of all unity of love.

God's People Israel

There was yet another journey that came as a result of the weeks and months of seclusion. This time not to our Christian brothers in other denominations and fellowships, as in the journeys of reconciliation, but to our elder brother Israel. It all began in the summer of 1954. In those days we did not yet possess a prayer garden or the land of Canaan, but north of our Mother House, where the 'House of God's Goodness' now stands, we had leased a small plot of wooded

* *Well-spring of Joy*, No. 131.

land where the Sisters could withdraw for prayer. One day my daughters prepared a lovely surprise for me there; they had built a small shelter so that I could have a quiet spot for my prayer ministry during the summer months.

On the first day I spent there the miracle of the incarnation was unfolded to me in a new dimension, even though it was midsummer and Christmas a long way off. As I thought of the life of Jesus, I was deeply moved. From the day of His birth He lived in the shadow of the cross, and in His infancy He was acquainted with suffering and grief. Without making any conscious effort, I began to compose a number of Christmas songs about the Child Jesus, the Child of Sorrows.

These thoughts, which were so clearly inspired by the Lord, made a lasting impression on me. Even as a Child, Jesus had a cross to bear; He was persecuted, hated, exposed to the evil about Him. And this Child was waiting to receive our special love that Christmas. He was to bring us to deeper repentance because of our attempts to avoid every burden, every cross.

Shortly before Christmas while I was contemplating all this, the Holy Spirit showed me God's suffering because of His chosen people. Today, just as in the past, Israel is a people especially loved by God. Referring to Israel, Scripture says, 'The gifts and the call of God are irrevocable' (Romans 11:29). Israel's long history of severe trials and afflictions testifies to this election, for God leads only His elect along such paths of suffering, purifying them in the 'furnace of affliction'. But as a nation Israel has not yet turned to God and responded to His love, since they have not yet recognised their Messiah Jesus, although He came to them and laid down His life for them.

Whoever loves Jesus cannot bear to see Him wait in vain for the love of His people. This waiting, which is part of His sufferings today, filled me with distress and drove me to prayer. We have a custom of bringing God our special requests for the coming year at Christmas, since that is the festival when the Father manifests His loving goodness and blessings. While I was meditating upon Jesus as the Child

216

of Sorrows that Christmas, the Holy Spirit laid two requests upon my heart as the most urgent ones: 'Awaken souls amongst Your chosen people Israel to love You like a bride so that one day they may be with You in the City of God, upon whose gates the names of the twelve tribes of Israel are written [Revelation 21:12]. And please – a visit to Israel.'

My first wish was an expression of my innermost experiences during those months of seclusion when the suffering of God left an indelible impression upon my heart. Not only had His people failed to receive Him two thousand years ago as the Child of the Cross, but to this very day Israel has not yet found her way back to her Messiah, to Jesus. My second wish, however, came from the realisation that as Christians we are also at fault – especially those of us from Germany – if His people cannot perceive His love. Instead of showing special love and deference to God's chosen people, our nation committed unspeakable atrocities against them. Not only did we harm 'the apple of His eye' by despising them and bringing them into disrepute, but we also inflicted inhuman suffering upon them in concentration camps and millions were brutally murdered. As a nation we heaped immeasurable guilt upon ourselves because of this crime.

In my heart a deep feeling of contrition broke out, because in the hour of greatest distress for God's people I had taken too little trouble to show love to my Jewish brothers. Full of grief I could only cry from the depths of my heart, 'How can we heal the wounds that we have inflicted? How – if it is at all possible – can we make amends?'

During a week of prayer and fasting I was led by the Lord into deep intercession for Israel. In the creative power of His Spirit, who calls into existence the things that do not exist, God awakened in my heart a powerful love for Israel, His chosen people. Indeed, God's plan of salvation for Israel had always been important to me and I had openly held lectures on this topic throughout Germany even in the years from 1935 to 1944 despite the great risks involved. But this time a greater, more fervent love was granted to me. With this event God's Holy Spirit gave me a commission that was to involve the whole Sisterhood – the Israel commission. During the talks I gave to my daughters about this new ministry in February 1955, repentance broke out amongst them – most of them had lived through the Third Reich as children or teenagers. As a small token of our contrition, for the following fifteen years while we were only German Sisters, we stood in silence during breakfast in memory of the crime of our nation against Israel. We used this time to bless Israel in our prayers. Today, since we have many Sisters from other countries, we hold this prayer for Israel in a different way.

By granting us repentance, the Lord changed our attitude. No longer did we try to avoid the houses in our town where Jews lived, because we felt ashamed of the crime of our people; instead we began to pay calls on them. Our first attempts at visiting Jewish people were met with marked reserve – a reaction which was understandable in view of the past. But in His grace God granted us a sign of His forgiveness; not only were we received in Jewish homes, but ever since then we have had the privilege of welcoming Jewish visitors from all over the world. The entire Sisterhood was inspired with this love for Israel and from that time on Israel has played an important role in our life. Her sorrows and joys are ours as well.

Now the spiritual experiences I had during these months of seclusion were to materialise and to have outward effects. God granted my prayer for a journey to Israel. I scarcely trusted my eyes when I read the postmark on a letter that was slipped under my door one day. It was from Israel and contained an invitation. In those days it was necessary for a German to have an invitation from Israel in order to apply for a visa, although this was no guarantee that a visa would be granted. Until then few Germans had the opportunity of visiting this country, but without any complications Mother Martyria and I received the necessary papers – God's confirmation for the journey. Also, quite unexpectedly, we received a gift of money to cover the travelling expenses. The way seemed paved for us to go there in the autumn of 1955. But eight weeks before departure I fell seriously ill; my life was in danger. This was to be a time of preparation for my commission. Since the visit was to have far-reaching significance, it had to be underlaid with suffering. Then by the Lord's grace I recovered sufficiently so that we could venture to make the journey, and step by step we discovered that the Lord Himself had planned it and made all the preparations.

It was an indescribable moment when I first set foot upon the soil of the Holy Land, the ground trodden by Jesus, the Son of God. There I was to come to know His people, who had returned home from many nations, and to learn about their way of life in Israel. I was to meet His people, whom I had come to love.

When I arrived in Israel, I was still quite weak physically. Moreover, on the second day I stumbled, spraining my ankle so that I could scarcely walk. Had the Lord led me there only to confine me to bed for the duration of my stay? On the contrary, God used this accident to lead me throughout the land within a few short weeks. He had selected a guide who was well-acquainted with Israel – a lady whom Mother Martyria met at a gathering. When this lady learnt of my accident, she offered to take me round in her car, where I could recline, while she drove me to all the important sites and holy places in Israel for about a week. Consequently, owing to my injury we not only acquired an excellent guide, but were able to visit places that we could never have reached without a car.

As a result of God's wonderful leadings, we came into contact with many Israelis. We met them in the streets and squares or wherever the car parked. Since our guide spoke several languages, including Modern Hebrew, we were able to communicate with Israelis and learn of their sufferings, their hopes and their joys.

Immeasurable suffering had been inflicted upon the Jewish people because of the crime of our nation; their end had been planned. But God intervened and frustrated this scheme. He used the deep, unspeakable suffering for carrying out His eternal purpose to lead His chosen people back home to their land. The return of His people was prophesied in Scripture for the last times (Ezekiel 38:8), when all the land, including the desert, would flourish as God had promised. Our hearts were deeply moved at the thought of these events.

Since the dispersion of His people two thousand years ago, this land had lain waste and barren. But during our drives through Israel, which once more belonged to His people, we could see fertile fields and orchards everywhere. We were eyewitnesses of the wonderful fulfilment of God's promises for this country at the close of the age. The flourishing land was a sign that the return of the King to His people was no longer distant. On that day 'when they look on him whom they have pierced, they shall mourn for him, as one mourns for an only child, and weep bitterly over him, as one weeps over a first-born' (Zechariah 12:10). Who could remain unmoved after reading this passage? My love for this land of God and for His people grew more and more fervent. I began to understand better the great love God has for this people and was grateful that He gave me a measure of His love for Israel. I was also grateful that we could meet leading personages of the country and humble ourselves in deep contrition before them because of the crime our nation had committed against Israel.

At every encounter I was conscious of God's planning. The whole journey revolved round Israel, the people whom God loves, and the new God-given commission. Once when our car pulled up in a street in Haifa, a little boy came up to the car window. He told us cheerfully that his name was Gideon and then with childlike candour asked, 'Who are you? Where do you come from?' Suddenly he said, 'You must come to Israel and help us! We could use you.' It was a strange feeling. Was God speaking through this child to call us to His people in His land Israel? Did He have a commission there for us as Germans? We scarcely dared to mention that we came from the land that had brought such misery and horror to the Jewish people. But just as God had given this little boy an open heart for us Germans, we found the same openness in other Israelis whenever we came to them in deep grief and asked for forgiveness because of the cruel wounds that our people had inflicted upon them.

After our return home we received another call to Israel; this time not from a child, but from an influential person. 'Come to us! Help us!' God was waiting for our response as a fruit of repentance, and accordingly we sent two Sisters to Israel. After studying Modern Hebrew, they took up nursing in an Israeli hospital. Although our Sisters offered their services voluntarily, accepting no salary – as a token of repentance for the crime of our nation – the fact that they were accepted as *German* Sisters can only be attributed to God, to His purposes and commission.

Much as I loved Israel, I found it very hard to be parted from two of my spiritual daughters. For the first time two members of our spiritual family were to go to a far-off land, which even in those days was threatened by war. Both of them had attended the MBK and Mother Martyria and I had known them since their childhood. Yet I could only regard it as the grace of God and a tremendous privilege that we were finally able to send two Sisters to Israel in March 1957. The Lord had confirmed that the Christmas wish I had made in 1954 was according to His will. A new commission had begun: to live for Israel out of repentance and love, thus fulfilling one of the desires of Jesus' heart.

When I returned from my first visit to Israel, the fire that had been kindled in me continued to blaze, and under the prompting of the Spirit I wrote a small book entitled, *Israel – Gottes Frage an uns*, and later the book, *Israel, Mein Volk* (*Israel, My Chosen People*), which was then translated into several languages. I felt constrained to write these books in order to call others in our country, especially the Christians, to see our serious sin against God's chosen people. At the same time I had a burden on my heart to tell Israel about her election and God's wonderful purposes for her, His promises and the beginning of their fulfilment. The Lord granted grace and this book was well received by Christians in our country and also by Jews, some of whom rediscovered the faith of their fathers as a result.

But the fire did not die down in my heart. Love, especially when repentance is its fuel, constantly seeks new ways and means of expressing itself. Even before my journey the Holy Spirit constrained me to write a proclamation play about Israel. In the summer of 1956 in Frankfurt we performed it at the German Protestant *Kirchentag** – the first Herald Play we performed at this bi-annual convention. Although it bore no resemblance to modern drama, it made such an impact that people came by the thousand to see it. The spacious church was not large enough to hold the crowds of visitors, although performances were held twice daily. One night we even had to give an additional performance at 10 o'clock. Later this proclamation play about Israel was presented at other *Kirchentage* and in many cities in West Germany. As various ministers told us, it helped to change the attitude towards Israel in churches in many parts of the country.

Thousands of guests attending our retreats over the course of the years have learnt of Israel's significance in God's plan of salvation. And those who were German have come to realise more deeply the seriousness of the crime committed by our nation. Our guests have taken part in our Prayer for Israel, which is held every Friday evening, and many have experienced a change of heart towards Israel.

But the Israel commission did not end there. In 1959 God showed me that a small branch of the Sisterhood – Beth Abraham – was to be established in Jerusalem and that we were to receive the house in answer to prayer and faith. For His beloved people it would be a place where wounds would be healed and hearts would learn to trust God again. Through the ministry in Beth Abraham His people would be prepared for the coming of the Messiah. In spite of great difficulties and impossibilities, the Lord, true to His name,

* National rally of German Protestants.

which is Yea and Amen, gave us this house a year later in a miraculous way.

It was all part of God's plan that the dedication of Beth Abraham happened to take place at the same time as the opening of the Eichmann trial in 1961. All Israel was in a state of great inner turmoil as the terrible wounds of the past (1933–45) were re-opened in public. For the first time many of Israel's young people began to comprehend the extent of our guilt as a nation; in order to spare their children, many parents had concealed the events of the past from them. At first I was deeply distressed; it seemed most unfortunate that the date of the dedication of Beth Abraham and the date of the Eichmann trial should coincide. We feared that no Israeli would attend our dedication ceremony. Who would step inside a house belonging to Germans, and Christians at that, in the present situation? Yet over a hundred Israeli guests came and the Lord in His grace used this gathering to bring some relief to their grief-stricken hearts. They could sense our love for them and that helped to melt their natural reserve and to assuage their pain.

The former mayor of Jerusalem was also present on the day of dedication, and as he gave his address, I began to understand the wisdom and love of God in allowing this festival to take place at the beginning of the Eichmann trial.

Now, as this terrible trial is in process, I can see the difference between this man, whose name I do not even wish to mention – especially not here – and the love I see in you. I have heard your reasons. I have also understood the cause. The source, the origin is contrition, atonement, repentance . . . The purpose is love, the means faith, trust, hope. This is what led you to open this house . . .

And a Jewish author said:

If in these days as Jews we are in danger of repaying hatred with hatred, you have helped us to overcome this temptation. There is only one weapon against hatred – and that is love. We thank you for saving us from hatred, from collective hatred in this hour of temptation.

How much has come as a result of that holy hour in 1955 when the Lord linked us together with Israel! Today our house Beth Abraham is a place were Israelis, especially those who have suffered in concentration camps, come for a time of refreshment in body and soul. In addition, Beth Abraham is a place of prayer and thus a source of blessing.

Israel had become part of our life; her joys and sorrows were our own. For example, when we heard of new incidents of anti-Semitism or when war had broken out in Israel – as in the case of the Six Day War or the Yom Kippur War – we felt all the more constrained to pray for God's people. We longed to send a word of encouragement to Jewish communities and the many Jews whom we have come to know over the course of years both in Israel and Germany.

The invitations to Israel were repeated. Doors were opened and I was privileged to hold lectures in His land. Requests were made to hear 'the unusual and incredible story of the Sisterhood'. Astonished and ashamed, I saw how Jewish people – some elderly and sick, some who had come from long distances – flocked to my talks, in good weather and bad. Although the majority had only heard of the meeting by word of mouth, they came all the same. Among other things I told them about the miracles that had taken place on our little land of Canaan and they followed my lecture with keen interest and evident warmth. Their gratitude overflowed. They said that they had received fresh inspiration, that a breath of biblical life had been brought back into their biblical land and that the shattered faith of some had been restored. I felt that such responses could only come from the people God had chosen as His possession – and I had been speaking to secular audiences. For example, the day after I had held a lecture in Haifa, a newspaper review drew the following conclusion, 'The governmental departments should begin to walk the pathway of faith, trusting in the living God; then there would be an improvement in the country.'

Also in the United States and Canada, Jewish communities asked me to come and speak at their synagogues, at rabbi meetings and student meetings, and even to hold the 'sermon' during their Sabbath service. The call to repentance, arising from personal contrition and confession of guilt, reached people's hearts.

Because God's suffering for His people weighed heavily on my heart, I was sad that for a long time all I wrote for Israel and about her only reached a few individuals in Israel. On the whole the doors were closed to my writings. At that time my books could not be published in Modern Hebrew, and the German and English editions were in little demand in the bookstores. Apart from that it was dangerous to show an interest in them. At a book fair in Jerusalem police were sent to guard our stand. It did not seem to matter which topic I wrote on, there was little response. This seeming futility was also a heavy burden for my daughters in Jerusalem; the spark of faith needed to be rekindled in them repeatedly.

Years passed by. I have undergone more suffering for Beth Abraham, our first branch, than for any of our other foreign branches. As Germans we feel called to serve in atonement, and because of our national crime we cannot have a missionary commission to His chosen people in the usual sense. Our commission is to help heal Israel's wounds out of repentance. Yet because we believe in Jesus Christ and love Him, we can only declare our true allegiance to Him and what He means to us. Our lives are meant to be a testimony of the everlasting joy which Jesus alone can give. But nothing is harder than finding no response to this particular message.

Even so it was like the dawning of a new age. We could see small forerunners of the day for which God has been waiting almost 2,000 years. I shall never forget the evening a well-known Jew spent with us in our Hall of Zion. Sitting opposite the crucifix, he joined us in singing songs of praise and adoration. And when I asked him if he had any special choice, he requested the verse:

O Jesus, fairest Treasure,
I love Thee, I am Thine.
Thy holy, godly nature
Is love, pure love divine!
Whoe'er hath caught a glimpse of Thee
Cannot resist Thy love.
He has to love Thee solely,
O fairest Lord above!

The first time I met this Jew was at an important institution in Israel where he held a leading position. A spirit of even deeper repentance came over me as I asked him for forgiveness on behalf of my people. Many a significant encounter followed. And years later I wept tears again – but this time tears of joy – to see a son of Israel, who had been cruelly tormented by our German people, come to Jesus shortly before his death.

The seeds that had been sown slowly pushed forth shoots, although they remained hidden to all but the expectant eyes of love. Beginning with the Six Day War, *Die Stunde des Messias* (*The Hour of the Messiah*), a book that I had written in Israel years ago, was suddenly in demand. Excerpts that were taken from the book and spoken on tape were made available for many, and keen interest was shown. My book *Sinai heute* all at once became popular because Mount Sinai had become a focal point of interest for all Israelis. A book that I had written especially for Israel after the Six Day War, *Um Jerusalems willen* (*For Jerusalem's Sake I Will Not Rest*) reached many hearts. Offers were made to translate the literature into Modern Hebrew, and it was a Jew who published *Realitäten* (*Realities*) and part one of my autobiography in Modern Hebrew. The call to repentance in *Wendepunkt* (*Turning Point*), a leaflet that I had written for Europe after Czechoslovakia was invaded in 1968, was introduced into the Israeli press by friends from Holland. Nine Israeli newspapers printed the text in six different languages. A few months later a Jew with a leading position in public life told me, 'From the Orthodox Jew to the modern Kibbutz youth – one and all heeded your words; some even carried the newspaper with them in their jacket pockets. By means of this message you have reached hearts in Israel.'

Thus there had been a special purpose in God's calling me to seclusion in the summer of 1954 instead of letting me take an active part in the life of the Sisterhood. While I was in the solitude of prayer He implanted in my heart the seed of love for Israel – love that arose from repentance. Looking back on all that has grown from this seed, I can only marvel at the heights and depths of the omnipotence and goodness in God's heart. Suffering is but slight and momentary compared with the fruit and rewards that He bestows.

Canaan – A Foreshadowing of Jesus' Kingdom
1955–1957

May 4, 1955 – God's Moment Had Come

Once before, the fourth of May had introduced a new chapter in the life of the Sisterhood of Mary. That was in 1949, when God inspired me to build a chapel where He would receive much adoration and thanksgiving. The year before that, Mother Martyria and I had committed ourselves to go the way of faith with respect to the future of the Sisterhood and its ministries. But just what this way of faith involved I discovered after God unexpectedly gave me the commission to build a chapel. With that He set my feet for good on the pathway of faith, which now began to assume undreamt-of proportions.

There are hardships that we forget after everything turns out well, but the harsh reality and the severe trials of those first years along the path of faith I shall remember for the rest of my life. Most of the time the responsibility for financing the construction weighed heavily upon me, and God constantly kept us at the edge of the abyss. Time and again in my distress I would cry to the Father for help, which often did not come until the very last moment, after He had brought us to contrition and repentance once more. Along these ways of faith it seemed as though the Father was aiming at drawing the last ounce of trust from my heart.

All my life I was particular about having my financial affairs well ordered and accurate – another reason why I found this walk in faith so difficult. Debts were unthinkable for me. But these sufferings were only secondary. That which caused me greatest distress of mind was that God's honour was continually at stake. Government officials, workmen, firms, the press, the clergy, parents of our Sisters, friends and foes – many eyes were focused on our construction site. This project was to glorify God, who intended to use it to magnify His name in the sight of all.

People would either believe that God performs miracles or doubt His power – or even scoff – depending upon the outcome of this project. If it all ended in debts and bankruptcy to the disgrace of God, it would be my fault, since God had given me the commission.

At many stages along this path I could only cry out, 'I believe, help my unbelief!' And occasionally I sighed to myself, 'Oh, if only I were in heaven! In heaven it will no longer be necessary to keep faith, since there I shall be able to see everything.' How often my fervent entreaties were expressed in my diary during those years!

No money. The situation seems utterly hopeless and we are in the process of building. Tears are my daily companion. But You will carry us through. You will not let Your honour be dragged in the dust.

For weeks now we have received hardly any money, but I commit myself to You, Lord. I will hold out to the end. I will endure the suffering, for Your honour is at stake. And one day this path will come to an end.

And the path really did come to an end – to His glory. Without debts our Mother House and Chapel were completed in 1952 and the building 'Jesus' Workshop' in 1954. When the last bill was paid, I thought it was the end of this type of venture and that there would be no more piles of bills to overcome by faith.

But then the day came, in 1955, again the fourth of May – six years to the day. In the small hours of the morning the Lord suddenly granted me the commission for our future land of Canaan. It was a vast commission, almost too great to comprehend! I happened to be sick in bed at the time and when Mother Martyria came to bring me breakfast, I shared with her what the Lord had disclosed to me, and painted her a picture of the future land of Canaan. Years later Mother Martyria would relate how she nearly dropped the breakfast tray, because she was so horrified. A new and far greater venture of faith had begun, surpassing all previous undertakings. On that fourth of May, God's time had come. It was a special hour of grace as God not only gave me a new, vast commission but also equipped me with the necessary faith and dedication, since by myself I was incapable of carrying out such a project.

During the previous weeks I had undergone the spiritual preparation for this new stretch, while praying in seclusion. Once again it was Lent, a season when I was usually more absorbed with the Passion of Jesus than at other times of the year. But contrary to my expectations, Lent 1955 was quite different.

One night I awoke, conscious of the very real presence of the heavenly Father. My heart was filled with love, and two words resounded within me, 'My Father, my Father!' A feeling of deep blessedness came over me; I was over-whelmed by the privilege of being a child of the heavenly Father. For years I had had a childlike love for God as my Father, but this time my love was immeasurably deepened; I was granted an even stronger and more intimate love for Him in a father-child relationship.

God the Father revealed Himself to me through His Spirit in a new way. He yearned to have a greater impact on the life of the Sisterhood of Mary and to display His power in our midst. All my daughters were to learn to be more childlike and to come into a personal relationship of love to the heavenly Father. And indeed, through the acquisition and development of the land, Canaan would be a living testimony for countless numbers that God lives, answers prayers and works miracles. As a symbol of the reality of God, Canaan would stand like a rock later in the turmoil and upheaval of a world that has largely turned its back on God, and in a Church where the 'death-of-God' theology prevails and the Bible, in many cases, has been demythologised.

A few weeks later, on a bright, sunny August day, Mother Martyria and I went with all the Sisters to the ruins of a nearby mountain castle, so as to view Canaan – the land that had been promised to us.* After walking through the woods for an hour and a half, we sat down on a grassy slope near the summit and sang our first song about Canaan, which the Lord had given me that day.

> Canaan, fairest of all lands,
> Fashioned by the Father's hands,
> Chosen as His possession.
> Here on this land God's eye doth rest,
> His love in mighty deeds expressed.
> This is His land, His treasure.

When we had climbed up the castle ruins, far below us we saw a stretch of land next to our Mother House – fields and

* This event is portrayed in a scene in the Canaan colour film *God Lives and Works Today*.

meadows bordered by forests and the suburb Eberstadt. A land that was unattainable in every respect. Yet at that moment God in His goodness turned my eyes completely away from the human factors of the situation and directed my gaze on Him alone. Thus before the entire Sisterhood I was able to illustrate the marvellous plans and goals God had for Canaan, as if this little land already existed – complete with its houses, gardens, residents and various ministries.

I shared with my daughters all that the Lord had shown me with regard to our future land of Canaan and they kept it in their chronicle.

'The biblical CANAAN is the land of promise – a land of God's miracles. Thus we shall only receive our land of Canaan if we believe the promises of God, clinging to them in faith. It is a land that will not be acquired by the usual human means, but through the personal intervention of God the Father.'

Seeing the questioning eyes of my daughters, I continued: 'God had intended the biblical CANAAN to be a land of joyous festivals and a place where songs of praise would resound. As the Holy Scriptures say, "They shall come and sing aloud on the height of Zion . . . Then shall the maidens rejoice in the dance" (Jeremiah 31:12a, 13a). With trumpets and drums Israel would often give praise to their God for many days. There must be such an atmosphere of rejoicing on our land of Canaan too that other people visiting us – whether on their own or in groups – will naturally join in the festivals and singing. No one may leave without having had a taste of this joy. Nothing pleases God more than to see His children happy. How the heavenly Father will rejoice to find a little land of festivals and abundant joy!'

I went on to tell my daughters that the land the Father had chosen for His people was a land where milk and honey flowed. So we too would have cows and bees on our land of Canaan. It would be a fertile land with the blessing of the Lord, a little 'paradise', a beautiful and fruitful land. And a spring must also be found.

The biblical CANAAN was destined to be the centre of blessing for all nations – likewise our land of Canaan would be a spiritual oasis for people from all over the world who love Jesus. But the more Canaan is visited, the more care must be taken to preserve an atmosphere of quiet for the hidden prayer life. The Mother House courtyard and prayer garden would no longer be open for tours and accessible to visitors, for if we wished to carry out our commission properly, we must guard the communion of the heart with God in the stillness.

The biblical CANAAN is also a 'holy land'. Accordingly, nothing unholy would be able to remain in our land of Canaan; all sin would be exposed in the light of God and brought under the blood of the Lamb. Every fellowship in the light must be kept holy, so that Canaan and its residents might increasingly reflect God's nature; every task must be done lovingly to the glory of the King and the whole of Canaan must be filled with light, dispelling all darkness. Every time I shared a new aspect of God's plan for Canaan, we sang songs of faith. Joy broke out in our midst and I continued to share what was on my heart. The hours simply flew by.

'The biblical CANAAN is a land that the Lord Himself watches over. He alone is its Protector. He will look after our land of Canaan as well, taking care that the houses are built and the high building costs covered, and providing good gifts for every mealtime. Since He has given us this land as our inheritance, He will take charge of it personally. We must fill this land with our prayers so that God can pour forth His blessing according to His promise. And when Canaan is finally ours and the land developed, we shall see God's promises being fulfilled like a miracle before our eyes.

'Since CANAAN is the land where Jesus' resurrection and ascension took place, we must sing never-ending songs of victory on our land of Canaan and everyone who comes here will learn to wave the banner of victory with us. But they will also learn to share Jesus' sufferings, for CANAAN is the land of Jesus' Passion. Here too on our little land of Canaan the Passion of Jesus will become real for us and touch many hearts. The passion plays will also help to this end.'

We spent a long time at the castle ruins. Overjoyed at what the Lord had planned for Canaan, we sang verses and claimed the land in faith. It was a mountaintop experience. All my daughters sensed the significance of this day regardless of how much each was able to take in at that point. This new commission of God was to set us fresh goals of faith and determine the course of the Sisterhood in the coming years. It was indeed a very special day.

Ever since I began my walk with the Lord, I yearned for a foreshadowing of the kingdom of heaven, for the dawning of Jesus' dominion here on earth. I longed to live my life to this end. This kingdom must have been God's desire even before the foundations of the world were laid – and it must be His desire today. All God's leadings with His people Israel were directed to this goal. John the Baptist announced Jesus' coming with the call, 'Repent, for the kingdom of heaven is at hand!' During His ministry Jesus proclaimed the same message, later commissioning His disciples to preach it and teaching them to pray, 'Thy kingdom come!' During the forty days after His resurrection He spoke with His disciples 'of the kingdom of God'. And the Bible ends with the prophecy for the close of the age, 'The kingdom of the world has become the kingdom of our Lord and of his Christ' (Revelation 11:15).

Can there be a more glorious purpose in life than to live for the dawning of Jesus' kingdom wherever God has placed us? Now God intended to fulfil this spiritual aim of mine by establishing a land with houses and grounds, inhabited by people who live under the dominion of God and keep His commandments – although naturally on earth only a dim reflection of this kingdom is possible.

First of all it meant climbing down the mountain – not only physically, as we left the castle ruins and wended our way back to Darmstadt-Eberstadt, but spiritually, by entering the wilderness of harsh reality where we were confronted with numerous difficulties. It meant taking up the battle of faith, following dark pathways that would lead to the land of Canaan and the fulfilment of God's promises.

One complication arose after the other. Only by the grace of God was I able to remain steadfast during the coming years in the acquisition of the land when confronted with such impossible situations. The doors of Canaan seemed tightly closed, but not only because of the flat refusals of the city officials. The land was also in the hands of twenty private owners and inheritance laws complicated the issue. Naturally, in a time threatened by inflation no one was willing to sell property. In addition, other plots in this territory belonged to the City of Darmstadt, the local church and the State of Hesse. To obtain decisions from these quarters meant going through a lot of red tape and waiting a long time for council meetings to be held. Moreover, it was almost hopeless trying to explain the necessity of Canaan to the property owners. God had called Canaan into existence at a time when the necessity of an enterprise was judged almost entirely by its social-political value. Who would understand, recognise and endorse Canaan's social significance as a centre beneficial to the spiritual renewal of man?

Even if this miracle did happen – although, humanly speaking, it was one hundred per cent unlikely – what would be the benefit? Even if God did open the doors to Canaan, even if permission was given to build on these strips of land, and the various property owners were willing to sell – where would the money come from?

Were we not tempting God with this venture of faith for the acquisition of Canaan? Ought I not to be afraid of assuming the far greater responsibility involved in this enterprise of faith? But God Himself had entrusted me with this commission and filled me with the burning desire to glorify Him. As I wrote in my diary, 'Canaan must be established and everything must be a living sermon, testifying to God!'

The Father, the Triune God, was to be glorified on

234

Canaan so that many would be inspired to love and honour Him. For this reason I felt compelled to take the risk in faith and acquire Canaan and develop the land – even if the suffering involved were far greater than that of our previous venture of faith.

Chastenings – A Special Token of God's Love

In the seclusion of the small Trinity Chapel I discovered what it is like to have a true childlike relationship with the heavenly Father. This was before the Canaan commission was granted. During the following months and years I was to experience the reality of this relationship in discussions with the local authorities concerning the acquisition of Canaan. When we are in need and distress and being disciplined by the Father, we come to know Him better than ever. By consenting and submitting to God's chastening with a YES, we have the key to His fatherly heart and all His blessings and favours, and *afterwards* when the chastening is over, He will overwhelm us with even more goodness. Since God intended to bestow His blessings upon us, He had to lead us along pathways of chastening before we could reach Canaan.*

Along these paths it seemed as though the Father was not contending for the commission that He Himself had given us, since His miracles grew few and far between. I was to learn that when God appears to oppose us, He is actually fighting for us. Many tears were shed in the following years, but my plight drove me all the more into the Father's arms where I was to experience His goodness in the end. A helpless, tearful child belongs in his father's arms.

The first test of faith came when plans were announced for a large bypass that would cut across our prospective land of Canaan. Our whole commission was at stake. It

* *Realities – The Miracles of God Experienced Today*, beginning at p. 100 (British edition) and p. 107 (American edition).

was an either-or situation. It was either Canaan or the by-pass, but not both. The situation grew more and more hopeless, though at times – as is often the case in ventures of faith – the victory seemed to be very near or even ours. One day we broke out in praise and thanks that God had heard our prayers for the bypass to be relocated. The Chapel bell rang for ten whole minutes! But our joy was short-lived. Not long afterwards came the crushing news that the bypass was to be built across the future Canaan after all. We were informed that the bypass was necessary at this location to alleviate traffic congestion and that the authorities in Bonn had turned down our petition once and for all. I wrote in my diary:

> I know that my Father cannot leave us at the mercy of our adversaries; we are His little flock. He cannot have given us all those promises, which are known to thousands, only to withdraw them. He cannot have overcome the municipal council, only to let the matter come to nought. He cannot deceive us. He cannot lead us along the wrong track when we have been praying for His intervention in the midst of all these difficulties. My Father, that You cannot do, for You are Love and Faithfulness. I am utterly convinced that You will give Canaan to us and us alone. But first You have to put obstacles in our way, because we are sinners and need these hindrances as a means of preparation. The greater the suffering, the greater Canaan's fruit will be.

The difficulties in purchasing the various acres of land were innumerable. One owner planned to have a filling station on his property, since its location would have been favourable due to the proposed bypass. Another was reluctant to sell or exchange his land, since his relatives, who were in America, had to be consulted first. A third was involved in an inheritance lawsuit, and thus not in a position to sell land. Each case was a problem in itself, and we were dealing with roughly twenty fields as well as another twenty plots in the vicinity to offer in exchange.

In addition, almost all our visits to the city authorities to ask them to sell the city property in the area marked out for Canaan proved to be fruitless. Finally a meeting of the municipal council was arranged and we prayed a great deal for the outcome. But when the session was over, the mayor, the assistant mayor and the municipal council sent us their unanimous resolution together with a map showing Canaan reduced to almost half its size. This was their final decision.

In tears I laid this map before the Lord and with my pencil I crossed out the border line. I clung to God's commission and promises in faith, trusting that He would still accomplish His purposes.

Two thirds of the land in question was owned by the State of Hesse, and the government flatly refused to sell or exchange this property. In those years I was greatly comforted by the verses of Scripture that the Lord gave me from time to time during my many prayer battles for Canaan as a strengthening of faith. Later, out of thanksgiving to God, and to His glory, I had monuments erected at the entrance to Canaan engraved with some of the Bible verses:

Fear not, you worm Jacob, you men of Israel! I will help you, says the Lord.   Isaiah 41:14

He who calls you is faithful, and he will do it.
                                                        1 Thessalonians 5:24

Behold, I have set the land before you; go in and take possession of the land.   Deuteronomy 1:8

What father among you, if his son asks for a loaf, will give him a stone; or if he asks for a fish, will instead of a fish give him a serpent?   Luke 11:11

When I look back now, it is a miracle to me that I was able to keep faith in the midst of these difficult times. Indeed, I could sense that it was not my doing; it was God who carried me through the most agonising moments when no one was able to stand by me any more. The advice of close friends, however well meant, was in actual fact the hand of the

Tempter, offering an easy way out. 'Give it up! Give in! No more battles of faith, no more struggles!'

How often I cried to the Lord from the depths of my heart, 'What is it in me or in the Sisterhood that is standing in Your way and preventing You from moving Your arm to help us?' Yet the conviction that I had to continue on this path never left me entirely, and in my innermost being I did not wish to go any other way. This pathway was part of my life and by following it I had the privilege of glorifying my heavenly Father. As I wrote in my diary:

I yearn to give myself to You, O Lord,
To be for ever faithful – through Your blood –
Departing never from the darkest paths of faith.
I long to stay with You and share Your way,
Beholding Your fair countenance one day
And seeing all that I believed on earth.

During those years there were times when the Father interrupted His chastening. It was as though black clouds were parting for a moment to let the bright sun shine through. God would suddenly show us the radiance of His countenance, revealing His heart once more to us and letting us taste His goodness and mercy. Sometimes He reserved special dates for these occasions, such as the Sisterhood's tenth anniversary. Shortly before that we had received three flat refusals as the final decision from the highest officials in both the city and the state. Although my daughters were most upset about this, I felt that there was all the more reason to hold a thanksgiving festival in honour of the Father. And in His goodness He had prepared a gift for us on this day. At the beginning of the afternoon service, the chief city engineer personally brought the news that the local government had given us first option to the territory in question, having withdrawn its plans for housing projects there. The news could be announced to the congregation that was as deeply moved as we were. Many passed on to others this testimony of God's fatherly goodness.

The Father gave us other rays of hope and moments of

consolation, by suddenly inspiring influential men to assist us and take up our cause in particularly critical situations, since we had no power or influence whatsoever. For a while it was the late mayor of Eberstadt, then a former university professor of mine who had become minister of education in another state and two dignitaries from the Church. But above all, it was the chief city engineer. The Father, however, had reserved His greatest and most touching gift for the twelfth anniversary of the Sisterhood, which I shall mention later.

Whenever we were promised a strip of land or given first option, it meant paying. Our financial difficulties in this venture of faith with Canaan seemed almost always insurmountable. Instead, as I noted in my diary at that time:

My Father, You will not forsake us, for we are Your children, even if we are sinners. We are needy children, true orphans, with no people, no organisations, no institutions to back us. We are relying completely on You and Your goodness. All our hopes are placed on You; You could never disappoint us or let us be put to shame. My Father, are we not living to magnify Your name, to reveal Your love and suffering? Surely You will care for our basic needs, granting us gifts out of the abundance of Your wealth – just as an earthly father would do for a child that loves him. Indeed, it is impossible for You to do otherwise, for You are pure fatherly Goodness.

'How are the finances?' That was the vital question for me every day. Although I understood little of money matters, my daughters were often amazed at how well-informed I was about our financial state. The simple truth was that our walk in faith especially concerning our finances had brought me great suffering. Sometimes during mealtimes when our treasurer, one of the Sisters, was unexpectedly asked to give a general survey of our financial state, she was unable to do so at such short notice. But I could reply for her. For many years I had a list of all the invoices due each month hanging up in my room. Day by day I would beseech the Father earnestly, laying before Him the outstanding bills, for time and again we found ourselves in straitened circumstances without the money to pay them. When the money did come, I would cross out every bill after it had been settled, writing beside it my thanks to the Father.

Our financial matters gave rise to other hardships as well. God was testing us. An entry in my diary reads as follows:

> I feel as though a sword has pierced my heart. We are following these dark avenues of faith so that You will be glorified, but our venture has just the opposite effect. Not only in Darmstadt but throughout the country the rumour is going round that we have large donations from abroad and do not know what to do with all the money. Consider my tears. It is for *You* and to Your glory alone that we want to erect the buildings.

Later when Canaan was under development and we had fallen into the severest financial straits, the news came that public institutions that had also bought land in the vicinity were paying an additional sum after the sale owing to the rise in land prices. We were not bound by law to follow their example. But because we longed to live according to the Sermon on the Mount as disciples of the Lord, we felt obliged to make the additional payments to the landowners who had sold to us. Since there were twenty private owners, it proved to be a very substantial sum. I shall never forget how I cried to God in that hopeless situation, 'My Father, we are sinking. Have mercy on us!'

These paths of chastening were necessary for me personally, so that my trust in the Father might be tried and proven. But such suffering is a small price to pay to be cleansed of all the blemishes that would make us unfit for His kingdom. The glory which God has stored up for us in eternity as a recompense surpasses all comprehension.

This chastening was also necessary, since Canaan was to be a place bearing testimony to God's fatherly love and

His miracles. Many people visiting Canaan later were to learn to commit themselves anew to the Father's chastenings and thus discover the depths of His heart. But if Canaan was to live up to its commission, the foundations had to be laid with as many acts of dedication as possible.

There was yet another purpose to these leadings of God and His chastenings. Canaan was to be established in an age when riots and revolutions would sweep across the whole world. Often in spirit I could see the many clenched fists raised in defiance against our heavenly Father. I could hear the torrent of blasphemy and accusations coming from countless numbers, including many Christians, as they hurled reproaches at God, saying, 'And He's supposed to be a God of love?' 'Why doesn't God help us?' 'How can He possibly allow such things to happen?' 'I can no longer believe in God . . . ' I was filled with grief at these bitter words, whether they are spoken aloud or retained in people's hearts, and at the cries of rebellion that openly taunt and blaspheme God. Because our heavenly Father was being treated so shamefully, we longed to show Him that we trusted His love as He led us to Canaan along this desert road, through tests of faith, disappointments and suffering. Then all the world would see that God is faithful, God is Love. No one can say with all his heart 'Father, my Father' and testify to the Father's love with more conviction than he who has learnt to trust the Father in the midst of deepest distress and chastening, and then experienced His help.

Trials and Temptations

A person is able to persevere and bear a great deal, if he has the inner conviction that a leading or a commission is from the Lord, and if he is not tempted on this point. Satan, well aware of this fact, makes use of his most effective weapon, temptation, to make us doubt and swerve from our conviction. Thus I discovered that the more firmly closed the doors to Canaan were, the more intense were the attacks of the enemy. In the winter of 1956 it seemed to me as though my lifework were doomed. In my eyes it was like a shrivelled leaf, about to disintegrate and die – never to live again. What was the point in persevering in faith with regard to Canaan or in keeping up the struggle? As I wrote in my diary:

> There is no depth to the passion plays; they make no impact. However, it was partly for their sake that we wanted to establish a land of Canaan – and now we are engaged in 'mortal combat' to obtain this land. Yet in reality Jesus' suffering has little place in all our hearts. If I had realised that a year ago, I'd never have made plans for a land of Canaan complete with a Herald Chapel. Everything has collapsed before me. All I see is a heap of ruins. Our passion plays this year drew smaller audiences than last year. Countless numbers of committed Christians have been warned not to read my books, and in certain groups they are strictly forbidden. Consequently, many Christians are kept from coming to our Herald Plays. It is like staring death in the face. I feel as though the death sentence has been pronounced on the commission Jesus entrusted to me . . . Was it sheer madness to want these spacious grounds and plan all these houses?

Another voice in me said, 'How long will it take to establish this land of Canaan? How long will it take to build the houses and lay out the gardens? By that time war may have broken out, making it impossible for Canaan's commission to be fulfilled.'

And in the Sisterhood questions were raised as to whether we ought to limit ourselves to half the land. 'Perhaps we were aiming too high? Would it be better to avoid planning on such a large scale? Would it be more advisable to have fewer houses and less land? Life on Canaan could easily become hectic and more of a commotion, and thus lose its appeal.' In addition, friends advised me to drop the unrealistic plan for a large Canaan, which, they declared, could only result in a fiasco for the Sisterhood.

Had I really been mistaken? I was in the throes of temptation. If the commission for Canaan was not from the Lord, then I wanted to abandon the struggle at once. Yet deep down inside a voice said, 'Woe, if you do not persevere in faith now and follow this path of chastening and suffering to the end in obedience! It is the Lord, and He has given this commission, intending Canaan to be a foreshadowing of the kingdom of heaven.' As a confirmation the Lord gave me the Bible verse, 'And your ears shall hear a word behind you, saying, "This is the way, walk in it" ' (Isaiah 30:21). Thus, I did not yield, but remained steadfast, believing that the inner conflicts would serve to humble me and prepare me for the future commission of Canaan.

When the enemy attacked with his weapons, it meant taking up the stronger weapons of God and fighting the temptations with the faith that hopes against hope. For this reason I wrote a newsletter to our friends describing our future land of Canaan, its grounds and houses, together with sketches. Everything that the Lord had shown me I wrote down in this letter.

However, to publish such a declaration of faith in the present situation seemed like madness, and with every fibre of my being I resisted the idea. It meant taking a leap in faith. Mother Martyria also felt it was impossible to send out this letter in view of the circumstances: the gates to Canaan seemed to be closed for ever. Yet I could not dismiss the thought that later when Canaan really did materialise, the Father would receive all the credit, since nothing had been achieved by human means. He would receive glory and adoration, since it was by His intervention and miracles alone that the land had been acquired and developed. But the Father could only be glorified if we had the boldness of faith to write this newsletter in that humanly impossible situation. It called for our public testimony, 'God's promise is valid and thus we believe that Canaan will be established in the end, although the doors are closed now.' If we did not proclaim the plans for Canaan at this point, the glory of God could not be proclaimed later.

With much trepidation the letter was sent out, but the inner conflict remained, although when Mother Martyria and I prayed about the matter beforehand, we received Bible verses that confirmed my innermost impression. 'Always be prepared to make a defence to any one who calls you to account for the hope that is in you' (1 Peter 3:15) and 'He who began a good work in you will bring it to completion' (Philippians 1:6).

Further trials arose. It was very hard for me to cling in faith to God's promises, believing that His intention was to grant us a foreshadowing of the kingdom of heaven and a foretaste of paradise. Disappointments in my daughters reached a culmination at that time and my goal of faith seemed almost shattered. I found myself cast into such great spiritual darkness that I could only weep and lament in my heart, 'They are not willing. All my prayers and hopes for them seem to have been dashed to pieces.' There was so much spiritual apathy, self-centredness, self-righteousness, and lack of love among them, which were blocking God's commissions. I was forced to think of St Francis of Assisi, whose lifework was ruined because of the conduct of his spiritual sons. The last years of his life he spent in tears as he faced the collapse of all that he had worked for. I too had to suffer bitter disappointment; God's commission seemed to have been destroyed because of my daughters' conduct.

In spite of all God's unmistakable and continuous judgements as He disciplined us in every possible way, a number of them were still unwilling to repent in true contrition. We had to ask some to leave, since they had become like a dead limb; others left of their own accord. Their love for Jesus had died out and they were not prepared to turn from their old ways. Such gaps in our spiritual family caused deep wounds for Mother Martyria and me. In those months of severe inner conflict I wished I could have laid aside the leadership of the Sisterhood of Mary, but God did not permit me to do so. He helped me to overcome these disappointments by showing me the unending patience He had with me as well. In His grace He inspired me with fresh hope through these words of Scripture, 'Let salvation and righteousness sprout up together from the earth. I, Jehovah, created them' (Isaiah 45:8, *The Living Bible*). And He strengthened me so that I could remain steadfast in faith.

Moriah – The Hour of Testing

The most crucial decision in the life of a Christian is not made at his conversion, nor when he suffers some great loss, nor when he is being chastened, but on occasions that can be called 'Moriah experiences'. Father Abraham is given to us as an example. Although it was extremely hard for Abraham to bring his child as an offering, the fact that he had waited for this child for twenty-five years made it harder still. Yet the greatest sacrifice of all that Abraham had to make on Mount Moriah was the sacrifice of God's promise. For a long time the Lord had promised Abraham that all the nations of the earth would be blessed through the son God would give him quite miraculously in his old age. At Mount Moriah Abraham was being tested as to whether he would lose faith in God when God appeared to deny Himself, when His actions contradicted His promise.

In such situations when we are disappointed in God, we are at breaking point. If we stand the test, however, we shall come into the deepest unity of the will with God, which is the highest privilege that God can grant us. Yet to come through victoriously it is necessary beforehand to make countless acts of self-surrender, to dedicate our wills in everyday life as we follow dark pathways when we can no longer understand God and His actions. God intended to use the spiritual struggles amid the external complications in acquiring Canaan to lay a cornerstone in my life.

During the course of the years God had given me a

promise for that which I considered to be the greatest and most blessed gift that a person could receive from God. For a long time in advance I had been preparing myself inwardly and all of God's leadings were directed towards this goal. In September 1956 the time of fulfilment seemed to have come. It was a special hour. The holiness of God was more tangible than ever before – but then I understood the true significance of Mount Moriah, the burial of God's promise. I consider it one of the greatest blessings in my life that, on that twenty-seventh of September 1956 when I was sorely disappointed, I did not lose my trust in God.

During that darkest of moments, which cost me more than any previous difficult leading in my life, God enabled me to give Him my consent. As an indication that I still trusted in His love, I laid some pebbles on the ground to form the words, YEA AMEN, at a place where I frequently withdrew for prayer. Even though my heart was full of anguish, God helped me to write in my diary, 'My Father, I do not understand You, but I trust You.' Later many people throughout the world mentioned how much these words in particular have meant to them. This saying has helped countless souls at dark moments in their lives, for according to a spiritual law in the Kingdom of God, the more something costs us, the more effect it will have.

Because God granted me the deepest unity with His will when His leadings seemed totally incomprehensible to me, the darkest day of my life became the day of greatest blessing. Afterwards I realised that God had fulfilled His promise – but not as I had expected. Much that I experienced later in the way of fulfilment, also during the acquisition of the promised land of Canaan, was related to this Moriah experience.

From 1956 to 1959, I frequently had to undergo minor Moriah experiences when time and again the promises concerning Canaan failed to come true. Instead of obtaining permission from government officials, we received an absolute refusal from the highest authorities. In 1958 our work of faith seemed to have come to an end, especially since I lay in hospital at the point of death. All our commissions seemed doomed. That which helped me to keep faith in this situation was my first and hardest Moriah experience when I composed the song,

I praise Your name, O Lord,
'Yea – Amen' evermore,
E'en when I cannot understand.

Ever anew my testimony was that God is Love and always will be, as I so often said to Him during those dark moments:

On paths of suffering
When night envelops me,
I praise the blessing that will come.

Your will is goodness
And loving-kindness,
And good the ways You lead us on.

Praising His will helped me to remain steadfast during those times.

The meaning of the words spoken to Abraham after he had stood the test became real to me, 'Now I know that you fear God' (Genesis 22:12), and I discovered how wonderful it is afterwards when God inclines Himself to us and showers us with His gifts.

Not far from the place where I had this Moriah experience, now stands a monument with the inscription,

Moriah – God sees you, O man, in your fear and agony.
Moriah – God is testing you, O man, as gold is purified in the fire.
Moriah – God loves him who is prepared to offer his best, his all.
Moriah – God, who sacrificed His Son, bears your grief today.

Everything depends on our standing the test in such Moriah experiences. The enemy takes advantage of these times to make an all-out effort to reach his objective when

247

he has failed with all other temptations. Realising this, I later wrote to my spiritual daughters:

. . . Whoever has not yet encountered God as a paradoxical God in his life does not know God. Whoever has not stood the test when he could not understand the paradoxical God has not yet proved his faith in God. Do you know times in your life when God seems paradoxical? Do you know times when you can no longer understand His actions, when He appears to be leading you in the wrong direction, when your hopes are shattered, and when you think your venture in faith has ended in utter disappointment?

Believe me, if a person wants to enter the glory of heaven one day, he must endure acute disappointment, passing through phases of utter darkness. During such spiritual night we feel as if we are lost in a maze, far away from God and unable to understand Him, since we receive no more answers from Him.

Whoever wishes to taste heaven for all eternity must endure short stretches of great darkness in this lifetime because of his sins. Our Lord Jesus underwent this suffering for us at the end of His Passion when He was crucified. There on the cross He cried out, 'My God, my God, why hast thou forsaken me?' He bore this agony, although He was sinless. But as sinners we deserve this suffering. If we belong to Jesus, we must have our small share of spiritual night in this lifetime – though we are never forsaken altogether. Jesus is with us in the midst of our distress. In such suffering we are actually very close to our Lord Jesus Christ.

Disappointments in our life are the criterion as to whether or not we really trust God and have completely surrendered our will to Him. In such instances, it becomes evident whether God can do with us as He pleases and whether we continue to surrender our will to the Father all the same, following His guidance to the end, as obedient children, loving and trusting Him fully. If we do so, we shall discover that His heart is truly love and that He always leads us out of the darkness into the light. Such times of severe testing are rewarded immeasurably.

' . . . until the wrath is past'

Later our little land of Canaan was to testify to the greatness of God and His manifold attributes. *So ist unser Gott* (*This Is Our God*) – the pictorial jubilee book published for the twenty-fifth anniversary of our Sisterhood – was to bring this testimony into all the world. *So ist unser Gott* (*God Lives and Works Today*) was to be the title of our colour film about Canaan, a factual account of what the Lord has done and is still doing. This film also was to spread the message of the greatness of God throughout the world. But before we could pass on this testimony to others, it was necessary for God to reveal every aspect of His character during those fundamental years while Canaan was being developed. Thus I came to know Him more fully – in His mercy and forgiveness, His chastening, guiding and disciplining; in His power to work miracles and in His omnipotent deeds; in His fatherliness, His patience and faithfulness; when He spoke and when He remained silent. Indeed, as I experienced, He is a Father of love. But one distinctive feature of His character, which is also an expression of His love, had not yet been disclosed to me.

In 1957 I spent some quiet days in prayer in a small country village, where friends had given us permission to use their summer cottage from time to time. Since I had experienced precious moments there in the past when God drew very close, I looked forward to a time of undisturbed prayer, once more expecting to be greeted by His loving presence. But the first instant I stepped into my room, I was aware of a completely different atmosphere. This time God's presence made me tremble with fear. I scarcely dared to breathe. The very air seemed to be charged with the wrath of God. A new feature of God's nature was revealed to me. Although theoretically I knew that He is also a God of wrath, I had never encountered Him in this way.

I had always been aware that God the Father is often forced to send judgement upon His children, pouring out His wrath upon them much to His grief. He has no other choice when they continually refuse to respond to His love and goodness, ignoring His chidings to turn from sin and come back to Him. Now for the first time I realised that God's heart is almost overflowing with grief and wrath as the Book of Revelation indicates for the last days, the era of God's wrath. Suddenly my eyes were opened to this attribute of God's nature, which is described in many passages in both the Old and New Testament that speak of the wrath of God. These Bible passages usually refer to the last days when the wrath of God will be poured out upon mankind like flowing lava. He will cause the world to go up in flames as He executes judgement (Revelation 15:1; 2 Peter 3:10). With every fibre of my being I understood what the Bible meant when it says that the whole earth will tremble, that men will no longer turn to Jesus as their Saviour, but instead seek to hide themselves from the wrath of the Lamb (Revelation 6:16), even beseeching the mountains to fall upon them, since the erupting wrath of God is so terrifying.

I could sense a little of the measure of God's overwhelming grief because of His lost children, of His anguish which is like a torrent rushing down the mountainside. His heart seemed to break out in the lament that once came from Jesus' lips, ' . . . and you would not' (Matthew 23:37). They refuse to return home; they refuse to be children of the Father; they spurn the redemption in the sacrifice made by His Son; they reject His light, preferring darkness and sin instead. Consequently they will die in their sins and in the torment of hell.

It was like a foretaste of the day when the anguished wrath of God the Father will shake the foundations of the world and thunderbolts of wrath will proceed from His heart. God is holy, thrice holy in His grief and wrath, which will not come to an end until all the world pays homage to Jesus.

At the same time God's sorrow gripped me with a previously unknown intensity. Although He lavishes love upon His children, scarcely one of them returns His love fully. My heart was filled with this grief of God over us, His children. Suddenly I broke out in singing, in melodies of lamentation that I had never known before. My voice, which normally was weak, was borne along by supernatural strength. I was immersed in the deep anguish of God, and for hours I could only lament His suffering in melodies that the Holy Spirit gave to me.

The days that followed this experience of God's suffering and His anguished wrath over the world introduced a new phase. Even years later I could only describe those days as terrifying. I myself tasted a measure of the fierceness of God's wrath as it erupted over me, and I felt as if He had dashed me to the ground. This experience with God was totally different from anything else I had encountered. On many occasions in the past I had come to know God in His chastening and discipline. But this time God came to me, a sinner, in His holy anger. His stern silence and wrath made me feel that He had become a total stranger. Fear befell me. I felt as though He had cast me away, and my heart was numb with anguish. An atmosphere of death engulfed me – its grimness almost tangible. During those days it seemed as though I was exposed to God's holy wrath over sin in general and over me, a sinner.

The wrath of God pursued me wherever I went. When I went to the woods because I could no longer bear being in my room, His wrath would follow me there too. His fury seemed to have been unleashed in nature as well. A violent storm had broken out, which lasted all those weeks. Lofty fir trees, snapping at the trunk, crashed to the ground. In the woods one could easily be struck dead at any moment, and I was reminded of the words of Scripture, 'Enter your chambers, and shut your doors behind you; hide yourselves for a little while until the wrath is past' (Isaiah 26:20). The wrath of God seemed so great that I felt it would destroy me.

Later I realised that I had to undergo this suffering in order to write about the coming judgements of wrath that would soon descend upon the world in the last days. I could only do so if I had experienced God's wrath personally. Little did I realise in 1957 that very soon the sins of mankind would be piling up to heaven, thus provoking God's judgement. In a short while more demons than ever would be unleashed in the world leading men astray, causing them to indulge in blasphemy and all kinds of immorality. Even Christians would fall under their sway. In those days one little dreamt that ten years later criminality and violence would deluge the world as a direct result of man's rejection of God's commandments, when figuratively speaking, the tablets of stone with the Ten Commandments would be smashed to pieces once again, thus opening the way for hell to come on earth.

Yet even at that early date – 1957 – I recorded in my diary:

The message of the grief and wrath of God over the sins of men in the last times is highly relevant, since we are heading for the great judgements of God.

Three years later I could see more clearly what the Lord had wanted to achieve in my soul with this experience of His wrath. From 1960 onwards I began to write on the topic of eschatology at the prompting of the Holy Spirit. I was able to write about the times ahead – the calamities and the eruption of God's wrath – since these coming judgements and His wrath, which are the expression of His holiness, had become so real to me in May 1957. The experiences of that year also enabled me to see in a completely different perspective all the atrocities and perversions that began to change the face of the earth in the following years. I could see them more in relationship to God's grief and His holy wrath. This insight made me willing to have a foretaste of His judgements, to undergo the suffering involved and to write about the coming judgements so that many souls might still be saved.

After having had this personal experience of the wrath of God, I could appreciate the bounteousness of His grace as never before. Only if we have encountered God's judgement and tasted His wrath, can we comprehend the meaning of grace. This experience alone lets us see more fully the significance of Jesus' becoming the sacrificial atonement for us so that all who truly believe in Him would not be destroyed by the wrath of God. Thus when I was commissioned to write new books in the coming years, I was able to testify that God's grace is even greater than His judgement, provided we repent and bring our sins to Jesus now before it is too late.

The urgency of this call increases daily, for the preliminary judgements of God have taken on alarming proportions as an indication that the day of the Lord is imminent. No one can escape it. 'Behold, the day of the Lord comes, cruel, with wrath and fierce anger' (Isaiah 13:9a). If only we would hear His voice today – while there is still time!

A Year of Death – God's Promises Are Buried and Brought to Life Again
1958–1959

One Blow after Another

1958 was to bring fresh ordeals and trials, including death itself. During that year I was tested as to whether I would truly cling to the Father's love in times of severe affliction.

First I met with a great disappointment with regard to the acquisition of Canaan. The State of Hesse had given us their final decision – a flat refusal as the result of our endeavours and spiritual struggles and the efforts of influential men on our behalf all those years. The authorities wished neither to sell nor to lease the state property in this area. Thus once more the commission for Canaan was as good as buried.

That year I had a new opportunity for giving the heavenly Father my consent when it cost me a great deal. Again I was able to reply:

> My Father, I do not understand You, but I trust Your guidance, which is always right, for what You do is always good. Just as You raise people from the dead, You can bring back to life this promise for Canaan, which seems to be buried.

Then came the second blow. We found ourselves in severe financial straits such as we had seldom experienced. It was almost necessary to stop construction on the retreat house 'Jesus' Joy'. By no means could we incur debts. Since the responsibility weighed so heavily on our hearts, the work could only proceed slowly.

But the waters of affliction continued to swell when the Sisterhood was struck by sickness and even death itself. Until then the Lord had been very gracious to us. Very few of our sixty young Sisters had ever fallen ill. And when such an occasion arose, healing was granted through prayer and the laying on of hands or in some cases through medical treatment.

The Father had shown special kindness in the case of Sister Angelika. She had been drafted to work as an anti-aircraft spotter and after the war was over, she returned home critically ill. When she joined the Sisterhood, the doctor gave her only two years to live, but she continued to live for ten years. It was literally a miracle of God.

At the end of 1957, however, the whole situation changed. Quite unexpectedly that autumn our Sister Margaretha became seriously ill, and the diagnosis was cancer. We prayed and believed that the Lord would perform a miracle and heal her – she was only thirty-three years old. But the Lord did not intervene. He led us through the fiery furnace of trials and temptations. Time and again we struggled through in prayer to the point where we could believe that the Lord would still perform a miracle of healing. Sister Margaretha also hoped and believed that God would intervene this way. Yet at the same time we saw how her condition worsened steadily, and after half a year of suffering she went to her eternal home in May 1958.

The first time I saw one of my spiritual daughters on her deathbed, I thought my heart would break. Sister Margaretha was still so young, and we loved her dearly. Our Sisterhood was not a vast, impersonal organisation, but a family, particularly since Mother Martyria and I had known a number of the Sisters since their childhood. We felt that they were our spiritual daughters in a double sense. They had a special place in our hearts and we were loved by them in return. We were such a happy family that it was a deep grief for Mother Martyria and me when one of the young Sisters was called to her eternal home.

With a heavy heart I left Sister Margaretha's deathbed to break the news to Sister Angelika, not knowing that a second blow would strike me on the same day. As I spoke with Sister Angelika, it was clear from her words that she expected to follow Sister Margaretha soon. In the previous night she had lost half her sight – a sure sign that her kidney disease had taken a fatal turn.

Bubbling over with life, Sister Angelika, the second young Sister to die that year, seemed the last person to be a candidate for death. She played an active part in the Sisterhood, for not only did she hold a responsible position, but she was also our sculptress and the director of our Herald Plays. Her presence would be sorely missed. My daughters asked me whether the commission for our Herald Plays would then come to an end. I answered that a commission from God is not bound to a specific person, but I myself could not see how we were to continue without Sister Angelika. Sorrowful months followed at Sister Angelika's bedside. She suffered great pain before she was finally called home half a year later in December 1958.

Yet it seemed as if death were seeking further victims that year. More Sisters fell seriously ill – one of them critically – and it was feared that others had been infected as well. There seemed to be no end to the bad news; the number of Sisters who became sick increased, but not once did the Lord grant healing. My heart was sorely wounded by all these chastenings of God. In the midst of this affliction I could only humble myself beneath the mighty hand of God and in tears give my consent to His will.

Not only did our prayers for the sick remain unanswered, but we continued to receive no help in the acquisition of Canaan, although God Himself had given us the commission. It appeared as though His promises would not be fulfilled. In addition, our ministry in the retreat house 'Jesus' Joy' seemed to have been nipped in the bud. As early as 1954 the Lord had given me the inner commission for this retreat house while I was in seclusion. There people were to have an opportunity for a time of quiet, to study the Word of God and see themselves in His light. In this retreat centre they were to discover the pathway of repentance which would lead them to bridal love for Jesus and uncompromising discipleship; they were to come into a father-child relationship with God, learning to depend upon Him and trust Him. Then the inexplicable occurred, although it was so clear that this commission was from the Lord. After many sacrifices had been made for the completion of this new retreat house with its fifty rooms, we received only six or seven registrations for one of the first retreats. Previously, when we lodged our guests in the small rooms in the upper storey of 'Jesus' Workshop' beneath the sloping roof and in makeshift quarters, we often had far more applications than we could handle. Now that we finally had all the facilities to carry out this commission, everything seemed to stagnate.

No fewer difficulties were presented by the large Herald Chapel, which was in the planning stage. In obedience to God I had tried to explain to the chief city engineer why we needed such a large building. Since the Mother House

Chapel was so small, the Sisters sometimes had to give up to three performances of a Herald Play on a single day. Yet when the plans for the Herald Chapel were under way, the Mother House Chapel was frequently half empty, and once our Sisters put on a passion play for only twenty people.

All these burdens weighed heavily on Mother Martyria and me, not to mention our financial problems.

In the Face of Death

The cup of suffering had not yet been drunk to its dregs. In December 1958, the same month that Sister Angelika died, I too was brought to the doorstep of death. Quite unexpectedly I became seriously ill and was taken to hospital. As I lay there, death seemed to have placed its imprint on my body, soul and spirit. It was Christmas. But the Mother House was shrouded in sorrow in contrast to our previous Christmases, for that Christmas Eve Mother Martyria received news from the hospital that my life was in grave danger.

A dark shadow had fallen upon the Sisterhood. Mother Martyria and the Sisters were not only faced with their personal grief of losing me, but when they heard of my critical condition, they felt as though the Lord was dealing the deathblow to our Sisterhood, since up to that point He had given me the main initiatives for the spiritual and external development of our Sisterhood according to His calling for my life. And I wondered whether I was to die without seeing the fulfilment of the promises and Canaan becoming a reality. Was I to die at a time when in almost every aspect my hopes were disappointed, the promises unfulfilled, the ministries incomplete and the whole commission seemed to lie in ruins? Was death to part me from the Sisterhood before God's promises for it came true?

As I lay on my sickbed, the thought of all the commissions that had not been fulfilled haunted me. The Sisterhood of

Mary, the lifework that had been entrusted to me, was still in its early stages and greatly in need of guidance along the path that the Lord had shown me. Not only did Canaan have to be built up, but it had to carry out its ministries for a while at least before the coming time of affliction. Yet I was faced with a commission that lay uncompleted.

Was my life to end before I could help my spiritual daughters reach the inner maturity that I so longed for them to attain? That very year I had been severely disappointed in them again, and I was sorely distressed. A special time of God's judgement in the summer of 1957 and those hard months as Sister Margaretha lay fatally ill brought to light many uncleansed sins, hardness of heart and unwillingness to repent. In spite of God's hard blows several Sisters remained more or less unmoved, their hearts could not be reached. It seemed impossible that the Sisterhood – and later the whole of Canaan – would one day be a foreshadowing of the kingdom of heaven – the kingdom which Jesus proclaimed at His first coming. Was I to go to my eternal home in this situation? It was these thoughts that caused me the greatest agony and inner conflict.

For weeks I lay in hospital, feeling extremely weak and tormented in soul and spirit, since I felt as though God had forsaken me. I was in spiritual night and in the throes of temptation because of all the unfulfilled promises. In my diary I wrote:

> The doors to Canaan remain closed. Nothing has come of the Herald Chapel or the Franciscan House, and it seems well nigh impossible to continue with the Herald Plays, since Sister Angelika, the director of the plays, has died. My strength is broken; everything has collapsed. Yet the Lord has given me repentance, which is the most precious blessing of all, and the commission will come to life out of the ruins.

God was using this critical illness as one of His disciplinary measures to lead me into a deeper walk of faith, for He yearned to hear me say, 'Yes, Father'. This prayer would cost me more than ever before, but it would be all the more precious to Him. For this reason I had to suffer this critical illness and thus face a total collapse in every sphere of my life. In actual fact, this experience was an answer to my long-standing prayer that God might be glorified in my life through repeated dedications of the will. I knew that the surrender of the will means more to God than a thousand prayers of adoration in His honour. I knew that the most precious prayer to Him is 'Yes, Father', said in dark moments, especially at times when His will brings us great suffering and we cannot understand Him.

Every time the Father leads us along dark pathways of chastening, we can imagine Him watching us closely and asking us, 'My child, will you also trust Me now? Will you still believe that My heart is full of love? Will you continue to consent to My actions, My leadings, My hard blows when you do not understand what I am doing? Will you commit your will to Me this time also? If you do, you will be closely united with Me, for the dedication of your will is the key to My heart and to the heavenly kingdom above.'

Will of the Father, how sublime,
God's heart expressing all through time,
Eternal love revealing!
O will of God, sublime and great,
From Your hand I shall take my fate,
'Tis all by love designed.*

Such unity of the will yields glorious fruit, immersing us in the divine nature of God. It is the deepest union of love between the soul and God, as I was to experience.

The foundation for Canaan's commissions was laid with such acts of dedication. The Father intended Canaan to be a spiritual centre and a living testimony to His amazing love. However, if Canaan's witness was to have power, even greater dedications of the will would be required. The first difficult stretches along the path of faith for the acquisition of Canaan and the financial impossibilities of carrying out

* *Well-spring of Joy*, No. 205.

this vast commission were insufficient. A year of death was necessary, for one day Canaan was to bear witness to the Triune God; it was to be the centre of a world-wide commission. Thus, a larger measure of suffering had to be laid in the foundations of Canaan; the Father had to receive even greater proofs of the dedication of my will at times when I was enveloped in darkness. It had to be a whole burnt-offering – that is, all the promises concerning Canaan had to be returned to God. Only this sacrifice could bring forth fruit, so that one day visitors on Canaan would also be inspired to trust God the Father along dark avenues of faith and to show Him genuine love. The way had to be so dark, the temptations and ordeals so great, since a tremendous commission was at stake.

'I shall not die but live!'

After I returned from the hospital at the end of January 1959, my heart condition was so critical that I remained on the threshold of death for the next couple of months. During this time I frequently felt utterly abandoned by God and He let me undergo many severe trials because of the unfulfilled promises. Inwardly I was being led through the valley of the shadow of death. I was extremely weak, scarcely able to speak, move or even write. I felt cut off from my daughters. Though I yearned to be with Jesus in heaven, my critical condition frequently alarmed me, for I felt I had not gained the victory in certain aspects of my life. Thus the thought of being called home to the Lord at that point caused me much inner distress. During those difficult weeks three sentences helped me to endure. At a time when I was scarcely able to lift a pen, I wrote them down in my diary as a testimony:

Yes, Father, Your will be done.
I trust in Your fatherly love.
I give myself to suffering.

It was during those days when death was knocking at my door again that the Lord gave me the inner assurance through His Spirit that I was going to recover. That was an unforgettable moment. The joy of Easter welled up within me. I was to rise again and live to complete my commissions. This gift was almost beyond my comprehension. God's promises would come true after all! Canaan would still come into existence and be a foreshadowing of the kingdom of heaven to the glory of God. I was overjoyed. He would complete all that He had set out to accomplish – in me personally as well. My life would not end abruptly. I could not grasp His loving-kindness; it was like a miracle to me after I had already surrendered myself to His will and to death. My heart was overflowing with songs of praise and thanksgiving.

Indeed, that April the Lord let me recover so that I was able to speak and write once more. It was like being raised from the dead. To be able to complete a lifework seemed a very great privilege to me. It would be pure grace if God accomplished His work within me as well and if I could reflect His image to His glory and bring Him joy.

During my serious illness God had shown me clearly all the dross that still needed to be purged from my life. Thus I was certain that He would continue His process of purification within me to His glory. Through the power of His holy blood, by taking me along paths of chastening and repentance, by leading me into greater battles of faith against sin, He would transform me more and more into His image. My prayer was that I might be able to make many amends, to show far more love, and to love my adversaries and enemies as well. I was consumed with a fervent longing for God to be glorified. Indeed, it was for this reason that He restored my life to me.

Thus the Lord granted me health, infusing new strength into me. He also gave me new commissions. Everything that I had laid on the altar during the past months was returned to me in greater measure after being purified.

It was May 1959. I was lying in the garden, enjoying

the spring flowers and the fresh green foliage, as I was recuperating from my serious illness. In His grace the Holy Spirit granted me new incentive to write. It was as if the Lord wished to accomplish in two weeks everything that had to be laid aside during the past months while I was ill. Day after day I worked from morning till night, almost without pause, writing small books and the texts of many festivals.

Several weeks later we were enjoying a happy time together when suddenly some of my daughters came in, pulling a miniature 'harvest wagon'. On it were hanging twenty new booklets with attractive cover designs – the effect was picturesque and cheerful. Then the Sisters pulling the wagon sang a little song they had made up. 'There is a harvest wagon to see of writings that have come to be – the fruit of days of suffering.' And we all sang together, 'O come, praise suffering with all your heart, for it has wondrous joy to impart on earth and in eternity.'

In those weeks God gave me the inspiration and the texts for our festivals, which had been a special burden of prayer for me. For a long time my fervent desire was that festivals would be held in our Herald Chapel, so as to inspire many hearts to join in worshipping the Lord, and my request was granted. Now on Canaan the great festival days of the Church do not end with the morning worship service. In the afternoon, services of praise and adoration are held for the entire congregation, and the songs of adoration continue in the evening when the Sisters come together. During these festivals those who long to glorify God have a foretaste of heaven where the Lamb upon the highest throne is worshipped and adored. Anthems of praise resound and the members of the congregation respond by singing the hymns and joining in the prayers, or by silently lauding His name and humbling themselves in the presence of His glory and majesty.

Jesus, Lord and mighty King beyond comparing,
All disgrace that Thou art bearing

Fades as we now honour Thee.
Crowned with many crowns of glory,
Sov'reign Lord o'er countless thrones,
We worship Thy great majesty.
All of heav'n the song of glory raises,
Endlessly retells Thy praises.
We worship Thee, the Lamb,
Glory and honour to Thee, the Lamb! *

In those days I did not realise the significance these services and festivals would have one day. They would help stem the tidal wave of outrageous blasphemies that would sweep across the world about thirteen years later.

In the months following my recovery I received new songs from the Lord – not only the words but the melodies as well – something that I had never imagined possible. One day as I listened to the birds vying with each other in song, and the world was lush and green and all aflower, I wrote down one song after the other praising our Creator, immediately singing the tunes on to my little dictaphone. An entry in my diary reads:

I feel as though I have entered a completely new sphere in my life, and as though my heart has been expanded.

And I wrote to my daughters:

What could be more glorious than bringing the Lord worship and honour? It is a privilege, a truly divine commission. In heaven we shall be seized with a holy ardour. Like the four living creatures at the throne we shall be constantly inspired to give praise and glory to the Father, the Lamb and the Holy Spirit . . . To God be the glory! This alone must be ringing in your hearts. Your souls have been created and redeemed to revolve round God, just as the four living creatures at the throne revolve round Him, and Him alone . . .

* *Jesus, O Joy Eternal*, a long-playing Canaan record.

But the blessings did not end there. In His grace God expanded my writing ministry by giving me larger books to write, which would later be translated into many languages and make their way throughout the world, to glorify God and inspire many souls to love Him.

How grateful I was when He gave me the inspiration to write a book about the Mother Mary and her discipleship (*Maria – der Weg der Mutter des Herrn*), and when some of the first responses came from well-known Protestant theologians who commented that the book was biblically sound and essential for the Protestant world. The Lord granted my prayers for this book and it was constantly in demand, widely read and translated into other languages. On the other hand, it brought me much disgrace, earning me the disapproval of those who could not accept a biblical approach to the Mother Mary because of their anti-Catholic attitude.

Another book followed in those weeks entitled *Busse – glückseliges Leben* (*Repentance – the Joy-filled Life*), which helped many to come to a spiritual breakthrough. How grateful I was, since repentance as a source of joy was *the* experience of my life. It all began with a letter to Mother Martyria in 1936. 'Who is a God like thee, pardoning iniquity . . . ' * At that time a wave of repentance had swept over us both, transforming our lives, spreading then to the MBK and later taking our spiritual daughters in its flow. Many of our guests whose concept of repentance was largely associated with sadness and legalism, as they told us, discovered that repentance transforms everything, solves problems, brings joy and grants reconciliation in families, churches, villages, towns and even between members of different nations.

The fact that a book like *Repentance – the Joy-filled Life* has become so popular shows that nothing is more precious than repentance. Thus I wrote a word of encouragement to my daughters:

* See page 94.

We must be willing to pay the price, to pray earnestly and consistently for this treasure until we have regained possession of it – particularly when our hearts have hardened. A person lacking contrition lacks everything. If he has contrition and repentance, he has everything he needs, for repentance draws down God's grace. Believe me, the way to joy, to a truly happy life, is repentance. Repentance is a fountain overflowing with joy and love for Jesus. If our heart is a spring of repentance, streams of joy and love will flow from us.

Easter

After that year of affliction and death there seemed to be no end to the blessings and favours that Jesus showered upon me. I had a foretaste of what it will be like in heaven when the Lord will comfort us after our suffering, bestowing us with even greater gifts of goodness, as His Word promises us.

It was Maundy Thursday 1959, the twelfth anniversary of the Sisterhood of Mary, when singing and rejoicing broke out in the Mother House. What was the cause for this sudden jubilation? Had I not seen the commission for Canaan buried before my eyes during that agonising year of death? Had we not received the flat refusal for our request once and for all from the highest authorities in the State of Hesse? But God intervened! On that Maundy Thursday a telephone call came with the news that the president of the state government had given written permission for the state property within the boundaries marked out for Canaan to be sold to us. No one could understand the sudden turn of events. It was a miracle. The refusal was turned into a consent.

Easter 1959 was an unforgettable experience – truly a day of resurrection for Canaan! At the same moment that my life was restored to me our Canaan commission rose to new life. Canaan was to come into existence after all, heralding the kingdom of heaven as God had promised. Light was to shine on the dark avenues of faith. All the disappointments were to prove worthwhile. My daughters were so overjoyed that they felt as though they were dreaming. I myself could only weep when I heard the news; all the disappointments and the suffering because of Canaan had left too deep a wound in my heart. I could hardly believe that the miracle had occurred. So often Canaan had been granted to us, only to be taken away again. This time, however, the Lord gave us the land for good. Completely overwhelmed by the grace of God, I wrote in my diary:

> God has kept His word. My Father, how faithful You are! Your name is Yea and Amen. I can only weep for joy over the grace You show to Your erring children, and because You have not failed me. How good You are! I can scarcely believe that You have given us Canaan and kept Your promise. Dearest Father, I am not worthy of such goodness.

When I asked the Lord in prayer for a Bible verse as a confirmation of this event, He gave me a verse that had often brought me consolation, since it speaks of the ultimate goal of God's leadings.

> You know how we call those blessed (happy) who were steadfast – who endured. You have heard of the endurance of Job; and you have seen the Lord's [purpose and how He richly blessed him in the] end, in as much as the Lord is full of pity and compassion and tenderness and mercy. (James 5:11 *The Amplified Bible*)

What a Father we have in God! He had prepared a marvellous outcome for all the suffering that I underwent because of Canaan and all the unfulfilled promises.

Canaan was really ours. That meant the Lord would also take care of the development of the land, which was the next stage, and provide the necessary money. Moreover, He would perform the greatest miracle of all and accomplish

His spiritual goals for Canaan. The very purpose of Canaan's existence was that on this small land God might be glorified and His fatherly love praised, and that Canaan might be a foreshadowing of the kingdom of heaven – a place of love and joy, since its residents would live in reconciliation. Just as the Lord had led us along those thorny paths of faith and suffering in acquiring Canaan, He would carry out His plans for Canaan's spiritual life. The only reason why He let us undergo all these humiliations was to make us humble, so that *He* might be glorified on Canaan and we could not take the credit. The Lord took care to lead us along pathways of chastening, so that all self-praise would be impossible. In my heart I could only rejoice, 'It is grace, grace, amazing grace!'

A Life Returned and New Commissions Granted
1959–1962

The Holy Land Ministry

The stream of God's goodness did not end with the gift of Canaan. Amongst the new commissions the Lord gave me now was one that was to bring me great blessing personally – and that was a commission in the Holy Land, in the biblical Canaan. Before I was taken critically ill, the Lord had gently knocked at the door of my heart, introducing this new ministry, although the possibility of carrying it out seemed very remote to me. And now the Lord repeated the call to seek out the places where He had lived and suffered, to help make them come spiritually alive through love and prayer.

The Holy Places, the memorials of Jesus' earthly life, His

suffering and His love – surely every Christian heart is drawn to them! The Kidron Valley, for example, almost untouched to this very day, beckons to us. Do we not feel the longing to take the path through the valley where the tears of our Saviour fell upon the earth? Do we not long to follow in His footsteps? Whoever loves Jesus will feel moved to give thanks and to worship Him at the sites of His sufferings – as far as it lies within his means. And if a person loves Jesus, he is grieved when the Holy Places are visited more by tourists on a sightseeing tour than by true pilgrims inspired by love.

Spiritual death reigns at some of the places where Jesus set foot, although these are places where He performed miracles and tarried in prayer, places that heard His lamentation and fervent pleading. I was moved at the thought of Jesus waiting at the Holy Places, longing for people to recommit themselves there, in prayer, to bear their cross lovingly with Him in everyday life. When thousands from all over the world visit these sites, the Lord waits for heartfelt praise and adoration in response to all that He has done for us. I felt as though Jesus were lamenting, because His own are so indifferent towards the places associated with His earthly life and because so little attempt is made to keep them holy.

Yet what could I do? How could I help? Although my life had been restored after my critical illness and I miraculously received new strength hour by hour to fulfil my commitments, a journey to the Holy Land was quite another matter. Since the doctor feared for my life, he only gave me permission to go at my own risk. However, I knew that if a decision to take steps in obedience to a call and commission from God has been confirmed, it cannot be contested – and in this instance, the confirmation came from Mother Martyria and from others. As in the case of the other commissions I received assurance from the Lord that 'I shall not die but live', that He Himself would enable me to fulfil this task and would carry me through – as indeed it happened. After my visit to the Holy Land our family doctor was amazed to see that my health had actually improved.

God touched my heart, not only imparting physical strength, but setting it aflame spiritually when, in 1959, I visited the Old City of Jerusalem and the Holy Places in the surrounding area. Whenever I set foot on one of the Holy Places, Jesus was very close; at each site His words and actions, His love and suffering there were so vivid that the events of the past became a present-day reality for me.

In spirit I was drawn into the events that took place at these sites: His humiliation at Lithostrotos, where He was crowned with thorns, His agony in Gethsemane, His suffering in the Kidron Valley where He was led off as a prisoner, like a lamb to the slaughter. In my heart I wept and lamented over the wicked arrogance of men in daring to bind the hands of Him who created the world. In the Pater Noster Grotto on the Mount of Olives, where Jesus is reputed to have held His talks about the end times, the Spirit of God constrained me to write on the subject of eschatology. An excerpt from my diary written at that time reads:

> Teach me about the last times so that I may help to prepare Your own for these days. Holy Spirit, come upon me as the Spirit of knowledge. Lord, grant me insight into Your hidden purposes. Give me books to write on this topic about the approaching end – books for this country and ours...

Little did I realise how wonderfully God would answer this prayer in the coming years.

At each of the Holy Places Jesus drew near to me, granting me songs and devotional readings about His love and suffering. Owing to the constant flow of people at the sites, it is normally difficult to find a quiet spot to retire for a while in prayer and contemplation. But since this prayer ministry was from God, He opened the way wonderfully. In Gethsemane I could spend several hours in the church by myself, lamenting Jesus' suffering in free melodies given by the Spirit of God. Even when the church was closed, I was allowed to remain. The Franciscan monk in charge was moved when he heard me sing about Jesus' Passion and he granted me permission to enter the church at any time and to pray by the rocks beyond the church. At Calvary, owing to the noise and commotion, it is usually impossible to kneel at the altar – the site of the cross – for more than a few minutes. Yet I was able to remain there undisturbed for a long time by myself. There the events of Calvary became more real to me than ever.

The inner compulsion from the Holy Spirit was so great that in spite of my physical weakness I went along the pathways taken by Jesus through the Kidron Valley and the Via Dolorosa. Humbling myself in spirit, I followed in His footsteps, sometimes kneeling on the ground. Deep joy filled me at the privilege of accompanying Jesus along His pathway. Thus I could continue with my testimony. At all the sites I visited on my first true 'pilgrimage to the Holy Land' I had a living encounter with the Lord, rather than an intellectual experience. I sensed that during this journey the real foundations of the new ministry were being laid through the revelation of His presence at the Holy Places. Just as fruit originates from seeds, everything would develop naturally from these encounters – as indeed it happened.

The possibilities for a ministry at the Holy Places had now been shown, and one thing led to another. Songs, texts and devotional readings, most of which I had written during this visit, were compiled to form a book for pilgrims, *Heiliges Land – heute* (*The Holy Land Today*). Excerpts were made, translated into various languages and printed separately as booklets or leaflets. In the following years they were distributed by the thousand at the Holy Places, and tourists were supplied with them in hotels. People applied for tours to the Holy Land under our leadership. The first pilgrimage, which I conducted myself, resulted in many others under the leadership of our Sisters.

The pilgrims were so on fire that they kindled others. One person wrote, 'At the Sea of Galilee several groups paused to hear the spiritual message . . . on the Mount of

Beatitudes we were joined by hippies who were full of spiritual hunger . . . at Calvary many were moved to tears by the sufferings of Jesus . . . On Mount Carmel everyone present joined in our songs quite spontaneously . . . our supply of literature was gone in no time at all. Everywhere at the Holy Places I saw a number of tourists reading and praying from the Holy Land book, and as we sang songs of adoration, others knelt with us.'

Yet the Lord yearned for more, for visible tokens of love that could always speak to people's hearts, even when there was no guide, and the churches and sites were closed. Accordingly, we manufactured herald plaques for the Holy Places with an inscription about Jesus' love and suffering. They were intended to draw people's eyes away from the excessive display of souvenirs and the other attractions, and to remind them of the true purpose of the visit. When human voices are silent, the plaques were to cause the stones of the buildings to speak and bring the places to life – as in actual fact they did.

Jesus, once filled with sorrow because of Peter's sin, is now gazing at us. He longs that we too might shed tears of repentance over our sins. The more we weep in contrition for having grieved Jesus, the more fervent our love for Him will be.

St Peter in Gallicantu

The glory of God shall be seen by those who in times of greatest distress and hopelessness put their faith in Jesus in the assurance that He is greater than any distress, greater than death itself.

Tomb of Lazarus

The hour of transfiguration came for Jesus when He was about to enter the night of suffering and death. As members of His Body, we can only receive the grace of transfiguration, which He has won for us, by following the same path – the pathway of humiliation and purification.

Mount Tabor

This undertaking roused the enemy to fury. For instance, after we had mounted a plaque on the wall of a house along the Via Dolorosa, with the owner's permission, there was almost a riot in the Old City of Jerusalem. The crowd was in an uproar, and the police led us away while the plaque was being removed. After interrogating the Sisters and me, the Governor of the Old City of Jerusalem forbade us to make any further attempts to mount plaques in his district. The Holy Places themselves came under special protection as historical sites. Furthermore, they were under the jurisdiction of the Orthodox and Catholic Churches, which, understandably enough, at that time were not in favour of Protestant Sisters cementing plaques on to the walls and entrances to the holy sites in their charge.

A few years later, however, our plaques were at almost every one of the Holy Places – including the Garden of Gethsemane. God took care of everything, paving the way and changing people's hearts so that the commission He had given could be carried out. As we learnt later, many pilgrims and tourists were challenged by the words of the plaques, which were responsible for a vital, personal encounter with Jesus. This was all part of God's plan. Responses would reach us, such as: 'These plaques made the cold, dead stones come alive for me.' 'They were responsible for a turning point in my life.' 'For me they were like a spiritual guide to all the places of Jesus' earthly life.' Many of the guides pointed out the plaques to their groups, and guardians of the Holy Places asked to have them mounted and took them under their care.

My longing to bring joy to Jesus at the Holy Places increased even more. If only some of my daughters could establish residence on the Mount of Olives – the place of Jesus' sufferings and the site of His return! With the Mount of Olives as their base, they could sing and pray at the Holy Places and perform their ministry amongst the pilgrims. And if only our future land of Canaan could have a permanent memorial to the love and sufferings of Jesus! I shall never forget the drive through Samaria when God suddenly inspired me with this commission. A flame was kindled in my heart. One day Canaan was to have a large prayer garden called 'The Garden of Jesus' Sufferings' so that everyone who came to Canaan would be reminded of the suffering Jesus underwent for our sakes and would be moved to respond with gratitude, love and adoration.

The Lord fulfilled all this. Some years later the Garden of Jesus' Sufferings was laid out and for countless numbers of people it has become a place of prayer portraying the love of Jesus that seeks a response. Likewise, God had pronounced His 'yea and amen' over the aim of faith for a house on the Mount of Olives. Ever since 1962 we have had Sisters stationed in our branch there. 'Beit Gaudia Dei' with its panoramic view of Jerusalem has become a spiritual centre for many pilgrims and visiting groups from all denominations and all parts of the world who come to join our Sisters in prayer and worship. How great is God's faithfulness!

In 1959 when I returned home, God gave me the text for our 'Passion Meditation'.* It was the outcome of the deep experience of Jesus' sufferings that I had during this journey, and an answer to my fervent prayer.

Grant me something for my daughters so that every Maundy Thursday and Good Friday they can truly accompany You in spirit along Your path of suffering. Help me to give a vivid representation so that their love for You may be set aflame and they may bring You real comfort and adoration during this holy night.

This was the prayer I had written in my diary before my journey.

The Lord enabled me to describe His suffering vividly as I spoke about His Passion on tape; the recording, which lasted many hours, was interspersed with hymns and prayers. A burden had been laid on my heart to inspire

* A service commemorating Jesus' sufferings on Maundy Thursday and Good Friday.

others to give Him the love that is His due as a response to all His sufferings. The secret of Jesus' sufferings was disclosed to my daughters more and more as they came together for this Passion Meditation every Maundy Thursday and Good Friday. Likewise, guests attending our retreats on Canaan, where similar hours of worship and adoration in memory of the Passion are held, have come into a deeper relationship to Jesus' sufferings.

Thus my prayer was fulfilled. It was my ardent plea that Jesus might reveal Himself and His suffering more to those who believe in Him and that He might receive an even greater response of love and gratitude, whether it be at the places of His suffering in Jerusalem, in our Mother House, or at our retreat centre on Canaan.

With each of these new commissions I literally discovered that times when God is distant and seems to have forsaken us are followed by times of grace when He inclines Himself to us and draws near. As I experienced, periods of deep affliction are followed by periods of supreme joy, and severe illness by a new surge of life. God is a Rewarder indeed! After those trying months when I recommitted my will almost hourly to the incomprehensible leadings of God, I found that such dedications opened the heavens for God's stream of grace to pour down.

Fill All the World with the Praise of God

Some of the most moving passages of Scripture are those where Jesus expresses His desire to glorify the Father, or where, as in the prayer He uttered at the end of His earthly life, He says that He has glorified the Father. If there is one thing that I longed to live for – doing my small part – it was to glorify God. Accordingly, every one of our various commissions can be traced back to this one source: to give God the love and glory that is His due.

Love for God is an incentive to erect signs and monuments that call people to give love and glory to Him who alone is worthy of receiving love and glory. As an expression of this love I had a crucifix erected in the woods behind our Mother House as early as 1952 at a spot we call 'Jesus' Abode'. Four years later I received fresh inspiration while I was staying in Aeschi, Switzerland. Overwhelmed by the lovely Alpine landscape of meadows, lakes and snow-capped mountains, I had a deep longing to express my love and gratitude to God our Father, who had created the glories of nature with such love for us, His children. In a letter I wrote to my daughters during my stay in 1956, I shared with them my heart's desire. 'Most of all, I yearn to build chapels everywhere and set up monuments to His glory.'

So far I was not sure of the next step to take and the commission that the Lord had laid upon my heart failed to materialise. But after I had recovered from my critical illness, the yearning to glorify God was rekindled in me and set ablaze. I felt as if God were asking me where the monuments were that I had wanted to raise to His glory. With new incentive I sought ways and means to perform this ministry before disaster would overtake the world. Cost what it may, I longed to erect visible signs at various places – signs that would inspire people to glorify God.

One day in 1960 a Sister gave me a small fired clay tablet as a little surprise. Upon it were engraved the words, 'God is Love'. As I picked up this tablet, it suddenly occurred to me that such plaques in a larger size could serve as small monuments to remind people of God. We could have the plaques engraved with a Bible verse and a stanza of a hymn and then erected at scenic spots as a means of calling others to praise God. The next step had been shown!

It was a special day when Mother Martyria and I, together with some of our spiritual daughters, set out on our first praise outing in the summer of 1960. Our car was like a travelling praise chapel. As we drove through the Bavarian mountains in all their splendour, our constant refrain was a song composed on this occasion.

Glory to God belongs!
Therefore, we raise our songs
Our Maker's love to praise,
And thank Him for the grace
His choristers to be.*

Improvising on the spot, I lifted my anthems of thanksgiving to the Father. As the first praise choristers from Canaan, we visited the regions and sites where in earlier years God had revealed to me His glory as the Creator and granted me songs in His honour. There we intended to mount plaques as a token of our gratitude.

But soon I learnt that this commission, like most of the other commissions God had given me, presented almost insurmountable obstacles. This was inevitable, since divine commissions are meant to glorify God, and God can manifest His glory and demonstrate His deeds best of all when we have come to the end of our own resources. The praise ministry seemed to have been nipped in the bud before it could make a proper start because of the many practical difficulties that ensued.

The most beautiful scenic spots were seldom owned by private individuals. Sometimes they were even in preservation areas – and, as we were told, it was hopeless asking for permission from the authorities concerned. Moreover, our first attempts to mount plaques proved to be highly dramatic. At a popular tourist centre in a neighbouring country we had obtained permission to erect plaques, but there was a great stir; feeling ran high amongst the local residents, who objected strongly and even let the air out of our car tyres to drive the point home. Thus our first endeavours were most discouraging. Considering the commission from the human point of view, I felt that it had been stamped as 'impossible'.

However, faith shatters iron bars and stone boulders. Faith is not deterred by any barrier – especially not when it is a matter of furthering God's cause. I knew that nothing

* *Well-spring of Joy*, No. 146.

is impossible for God. Moreover, my prayer was a prayer in Jesus' name, since His greatest longing was that the Father be glorified and human souls saved. And the praise ministry was also designed for outreach, for next to the praise plaques and monuments we intended to erect 'outdoor herald boxes' containing short sayings and leaflets for passers-by to take home with them. What an opportunity to call people to Jesus, if these herald boxes were strewn throughout the country, at scenic spots where hundreds, even thousands, would come for outings in the summer! The hearts of my daughters were set on fire. During this first praise outing we sang songs of faith and verses that we made up on the spot, bringing the Lord our specific prayer requests.

Our 'aims of faith' were pinned up high – aims to which only a bold faith could aspire – since the circumstances could not have been less favourable. In Switzerland, for instance, a land of outstanding natural beauty, the prospects were depressing. Nevertheless, we prayed to the heavenly Father and in faith we thanked Him in advance for all that He would do. Our goal was forty praise places at the most lovely look-out points in the Swiss alps! Later God put us to shame, for our faith proved to be far too small. Within a few years over one hundred praise plaques, scattered throughout the Swiss alps, bore the challenge to praise God. The plaques, which have found their way to the highest and loveliest mountains, such as the Jungfraujoch, brought glory to God the Maker through the Bible verses and songs engraved upon them.

Our praise outing took us to the Rossfeldalm overlooking Berchtesgaden in Bavaria near the Austrian border. Part of this mountain once belonged to Adolf Hitler, a God-hater, a man who let himself be deified by millions. Because of all the blasphemies that were committed there a deep longing was kindled within me for a monument to be set up in this vicinity to the glory of God, the Creator – and later, much to my joy, it was erected. During our visit there I could see across the Austrian border to the chain of mountains stretched out before me in solemn majesty and grandeur, and as I gazed at this view, a song that I had written at this very spot some years earlier resounded in my heart.

Worlds unnumbered pay God homage.
At His word through endless ages,
Mountains shuddered, melted, fell.
All high places bring You honour,
Grand indeed is Your great splendour,
Father, Maker, Source of life.*

During this excursion in the summer of 1960, the Lord laid a special burden on my heart, showing me that He was waiting above all for a group of praise choristers, for people who would spend themselves that God might be glorified. Such praise choristers would help to deter the coming destruction. Wherever signs are raised testifying to God, wherever He is worshipped in truth and is glorified, Satan will be checked from fully accomplishing his schemes.

In those days who could have imagined that seven or eight years later the 'death-of-God' theology would sweep across the world, and that today it would be so widely accepted and adopted in the Christian world? Who would have thought that God would soon be forced to give up mankind to shameless passions, because man had refused to give his Maker the glory? (Romans 1:18-32). Who would have dreamt that church services – instead of being kept as times to worship God and give Him the glory would be turned into discussion sessions for everyone to air his views? And who would have foreseen that blasphemous musicals degrading Jesus, portraying Him as a clown, would even be performed in churches and applauded by Christian audiences?

At that time who spoke of pollution? Who could have suspected that rivers and lakes, which were still relatively pure, would soon be contaminated? Who could have known that millions of dead fish would be washed up on the shores, that pure drinking water would become such a rarity that

* See *Well-spring of Joy*, No. 159.

bottles of 'Norwegian water' would be sold in West Germany? Who gave thanks daily for the pure air before the day of smog alarms in major cities? And who realised that our glorious forests filled with rejoicing song-birds were already doomed to die? Yet even at that early date the Lord drew my attention to Revelation 14:7, a verse of far-reaching significance for the end times, in which we are living. I then had this verse inscribed in mosaic on the chancel wall of the 'Glory to God Chapel', our second praise chapel in the Bernese Oberland, Switzerland, and at the dedication of the chapel I spoke on this text. 'Fear God and give him glory, for the hour of his judgement has come; and worship him who made heaven and earth, the sea and the fountains of water.'

In those days very few realised the relevance of this command of Scripture. In view of the future, however, the Lord laid a burden on my heart for the praise ministry at home and abroad. Praise places were to be established and praise outings arranged so that the time left would be used to the best advantage to the glorification of God.

I wrote in my diary:

These praise outings have a two-fold purpose. They will also be conducive to unity between Protestants and Roman Catholics, as people join together in praising the Creator and worshipping Him.

And indeed this came to pass a few years later.

But I was not spared the inner conflict that accompanied every ministry God gave me. I was haunted by such questions as: 'Would the response make it worthwhile spending so much effort on this expensive and time-consuming project? Would the plaques really speak to people's hearts? Would they really cause a turning point in people's lives?' Suddenly everything seemed so pointless – including the outdoor herald boxes, which were damaged time and again. Moreover, I continued to doubt whether there would be enough people willing to devote time and energy to the praise ministry so that it could be carried out effectively. A diary entry from that time indicates my burning desire.

A campaign really ought to be started now. Our friends should be mounting plaques and erecting outdoor herald boxes everywhere. All that our Sisters have accomplished so far is too little. Please help me to write an inspiring letter to our friends to set them on fire for the praise ministry.

Shortly afterwards the newsletter was sent out to our friends, but to my great disappointment there was no response. I discovered how hard it was to arouse interest and gain understanding for the praise ministry, which was almost entirely unknown until then and which even caused antagonism in some cases. We were expected to perform 'useful' services. This attitude, which had caused us much trouble from the very beginning – from the time we started building the Mother House Chapel – confronted us again in 1962 as we planned to build a small praise chapel in Aeschi, Switzerland. Even friends raised their voices in protest. 'Build chapels for God? Surely it would be better to build hospitals?' When money is spent for charitable works, people are grateful and appreciative. But I discovered that when money is spent for the glorification of God even committed Christians voice their disapproval, as if such expenditures were a waste of money, despite Jesus' words in Mark 14:6–9.

As I recorded in my diary:

Both the commission to erect herald plaques at the Holy Places, and the praise ministry are a battle against overwhelming odds. To many, our ministries seem foolish and meaningless, since they are not primarily intended as service to mankind, but originate from the desire to honour and glorify God. Our ministries, whichever you name, are strange and novel to the Christian world . . . One of the Church's most precious heritages, the adoration and worship of God, has fallen, generally speaking, into oblivion. But how can it be revived and how can we learn to appreciate it again if no one is willing to pay the price, if no one dares to face opposition and be considered a fool?

When we finally commenced with the building of the praise chapel in Aeschi overlooking Lake Thun, the enemy seemed to be infuriated. No doubt he sensed that this chapel would be a place of never-ending praise for God, since later thousands of holiday-makers from all over the world would come to visit the chapel, on their own or in groups. Accordingly, the enemy made an all-out effort to prevent the construction. We were accused of being a sect, we had to face many bitter foes, and innumerable obstacles cropped up.

Although the date of dedication had been publicly announced for Ascension Day, May 31, 1962, it seemed unlikely that we could keep it. Owing to false statements made about us, the authorities refused to grant us a building permit. But the word of assurance I received from the Lord was overwhelming. 'Take courage! Do not let your hands be weak, for your work shall be rewarded' (2 Chronicles 15:7). Thus, against all common sense, I believed that God would complete this project.

Since there seems to be no end to the tears shed because of the Aeschi chapel, it will be a chapel of never-ending praise – and this flame of praise will not die out in the coming time of destruction. You will complete Your marvellous work. Glory will be the final outcome, for suffering always ends in glory.

At the last moment God intervened. Almost overnight we received the building permit – three and a half weeks before the date of the dedication ceremony! That was the first miracle God performed. And the second followed. In those three and a half weeks the chapel was built and ready by Ascension Day!

Since then the chapel has been a visible testimony to the superior strength of God. Even when the powers of darkness are up in arms because monuments are being erected to the glory of God, He is triumphant. God is not deterred by any man's refusal. He accomplishes His purposes majestically. Although the praise chapel in Aeschi is off the beaten track and to outward appearances small and insignificant, thousands visit this site of never-ending praise. Here countless numbers of people have been inspired to glorify God, while many a counselling talk has ended in unburdened hearts and true, joyous worship of God.

Everything that had been laid into the chapel's foundations had proved worthwhile – the sacrifices, the disgrace, the suffering and faith, and even the money invested, which we had received in answer to prayer along dark avenues of faith. Indeed, we should give unstintingly to magnify the glory of God.

But where were the praise choristers? Where were the souls inspired by the love of God to establish places of praise throughout the world? There was still a long way to go before the praise ministry could make headway. Only by paying no heed to the voices of opposition and by attuning my ears to the voice of God alone, was I able to remain steadfast and continue this ministry. I knew that since God's thoughts are higher and different from human ways of thinking, His commissions are bound to appear foolish in the eyes of men. Thus in obedience to God I had to follow unusual leadings, which were not appreciated by others. I had to follow such pathways, even if the whole world stood against me.

The following lines I wrote down as a spiritual legacy for my daughters:

My dear Daughters,
For every God-given commission, for every hour of divine inspiration, there is a price to be paid. Every time God inclines Himself to us in such an hour of grace and revelation, we must pay for it – and usually dearly. So do not lose faith when hard times come, when it almost seems too difficult to carry out the commission, when great

obstacles arise and you begin to doubt seriously whether the commission was really from the Lord. On the contrary, inner conflict is a sure sign that a commission is a revelation from God, a commission from the Holy Spirit. The unmerited favours of God must be spiritually absorbed and assimilated into our entire being; His blessings must yield fruit in us. And this will occur, if we are willing to pay the price for a commission by suffering – which also includes undergoing trials and temptations. God always works on us first before using us as a channel of blessing for others. It is not enough for a person to receive blessings for himself. Many who have experienced blessings did not bear any fruit, but rather became a stumbling block and an offence for others. And why? Because they did not inwardly digest these blessings, but snatched them as their rightful prey. They were unwilling to undergo the process that would make the blessing fruitful, unwilling to follow the path of chastening, inner conflict and suffering. But choose this path. Then the blessing will increase a hundredfold.

Since this praise ministry was from the Lord, it bore divine life, and in spite of everything it made headway – first with our Canaan Friends, and then with many others. When God gives a commission, He will provide an opening. He calls people to carry it out and grants moments when His 'yea and amen' unlocks the doors of fulfilment. Thus the tide turned for the praise ministry also, as the following incidents demonstrate. An official of a City Park Commission in the United States remarked, 'Why, it's a privilege and an honour to have these plaques in our parks!' The Chief Forest Ranger in the Oden Forest in West Germany permitted several praise places to be established simultaneously. After having seen some in Switzerland and the Black Forest, he was enthusiastic about the idea. In Ghana, a tribal chief helped mount the plaque himself and promised to make it known to others and to protect it from vandalism. On the island of Heligoland, off the coast of northern Germany – as in many other places – a shopkeeper said that he had to arrange for postcards to be made of the praise place, since so many people had asked for them.

A Canadian wrote about the plaques, saying, 'They are filled with the love of Jesus, and people almost gasp as they look at them.' And a missionary from Argentina related, 'We organised an excursion . . . to a natural "window", at the top of a 4,000 foot high mountain. This window is a tourist attraction, and more than 50 Christians came together at the foot of the hill, and some 35 climbed up to the top where we cemented the plaque . . . After this we took time to praise the Lord for His works . . . We hope that we can go on together and fill national parks and other beautiful places in Latin America with such testimonies to the glory of God.'

'Wherever I go – whether it be to Gethsemane or La Verna, Assisi [Italy], Switzerland or the Oden Forest – I always come across plaques with inscriptions praising God,' wrote the head of deaconess house in a letter. In Arizona, USA, a forest ranger was very interested in having praise plaques in his territory and gave full permission for them to be erected. He even promised that his men would bring rocks to mount them on if there were none at the site.

Hundreds of praise places with plaques written in many different languages have imprinted the seal of God upon the loveliest and most popular scenic spots and historical sites throughout the world – from the Norwegian fjords to the Pauline sites in Greece, from the lonely Himalayas to the Grand Canyon in the United States where 20,000 sightseers come daily during the summer months. Nothing is impossible for God.

Every time a letter arrived with the news that a plaque had been mounted, I rejoiced in my heart and gave thanks – another sign of testimony had been set up to remind people of the Lord and to call them back to Him, and the herald boxes would be a further means to this end.

The zeal of our friends for this commission increased greatly. There are no words to describe their spirit of faith and the countless sacrifices they made as they worked for the glory of God. In spite of overwhelming obstacles they did not give up before the praise plaques were mounted, and if the praise plaques were torn down, they resumed their efforts. Many of our friends were so on fire for this ministry to give God honour and glory that by 1973 there were already about 600 praise places established in West Germany and over 120 in Switzerland. In health resorts at the height of the season there would be weekly gatherings at praise places for open-air services of worship. In Britain a county borough council permitted a praise plaque to be erected near the edge of a sheer cliff where many had taken their lives so that the plaque would not only give glory to God but prevent people from committing suicide. Indeed, we have heard of instances when praise plaques, which had been primarily erected *for God*, have kept people from putting an end to their lives.

Giving God the glory and worshipping Him is the true purpose of our lives. The balance of nature is only maintained when man and the whole of creation reverence God without pause, making Him the object of their worship, as the morning stars did after the creation of the world, when they brought the Lord homage and adoration, rejoicing in Him and encircling Him like planets orbiting round the sun.

What a tremendous privilege to spend ourselves in this lifetime that God might receive praise and adoration in the vast expanse of creation through small visible reminders! And who is the object of our worship? The Ruler of all heavens, the Sovereign of the universe, the Omnipotent, the God of creation, who is the source of wisdom, whose purposes are unsearchable, the Lord Almighty, from whom all existing things come and to whom all existing things return. How wonderful to revolve round God alone and to glorify Him! The praise ministry has been a great blessing for me and through it the Lord has enriched my life immeasurably.

Now that the Lord had restored my life after my critical illness, granting me new commissions, it meant living at the 'end of time'. True, in the early 1960s there was little indication that a new era had begun. Over the course of the years, however, people were disquieted by the development of the world situation: the commandments of God were being dissolved; immorality was spreading; revolutionary currents were making headway; and in many areas of the Church the very fundamentals of the Christian faith were being whittled away. But few suspected that apostasy would begin to sweep through all branches of Christianity within a few short years. At the time everything seemed relatively peaceful.

In the winter of 1960 I was once more in the small Trinity Chapel for several weeks of seclusion and prayer, when quite inexplicably the Lord filled my heart with a burning zeal to warn others so that they might be saved. Under the prompting of the Holy Spirit I felt constrained to write without pause. A new book was to be written, *Das Ende ist nah* (*Lo, He Comes*). The Father knew what awaited mankind in the coming decades, and in His love He wished to use this book as another means of urging people to make good use of the time left. When Jesus returns, He wishes to come as Bridegroom to His own, to take them to Himself, and lead them into immeasurable joy and glory for all eternity. He does not wish to come as Judge to those who actually belong to Him, or to pronounce the terrible verdict, 'I do not know you!' He longs to spare them the dreadful experience of standing before a closed door and finding they are too late, for on that day no cry of despair will be able to change God's verdict.

These thoughts constrained me to pass on the warning to others, for I perceived that we were living in the last times. An avalanche was gathering force. Apostasy would soon be rampant; the antichristian era was drawing close, and thus the severe judgements of God upon mankind were no longer distant. The day of the Lord's wrath was approaching swiftly. This realisation was followed by long, dark weeks when I was alone with God, away from everyone else, writing about the end of time. Before writing about this topic, I had to undergo in the spirit the suffering involved. I had to experience God's anguish anew, His grief and wrath over man, who was at the point of drowning in the quicksand of iniquity, although God had created him in His own image and redeemed him by His only Son. In an earlier chapter I mentioned how I had had to taste the wrath of God in order to testify to it, and indeed, the experiences of those weeks in 1957 had given me the necessary preparation for writing this new book. But even now, as I was writing it, I again had to suffer in spirit the frightening reality of the judgements threatening to descend upon mankind, and to face the alarming upsurge of sin throughout the world.

During this period (winter 1960–1) I wrote:

My heart is like an abyss of grief. I feel as though I have lost my dear ones. The abominations of our times tear at my heart. I suffer agony as I perceive God's grief over the world that He has created, but which has turned its back on Him and is thoroughly corrupt. I feel driven to write this book, *Lo, He Comes*. Incalculable suffering fills the depths of my soul. Never before have I had to suffer so much in writing a book ...

Yet here again it all seemed pointless, for my common sense argued, 'Who would read this book?' Those who had always been against my commission and the way God was leading me would find all the more reason to say, 'Look at the fanatic, the doomsday prophet with her talk about the end of the world, painting such a gloomy picture!' My books would be forbidden even more so. But the love of God was victorious in me; I was moved by His compassion. In His love He suffers and cares for His children, especially for those who call themselves by His name. And in the power of the Holy Spirit I was driven by this love to win souls for God, to entreat and warn people so that those who believe in God might prepare themselves for the time ahead.

I had hoped that this would be the only occasion when I had to present such a grave message, but the Lord ordained it otherwise as I discovered at Christmas 1960. In the Mother House a Christmas song resounded triumphantly – a verse from Isaiah set to music, 'For to us a child is born, to us a son is given; and the government will be upon his shoulder!' (Isaiah 9:6). That Christmas the Spirit of God unfolded a special secret to us: when Jesus was born as a child into this world, He was already King, bearing the government upon His shoulders. While I was in seclusion, the Lord had revealed the spiritual truth to me that the King who will come again in glory was already present in the Child Jesus; His future majesty was only veiled from our eyes. What a joyous and triumphant message this is in an age when Satan's power is increasing! When Jesus comes again in glory, He will be King over all the dominions of the world!

On the Second Day of Christmas our Hall of Zion resounded with songs of adoration as we worshipped the Child Jesus as the little King. 'Crown Him, crown Him, Lord of all!' After the last strains of the song faded away, and we were talking about the different ways of glorifying Jesus, the conversation turned to the dedication ceremony of our Herald Chapel, which would take place in May 1961. We agreed that the programme must include a Herald Play about the return of Jesus as King at the end of time. 'Please write one, Mother Basilea,' my daughters pleaded. 'We'll pray for it!' 'Then tomorrow I shall withdraw and see whether the Holy Spirit will give me a script. But I'm afraid you will have to forgo our time of worship and praise, and come together in small groups instead to pray for the play.' It was the right moment; I could feel the prompting of the Spirit.

The following evening I returned to the Hall of Zion and our hearts were filled with thanksgiving as we listened to the tape recording of the Herald Play that God had graciously given in answer to prayer. His Spirit had granted the inspiration. Like a miracle the play was given to me within a few hours, during which I dictated the script on to the tape, singing the songs extemporaneously.

Although we were overflowing with gratitude on that evening, there was a burden weighing heavily upon me. I sensed that the book, *Lo, He Comes*, and this new Herald Play about the end-time events were only the beginning of a lasting commission. In the following years I was led to write one pamphlet after another dealing with current developments in the world. But such a commission entails having a foretaste of the suffering and judgements that will come as a result of the sins of our nation, as well as the sins of the Church and the whole world, since iniquity would soon be universal. In a prophetic ministry one must be willing to pay the price involved in foreseeing the coming events, in suffering and experiencing them in advance. Only then can the warning be passed on.

All the new ministries entrusted to me after my recovery brought various types of sufferings – trials and temptations, antagonism and humiliation – since they were folly in the eyes of men. But the anguish and hardship that accompanied this commission was even greater, for there was a price to be paid spiritually for every new booklet about the current situation. Part of the suffering arose, because I had to read so much material about the apostasy and corruption in our world, and it was a painful experience to confront the terrible power of evil.

In this ministry I was especially isolated and misunderstood by many Christian groups, for this message about the end times was seldom heard in the Protestant Church, and the Revelation of John was sometimes even considered to be a legend rather than a biblical message. Pietists have always respected this Christian heritage and have repeatedly endeavoured to interpret the signs of the times. However, a misunderstanding about conversion and the rapture has lulled countless numbers of Christians into a false state of security. And although newly arisen revival groups and charismatic fellowships have rediscovered the biblical reality of the gifts of the Spirit and written about the gift of prophecy, they usually found it hard to understand that we must repent today, since the last times have come and judgement is impending. In their opinion it was a gloomy topic – too much to expect of modern man.

Even at our retreats it was difficult to share this message with our friends and guests. Whenever I could speak on other topics, it was easy to reach the hearts of the listeners. Yet I was aware of a certain amount of resistance when it came to this message, which Jesus Himself had preached so often and which is a recurrent theme in the Bible. Each time it was a struggle for me to follow the suggestion of my daughters for a large-scale mailing of any of the booklets dealing with current developments. Nothing could have been more foreign to my nature. As a woman I found it particularly hard to have written such literature and have given permission for its distribution, but I felt it was the Lord's will.

From then onwards this ministry was to be an integral part of my life. But only a deeper love for God could enable me to share His great grief over the vileness of sin (Genesis 6:6) and equip me to carry out this ministry. Mankind was running headlong into destruction; I needed a greater love for my fellow men in order to win them back to God, to raise my voice in warning time and again, regardless of the counterstrokes that would come as a result of this message. In answer to prayer the Lord increased my love for Him and my fellow men, and this love alone kept me from laying the task aside when the cry of despair rose in my heart, 'Oh, if only I did not have to know, hear or write anything about these terrible matters!' However, the ministry continued, and since the Lord had entrusted it to me, He saw to it that I almost knew more about the current events than the Sister who had the assignment of reading the daily newspaper to keep the whole Sisterhood informed. It was as if the Lord had turned my heart into a receiver for the serious problems of our times.

Over the course of the years a whole series of booklets

dealing with relevant topics was issued* – in fulfilment of God's promise. When the first booklet *Heute – eine Zeit wie nie* (*Today a Time like None Before*) was being written in 1962, I noted in my diary:

> Disaster is inevitable. I can clearly see it coming. We are living in the age of the wrath of God, the end times, when people will be fainting with fear and foreboding of all that is coming on the world. The frightening spectre of future events looms up before me. The air is pregnant with doom; destruction is threatening – destruction such as the world has never seen before . . . The thought of all the dreadful and appalling things that await my daughters weighs heavily on me . . . It is a race to carry out the commission entrusted to us before disaster strikes . . .

My great concern was that my daughters would no longer evade the issue in the present world situation, suppressing the truth, but come to grips with it by making dedications to suffering. I longed for them to see Jesus in such splendour that their fears about the future would be overcome. Then they would be strengthened and filled with consolation for the time when affliction comes. I wrote down many words of encouragement from the Bible for them, and later the Lord gave me a booklet to write about overcoming fear and learning to trust the Father.

All these spiritual experiences were to set the tone of the following Christmases (1961 and 1962). Christmas 1962 in particular brought a great deal of comfort to our hearts, as we felt the reassuring presence of the Lord, who came into our dark world as a child to save souls and overcome the powers of darkness. Our constant refrain was a song composed at the time.

* A selection of booklets dealing with relevant topics: *To-day a Time like None Before*; *World in Revolt*; *Never Before in the History of the Church*; *Pollution – but there is an Answer* (American edition: *A Matter of Life and Death*); *Countdown to World Disaster – Hope and Protection for the Future*; *The Eve of Persecution*.

Dearest Child, You came to darkness,
Brought Your gleam to this earth's night,
For the world is ripe for judgement,
Helpless in its woeful plight.

Yet Your radiance shines the brighter
O'er our sinful misery,
And You lead mankind in triumph
Out of death to victory.*

Later these songs, together with the little booklet about overcoming fear and other books offering solace were published.† In writing about these relevant topics I was grateful that I did not only have to warn others, confronting them with the facts, but could bring them comfort and encouragement in their fears and distress. Having tasted the misery and hardship in advance, I was able to write about the source of help for such times when comfort will be scarce. Amongst my spiritual daughters I could see the deep trust that filled them, and the peace and joy that broke out in their midst at the knowledge that during the coming time of affliction they would have an experience with the Father as never before.

The responses from other quarters also showed me that my dedication to carry out this ministry had been worthwhile. The task of warning others of the impending disaster – the hardest task of all for me – had not been in vain.

Songs and Festivals of Heaven

Was I really a 'doomsday prophet' as my adversaries claimed? That could not be, since all my life every experience I had had in the spiritual and practical leadings of God had given me quite a different outlook. I had learnt that after hard times of judgement and chastening light shines

* *Well-spring of Joy*, No. 44.
† Such as *Father of Comfort*.

forth; suffering is followed by tremendous joy, for with God suffering is never the final outcome. God is Love; He accomplishes His marvellous purposes. The raging of hell today announces the imminent coming of heaven. Later, when the fury of the Antichrist reaches its peak, the shout of jubilation will begin to resound through all the heavens. 'The kingdom of the world has become the kingdom of our Lord and of his Christ' (Revelation 11:15). 'The marriage of the Lamb has come' (Revelation 19:7). Every booklet in the series about relevant topics contained this joyous message. One person wrote to us, saying, 'I always underline the passages about heaven, Jesus' second coming and His glory in bright yellow, and in your booklets about current matters I have whole pages in yellow! The joyful expectation of the coming glory makes my heart beat faster . . . '

After that 'year of death' the Father was to grant me a renewal of the blessing I had received after my Moriah experience – a foretaste of heaven. But this time I was able to share the blessing in a new way. Although I had previously written booklets and many songs about heaven, I did not have the impression that there was a great deal of receptiveness amongst my daughters, or our guests and friends. My diary mirrored my feelings as I began to write these songs in 1956.

I pray now that heaven will come down when these songs about heaven are sung later. Please perform this miracle so that when people sing of heaven, it really breaks out in their midst. Work on their souls as they sing, so that the words of the songs come true for them. You know how hard I often find it to write these songs, since I feel they are irrelevant, a waste of time. But today the presence of heaven is very real and I can sense that the songs are from You – just as You promised. Please grant my prayer and say 'yea and amen' to it.

After 1958 – that year of strain and hardship – the Lord began to answer this prayer also and soon the stream of heavenly joy flowed down, carrying my spiritual daughters along in its current. Thus we began to celebrate 'festivals of heaven', in a way we had never done before. Whenever heaven comes down, there are bound to be festivals, for as the Bible says, 'You have come to Mount Zion . . . the heavenly Jerusalem, and to innumerable angels in festal gathering, and to the assembly of the first-born who are enrolled in heaven' (Hebrews 12:22f.). In heaven above there are festivals and festive gatherings, and the sound of praise and adoration reverberates throughout its spheres.

This greater responsiveness of my daughters now for the heavenly world could be partly attributed to the more thorough cleansing process that many of them had undergone. They too had learnt to fear and love the holy God even more deeply, having tasted His wrath during times of divine visitation. In accordance with a spiritual law the natural outcome was festivals of heaven. A minister from abroad once expressed it this way, 'It seems to me that "to feast the Lord" is a special charisma that He has given you on Canaan. This is why I feel especially drawn here. Joyous festivity is what makes heaven heaven, and as I have discovered, the greater the repentance, the greater the joy.'

These festivals of heaven were not 'organised'; they did not run according to a set programme. We simply came together and as we began to sing, it was natural for us to worship the Lord Jesus, and to praise Him, the Diadem of heaven. We brought Him adoration in many songs: Our hearts were seized with a deep desire to proclaim the glories of the King of heaven – Jesus, the Lamb of God seated upon the throne most high. Improvising melodies, we extolled Jesus, constantly seeking new ways of expressing our adoration. Then as we began to sing of the glory that awaits His own in heaven, joy broke out in our midst, so that even the sad of heart were uplifted. Soon our Hall of Zion was immersed in the splendour of heaven. When we prayed for heaven to come into our midst by singing the song, 'Oh, that we were there . . . ', we usually wanted to sing it all over again – even though it had almost thirty verses – for we never tired of proclaiming the joy of heaven.

This song was composed at a time of deep sorrow. Sister Angelika was lying on her deathbed in great agony, and I was filled with grief, longing to comfort her, but not knowing how. Leaving her bedside, I went into my room to pray, and as I did so the Lord let the radiance of heaven shine into my heart; one verse after another flowed from my pen and I hastened to Sister Angelika to sing this song of heaven to her. Suddenly her pain seemed to vanish. Sister Angelika's face grew more and more radiant, and despite her weakened condition she sang with me. Heaven had come down.

In the following years not only my daughters, but many others as well, sang this song. In particular, I remember one festival of heaven that we held in the Herald Chapel with many retreat guests; a large percentage of the gathering was young people. That evening I went to the festival with some trepidation, for during the morning Bible study I had talked about the harsh reality of the coming times. Addressing the young people that morning, I said that they had been born in the 'age of death' when destruction was threatening them in body, soul and spirit. I also felt led to refer to the advancing Satanic powers, which were increasing their influence, and to point out that persecution of Christians was on the threshold and that some of them might be called to lay down their lives as martyrs. Yet at the same time I told them that they were a privileged generation, who might live to see the final outcome of all this misery and grief – the revelation of the glory of Jesus Christ. The developments in the present world situation all point to the imminent return of the King. I encouraged them, saying that if they were numbered among those who love Jesus and have learnt to overcome in trials and temptations, they could well partake in the event that every generation in the past two thousand years had yearned to see – the return of Jesus to His own for the rapture, the day of supreme joy and glory.

As a result of this Bible study tremendous joy broke out in the Herald Chapel that evening during the festival of heaven, such as we had seldom experienced in previous years. The morning Bible study had confronted the young people with the future trials and distress. They heeded the call to repentance and surrendered their will in the prayer, 'Yes, Father'. And the harder it was for them to make this committal to suffering, the greater was the joy they experienced, for the measure of joy corresponds to the suffering, if we consent to it willingly. They were filled with longing and deep bliss as they turned their gaze heavenwards. Brimming over with joy, they sang songs about heaven with us and waved green branches as they worshipped Jesus, the King of heaven, the Love of their hearts. Together they lifted their songs in praise and adoration of Him. Indeed this festival had brought down the presence of heaven. Those who had had a hard battle that morning and were oppressed by the hardships of these last times were still singing as they left the Herald Chapel. Even after the festival was over, the songs of heaven were carried from one end of Canaan to the other. Since then we have experienced many other festivals of heaven with such an impact.

How glad I was that the festivals of heaven were having so many repercussions now. At first, when we only had one festival of heaven a year, we received a letter saying, 'We'd like to come, but please could you explain to us what you mean by a "festival of heaven"? We are quite mystified.' Yet in the end the festivals of heaven turned out to be the highlight of the retreats and a standing favourite for the summer youth community. On one occasion the boys of the youth community had not been asked to attend owing to the space shortage, but one boy prayed that God would lay it on my heart to invite them as well. He prayed until God intervened and the invitation was actually extended to them also! Another time there was a long-distance call. 'We are holding a festival of heaven tonight just as we have learnt to do on Canaan.' A minister who had brought a busload of people from his parish to the Herald Chapel told us later that although weeks had passed by, the festival of heaven had not lost its lustre; his parishioners would still sing with enthusiasm, 'Jerusalem, thou city fair and high.'

Once I wrote to my daughters:

Think of heaven and your suffering will suddenly grow insignificant, for it is not worth comparing with the heavenly glory that is to be revealed to you for all eternity. When you hear the word 'heaven', remember that the future joy is eternal and that your present suffering will come to an end. Live more in the heavenly realm! Concentrate more on the things above! It's worth it, for your home is above where you will abide for ever. Then you will see matters in the right perspective. Trivialities will be reduced to their proper size, while the things that count for all eternity will grow important to you. Sing about heaven! Celebrate festivals of heaven amid the gloom of our times. Only heaven can banish hell. Heaven is stronger than hell, since Jesus is the Lord of heaven. Blessed are those who weep here, for they shall laugh. So if you wish to taste heaven, commit yourself to suffering.

As I have personally discovered and repeatedly shared with my daughters, there is great power in contemplating and singing about heaven. Not only is our suffering diminished, but it fades away in view of the heavenly glory that will soon be granted to us. Ever since 1956 I have experienced that when heaven comes down, our deep longing becomes a fervent plea, 'Grant me the heavenly nature and mould me into a true citizen of heaven. Adorn me with the heavenly virtues – with the attributes of Jesus.' Only those who have reached spiritual maturity, the overcomers, the blessèd ones, can attain the goal of heavenly glory.

Although I found it hard to raise my voice in warning about the coming judgements and afflictions, and to speak about the reality of sin and demonism in our times, I was grateful for the privilege of telling others about the glory of heaven and the imminent return of our heavenly Bridegroom. Thus in His great love the Lord had granted me a double ministry amongst the new commissions – the twofold message that Jesus Himself had preached: 'Repent, for the kingdom of heaven is at hand!'

Of all the suffering I had to undergo during my critical illness in 1958 the most bitter was that of having to see the burial of one of my heart's desires, which the Lord had promised to fulfil. Ever since the founding years when He showed me that we were to have a foreshadowing of paradise and that heaven was to dawn in our midst, this was my aim of faith for the Sisterhood of Mary. But so far this request had not been fulfilled.

Yet during this time of recompense after my serious illness I was to see the beginning of this fulfilment. God, in His loving-kindness, intended to do more than restore and return everything. Even greater blessings were in store. He let me discover the reality of the verse, 'Where sin increased, grace abounded all the more' (Romans 5:20). What a mighty Redeemer Jesus is! Canaan was gradually taking shape, but that which gave it its special character was not its grounds or buildings, for there are grounds set in a more beautiful landscape and there are other buildings that have been built by faith alone. Jesus is glorified on Canaan most of all by its residents, who live in reconciliation with God and their neighbour. The nucleus of the Canaan family is formed by our Sisters, who after having followed God's long paths of discipline are a witness to the power of Jesus' redemption. If the Apostle Paul could write to the Church in Thessalonica, saying that they were his glory and joy, I was able to say the same of my spiritual daughters by now.

In the very beginning when we were still living in the Steinberg House, my greatest prayer request was that God's promise might be fulfilled in our midst. 'The Lord has chosen Zion . . . here I will dwell, for I have desired it' (Psalm 132:13f.).To me the fulfilment of this promise seemed like the dawning of the kingdom of heaven, a foreshadowing of paradise, which I was able to experience now in the midst of my daughters, after having met with so many disappointments. As a result of our times of fellowship in the light when we accept the truth about ourselves ever anew and acknowledge our sins, thus submitting to God's chastening, He was able to make His dwelling in our midst, for He dwells in penitent and humble hearts (Isaiah 57:15).

I still remember the feeling of great joy and thankfulness that once came over me when I returned from a long journey. As I entered the Hall of Zion where my daughters were gathered to welcome me, I felt as though I had come into a brightly-lit room – not because of the good lighting, but because of the inner radiance emanating from my daughters. I could see Jesus in them, shining like the sun.

In the time following my critical illness, the Lord showed me that there was to be a foreshadowing of the kingdom of heaven, of paradise, not only on Canaan, but in small centres abroad. I was to see to it that branches were opened up in other countries, beginning with Jerusalem, the heart of the world. The Lord desired many of these centres – little Canaan centres, oases radiating love, peace and joy – as a small foreshadowing of God's dominion, the dominion which is His ultimate goal in His plan of salvation for mankind.

Since the New Jerusalem will be comprised of the bride of the Lamb, the bride of Jesus on earth will naturally live and pray for a reflection of the heavenly Jerusalem in her particular surroundings as her goal of faith. A foreshadowing of the New Jerusalem! That was my constant longing for Canaan and later for our foreign branches, which we sometimes call little 'centres of paradise'. My aim of faith was that they might reflect the light of the City of God and its transparency, and accordingly every Sister was to expose herself fully to the light, to acknowledge the truth about herself and admit her sins. It was my yearning that the holy presence of God would descend there and that His fire would consume all that stands in His way, and that His transforming light would shine through those who endure it.

The foreign branches were to reflect the splendour of His city and its radiant joy. They were to give a foretaste of the singing and rejoicing that is so characteristic of the heavenly city. They were to be a visible testimony that tears of repentance result in laughter and tremendous joy. Love was to be the predominant feature and everything was to centre on Jesus, the Father and the Holy Spirit, not only during worship, but in the normal routine of life – just as the living creatures before the throne and all the heavenly host constantly revolve round God. The Sisters were to live together in the unity of love, while in their houses an atmosphere of peace and reconciliation was to prevail, which in turn was to affect other people's lives. That was how I visualised the foreign branches, the little centres of paradise.

The more our world resembles a raging, heaving sea, constantly churning up filth and sin, the more God needs sanctuaries, little islands emanating His holy presence, and our foreign branches were to help serve to this end. Such islands would send out rays of light and divine energy. From them the lifeline of love would be cast out to people, drawing them to Jesus Christ, their Saviour, enabling them to discover the love of God. Many souls at the point of drowning would reach out for the lifeline of love; the lost would be saved, and Christians led into a deeper and stronger faith.

The raging sea will not be able to deluge these islands, these sanctuaries of God, if they are founded on contrition and repentance – that is, if we remain humble and penitent in heart. Although the powers of darkness may assail them and bring suffering upon them, they are unable to destroy these sanctuaries, for as Jesus said of His Church, 'The gates of hell shall not prevail against it' (Matthew 16:18 AV).

Even though our foreign branches are a mere dot on the map, I knew that their influence would be felt throughout the land – as long as the fire of love was kept burning. And in each country those who felt called to live for the manifestation of the Kingdom of God would be united in spirit. Through daily repentance people would enter the door to the kingdom of heaven and thus be inspired to live according to the laws of this kingdom. They would be prepared to die to self so as to help pave the way for the realm of love, the Kingdom of God.

I was filled with gratitude that God had such wonderful plans for the life He had restored to me. Truly, He had 'thoughts of peace and not of evil', and soon He began to accomplish His purposes. As early as 1961, while Jerusalem was still divided, He gave us the house 'Beth Abraham' in the New City and a year later the house 'Moriah', the predecessor of our present 'Beit Gaudia Dei' on the Mount of Olives. These were our first two foreign branches – and both of them in His land!

Mount Sinai – The Climax of My Life
1963-1969

Weeks of Solitude at Mount Sinai

The year 1963 was highly significant for me, since a new chapter in my life began with a stay at Mount Sinai. For some time, in response to God's summons, I had been contemplating the idea of going there for a time of solitude in order to receive further directives from the Lord concerning our commission and ministries. But when I began considering how to carry out this plan, many questions arose. Was it a genuine call from the Lord? Was it truly His will? Could He not disclose His purposes to me equally well in my small prayer room in the Mother House? My intellect constantly presented new difficulties; I was in a state of great inner turmoil. With every fibre of my being I resisted this call, even though the Spirit of God kept reminding me of the verse, 'My thoughts are not your thoughts, neither are your ways my ways' (Isaiah 55:8). God's way of thinking is higher and different from ours; His thoughts are unsearchable for the human mind, which is so small and limited.

Yet why should the Lord not plan for an encounter in the tranquillity and solitude of the desert if He should choose to do so? There at His holy mountain, far away from the tumult of the world, He intended to give me a new ministry that would embrace the nations. I consented to go, and joy and expectation began to fill my heart.

But when we received a traveller's report about Mount Sinai, my inner conflict was not only rekindled, but increased. According to this account the atmosphere was not conducive to prayer because of the worldly noise created by tourist groups in the monastery fortress. There were no single rooms and it was almost impossible to leave the confines of St Catharine's Monastery on one's own because of the bedouins, who had a reputation for being dangerous ... Thus to all intents and purposes the journey seemed futile; it did not seem that the preconditions for a time of prayer, which was the main purpose of a stay at Mount Sinai, could be fulfilled. To complicate the issue I read that world travellers rated the journey to Mount Sinai as one of the most strenuous expeditions. From the very outset the journey seemed out of the question for me owing to my physical weakness – and that summer my health was especially poor. All in all it was a trying time when I had to undergo many inner conflicts. Also it seemed irresponsible to pay such high travelling costs.

On the other hand, I was afraid that I might be opposing God, should it be His will for me to go. Often enough I had seen how supposedly foolish, irrational leadings resulted in great commissions of God. Although I knew that the 'foolishness' of God is actually His wisdom, I felt as though I were being tossed from side to side by the waves of inner conflict. But that was part of God's plan. Encounters with God are always preceded by times of spiritual night and inner conflict, when we are obliterated so that His light, which cannot blend with the light of our fallen intellect, will pervade us. Figuratively speaking, there was only one way to His holy mountain – the way through the wilderness of trials and temptations that would serve to make me humble and lowly, and prepare me to meet the high and lofty God.

Then as a confirmation of His call, the Lord gave me an

overwhelming verse of Scripture for this journey – Genesis 46:3f., 'I am God, the God of your father; do not be afraid to go down to Egypt; for I will there make of you a great nation. I will go down with you to Egypt, and I will also bring you up again.' (In those days Mount Sinai was still within Egyptian territory.)

I actually received the visa for Egypt, although anyone familiar with such matters could have told me that it was impossible, since I had written a book entitled *Israel, My Chosen People*, and we had a branch, 'Beth Abraham', in the Israeli part of Jerusalem.

It was October 8, 1963. Feeling very frail and almost ill, I set out on the journey to Mount Sinai, and on the very first day a miracle occurred – the Lord touched me with His healing hand. New life flowed into my body, soul and spirit. Although it meant travelling three days and three nights without much sleep, I stood the journey well, for God had imparted new strength to me. The drive from Suez through the desert sands lasted many hours and on the way I was greeted by the mountains with their unusual rock formation glistening in the hot sun in varying shades of colour. Eternal silence reigned throughout the desert where no sound could be heard, no person seen except at the oasis Rephidim. When we finally arrived at Mount Sinai, I was deeply moved by the grandeur of God resting upon the desert mountains of granite and gneiss. The mountains stood as solid and immovable as the commandments that God had given to His chosen people at this site.

At the foot of Moses' Mountain in the midst of the imposing Sinai Massif was St Catharine's Monastery – a miniature city with buildings and chapels surrounded by high walls. Since the sixth century Greek Orthodox monks have been living there and one wing is set aside for visitors. As we entered the monastery precincts, there was one question in my heart. 'Would the Lord perform a miracle and give me a single room where I could pray in silence?' The Sister accompanying me spoke with the monk in charge of the guests, asking if I could have a single room. At first he objected to such a request, since the guest wing only provided mass accommodation. But then quite suddenly during the conversation the Lord gave him a change of heart and I was given a room for three where I could be alone. The heavenly Father had made this arrangement, thus confirming the summons to spend some weeks in seclusion at Mount Sinai. I was deeply touched by His love. From my room I had a view of Moses' Mountain, which greeted me every morning at dawn with a reddish hue in the sunlight.

In His goodness God had prepared yet another place where I could be alone in prayer – the flat roof of the house. There I could remain almost all the time undisturbed as I spent the day praying and writing. Giant-sized mountains towered above me on either side and in their hollow a wide desert plain stretched out before me to the west. This was the 'Raha Plain', which had witnessed a special act of God. The Israelites were encamped here when God made the covenant with them and gave them His laws on Mount Sinai.

Thus I was spared the noise and commotion within the monastic fortress. All my inner conflicts were silenced. Throughout the journey God's promises for it were fulfilled in actual events. In those days a strict time-honoured rule did not permit tourists to stay longer than three days in the monastery, but God overruled so that an exception was made in my case and I was granted permission from the highest authorities to extend my stay for several weeks. This was a further confirmation that God had called me to Mount Sinai.

We also experienced the grace of God and His provision in regard to our daily needs. It was quite a risk considering that no food could be bought there; we had no means of cooking, and nothing could keep long in the intense heat. Furthermore, we were unable to bring enough provisions with us to last for several weeks. Yet we were constantly surprised by God's loving care. One day a monk from Rephidim brought us magnificent grapes, and shortly after our arrival the monks in the monastery kindly allowed us to partake of their bread, although it was not customary. In addition, tourists left us the remains of their provisions and a bedouin brought us eggs and some meat. Every day the heavenly Father provided for us – and sometimes in the most marvellous ways.

The Lord paved the way, taking care of all the details, for He intended me to have an encounter with Him in the solitude of the wilderness such as I had never experienced before.

Mount Sinai – the holy mountain of God where He made a covenant of love with men, with His chosen people (Deuteronomy 5:2). Mount Sinai – the mountain where Moses was privileged to have a divine encounter and where God spoke with him. Mount Sinai – the mountain where God disclosed His will to His people and thus to the rest of mankind by giving them His Commandments. A mountain of divine revelation! How could I approach this holy site without having first undergone a year of preparation – of physical suffering and sickness, of severe inner conflict and much anguish of soul?

Within the first twelve days the Lord began to speak to me and the events of Mount Sinai became a present-day reality for me. My experience of Mount Sinai as the place where God gave His Commandments as the yardstick for our lives to show us where we sin and fall short of His standard marked the beginning of my stay. In the booklet, *Daily Texts**, the Scripture verse for October 13, 1963 – the first day of my stay – happened to be 'You shall love your neighbour as yourself' (Leviticus 19:18), and the text for that week in the Church year was 'And this commandment we have from him, that he who loves God should love his brother also' (1 John 4:21). Even though these commandments of God were so familiar to me, they now cut me to the quick as if I were reading them for the first time. From the depths of my heart I wept in repentance for all the times I had failed to keep these commandments and had not acted

* A well-known booklet published by the Moravian Church in Germany, containing Bible texts with hymn verses and prayers for every day in the year.

in love. Before I could ascend the holy mountain, Moses' Mountain, I knew I had to bring my sins to the Lord for the blood of the Lamb to wash them away. First of all I had to climb down in spirit – lower and lower – before the Lord could uplift me. This I did also on behalf of my daughters.

Then came the blessèd day when I was to ascend the mountain, and on that day, which happened to be my birthday, God poured out His grace upon me as I had seldom experienced before. The sun shone brightly, but it was not too hot. With its contours clearly outlined against the sky, Moses' Mountain was a strikingly beautiful sight at six o'clock in the morning as I rode a camel for the first stretch of the way to the summit. Deep joy and bliss welled up in my heart. It was as if the Lord was expecting me above where the little 'Chapel of Moses' stands, and I was eager to reach the summit to come to Him in prayer. When the camel ride was over, there was yet another three-quarters-of-an-hour to go, and in spite of my weakened heart condition, I fairly flew up the huge, steep, roughly hewn, granite 'Steps of Repentance' that led to the peak of Moses' Mountain.

Standing on the summit of this holy mountain of divine revelation, I could see a rolling sea of enormous mountains before me in their primeval splendour. I was overwhelmed by the majesty and glory of the sight: a ring of innumerable mountains surrounded the Mountain of Moses like huge giants. There the meaning of the name of the Lord 'Yahweh' was disclosed to me – 'I AM WHO I AM' (Exodus 3:14). And I experienced the truth of His words, 'I will make all my goodness pass before you' (Exodus 33:19). The Lord inclined Himself as the God who makes a covenant with a human soul, a sinner, for the blood of the Lamb washes away all sin.

That which the Lord now granted me on the top of Moses' Mountain was a reality. As a gift of His Spirit, who calls into existence the things that do not exist, He gave me a love that I had not known before. It was a love for the nations, which He had created to His glory, since love was the prerequisite for the new commission to the nations that

God intended to entrust to me.

He filled me with the spirit of compassion and pity for the nations of the world, which are facing collapse as the result of their disobedience to God's commandments. From then onwards I felt inwardly compelled to lift up the nations to Him in prayer daily so that souls might still be saved in this corrupt and sinful age. This newly awakened love made me zealous to do whatever I could for the nations – whatever the Lord showed me and whatever lay within my power. Above all, the lifeline of love – the commandments of God, which are given to save us from disaster – was to be thrown out to them.

The nations now had a place in my heart; I had to share their life, give myself for their sake, love them and suffer on their behalf. Without this experience I could not possibly have given my daughters for the sake of other nations, sending them out shortly afterwards to foreign countries, where they would be rejected, and their lives imperilled. On that day the Lord graciously equipped me to step in the breach for the nations of the world in a priestly fashion out of compassion for them – a momentous event for our commission. The Lord granted me yet another gift – the gift of faith for the vast ministry to the nations. Without this grace the burden would have weighed me down, since I was keenly aware of my utter helplessness and the impossibility of carrying out such a ministry.

The encounter with the Lord, however, was the most significant part of my experience on the summit of Moses' Mountain. God Himself was present. In that divine hour of grace He inclined Himself and then imparted a tremendous commission. As the Father's visible seal on all that had taken place, an impressive natural phenomenon crowned the events of that day. Late in the afternoon as I was three quarters of the way down the mountain, I paused again to rest on a projecting rock, when a magnificent rainbow formed a perfect arch over this spot, even though it had not rained. It was God's confirmation that the covenant had been made and the commission given. The events of Mount Sinai had become present-day occurrences for me. God had made all His goodness pass before me and revealed His nature to me, which is 'merciful and gracious, abounding in steadfast love and faithfulness'.

The day when I first ascended Moses' Mountain was the highlight of my stay, and many of the events of those weeks were associated with that momentous occasion. While I was alone in prayer, the Lord shed His light upon the seeming meaninglessness and struggles of the past years of my life, letting me see them in relationship to His eternal purposes and their marvellous goal.

Above all, the Father cast His light upon the future, indicating the further development of the Sisterhood and its commission. He inspired me to write down our rule – a number of texts expounding God's commandments as they appear in the Bible. These texts were given to help us to apply the commandments to the everyday situations of life, for which they were intended, to take them as more binding and to put them into practice in Christian discipleship. And how my daughters rejoiced to receive this little book, which has become so precious to them! In addition, I wrote the rule for our Sisters of Thorns (a group of women closely associated with us) and that which is known as the 'Canaan Commandments' for our Canaan Friends.* Later the Canaan Commandments were translated and published in various languages by friends in other parts of the world, and even broadcast as daily watchwords.

Only God could have foreseen that beginning with the following year the nations of the world would be more and more influenced by the spirit of lawlessness and the disregard for His commandments. In the latter half of the sixties the voices that had been disputing the validity of the commandments grew increasingly clamorous, so that even in Christian circles the commandments were more or less discarded. For this reason at Mount Sinai God stressed to me the urgency of proclaiming the glory and inviolability of His command-

* Men and women in Germany and abroad who wish to apply Canaan's spiritual guidelines in their respective walks of life.

ments, of letting this call resound throughout the world once more. It was to this end that He inspired me to write these texts expounding the biblical commandments.

Those days of grace at Mount Sinai when I received the vast commission from God and the 'Canaan Rule' were followed by a period of great affliction during which I suffered immeasurably because of the nations of the world. In spirit I could see them all heading towards disaster; the trials and affliction of the anti-Christian era were awaiting them. And through His Spirit God was calling my daughters to be a priestly host in such perilous times. One day some of them would have to be ready to launch out on their own, following dark avenues of faith and performing their ministry in our foreign branches even under the threat of war. Thus I had to experience beforehand the sacrifices this commission to the nations would entail.

Now the Lord was requiring more of me than the overcoming of my human weakness in this respect – that is, my natural concern for the well-being of the Sisters, most of whom were relatively young, and who would be faced with difficult enterprises in foreign surroundings, usually left to manage on their own. This was a battle of prayer on quite a different plane. As I wrote in my diary at the time:

I am already suffering the grief entailed in having posts abroad. God will give us these branches in the turmoil of the nations, which are growing increasingly antagonistic towards Christianity, and where my daughters will be exposed to the threat of persecution. I must undergo the pain beforehand. I can feel the grief of having to tear my daughters from my heart and sending them out alone into foreign countries.

This grief accompanied me wherever I went – whether I was on the flat roof, in my room or in the small Chapel of the Martyrs within the monastery fortress, or when I took a walk alone through the desert to Aaron's Hill, the place where the sin of the golden calf was committed.

Thus I came to associate Mount Sinai not only with great

blessing and joy but also with deep anguish and grief, which came to a head on November 8, 1963, an unforgettable day, when I had an encounter with the awesome God of Mount Sinai, who is a consuming Fire. As I was praying in the Chapel of the Martyrs, I was struck by the reality of the verse, 'It is a fearful thing to fall into the hands of the living God' (Hebrews 10:31). There I experienced how God in His holiness judges sinners, and in the presence of His divine majesty I shook and trembled. Before the great and almighty God, man is but a speck of dust. Thus I wrote in the chapel:

O God almighty, distant and holy,
Thou art eternal, a mighty Lord and King,
Veiled in fire, shrouded in mystery,
God of the heavens, whom none can ever see!
Thy divine eyes with lightning are flashing,
And man is cast far away from Thee.

Who can escape Thy terrible anger –
Thou who art distant, yet in wrath so near?
Who can approach Thy heart any longer
When fire alone is Thy dwelling here?
How my soul trembleth, O Lord, in terror!
Lord God – at Thy name, whole worlds disappear!

Yet at the same time I understood more fully the significance of the throne of grace: covered by the blood of Jesus Christ, we can enter the presence of the thrice holy God without being destroyed.

As those special days at Mount Sinai drew to a close, I made my last ascent to the summit of Moses' Mountain on November 13, 1963, the day before my departure.

Would the Lord seal the events of these weeks once more? – Indeed He did. On November 13, 1972 – the same day nine years later – a strange expedition set out from the foot of Moses' Mountain to a spot not far from where the mountainside begins to rise almost vertically and where Moses is reputed to have raised the boundary to enclose the holy mountain. The two camels must have looked on in amazement as two of my spiritual daughters, assisted by an Israeli guide and two bedouins, used a drill to mount a large plaque on the face of the mountain with some iron bolts and cement. It was our monument for Mount Sinai. Almost at the end of the camel path, in the vicinity where Moses must have begun his climb to the heights for an encounter with God, the plaque can be seen against the mountainside, with the peak towering high above it. The text reads as follows:

> The Lord our God
> made a covenant
> with us in Horeb. Deuteronomy 5:2

> Blessed are they
> whom God encounters here,
> to make the covenant of love
> with them,
> to unite Himself with them,
> to take them into His Heart and Being,
> on His path,
> the path of His commandments.

For years we had been praying that a visible sign could be raised for the Lord there – and for years this undertaking seemed to have been stamped as 'impossible'. Letters containing this request were turned down despite recommendations with the most imposing seals. The personal visits made by my daughters, friends, pilgrims or others who had taken up our cause met with the same result – every new attempt was frustrated. The door seemed to have been fastened securely with an iron bolt, which everyone assured us would be impossible to remove. But nine years later, once again on November 13, the day that I had ascended Moses' Mountain for the last time (for we know that God in His loving-kindness remembers the special dates in our lives), the door swung open miraculously.

All the arrangements seemed to have been made in heaven. The right people unexpectedly turned up to advise us about obtaining permission, and shortly afterwards permission was granted. Everything dovetailed beautifully. Our Sisters stationed in Jerusalem were able to make the journey. Willing hands assisted them in their task. And although our Sisters were not permitted to take any fuel with them for the drill as they boarded the aeroplane, the small amount they were able to procure upon arrival miraculously increased – a 'multiplication of the loaves' miracle! The project that had seemed utterly impossible in bygone years could now be accomplished with such ease that the Israeli guide who helped them commented, 'That was quite something! Strange, that no one came up with the idea before!' Indeed, the plaque's inscription about God's covenant with His chosen people may well touch a chord in their hearts.

The Lord not only sealed the events of those weeks at Mount Sinai with this plaque, but gave me the following verse of Scripture on that November 13, 1963, as a confirmation that it was He who had brought me there and spoken with me. 'You will be a witness for him to all men of what you have seen and heard' (Acts 22:15).

Travels Abroad – in Vain?

After my return from Mount Sinai I was faced with an altogether different situation from that which the Lord had shown me there for the ministry unto the nations. Canaan's commission seemed to be foundering. More libel had been published against us in the meanwhile and proved to be effective in that our literature was scarcely in demand any more. Our Herald Plays were not well attended. When the recipients of our newsletters were asked if they would like to continue receiving them, our mailing list was reduced to half its original size. Naturally, this turn of events had an effect on the donations made towards our ministry. Had the moment really come for the message of Canaan to go abroad into all the world?

Even amongst my daughters disappointments awaited me,

which surpassed all previous ones and caused Mother Martyria and me much anguish of heart. At Mount Sinai I had imagined what a joyful time we should have together when I returned home with all the spiritual blessings. From now on new festivals would be held in the Sisterhood at various times of the year. My daughters were to share in all the blessings that God had granted me. Even the Sisters serving in Jerusalem were to come home to the Mother House for Christmas so as to receive everything firsthand. But now that we were all together it turned out quite differently than I had expected. The gift received at Mount Sinai seemed to have been shattered, and all these disappointments cut keenly into my heart as I held the week-long 'Sinai Chapter' for my daughters after Christmas. Although I had thought that it would be the most wonderful festival time that we had ever had, I had to wring every word from my lips. It was night in my soul.

Apart from that, not only was I surrounded by adversaries without, but I was apparently forgotten by friends. It even seemed as though God, who had granted me such marvellous experiences at Mount Sinai, had enveloped Himself in silence. However, God was holding me in His hand and did not permit me to sink. He was at work in this situation. Although I was not aware of any tangible comfort at the time, His promises soon began to be fulfilled in real life, and the events spoke for themselves – the greatest sign of confirmation. During this new phase, which began in Lent 1964, I wrote:

> I am consumed with zeal, my ardent desire is to fill all the world with the call of the last times, the call to prepare oneself before the destruction of the world and the coming of Jesus.

The darkness of the midnight hour, which was beginning to fall upon the world, filled me with deep agony and made me yearn all the more for souls to be saved. In great spiritual anguish I began to write the book, *Und keiner wollte es glauben* (*Hope for Man in a Hopeless World*), which con-

313

veyed the message of Mount Sinai. It was based on the urgent call to turn back to God's commandments – a matter of life and death for every nation. With this book about God's commandments, the commission received at Mount Sinai began to materialise.

During the spring of 1964, quite unexpectedly, the call came from God to go to North America; the time was ripe. However, the idea seemed irrational to me, since we had only a few acquaintances in North America in those days. But God's thoughts are higher than ours. The Spirit continued to urge me to make this journey, charging me to carry out this commission of God. And as Mother Martyria and I prayed for a confirmation, we received the verse, 'You shall be my witnesses' (Acts 1:8).

Then in the following weeks God granted me a visible confirmation that a speaking tour of North America was to be the first phase of the commission unto the nations. Suddenly one American visitor after another called at our Mother House – something which had never occurred before. Without realising what had taken place, most of them suggested a visit to the United States, inviting me to speak at their church or fellowship. During the summer months of 1964 plans were drawn up for an eight-week speaking tour – a miracle before our eyes, since we were almost completely unknown in North America at that time. The Spirit of God was at work. I was set on fire for this commission as I expressed in my diary:

> The ardour of prayer is consuming me; my heart is filled with fervent entreaty for America.

Humanly speaking, this zeal was incomprehensible, for I could see no purpose in this commission. Not only did I feel inadequate for it, but I lacked the stamina.

Was I, then, to make long journeys in the following years of my life? Journeys to other countries and continents may be a life's dream for some, but for me they were a cross. We are given a cross, however, so that we may die to self. When I was in my late forties, in the prime of my life, I had gone into seclusion for Jesus' sake, but now when I was over sixty and my energy was spent, I had to make long, very strenuous journeys. Why? If the ministry was performed in human weakness, God alone would receive the credit for all that was accomplished.

In a state of great spiritual poverty and physical weakness I set out on my first journey to the nations, conscious of my inadequacy. Since I did not have a flair for languages and had only studied ancient languages at school and university, with the exception of a very brief course in English, it was impossible for me to deliver my lectures extemporaneously in English. But could I find interpreters who would translate in the right spirit? Furthermore, I did not feel equal to holding lectures in the many colleges and seminaries where the students were influenced by liberal theology, especially since I could not expect to find a good reception as a member of a religious order. Yet deep down in my heart I knew that all this was precisely God's intention, since He reveals Himself through the little ones, the incapable. It was fitting that this journey should be a dying process for me. Out of death, life was to flow like an invisible stream to others.

At the end of October in 1964 I set out for Canada and the United States. On this first journey to the nations I was to meet many disappointments. The audiences were usually not receptive to our message. Because our habit was strange for many, prejudice was evident, especially amongst evangelical Christians. Understandably, we also met with a certain amount of reserve, since we were Germans. In addition, the person who had arranged my speaking engagements for the tour in Canada proved unequal to the task, and some of the promises made about meetings turned out to be wishful thinking.

I was continually burdened with the dark atmosphere of the big cities where I had to hold lectures night after night. My speaking tour began in Toronto, Canada, and from there I went to the east coast of the United States and then across the country to the west coast. The engagements took me to New York, Washington D.C., Philadelphia, Baltimore,

Richmond (Virginia), Minneapolis, St Paul, Chicago, Dubuque (Iowa), San Francisco, Los Angeles . . .

My lectures were arranged for colleges of various denominations, for Lutheran, Presbyterian, Episcopalian and other Protestant churches as well as Roman Catholic ones. I was also expected to speak at ministers' conferences, youth rallies, in synagogues, at the Headquarters of the Union of American Hebrew Congregations, in Hebrew Christian fellowships, at deaconess houses, at retreat centres and in abbeys, as well as at prayer breakfasts, a 'Christian fashion show' and television interviews . . .

There was no pause between the speaking engagements – partly due to inexperience in planning the schedule, and partly due to the additional requests that we received daily en route. Owing to the medley of impressions created by the earlier items on the evening programme, the listeners were somewhat distracted, and thus it was often a struggle to bring the message across. In addition, it was reduced to half its length owing to the translation. In many places, the audience only expected to hear a brief word at the close of the evening rather than a long spiritual address. This was customary in the United States, but we were not aware of the circumstances beforehand. Consequently, during the talks there was not enough time for people's hearts to become still, attentive and responsive to God. There was little chance for unfolding the message or for the listeners to give the Lord their response.

Often I wondered if the message had come across. The grateful responses that reached me after the lectures were most heartwarming, but the voices of inner conflict within me were louder still. Utterly exhausted and perpetually faced with the meaninglessness of this commission, I often told myself it would have made more sense if my spiritual daughters had made these speaking tours, since they were younger, had more strength, and were proficient in the language with no need of an interpreter. At the time, owing to my heart condition, I usually felt so weak that I could scarcely collect my thoughts when I had to speak, but on every occasion the Lord concealed this from the listeners.

Yet there were some immediate results of the journey. In the United States our literature was readily accepted. Quite a large venture of faith had been involved, for in those days we did not yet have a publishing house in America. Apart from a few books that had been published in Britain, there was a number of poorly translated manuscripts which were printed on Canaan and then shipped in advance in large quantities to various places throughout North America. We had taken this step despite the discouraging comments made by some of our American visitors who declared that there would be little demand for this sort of literature in the States; in view of the expenses, this undertaking almost amounted to folly. But when we saw the great interest shown in the literature, we were glad we had made this venture of faith.

In the big cities I had a special burden on my heart to carry out the commission that God had given me at Mount Sinai. Strongly aware of the atmosphere, I wrote in my diary at the time, 'Darkness is covering the nations and cities. God has been ousted. A high standard of living is all that matters.' At the end of each day I felt that I had achieved little, and it could scarcely be said that our message was widely accepted. In the midst of all the disappointments of this journey I was encouraged by the love expressed in Mother Martyria's letters as she shared all the burdens.

It was a sad journey home, for I felt that I had served the Lord Jesus poorly. My heart was heavy laden. But on the way I asked the Lord in prayer to give me a Bible verse for the events of the past few weeks. And once again it was Genesis 46:3 – 'I am God, the God of your father; do not be afraid to go down to Egypt; for I will there make of you a great nation' – the verse I had received twice before for the journey to North America. How overwhelmed I was, for it was also the same verse that I had received for the stay at Mount Sinai – the place where I had been given the commission unto the nations.

' . . . make of you a great nation'? But how? By laying

317

the foundation with suffering and 'death'. In those days I could not have possibly foreseen that which now has become a reality before my eyes. A branch has actually been established in Phoenix, Arizona called 'Canaan in the Desert'. Retreats are now held on Canaan in Germany for guests from the English-speaking world, and year after year Americans have flown across the ocean to experience life on Canaan for a couple of weeks, then taking the message back to America.

Nor did I suspect at the time that an American publishing house would soon open up for my literature so that countless numbers of people could be reached by the message. A second publishing house followed, which was very diligent, once producing as many as six books in a year. We literally experienced that when God begins to reward, He does so abundantly – as I had discovered during the time following my critical illness. Should anyone be unacquainted with the heart of God, he could come to know His goodness by simply considering such facts. At times God appears to treat His own harshly, but only because He wants to reward them with an even greater outpouring of His love, after He has achieved His objective with them.

Who would have thought that our booklets dealing with current issues would be distributed by the thousand at American universities and also at a large international student conference in the States? Who would have imagined that American radio stations would broadcast the message and songs of Canaan for millions of listeners and that our song book, *Freudenquell Jesus* (*Well-spring of Joy*), would be printed in English and that its songs would be sung in many parts of the country? Little did I realise that a few years later two of the first members of our Canaan Franciscan Brotherhood would come from America, and that Sisters would come from America and Canada, who in turn would work untiringly on translations and radio programmes for their countries.

An American lady speaking at our Festival of Love for Jesus, which was held on Canaan, said, 'There are about twenty-five or thirty of us here from the United States, but we represent many hundreds, who had longed to be with you here today on Canaan. Through the visits of the dear Mothers in the States and through the many published books, the song of Canaan is being sung in our country from coast to coast . . . In really a very few years the Canaan commission, which is a new way – and yet a very old way, because it is the way of Jesus – has been brought to us in America.'

Even in Canada, where everything had seemed especially meaningless during my journey, the seed sprouted most wonderfully years later. A letter we received from my spiritual daughters while they were on a two-week speaking tour in Canada read as follows: 'We have reached about 4,500 people; 2,500 books and 10,000 booklets and leaflets have been distributed, and more literature had to be sent by special delivery, since we ran out of supplies.'

In retrospect I can only praise God for fulfilling this commission so marvellously after all those years. The seeds sown in hidden dedications, in acts of obedience and faith during travels in response to a call from God will one day bring forth fruit as a blessing for the country concerned. Meaningless paths taken in obedience to God have the greatest significance. Down through the years I have experienced the truth of this divine law.

Thus ever anew I brought my dedications to the Lord before each journey I made in the following years.

Gladly for You, dear Lord,
I'll follow where You will,
Whate'er You ask I'll do,
And never rest until
Your work is all completed.

Gladly for You, dear Lord,
Whate'er the cost may be,
My heart and will I give,
For You are all to me,
I give You all I treasure.*

* *Well-spring of Joy*, No. 229.

319

How could the message of repentance as the gateway to heaven be brought to countries that had suffered immeasurably as a result of the crime of our nation during the years of 1939–45 – countries that moreover lay behind the Iron Curtain? How could we proclaim the significance of God's commandments and the fact that we had embarked on a new era, the end times? How could we share with them about Jesus' suffering today, about the joy that comes from loving Him and about His glory? God knew. Ever since my stay at Mount Sinai I had been cherishing a plan in my heart to visit countries such as Poland and Czechoslovakia for the purpose of humbling myself beneath our grave national crime whenever the Lord gave me the opportunity, as I had done in Israel.

However, I was concerned that I should have the support of not only Mother Martyria and the Sisters, but also our Canaan Friends when I made this journey as a representative of many Christians in our country. Therefore, I wrote a prayer letter to our Canaan Friends with this request.

How can we enter these countries with this heavy burden of our national crime without opening up wounds when the people see us as representatives of the nation that had inflicted such terror and misery upon them? Only if we weep over that which we have done, can we reach their hearts. Only if we come to them in an attitude of contrition, will our proclamation of the Word of God be believed . . . We could never make amends if we failed to bring the comfort and aid of the gospel to those who were not only victims of the last world war, but who are now exposed to new hardships. We entreat you most earnestly to accompany us on this journey with your prayers. Pray that God may be moved by our contrition and grant forgiveness for the serious crime of our people – the terrible bloodbath of defenceless women and children, of the Polish and Jewish intelligentsia . . . We could not presume to enter these countries with the message entrusted to us if God had not charged us with this commission, but we shall not be able to carry it out unless we have your prayer support!

Kanaan-Ruf No. 35 (*Call from Canaan*)

Thus it was inevitable that this journey too should bear the imprint of suffering and the cross and be a dying process. At that time it was well nigh impossible for a German citizen – not to mention a member of a religious order wearing a habit – to receive a visa for these countries. However, when streaks of lightning flashed across the political sky, indicating the outbreak of war, the long-awaited visas for Poland and Czechoslovakia came. The arrival of the visas was a clear sign from the Lord to make the journey in spite of the threat of war. And on June 5, 1967, one hour after a Sister and I had crossed the Czech border, war broke out in Israel. Now I was behind the Iron Curtain, cut off from the Mother House for a number of weeks and unable to obtain any news from there about action on the front or about the fate of many close friends in Israel. I could not even find out whether my daughters in Israel were still alive. The suspense was very hard to bear; yet I wished to underlay my journey with this sacrifice in particular, for how many people in these countries did not know the fate of their dear ones for a long time, if ever, because of what we Germans had done during the last world war.

Seldom had I encountered such futility in a ministry as during this journey. Meaninglessness stared me in the face. The groups that I met were very small – smaller than usual owing to the critical political situation – and there was little sign of spiritual life. Understandably so, my views about Israel were not appreciated; they endangered us even more. The only large speaking engagement that had been planned was for a few hundred Roman Catholic nuns, who were looking forward to the meeting expectantly. However, due to an oversight on the part of the organiser the Sisters waited for me on the wrong day. Since I did not learn about this until afterwards, the meeting failed to take place. All I could do was to reply, 'My Father, I do not understand You, but I trust You', and to rededicate myself to the will of God hour by hour. In addition, I had seldom been so exhausted as during those weeks, and it was only with great effort that I could stand upright. I felt forsaken by God and man.

At every turn I was confronted with unforgiven sin, the bloodguiltiness of our nation – mass graves, memorials speaking of guilt, places reminding of gruesome events, the frightening statistics, the personal testimonies of survivors who had suffered torture during the Nazi regime; the death-rolls that included whole families. Wherever I went, there were wounds that were still smarting.

If God in His great mercy had not taken us along the path of contrition and repentance ever since the time of the revival and the foundation of the Sisterhood of Mary, I could never have made this painful journey to these sorely-stricken people. It was truly the grace of God that I had discovered the secret of the all-transforming power of re-pentance through the recognition of personal sin against God and man. This in turn led me to see our guilt as a nation towards Israel and our neighbouring countries. And now as I visited the sites where atrocities had been com-mitted and met survivors of that era, I could witness the power of repentance once more. Heartfelt repentance turned deep-rooted bitterness into forgiveness. Our grief and con-trition were like balm on the wounds of others. Many eyes were filled with tears, but this time because people were moved to see us humble ourselves at special sites com-memorating our national crime. At some places we were able to lay down tokens of our grief, with texts such as the following:

Have mercy upon us, O God.
Deliver us from bloodguiltiness.
Psalm 51

In deep shame and grief we remember all the victims who suffered and died here in torment at the hands of the German people.

The Evangelical Sisterhood of Mary

At the medieval synagogues in Prague that are only visited as museums nowadays, I was deeply touched when the Jewish guardians gathered round me to hear my opinion about the situation in Israel. It was evident that a new spark of hope had been kindled in their hearts.

We visited the sites of the Warsaw Ghetto, the former prison of Paviak, and Auschwitz; and in the former concentration camp at Theresienstadt and in Lidice (the site of a village wiped out by our German people) I met the head officials, who were moved by the purpose of our visit. As in Auschwitz they put our tokens of atonement in their museums at places where thousands of visitors pass by.

On my return journey I was met at the border by Mother Martyria, who had come to give me immediate news of the situation in Israel. The Six Day War was over, and our Sisters in Jerusalem were all alive. Both houses were still standing. However, our Sisters living on the Mount of Olives narrowly escaped death when their house was hit; a shell landed directly above them in a trunk filled with blankets, and thus the disastrous effects were lessened. Before my journey I had written a letter to our Israeli friends, drawing their attenion to God's promises for His people and the letter arrived in time to bring comfort to many. On the first night of the war, school children serving as postmen delivered the letters despite the barrage. Only he who has surrendered everything to God in weeks of complete uncertainty knows the joy when God the Father returns the sacrifice.

After some years the seeds that had been sown during this journey began to germinate. A lecture that I had held in Freiburg for Roman Catholic superiors was reprinted in a magazine behind the Iron Curtain with a wide circulation in the convents, thus more than compensating for the meeting that had failed to materialise during my journey. As long as the borders were open, many friends came to visit us. Canaan has become a spiritual home and a place of renewal for many.

God had greatly impressed upon Mother Martyria and me the seriousness of our national crime, and accordingly, further journeys ensued. Later our Sisters were able to erect plaques of atonement at places especially stained by our national crime. Such plaques expressing our grief were mounted in Denmark, Norway, Finland, Yugoslavia and Greece as well as at former Nazi concentration camps, and these small tokens have had their effect.

Such was the case in Karasjok, northern Norway, in the territory known as 'the scorched earth district' where only the old church was left standing after the German occupation forces destroyed the whole region as they retreated in 1944. At the ceremony for the dedication of the plaque it was said, 'We promised to give the plaque a worthy place, and could think of none better than next to the old church. Here we ourselves have received forgiveness and here we wish to stand with our brothers and sisters in the light of love that comes from heaven.' Articles about the ceremony with photographs of the Bishop and other personages present, as well as accounts and pictures of our Sisters' visit there were printed in the major Christian and secular newspapers of Norway as an expression of reconciliation. All this helped towards further reconciliation.

At Mount Sinai when I wrote down the Canaan Rule, little did I realise that one of these short texts would be also significant for our relationship to nations against whom we had sinned.

Be reconciled! Do not be estranged from anyone!
If there are feelings of ill will, go to the
other person – and let love be victorious.

Indeed, my experience at Mount Sinai was followed by one journey after the other to various countries to which I was invited. For instance, a bishop from the Church of South India who had once spent three hours on Canaan was the main initiator and promoter for a visit to India. Thus in 1969 I set out for India together with a Sister who also acted as my interpreter, and once again I found myself visiting Protestant and Roman Catholic colleges and seminaries. Other meetings were arranged where I reached hundreds of divinity students, ministers and church workers, college girls and women, members of Christian communities and even thousands of Hindus.

Months before my visit this bishop had organised a large prayer campaign; he was expecting great things of God. In order to bring the message to the leading men of the city, including the mayor who was a Hindu, he arranged a public reception for the day I arrived. And God acted according to his faith; over a thousand people, a good percentage of whom was Hindu, filled the hall for this reception, which had come as a complete surprise to me. Not only did God give me a message for this occasion, but like a miracle, my book, *Immer ist Gott grösser* (*God Is Always Greater*) in Tamil – the local Indian language – had just been published and was ready for distribution amongst the people, who reached out for it eagerly.

Apart from services of worship and various speaking engagements, the bishop planned a large open-air meeting. Owing to the excellent organisation the smallest detail was taken care of. Two thousand chairs had been placed on the grounds, which were floodlit with many neon lights; an extensive loud-speaker system had been set up. Throughout the town posters had invited the people. When the evening came, three thousand turned up, and half the number was non-Christian, much to the joy of the Christians; at the end of the meeting three hundred, including many Hindus, came forward as a public testimony of their decision to give their lives to Jesus, the crucified Lord, and to renounce sin and Satan. They were overflowing with joy and gratitude. The spiritual hunger of these Indians, the childlike radiance of the women who wished to be blessed, and the simplicity of the young people, who were so unsophisticated, was most refreshing.

The heavenly Father had blessed our finances before the journey and friends filled our hands with gifts of money to help in a material way where the need was the greatest. During my stay, the bishop's wife, who was especially devoted to the cause of the homeless widows, seeking to ease the hard conditions of women in distress, insisted, together with her husband, that as a patron I should lay the foundation stone for their 'Aged Women's Home'.

My experiences in this district of India were deeply moving in many respects. Above all, I could see the blessing that ensues when Jesus' last request 'that they may all be one' is followed. The spiritual receptiveness in this area was no coincidence. Previously, there had been much quarrelling – even amongst church workers. But now there was an atmosphere of love, true fellowship and oneness everywhere – as I noticed from the very first moment when about forty people – ministers, church workers and their wives – met me at the airport. Here the ground had been prepared not only by the great efforts and excellent organisation of the Christians, but by their life of reconciliation, and thus God was able to use them to call the heathen to Himself. Furthermore, it was an encouragement and a privilege to see that the commission God had given me at Mount Sinai met with such openness.

Apart from that, my stay in India was a most exhausting time – partly due to the intense heat – and often I scarcely knew what to say when I had to give a talk. Moreover, the grief of God over this vast land went to my heart, and I was drawn into His suffering. I was deeply distressed to see the poverty and the pagan idolatry. But the most painful experience was that of seeing how disunity, indifference and the influence of liberal theology prevented many Christians from being the salt and light for their pagan environment.

Yet in retrospect, it is all the more wonderful to me that a number of keen, influential Indian Christians have become Canaan Friends. They long to live in daily contrition and repentance, in reconciliation and bridal love for Jesus and are working zealously to spread this message in their country. From that time onwards my books and smaller writings as well as our Canaan Commandments have been translated and published in the Indian languages of Telugu, Tamil and Malayalam; Hindi and Kanarese followed – and the work continues. Since our English radio programmes have been broadcast in Eastern Asia, we have received many warm responses from both Christians and non-Christians in India – perhaps more than from anywhere else – and now broadcasts in Indian languages have begun.

The Moral Landslide – Mount Sinai Begins to Quake

In the mid-sixties the Satanic age began – according to a statement made by the 'Black Pope', the founder of the Church of Satan in the United States. It was like the bursting of a dam; a wave of demonism deluged the nations. Riotous living and the uninhibited gratification of carnal desires became the ideal of many. The mass media ruined the moral standards of millions; television and radio programmes – sometimes under the guise of art, research or education – gave lucid instructions in brutality, murder and sexual perversions, and promoted a callous disregard for unborn human life.

Evil practices, previously limited to the fringe of society and severely punished, could now assert themselves openly and were even encouraged and acclaimed. Qualms of conscience were treated as a symptom of unhealthy inhibition. Governed by his impulses, man was no longer held responsible for his deeds and was released from all restrictions and divine standards of right and wrong. Scientists, lawyers, doctors and theologians declared that law and justice must be adapted to the change in society's views on ethics, and with that, the moral landslide could no longer be held back. An avalanche had started to roll – the most terrible one of all, since it was the avalanche of sin. Men, even whole nations would be buried beneath it, for sin is a destructive force that inevitably leads people into ruin – as it soon became apparent.

I could almost feel a cry of despair rising in me. A generation of criminals would be raised. Soon the life of men and nations would be stamped by violence and crime, by physical and mental diseases caused by sin. In many cases people would end up with ruined personalities, bearing the seal of death.

The avalanche of sin, which had reached staggering proportions and was gathering force as it hurtled down the mountainside, filled me with anguish, and weeping inwardly I lamented. Sin! this fatal disease has infected men and nations. Sin! that destroys all joy, disrupts all peace. Sin! with its corruptive influence on the younger generation. Sin! that affects normally active, energetic and creative young people, making them apathetic and disillusioned, turning them into vegetating idlers, parasites, and even causing them to sink to the level of criminals. Sin! that wreaks havoc. Sin! that is fomented by Satan, who has but one goal: to ruin and annihilate the lives of persons, entire nations and the world!

For my personal life I came to see as never before the terrible nature of sin during the years following my stay at Mount Sinai. This became evident to me, for instance, as I reread one of my first books, . . . *er kämpfe denn recht*, which I had written years before as a spiritual aid for the battle of faith against sin. As I reviewed it now, I was struck by the book's lack of true effectiveness. After having comprehended more of the vileness of sin, of the power of Satan and the torment of hell, I knew that the book had to be rewritten.

It is imperative that we live in the presence of the holiness

328

of God, as I came to realise in greater depth after my experience at Mount Sinai. Sin inevitably provokes the wrath of God, and this is why Jesus had to undergo such terrible torment to make atonement for our sins. With greater perception I realised the gravity of our sinning in God's eyes especially since Jesus had suffered an agonising death in propitiation for our sins. Now I understood better why Jesus demands that we take such drastic measures against sin in the power of His redemption. He says, 'If your right eye causes you to sin, pluck it out . . . it is better that you lose one of your members than that your whole body be thrown into hell!' (Matthew 5:29).

He knows that sin brings hell upon earth and that after this transient life sin will condemn souls to the kingdom of darkness, a real place, 'where their worm does not die, and the fire is not quenched' (Mark 9:48), where they must undergo the 'second death' – continually dying without ever attaining death. Because Jesus loves us, He makes frequent reference to the terrors of hell and warns us against glossing over sin.

Thus at a time when the commandments of God were being dissolved, I wrote a new book entitled *So wird man anders* (*You Will Never Be the Same*) to replace . . . *er kämpfe denn recht*. The agony God suffers because of man's wickedness and the terrible consequences of sin for time and eternity – both were a constant source of grief to me, boring deep into my heart. Often I felt I could not hear any more about the perversions, because it filled me with such anguish that man, who had been created in the image of God, was sinking further and further into the quicksand of iniquity, immersed in filth, hatred and hideous vices.

Over the course of the years when I thought of the young people, I lamented even more. The young and mighty have been slain and are lying in the dust – but not as heroes who gave their lives to save their country. They died as the victims of lust, of alcoholism and drug addiction, having poisoned themselves. Satan and sin had led them down the path of destruction, ruined their personalities, driven them insane, made them physically and mentally ill, turned them into criminals and hounded them to death by the million.

Like the Prophet Jeremiah I learnt to mourn and cry out, 'Is there no balm in Gilead? Is there no physician there? Why then has the health of the daughter [and son] of my people not been restored?' (Jeremiah 8:22). Yet balm was available – in the Person of the Lord Jesus. But where were the people who would bring Him to the younger generation? Where were those who wept and lamented in deep anguish and sorrow over the fate of our young people? Where were the Christians who came together and called upon the Lord for intervention and sought ways of saving souls in view of the staggering increase in drug addiction?

Ever since this new era commenced, I asked myself daily, 'What can I do so that more souls can be saved?' I asked God to show me how I could prove my love for Him at this critical moment. I prayed that He would lead me to others who had the same burden, who shared the immeasurable grief of God over our nation and our young people, and who would thus be prepared to give their utmost for souls to be saved.

In the autumn of 1964 I had written an article about the terrible moral landslide for the first issue of our annual journal, . . . *in alle Welt* (. . . *into all the world*). This article resulted in a handbill with the challenge *What Can We Do?* We began to print leaflets and distributed them as a warning in front of cinemas that were showing obscene films. Two atrocious films, *The Silence* and *491*, were the main impetus for a tract called *Stop!* as well as for an *Open Letter* that private individuals and others could use to collect signatures and then submit them to influential personages and organisations.

Early every morning in the Sisterhood we came together for a special time of prayer, and many friends joined in doing the same. We used the *Prayer for Our Time of Distress*, which had been compiled from prayers I had written as early as 1962. It proved to be highly relevant and only needed to be altered slightly in view of the latest facts.

Now, in the autumn of 1964, Mother Martyria and I approached all the Christian women's organisations in the country with the request to seek joint ways of stemming the tide of filth. The Lord guided us in a wonderful way; one thing led to another. The 'White Cross', a group that deals with Christian ethics in the sexual context and does spiritual counselling in this field, sent us an invitation to a convention that was being held on this topic. Contact was made with other groups who were alarmed at recent developments. During a tour of Bavaria and northern Germany where we performed one of our Herald Plays, we collected signatures for our *Open Letter*, and Canaan Friends in other parts of the country contributed their efforts. Thus altogether 50,000 signatures were collected and the following spring they were sent off to the President of our nation.

These various undertakings led to a meeting that was held in our retreat house 'Jesus' Joy' at the beginning of December 1964 while I was still on my speaking tour in North America. Mother Martyria had invited a number of people in leading positions and other interested personages to attend, some of whom then formed the movement *Sorge um Deutschland* (*Concern for Germany*). They considered it their responsibility not only to gather pertinent information and make it available to the public, but to perform the priestly ministry of prayer and the ministry of warning. For instance, the executive committee of this organisation sent the book, *Und keiner wollte es glauben* (*Hope for Man in a Hopeless World*), to all the Protestant bishops in our country as 'a beacon in the fog of this day and age', and decided to have it circulated as widely as possible, since it helped many to see Satan's secret strategy exposed in the light of God.

Using our *Open Letter* as a basis, the executive committee drew up an appeal and sent it to prominent men and women, requesting their endorsement, and some of them – including church dignitaries – expressed their willingness to do so. This appeal, entitled *Sorge um Deutschland* (*Concern for Germany*), was then distributed in large quantities and a press conference was held so that the entire nation could hear the warning before it was too late:

> ... Disregard for the will of God has led to the present situation where all moral norms are being discarded ... Peril calls for the rallying of all those who have a sense of responsibility. The tide must be stemmed; a dike must be built. And people living in obedience to God can form this dam! It is imperative that we use every means at our disposal before it is too late to curb the powers of destruction that are ruining our people ... In the words of Scripture we are given the eternally valid standards of good and evil – the commandments of God – which shine forth in the fog and confusion of our times ... When people receive daily orientation from the Word of God, there will be light and renewal ... May everyone who longs for the renewal of our nation join us in the movement *Concern for Germany* ...

Within a few short weeks we received thousands of signatures in response to this appeal. The movement *Concern for Germany* spread. Part-time volunteers and later – owing to the mounting work – full-time co-workers offered their services. Circular letters were sent out, appeals were written on specific topics and evening lectures were given. Conferences of groups with similar aims were attended and a convocation for doctors was arranged. On Canaan we held retreats with Bible studies about priestly intercession and stepping in the breach on behalf of the nation and the Church for all those who were connected with the movement and interested in coming. Yet in view of the widespread rebellion against God and His commandments I also felt that we should have a special time of worship in the Herald Chapel, open to the public, so that the name of God the Father, Son and Holy Spirit could be magnified before the visible and invisible world. This form of 'testimony service' was held on Canaan and in various cities. Moreover, prayer groups for *Concern for Germany* were formed in many places throughout the country.

True, it could not be said that there were evident signs of success, since the situation was far too advanced – the end times had begun and the powers of darkness were exerting a strong influence. Yet it is certain that the distribution of the leaflets, handbills and posters against immoral films and sex fairs and above all the many prayer battles were not in vain. Every prayer, sacrifice and effort that is made helps to check the advance of the forces of evil and the power of sin, and to put people on the alert.

But there was no way of holding back the avalanche as a whole. Sin would soon be heaped as high as the heavens, provoking God to send judgement upon the world such as it had never seen before. The era of the anguished wrath of God was approaching. Soon God would be confronted with sin wherever He turned His eyes. God is Love. Yet in His holy wrath and anguish He would be forced to answer with consuming fire and death-bringing judgement. All this I could visualise in spirit.

Figuratively speaking, we, mankind, have undermined Mount Sinai, the symbol of God's commandments and shall soon cause it to tumble down. A British theologian said, 'The sanctions of Sinai have lost their terrors.' But God is holy. Even in those days I realised that as soon as man no longer respected God and His commandments, Mount Sinai would come crashing down, burying us alive. Yet what could be harder or more painful for God than to have to judge men and to vent His rage upon them, since they refused to heed the admonition of His Spirit!

One day words of lamentation flowed from my pen as an expression of the grief that filled my heart:

O the immeasurable sorrow of God! The time is drawing near when God, who loved the world so much that He gave His only-begotten Son as a sacrifice, will be forced to strike the world with thunderbolts of judgement and devastation, bringing death to millions. The divine heart of eternal Love is rent asunder when He is forced to be wrathful. No longer is He permitted to be gracious and merciful. He has no other choice but to hurl His wrath like streaks of lightning upon the world He created.

How foreign is this act to the Godhead! Once before God had to judge the world by sending the Great Flood and, so to speak, deny Himself, for He is the God of love and mercy. Yet God cannot be angry for long, for His heart breaks with sheer compassion. As a symbol of His grace He caused a rainbow to form an arch over the earth.

But now we are living in the last times; the world has become a Babylon of sin and the spirit of mutiny in the hearts of millions of people cries aloud to God in heaven. Oh, He who is the essence of love is forced to answer with unequalled wrath; He who desires to preserve life must destroy it, and He who delights in showing goodness to His children can do so no longer. He is compelled to send them affliction, agony and death.

The fields will no longer yield fruit, although God in His love had created them for this purpose. The forests will no longer delight us, providing us with shade and wood, since they will exist no more. The grass, which will be contaminated, will no longer provide fodder for the cattle; houses and cities that should provide dwelling places for people will be destroyed. The stench of putrefying corpses will fill the air. Terror and death will reign, because sin had reigned over the earth.

O worship the stern love of God. He inflicts the greatest suffering upon Himself when He is wrathful and metes out judgement. Yet He does so in order that through judgement a new world and a new generation will rise.

The hour of deepest anguish for the eternal God has now drawn near. Who stands by Him and shares His burden? Who bears the agony of God in his heart and consents to the judgement and affliction? God is searching for a soul who can fathom the depths of His anguish today – and a childlike soul who loves the Father would comprehend His grief.

The time has come when God is suffering great anguish.

Do not ignore this suffering, which surpasses all other grief. It is the Father who is suffering. It is your Father who is in such great agony.

In spirit I had a foretaste of the judgement of God upon our world, which would be incurred by the flagrant sinning of mankind. Indeed, God has no other choice but to execute terrible punishment so that sin will not hold sway over the earth for ever. As of old when God responded with a lament to Isaiah's question, 'Why is thy apparel red, and thy garments like his that treads in the wine press?' – I felt as though He were lamenting over our world today. 'I have trodden the wine press alone . . . I trod them in my anger and trampled them in my wrath' (Isaiah 63:2f.). And in this context the Lord asked who would stand by Him. 'The Lord saw it, and it displeased him that there was no justice. He saw that there was no man, and wondered that there was no one to intervene; then his own arm brought him victory, and his righteousness upheld him' (Isaiah 59:15b, 16). To stand by Him was my fervent longing, and He gave me opportunity to do so.

The tidal wave of lawlessness and sin constantly invaded more territory, so that the movement *Concern for Germany* was faced with a changing situation.

The age of student riots had begun in the meantime. Thus the *Concern for Germany* movement saw its main task in giving biblical orientation to young people in schools and universities, since they were exposed to this spiritual warfare. The first youth rallies within the framework of the movement were held on Canaan and it was amazing to see how many came and what effect the meetings had on these young people. Soon the youth conferences had increased so much that they could no longer be accommodated at our retreat centre owing to our tightly-packed schedule and many other commitments. Then the Lord graciously opened another door. The executive secretary of *Concern for Germany*, whom God had given a special burden for these young people, was clearly led to take over this ministry independently under the name of *Offensive Junger Christen* (*Young Christians on the Offensive*). The way was paved and he was able to continue the ministry in a new centre that he opened in Bensheim on the Bergstrasse.

Thus in 1969 the *Concern for Germany* movement developed into the *Young Christians on the Offensive* – a centre to help young people find the way to Christian discipleship, and Canaan, together with the Canaan Friends, continued to give prayer support for this ministry, backing it with our literature. At all times our priestly responsibility as Christians in today's world has remained at the heart of Canaan's ministry in these last times.

The moral landslide continued to develop. If God was grieved to His heart in the days of Noah (Genesis 6:6), His anguish must be all the greater now, especially since apostasy is rife in His Church, the House of God. The 'death-of-God' theology had been proclaimed, and was propagated at the large German *Kirchentage*. In 1965 when I read the study papers for the rally at Cologne, I wrote, 'The *Kirchentag* will be a rostrum for Satan.' Should we go all the same and perform our Herald Plays as we had done in previous years? It was heartbreaking to think of the thousands of Christians who flocked to the *Kirchentag* filled with spiritual hunger and great expectations, many of them not realising what they would be offered. And God gave us the inner assurance that we should carry out our Herald Play ministry there once more.

When we were in Cologne, Mother Martyria and I were very perturbed to see how the young people, who were present at the sessions in large numbers, were offered freedom from all restrictions. Sins that according to Holy Scripture will be judged and punished by God were no longer considered sins. Sexual permissiveness was condoned and God's commandments were diluted. Symptomatic of this trend, the programme for one evening was devoted to the readings of Berthold Brecht, during which a woman sang persuasively, 'How sweet is sin'. As an expression of our grief, we rose and left the hall.

This evening programme was an indication that Satan's entry into the Protestant Church was not only tolerated by Christians but even welcomed and acclaimed. Thus Dorothee Soelle gained her first applause at this *Kirchentag* with her 'death-of-God' theology. Later when we returned home, I told the Sisters everything that had happened, adding that in Cologne I could almost hear the death knell tolling for the Protestant Church. I was seized with a burning ardour to pray and filled with immeasurable grief. In my diary I wrote:

> Night has fallen. Instead of proclaiming Jesus, one introduces notions inspired by Satan. My heart is filled with anguish and lamentation over the pain inflicted upon Jesus. Apostasy has begun on a large scale, and after a number of years judgement will descend, since people refuse to listen. They prefer sin and lead the younger generation astray together with all who lack discernment.

I had but one yearning – that the trumpet be sounded in warning. Although it was clear to me that we could never participate in another *Kirchentag*, merely staying away was insufficient. Accordingly, I wrote a newsletter under the heading, 'An Answer to the German Protestant Kirchentag in Cologne', followed by a booklet about the dangers of false brotherly love, entitled *Mitmenschlichkeit*. Later, seeing that the Protestant Church was continuing to move in this direction, I felt urged to write more on this subject. Thus in 1970, although it cost me many a spiritual battle, I wrote the booklet, *Zum erstenmal seitdem es Kirche Jesu Christi gibt (Never Before in the History of the Church)*, elucidating this trend from the biblical perspective.

How grateful I was to God that such booklets could serve as beacons amid the deceptive lights of our present age. In all this suffering it was comforting to be able to bring God's light and truth to people who had been led astray, and to have the privilege of serving Him this way, not heeding the battle that ensued. Moreover, it was my fervent plea that this literature would help those who love God to raise their voices in lamentation. 'The living, eternal God, our Maker, by whom the world was created, the Giver and Sustainer of all life, is being declared dead! And man, having turned his back on God, the very essence of life, will be spiritually dead as a result, dead in sin.'

In the Garden of Gethsemane Jesus was abandoned by His disciples to combat the raging powers of darkness alone. Realising that Jesus was undergoing another Gethsemane experience today, I wrote a prayer entitled *Jesus Forsaken Once More* to help us to stand by Him in His suffering. In the Sisterhood we set aside special evenings for this prayer, when we sought to express our love in word and song, to humble ourselves and to bring Him comfort. Friends and retreat guests who had participated in such evenings on Canaan continued to pray in this way at home.

Lord Jesus,
We long to raise our voices in lamentation over Your suffering today. Your Church, which is commissioned to bear witness to the gospel, is becoming a place for discussion; believers are turning into revolutionaries; those who used to pray are becoming rebels; and people are exchanging their love of God for false brotherly love ...

Let us rise, Lord, from our slumber,
And with tears make supplication.
Let us bring our hearts' devotion
To relieve Thy bitter sorrow.
Let us sacrifice with zeal,
In disgrace beside Thee kneel.
Now to Thee my life I offer
As a sacrifice for ever.

Yet we were to become more acquainted with this theology through personal contact with one of its adherents. Our spiritual Father, Pastor Riedinger, said the last time he blessed me that the Sisterhood would never have another spiritual Father. This was the Lord's guidance for us.

338

Yet it became necessary to have a minister on Canaan to hold our Sunday services of worship and to counsel male guests, and above all, a theologian was essential for the movement *Concern for Germany*. A minister friend of ours was willing to come. We knew that he had studied under a well-known Bultmann scholar, but because he had become a Canaan Friend and expressed his great longing to grow more in the love for Jesus, we felt that we could walk together under the guidance of the Holy Spirit, in the light of God and the fellowship of love.

However, it was soon evident that there was a basic difference in our spiritual approach to the commission God had entrusted to Canaan. It came as a complete surprise to us when the minister resigned from the executive committee of *Concern for Germany*, which was his chief responsibility. During a talk with him, we realised that the difference between our conceptions and commissions was fundamental and had long since ceased to be a matter of form. Mother Martyria and I clearly saw that a separation was inevitable, although this step – together with its after-effects – was a painful experience.

But in His goodness the Lord gave us another minister for Canaan directly afterwards – Pastor Douwes, who came to live on Canaan with his wife, who is a Sister of Thorns. They are Dutch and have left their homeland, their parish and their grown-up sons. With great love they overcame their national reservations against us Germans, who had committed such a grievous crime against Holland during World War II. Our Canaan Pastor and his wife live with us according to the Canaan Rule, which is to walk in the light and live in reconciliation. They also share our walk of faith and are closely united with us in all our commissions.

Canaan – Final Foundations and Completion
1960-1973

Last Phase in Construction

Ever since 1955 when the Lord first gave me the commission for Canaan, the land of promise, it has had a special place in my heart. Taking its example from the biblical Canaan, this land was to magnify the glory of God. The living God, who answers prayers and performs miracles, was to shine forth from Canaan. Everything on Canaan, from the houses and residents to the plants and animals, was to proclaim the glories of His name, testifying to His unexcelled greatness. Here God was to receive the love of many hearts, and all who dwell in this little land were to reflect Him, because they live according to the Bible verse, 'If we walk in the light, as he is in the light, we have fellowship with one another . . . ' (1 John 1:7).

In the ups and downs of the battle of faith for obtaining the land, the victories turned out to be merely temporary, whereas the defeats seemed to be final. Frequently, after celebrating a victory with thankful hearts, we had to return that which we had gained. This state of affairs continued until all the promises for Canaan, which I had buried in 1958, that year of death, were resurrected and the whole of Canaan was ours!

The years from 1960 to 1966 were significant. During this period Canaan was developed, the land enclosed, the houses constructed, the hills formed, the bed of the lake paved, the fountain built, the monument erected at the entrance, the 'Garden of Jesus' Sufferings' laid out and the rest of the grounds planted. At the time this project seemed like an insurmountable task to me. Yet had not the Lord shown me that Canaan's grounds should help to make the events of Jesus' earthly life and His Passion come alive for us? Everywhere there should be quiet walks and places to retire for contemplation. Everything should be conducive to prayer – the 'Garden of Jesus' Sufferings', the 'Bethlehem Grotto', the 'Mount of Beatitudes', the 'Sea of Galilee', the 'River Jordan' and 'Jacob's Well'. Love for Jesus made me yearn that everything on Canaan would remind us of Him. To quote Luther, 'Would to God I could persuade the rulers and wealthy people to have all the scenes of the Bible painted on the walls of the houses, inside as well as outside, for everyone to see. That would be a truly Christian deed!'

No words could ever express my gratitude for the marvellous leadings of God our Father during those six years while Canaan was under development. Who could imagine what was involved in carrying out this great enterprise with neither a landscape architect nor professional help! At the same time most of the houses on Canaan were being built. And, of course, there was the financial aspect to consider. We were nearly speechless when we heard the estimated sums – whether it was for the buildings, the large kiln to fire the clay reliefs, the moving of the soil, the construction of the road or for the many other items.

But almost greater than the burden of these expenditures was the question, 'Can you accept the responsibility of spending these sums of money – even if they should be donated – for such landscaping?' This question caused me much inner conflict during those years while Canaan was being laid out and developed. Since it was I who had arranged for the layout of the grounds, the whole burden of responsibility weighed upon my shoulders. Had I been mistaken? Was I dragging God's honour in the dust? This type of inner conflict was long familiar to me; but in addition, trials and temptations now came from without. The layout of Canaan with its large grounds was considered a waste from the rational point of view, since this valuable building land was partly to be converted into a 'mere prayer garden' instead of becoming a necessary housing district.

However, I resisted the devil in such onslaughts until he was forced to yield and flee from me. I drew near to God, and He drew near to me again, giving me the conviction that when it comes to glorifying God, no sum is too large – especially when monuments to Jesus' suffering are erected to win Him love and gratitude. Had I forgotten how Mary lavishly poured out her costly ointment as an expression of her love for Jesus before His Passion? The disciples, not understanding, said that it would have been better to give the money to the poor; yet Jesus was comforted by this deed. Likewise, the purpose of Canaan's layout was that many might be inspired and moved to give Jesus their love and gratitude.

In these hours of inner conflict it would have been a consolation to have known that only a few years later, each summer thousands would pass through the 'Garden of Jesus' Sufferings' alone or in groups and that the Lord would accomplish great things in many lives. Moreover, there would have been no hesitation in my heart about this 'extravagance' for the glory of God if I had known that some years later many would strive for the cause of humanity, maintaining that money should be devoted exclusively to the relief of social needs, and considering church buildings, bells and organs to be unnecessary expenditures – an indication that God was no longer regarded worthy of honour and worship. And if I had known of the flagrant mockery and blasphemy of Jesus in theatrical performances, in films and on records, for which countless Christians would later give their money, all my doubts would most certainly have been dispelled.

But even at the time the Father made me feel ashamed of my doubts, and He comforted me by performing one miracle after the other. Left-over sand and soil from nearby construction sites were transported to our grounds free of charge and could then be formed into hills such as our 'Mount of Olives'. And even for the bulldozer work no charge was made. In addition, most of the small evergreens and other trees in the 'Garden of Jesus' Sufferings' were presented to us as a gift.

Within a very short space of time our Artist Sister completed the sculptures and reliefs for the garden, and our foreman, who had helped us to build the Mother House, generously offered his services and assisted the Sisters in erecting the small grottoes, edifices and walls. The quarry stones that we needed were donated, and we were lent lorries to fetch them. The town authorities, who were turning over to asphalt roads, had an excess of cobblestones, which they gave to us for nothing, and these could be used for paving the bed of the lake. Even the cement for filling up the cracks was donated by a firm. Indeed, every single thing that we needed came from the Father's hands. We suffered no lack, although normally these goods would have cost us a small fortune. I felt as though the Father had made it a point of honour to provide everything that was necessary for this project, which I had undertaken to glorify His name and to make the suffering of His Son come alive for others. Thus tears turned to laughter, dark avenues of faith ended in visible results, and supplications, in thanksgiving.

The Lord had taught me that it is right to be thrifty with our money, goods, time and energy in all areas of life, but never when it comes to glorifying Him.

Threatened by Pollution

It takes no great stretch of the imagination to visualise Satan's fury when a plot of land is consecrated to the glory of God. As the enemy of the glory of God and the foe of all human happiness, he cannot bear to see people living together in peace on a small plot of land where everything flourishes, where the earth brings forth its fruit, and the birds sing their joyous choruses in praise of the heavenly Father.

Accordingly, the enemy sought to harm Canaan with plagues – the same that afflict the rest of the world today – vermin! And when vermin appear, people use the appropriate means of pest control – poisonous sprays. This procedure inevitably results in the extermination of the beneficial insects also, the death of fish and birds, contamination of

343

soil and water – and finally the poisoning of man himself.

But when Satan launches an attack, it is a challenge for us to take up an earnest battle of faith against our sins. Although I knew nothing about agriculture, and pollution was not a topic of public interest at the time, the Spirit of God one day created in me a feeling of uneasiness about the whole situation. After calling our Sisters together, I shared with them the insight the Lord had given me. 'Poison does not belong on Canaan. God has other means of eliminating vermin than sprays that poison the things that He has caused to live and thrive. Once again we are being called to walk the pathway of faith in a new area, that is, we must combat the vermin that Satan has sent to invade Canaan, by fighting the battle of faith against sin. Then, if we live according to the will of God, we shall experience His intervention and miracles, for in His Word He declares, "I will rebuke the devourer for you" (Malachi 3:11) . . . .' With these new battles of faith the Lord was giving us an opportunity to glorify Him, provided that these battles resulted in victory over the vermin. The prospect of a new way of glorifying God filled me with joy.

In the beginning my daughters, especially the Sisters working on the farm, were opposed to this new leading; they were reluctant to give up the old method of using poisonous insecticides to combat the noxious creatures. This new course of action defied all common sense. Yet the Lord convinced them, and toxic sprays were laid aside. The test that followed was severe. When a person launches out in faith, the way usually grows darker at first. Our little land of Canaan, which lies at the edge of a forest, was invaded by hordes of 'devourers' – various species of plant lice that thrived in the dry weather, Colorado beetles, grubs, inchworms and the like, and at times by rabbits. The whole harvest was endangered. Yet it is written, 'The creature that serveth thee, who art the Maker, increaseth his strength against the unrighteous for their punishment, and abateth his strength for the benefit of such as put their trust in thee' (Wisdom of Solomon 16:24 AV).

In other words, God permitted Canaan to be afflicted with these noxious creatures in order to chasten us. Now it meant enduring this chastening until the Father had attained His objective with each one of us, rather than seeking to evade His chastening by employing means that disrupted the divine balance of nature. By leading us this way, the Father intended to teach us to rely on Him far more, to deepen our love for Him, and to strengthen our father-child relationship with Him. New repentance would let us experience His mercy and aid. And God did grant repentance. Many of us recognised the specific instances that called for a turnabout from sin and learnt to see the plagues in the right perspective. Thus the enemy had achieved just the opposite from that which he had hoped to accomplish. We were put on the alert in our struggle against sin, and with renewed vigour we took up the battle of faith that inevitably leads to victory.

Many evenings we came together to sing songs of faith. God's honour was at stake in the sight of all the visitors who came to Canaan. But the worse the condition of the land became, the more Mother Martyria and I encouraged our spiritual daughters to battle against the sins that God had disclosed, urging them to keep faith and by all means not to lose courage. Singing songs, we made a procession over our afflicted land. Separately or together we held up to the Lord the specific sins and faults that He had laid His finger on, determined not to desist until we experienced release in that particular sphere. In many of our times of fellowship in the light and private counselling sessions God shed His light into layers of the personality that had previously lain hidden – frequently a very painful experience. We called this summer 'the time of unmasking', because the holiness of God brought so many things to light in our midst. Yet it was during these months of chastening that some of my daughters who easily tended to be discouraged learnt what it really meant to keep faith and to persevere in their personal battle of faith against sin.

The Sisters also learnt that the battle of faith includes 'works' (in the New Testament sense of the word) – deeds, not to win us merit, but to give a token of our willingness. For instance, everyone joined forces in taking action against the vermin, using their time off to dig grubs out of the ground, to pick the inchworms and other harmful insects off the trees and vegetables and wherever else they could be found. When we had a plague of rabbits, the Sisters rose early in the morning to catch them by hand – just as Scripture exhorts us in view of our sins, 'Catch us the foxes, the little foxes, that spoil the vineyards' (Song of Solomon 2:15). Naturally our efforts could not remedy the situation (just as our battle of faith cannot free us from our sins); they could only be taken as an indication of our willingness. That summer, as in the case of all further plagues, it was the Lord who brought the turning-point – when His time had come.

With a heart brimming over with loving-kindness God responded to our faith. Jesus' victory was made manifest in the battle of faith against sin and against Satan, who had sent the vermin. After chastening us for several months with a drought, God sent us rain before it was too late, and in addition, many ladybirds to eat the plant lice, birds to devour the pernicious insects, and helpers who joined us in combatting the weeds. At the last moment the Father transformed the situation, giving His blessing so that we could reap a marvellous harvest. When the harvest festival came, the Sisters working on the farm – like the Israelites of old who had been sent to spy out the Promised Land – went from house to house on Canaan with poles on their shoulders, bearing the most magnificent fruit and vegetables. They sang songs of praise, full of thanksgiving and overwhelmed by the goodness of God. That was our first 'harvest of grace' as we called it, since the Scripture verse the Lord had given us for that summer was 'Where sin increased, grace abounded all the more' (Romans 5:20).

This new venture of faith, which we had begun at the end of the sixties, repeated itself year after year. Time and again the Father had to be stern with us in order to put us on the alert and to make us take up the battle against sin with renewed ardour. Our voluntary decision to be dependent on God in this venture obliged us to fight the battle of faith all the more. No words can describe the spiritual renewal that we have experienced in our Sisterhood over the course of the years as a result. And we can never give enough thanks for the amazing increase in our harvests. From then on we have reaped such an abundance of vegetables and fruit that all of Canaan's residents, and at times our guests and needy families in the town, could partake of the harvest.

Yet the full significance of this leading did not dawn on me until pollution had assumed such proportions throughout the world that the cycle of development had gone too far to be reversed and life on our planet was endangered. By taking us along this path, God had shown us how to live as Christians in a world threatened by pollution: the battle of faith against sin leads to a purified and deeper relationship with God, whose grace is absolutely essential in this question of survival. God, however, grants grace only to those who live in repentance and resist sin, which clings to us so closely. Only after I had personally experienced that for years now our land has yielded good harvests without the use of poisonous insecticides and that repentance and faith are the best means of 'pest control', was I able to write a booklet about pollution* in 1972.

Yet that was not the last struggle to be laid into the foundations of Canaan. If Canaan was to stand in the future, the foundations had to be laid deep, and indeed, further battles were to come.

Ephesians 6 – Combat with the Unseen

In the meanwhile God was graciously beginning to fulfil His promise on Canaan, 'Here I will dwell', and many people

* *Umweltverschmutzung und dennoch Hoffnung (Pollution: but there is an answer* – British edition; *A Matter of Life and Death* – American edition).

visiting Canaan could sense His presence there. Would that not provoke Satan to plan even greater onslaughts? And indeed, we came to experience his attacks. It was roughly nine months before the Canaan Festival of Thanksgiving to the Father, which had been arranged for July 10, 1966. We were looking forward to this day, preparing ourselves inwardly in prayer and attending to all the external arrangements – but then came a major attack from the powers of darkness.

During those weeks one of our young Sisters told me that ever since her childhood she had frequently suffered terrible oppression by demons. Time and again these spirits taunted her with the fact that her grandfather had sold her to the devil. For years she had experienced severe torment, but she had hoped to become free after her entry in the Sisterhood, though she had made no mention of her plight before joining us.

After a long talk with her when she brought everything into the light, fear and anguish befell me. Years before that I had read about Blumhardt's* battle for the soul of Gottlie-bin Dittus and consequently the prospect of confronting such powers was agonising for me. From Blumhardt's account I knew that hardly anything is more dreadful than engaging in warfare against these evil spirits, especially when they have taken hold of a human being. Such a battle seemed to me to be a task for a group of men like Blumhardt and his Christian friends. Yet God had placed this young Sister in my charge, and I could not leave her in her dire need. God was expecting me to enter the warfare that I preferred to avoid – the combat against demonic powers.

My fears were not ungrounded, for it turned out to be an extremely severe case, as others confirmed, who had experience in such matters. Months of anguish followed. All

* Johann Christoph Blumhardt (1805–1880), a pastor in Moettlingen, Wuerttemberg, who later became the leader of a Christian centre in Bad Boll. This spiritual counsellor was mightily used by God in bringing about a revival movement and was well-known for his ministry of healing the sick and delivering the demon-possessed.

prayers, entreaties, fasting, invocation of the victorious name of Jesus and claiming of His blood appeared to be in vain. The demonic powers only raged all the more. Yet I opposed these evil forces that refused to yield, by singing repeatedly:

'Tis only One who has such might,
'Tis Jesus, who once won the fight
And Satan's pow'r defeated.
And still He puts the foe to flight
And takes from Satan ev'ry right,
Our living, glorious Champion.

Our ransom has been fully bought;
All Satan's wiles must come to nought;
His claims on us are cancelled.
Our souls to Christ alone belong,
Who gave His life to right all wrong
And ransom us poor sinners.

I had also written a number of other songs of victory and prayers for the battle of faith* and called some of the Sisters together to form a small prayer group and to join me in this battle of faith. Yet all our efforts seemed of no avail; the more we prayed, the more the demons raged. It was an agonising experience and I could understand Blumhardt when he said that he underwent immeasurable suffering in his struggle.

I had seldom borne such a burden. Out of my anguished heart arose the cry, 'Where is Jesus' victory now?' Time and again I struggled through in prayer to the point where I could believe that He was truly Victor and had accomplished His act of redemption. 'The right hand of the Lord is exalted, the right hand of the Lord does valiantly!' It is the truth, 'He has the keys of Death and Hades.' Indeed, 'He disarmed the principalities and powers and made a public example of them, triumphing over them.' It is a fact,

---

* 7 × around the Walls of Jericho and In the Name of Jesus (two pocket-size booklets).

'He has bruised the serpent's head.' Indeed, it is true, 'The reason the Son of God appeared was to destroy the works of the devil.'* In prayer we held these verses before the Lord ever anew, praising His victory on Calvary that cancelled the claim Satan had over this soul.

The Festival of Thanksgiving to the Father was approaching, but was I to celebrate it with this immense burden on my heart? Yet God willed it so, and as I wrote at the time:

My Father, this was the gift I wished to bring You – implicit trust and submission to severe leadings that I cannot understand . . . But Canaan cannot live up to its name and be a land of God, or a foreshadowing of the kingdom of heaven, a land where the Lord dwells, if Satan has such power over a human soul and does not yield but triumphs. That cannot be, for the sake of Jesus' honour.

Thus I prayed unceasingly and persevered resolutely, declaring, 'Jesus, since the victory is Yours, it will be manifested in this situation too. "Even if the battle lasts all night, all day, my heart shall neither fret nor doubt the power of God . . ." '

During the acquisition of Canaan I had learnt to keep faith even when a hundred times over my faith was not rewarded by any visible results, when the opponents seemed to be victorious and the commission for Canaan appeared to lie in ruins before me. With a heavy heart I had to struggle through in faith ever anew, but this time my anguish was greatly intensified. It was not simply a matter of submitting to God's difficult leading, but of dealing with the demonic world itself. A human soul entrusted to my care was at stake. It was either deliverance from the power of the devil and his demons or eternal perdition depending on the outcome of this battle.

What was it that helped me to endure, and not to grow

* See Psalm 118:16; Revelation 1:18; Colossians 2:15; Genesis 3:15; 1 John 3:8.

weary in the struggle? That which Blumhardt shared about his experiences. When writing about his immense battle, which is given as a helpful example to the Christian world, Blumhardt stated that the spirits betrayed themselves when they confessed that his 'loathsome' praying and his persistence in calling upon the victorious name of Jesus made them abandon the struggle. Thus I knew that at all costs I must not give up, but press on in the battle of faith, proclaiming Jesus' victory, despite the countless times it seemed to be of no avail. Persevering faith is always crowned with victory!

Then the miracle happened. Jesus proved Himself to be the Victor, the Lamb of God that vanquished Satan's power. Satan was forced to depart from this soul; she became free. After one and a half years she lay at Jesus' feet weeping. Against her natural desires she had been blaspheming Him while under demonic influence, but now she brought Him tears of repentance and consecrated herself to Him out of love. In the following years the Lord made her a truly bridal soul, who became especially close to Him.

However, that summer the battle was not yet over, and when the Festival of Thanksgiving came, this burden still weighed heavily upon me and I had to bear the great disappointment that the Lord Jesus had not yet answered my many prayers. In this situation I was called to worship and give thanks to God the Father in deep gratitude, although I had not experienced His help in this matter. My worship was to have the one true basis where there can be no deception – the basis of suffering. I knew that songs of adoration raised in spiritual night would give the Festival of Thanksgiving to the Father its depth and note of true worship.

A song now is swelling,
From depths is upwelling
To honour God's will in its greatness and pow'r.
Those souls who have gladly
To His will bowed humbly,
Now worship, adoring, God's plan so sublime.

Our view is so bounded.
All doubts are confounded
When each of His promises God has fulfilled.
In worship adoring,
Our praises outpouring,
We humbly will wait till God's plan is revealed.*

In Perfect Love?

It was January 1966. I had withdrawn into seclusion again –
this time for a week of fasting and prayer for a spiritual
renewal in our Sisterhood. During those days a book came
into my hands that contained a report covering a number of
different Christian groups. The author, an evangelist who
had founded his own fellowship, was a complete stranger to
me and had never visited us. As I read his comments about
the Sisterhood and my person, I felt as though the waters of
affliction were rising over me. Although other fellowships
were also given unfavourable criticism in this book, in most
cases fewer pages were devoted to them than to us; the
Sisterhood of Mary was the evangelist's main target. I read
that my way of life was 'of a diabolical nature', and in a
second publication, which appeared shortly afterwards, the
same author wrote that I was 'destroying the body of
believers and creating a schism', that I 'profaned and blasphemed the name of God'. By way of proof each time he
listed names and events that were either fabricated or totally
distorted, and thus his statements amounted to nothing less
than libel. Furthermore, he maintained that we held heretical
views and that a false spirit had crept in, since I had opened
the door to pride – and pride, he said, was the cause of all
apostasy.

In order to support his claims that we were 'demonic', he
noted several points: 'Catholic tendencies', our 'religious
plays', 'much prayer and even fasting', our 'life of repentance, poverty and obedience', the 'word of warning' in my

* *Well-spring of Joy*, No. 208.

writings, the 'charismatic gifts of prophecy and speaking in tongues', and that in our Sisterhood missionary activities rather than nursing stood in the foreground. Furthermore, the report contained the observation: 'Paul writes, "If any one will not work, let him not eat." What do the Sisters of Mary do? Instead of earning their daily bread with the labour of their hands, they have "religious pastimes" with praying, fasting, theatricals [by which he meant our Herald Plays] and the like . . . '

In early 1966 an acquaintance of ours sought to point out the truth to this evangelist, mentioning among other things how God had let us experience answers to prayer and miracles along pathways of faith and how Canaan had come into existence by the grace of God. He replied that the devil could also perform great works!

Was this evangelist alone in his views; had he given play to his imagination? One would think so. Moreover, one would also assume that a book written in this spirit and without the backing of a publishing house could have no effect in circles of committed Christians. Yet this was not the case. Many groups that had been opposing the Sisterhood and me for years lent their support to this man. A long history of antagonism and even hostility that had begun with the founding of the Sisterhood reached its peak with this book. This time it was not merely a report about us in a newsletter, which reached only certain groups, but the publication of the accusations in a book, which the author and his associates systematically sent to Christian bookshops, as well as to preachers, ministers and Christian organisations. In addition, brochures for this book were circulated.

One of the leaders in the Confessional Movement wrote to me soon afterwards, saying, 'In the past few days I have received several copies of this book in the post, sent to me by friends and strangers alike with the request to break off contact with you.' This minister had ordered 25,000 copies of my report about the *Kirchentag* in Cologne and 25,000 copies of the booklet *Mitmenschlichkeit* (which notes the dangers of false brotherly love) to distribute at a large convocation. The warning against our Sisterhood was intended to prevent the proposed distribution from taking place, and these measures proved to be effective. A campaign against our Sisterhood and my person was underway.

Many tears were shed during that week, which I had set apart for prayer. The book was now in circulation in groups from which I had previously received many grateful responses for my literature. Readers had testified that my writings had helped them to come to new repentance and love for Jesus and to dedicate themselves more fully to a life of discipleship. I was filled with immeasurable grief at the thought that many who wished to follow Jesus earnestly would now become confused as a result of this libel and even doubt whether they were on the right path.

Another book published shortly before that contained the statement: 'With the Darmstadt Mariolatry the harlot spirit of the goddess of love and fertility, allied with a perpetually crucified and bleeding Christ, attempts to infiltrate the ranks of Protestant believers. It is the "spirit of Moloch". This spirit leads souls astray, making them fall into a state of apostasy, and tramples the glorious triumph and victory of Jesus Christ underfoot.'

Repeatedly I was told by believers that they could not understand how such libel could be published, but they reassured themselves that no one would pay attention to the incredible statements in these books. Consequently, they felt that this literature could not cause us any harm. However, twenty years of experience had taught me otherwise: lies and slander, no matter how incredible and preposterous they might be, are as effective as poison. Much is retained in the hearts of the readers of such books. At the very least it succeeds in discrediting an organisation. I had discovered that such literature has the power to ruin the reputation of a fellowship.

From the very beginning when our Sisterhood was established I had experienced that false reports, whether passed on by newsletters or in assemblies, spread like wildfire throughout the land. But with the appearance of this evangelist's book, a major onslaught had begun, for the author and his colleagues considered it their duty to send the book to prominent people and organisations not only at home but also abroad. The purpose of this undertaking was that we might be ostracised and our ministry ruined. The many instances of libellous abuse that I had had to face over the course of the years now reached their culmination. Whenever excerpts from my literature or songs appeared in Christian periodicals and calendars, in the *Daily Texts*, or elsewhere, the editors would afterwards be called to account by our adversaries. The publishers concerned were faced with the prospect of losing many subscribers for their periodicals and calendars if they continued to print extracts from my writings. It was humiliating to realise that everyone who came into contact with me and the Sisterhood was also subject to this disgrace.

The evangelist's book penetrated far into Christian circles. Friends of ours received letters warning them that I was the greatest demon-inspired heretic, that they should sever all connections with me and read no more of my books. Time and again people were advised to burn my writings, so that even in places where there was a scarcity of Christian literature, such as in East Germany, my books were 'placed on the bonfire'.

In the following weeks and months I was almost heart-broken, for time and again news arrived of instances where the evangelist's book had wreaked havoc. In my diary I wrote:

I have been stamped as 'demonic'; our ministry is undergoing its second 'burial' because of all this defamation. My heart is almost breaking from all this contempt. The wound is deep and I feel sick with grief. On all sides we are hemmed in by adversaries, and there is not a single ray of hope after this terrible blow.

Yet in view of the disgrace that came upon me because of this book, I committed myself all the more to humiliations.

This should serve to make me more humble and to let priestly love come to maturity in me. I beseech the Lord to use these many wounds and blows that are now being inflicted upon me to kill everything in my soul that is not love.

By the grace of God I was at peace in my heart and could humble myself beneath His mighty hand as it struck the Sisterhood and me personally with this large-scale attack of the powers of darkness. Although I found it hard to believe that this onslaught could not ultimately harm the ministry and message entrusted to us, I struggled through ever anew to the point where I could believe that God would let all things work out for the best.

This was the situation that faced us in the summer of 1966 as we prepared to celebrate the Festival of Thanksgiving to the Father. This festival was to be in honour of God, to praise His goodness in completing Canaan. Yet as God impressed upon us, neither the festival nor the specific commissions of Canaan were the decisive factor. His one concern for the newly laid out and developed land of Canaan was that it might depict a little 'kingdom of love'. And since the Lord had given me the commission for the establishment of our land of Canaan, the spiritual influence I exercised was important. Everything depended on my being merciful and loving in the face of these attacks. God had to fashion this love in me first. In my heart I knew that only if I were adorned with perfect love, that is, with unlimited mercy and overflowing love for friend and foe alike, could I represent the true Canaan and be a citizen of the kingdom of love. Otherwise Canaan would be dishonouring the Lord. Instead of living up to its calling, it would be a distortion of the kingdom of love. Yet only if Canaan were a kingdom of love, could it be endowed with authority to carry out its commission and become a genuine centre of blessing. Only then would the kingdom of heaven be 'at hand', for is not heaven the dwelling place of loving souls?

Love would give the residents of Canaan their radiance

and Canaan its atmosphere of joy. God had a definite plan for creating this love in me. Thus during that year when the final stages of the building and development of Canaan were being completed, He raised a man who used serious defamation to work against us. It was God's loving intention that by following this path of chastening I might receive this love.

The struggle to be loving had marked the beginning of my spiritual life. As a young girl I was frustrated in this struggle and thus, ever since my youth, my greatest plea was to be loving. The Lord helped me to come to my first breakthrough to this love some decades ago when I was living for a while with a difficult, hysterical person, who had wronged me a great deal. At the time the continual injustice I had to suffer embittered me, and I was estranged from this person. But as the Lord showed me how I had transgressed against love and I came to repentance and claimed the power of the blood of the Lamb over my bitterness, I experienced the first instance of release. The feeling of resentment was overcome; love flowed into my heart, and the broken relationship was mended.

The Lord continued to grant grace so that in later years after the Sisterhood of Mary was founded, when the waves of libel and slander swept over me, I had no room in my heart for unforgivingness or bitterness. Yet I sensed that I was a long way off from perfect love. As a true granddaughter of a lawyer I found it hard to bear injustice and falsehoods, and consequently the flow of merciful love was obstructed.

I had become very conscious of this some three years earlier, before the publication of the evangelist's book. In Berlin, where we were asked to present a Herald Play, many were deterred from attending the performance because of the libel spread about us there. The following morning I was asked to say a few words to the congregation after the sermon, but as I began to speak, some of the people rose in protest and left the worship service as a sign that they took my words for heresy. In the midst of this humiliation I could rejoice in my heart, since it was disgrace for Christ's sake.

Yet later when I returned to the Mother House, where I learnt that there had been further instances of defamation, and that opposition had been fanned into flame, I became upset, especially since the falsehoods came from those who sought to follow the Lord with great sincerity.

When the matter began to keep me awake at night, the Lord showed me clearly that it was sin. It was my ego that still found it so hard to bear injustice – that was the reason why I was upset and unable to sleep. Yet in the Bible Jesus had referred to such situations and shown His own how to react. 'If they have persecuted me, they will also persecute you . . . These things have I spoken unto you, that ye should not be offended' (John 15:20; 16:1 AV). Realising that I had let the Berlin incident upset me inwardly, I asked the Lord to grant me the grace to remain in complete peace in view of such libel, even though it was painful to know that libel would poison the hearts of people, cause division among believers and impede the spreading of the Lord's message.

The Lord answered this prayer, which I had often brought Him during these three years. Yet He was concerned about more – His aim was *perfect* love. During the sixties the theme of my diaries and songs was the prayer for perfect love towards my adversaries, since love is the greatest gift that God can grant us. The heart of God is pure love. We were created to love, and we were redeemed by Jesus so that we might love even our enemies with genuine love. I knew that this love would only be imparted to us if we constantly prayed for it, firmly believing that we have been redeemed through Jesus' sacrifice so that we might love. Time and again I sang in faith:

I am redeemed, to offer love alone.
I am redeemed; the victory, Lord, You won.

During those years whenever I walked along a certain path, I used to spend the time praying for this love; every step was like a cry from the depths of my heart.

Father, since I am Your child and chosen to bear Your traits, You must, and indeed You will, mould me into Your image of love. My Lord Jesus, I wish to belong to the bride of the Lamb, and since You have called me to be Your bride, You will make me like unto Yourself. It was for this reason that You shed Your blood. O Holy Spirit, You possess transforming power and You will transform me into the image of love.

Thus ever anew I entreated God, conscious that I did not have enough of this merciful love. As I prayed, I thought of Jesus' heart, which overflows with love. His first prayer on the cross was not for His friends, but for His enemies – 'Father, forgive them.' Jesus' very nature is compassion and loving-kindness, and by His holy sacrifice and His precious life-blood He ransomed us from the futile ways we inherited from our fathers so that we might be moulded into the image of God. My sole longing was not to disappoint Him.

I had experienced so many of God's miracles in my life. Should I not also believe that He would perform this miracle, which He must long to grant more than anything else? He yearns for His children to reflect Him and His merciful love. This love also embraces its enemies and shines upon the quarrelsome and the opinionated. This love, which flows like a river from the heart of God, has divine compassion on those who ill-treat, abuse and slander it. This love knows no bounds, has no reservations, and is not concerned about the hardships and humiliation it may incur. Should I not believe in this miracle when Jesus had laid down His life in order to redeem us by His blood and transform us into the image of perfect love? I had always found that if we claim the irrevocable promises of God, we shall experience what we believe.

But we must also be willing to be disciplined and to submit to God when He leads us along paths of chastening. Faith alone is insufficient. Faith and paths of chastening are intertwined as I had already learnt during the acquisition of Canaan. If the Bible says that we shall be cleansed by faith in Jesus' blood, it also states that we shall 'share his holiness' through chastening (Hebrews 12:5-11). A person that believes in Jesus' victory and praises the power of His blood, but refuses to be 'pruned' and chastened by the Father will experience little victory and produce no fruit. But if he truly claims the blood of Jesus, he will also be willing to submit to the Lord's disciplinary measures in order to share His holiness.

Thus God used a severe blow (the evangelist's book about the Sisterhood and my person) to answer my prayers to be transformed more into the image of His love.

In the following years, 1968–9, the Lord led me into new situations in order to test my love. Mother Martyria and I had painful disappointments, similar to the ones described by the Apostle Paul. Those who were close to him in the beginning, working together with him, later became his opponents. This was our experience with friends at home and abroad, even with those who had been especially dear to us. Every time new wounds were inflicted, I felt as though Jesus were watching to see my reaction. Would I be full of mercy as He was merciful? Would I love as He did? Would I be able to endure suffering patiently as He patiently endured?

In this situation the Lord engraved upon my heart that love is the decisive factor. The eternal and holy God will not inquire about anything else at the end of our lives. All our works that do not bear the hallmark of love will perish; everything that is not done out of love will pass away. Only love never ends. It is eternal and immortal, since it contains divine life.

The message of reconciling love was now entrusted to me in a special way; I could pass it on at our retreats and in our journal, ... into All the World, as well as in my other writings. Moreover, I was commissioned to travel abroad even as far as India to share this testimony about reconciliation in the love of Jesus, with heathens as well as Christians. The message of reconciling love had become my life's testimony. Time and again I was told after holding a lecture, 'That is the very word we need. In our town there are many quarrels and disputes among Christians and heathens alike. Everywhere hearts are embittered.' It was a privilege to see how this message, which was not a theoretical teaching, but a life's testimony, moved people to seek reconciliation.

God had accomplished His purposes, using those months as I struggled in prayer to attain greater love, that is, love for my adversaries, as a prelude to Canaan's great Festival of Thanksgiving. Since Canaan was to be a little kingdom of love, its first and foremost message had to be: Those who love Jesus are merciful. He who loves God loves his brother and also his enemy. The unity of love he has with God leads to unity of love with his brother, and even if his brother becomes his enemy, he continues to offer his hand in reconciliation.

Thus all these experiences, all these struggles to obtain perfect love, were laid into the foundations of Canaan before its completion and consecration.

Canaan's Festival of Thanksgiving to the Father

On July 10, 1966, the Father was to receive praise and thanksgiving for having fulfilled His promises and completed Canaan. This day was a milestone in the history of Canaan, the crowning event of all God's fatherly leadings for us.

On this bright festival day we could see the Land of Canaan stretched out before us, with its grounds laid out and developed. Over a thousand friends had come to join us in praising the Lord for His mighty deeds and on our little 'Mount of Beatitudes' twenty different flags were set up, representing the native countries of our guests, some of whom had even made an overseas journey from other continents. Marvellous things had taken place, and now they were visible for all to see. God's promises had truly been fulfilled. Along pathways of faith without any human resources or influence, the 'land of promise' had been obtained – by prayer alone. The 'immovable' bypass had been moved as well as the planned housing estate of the city and the proposed settlement for the American army officers. Through the grace of God the necessary funds were provided for the acquisition and layout of Canaan.

The deeds that God performed on Canaan were expressive of His loving heart and being, His fatherly goodness and overflowing kindness. He was indeed worthy of honour and glory for His marvellous acts. People made long journeys in order to join in the anthems of praise to the 'Father of Goodness'. A large and diverse festal congregation had gathered between our 'Mount of Beatitudes' and 'Sea of Galilee'. That Canaan had a small lake was a miracle in itself. Who could comprehend what God had done? Who could imagine the trials of faith and the suffering entailed before the water came? All those years while Canaan was under development it resembled a desert because of its infertile, sandy soil and the low precipitation of our area.

Only in faith did we venture to have the earth dug out and only in faith did the Sisters pave the bed of the lake with cobblestones. The authorities from the local water company had informed us that a drilling in our district would not be worthwhile. According to their estimates, the most we could expect would only be enough to supply the daily needs of a household of four to five persons. The outlook did not seem to improve much even when God granted a ray of hope by raising a man hitherto almost unknown to us to pray for water on Canaan and even to help to arrange for a drilling on our land. In the opinion of the experts it would take a miracle – like the ones in the Bible – for a drilling to provide a water supply for such a large territory like Canaan.

But now on this great festival day at the sound of a trumpet every head turned in the direction where rushing water could be heard. Jets of water spurted high into the air from the sprinkling system, and descended upon the fields and meadows. Nearby the Fountain of the Father's

Goodness splashed and in front of us the lake sparkled in the sunlight. Deeply moved, everyone began to sing, 'Holy God, Thy name we bless . . . '

What could be the cause for this feeling of awe? Amongst those present were many friends who in previous years had refused to believe that this 'water miracle' was possible. After reading our newsletter about this goal of faith for Canaan, they expressed their scepticism to me; some even thought that we were tempting God with this aim of faith. Indeed, before sending out the newsletter, Mother Martyria and I had seriously deliberated whether or not to share this matter with our friends and ask them for their prayer support in this goal of faith if perhaps only a few would understand it. We had asked the Lord for a Bible verse about water as a confirmation that we should announce a water miracle in faith before there was any sign of it. And He gave us the verse, 'With joy you will draw water from the wells of salvation' (Isaiah 12:3). In 1960, heading our newsletter with this verse, we asked our friends to join us in believing and praying for water on Canaan – and six years later, on July 10, they could really 'draw water from the wells' while we sang this Bible verse. They drank of Canaan's fresh water that flowed from the small taps at the Fountain of the Father's Goodness. After we had waited for years, undergoing inner preparation and humiliation, God actually performed the water miracle in 1964. Our well produces twenty-five times more water per hour than over a hundred other wells of the same size in this area. Deeply moved, a leading official from the city water company declared, 'A miracle has taken place here!'

Indeed, we have a God who performs miracles! These were the words that resounded like a canticle of praise from the 'Mount of Beatitudes', which was our outdoor stage for the day. There the mighty deeds of God were proclaimed; in many different ways our Sisters testified to our guests and friends of all that the Lord had done. The residents of Canaan stepped forward – young and old alike. Each one tried to outdo the other in thanking God for His goodness in granting us such a wonderful 'inheritance', the land of Canaan. The festal gathering gave its response. The worship, the songs of praise and thanksgiving and the rejoicing seemed to have no end – and before anyone realised it, three hours had slipped by.

The Fountain of the Father's Goodness with its constant flow of water was a symbol to me of the heart of God, which brims over with loving-kindness. His heart is indeed a well of goodness, as I could personally testify. As a token of thanksgiving to the Father we had His various names written in mosaic round the edge of the fountain – each name revealing a new attribute of His. All day long the songs composed about these names resounded over Canaan, the entire congregation joining us in the refrains of praise. 'Father of Goodness, Father of Love, Father of Grace, Father of Comfort, Father of Faithfulness, Father of Mercy, Father of Patience . . . '

Groups of guests wandered about Canaan, taking pleasure in all that the Lord had established there. Only three years earlier Canaan was like a 'desert' with unsightly mounds of earth and scorched patches of grass, but now it had become a lovely piece of land with sloping hills and well-watered grounds, a lake and fountain, as well as various monuments raised in thanksgiving to God. Everything praised the glory of God the Creator – the lush meadows, the blooming flowers, the newly planted shrubs and trees. All the houses on Canaan had been completed and no debts incurred. Who could fathom such amazing goodness of the Father!

The weather that day was yet another proof of the Father's goodness. Since most of the festivals and praise services were to take place out of doors at the 'Mount of Beatitudes', good weather was essential. Although heat waves and thunderstorms were a common occurrence in mid-July, the Father gave us the most glorious weather. It was a mild, pleasant day with no scorching sun and everyone could sit outdoors. It could not have been more perfect, and not until the last guest had departed did the first drops of rain fall.

In the morning as we held the festival worship service in the Herald Chapel, my longing was to praise God's fatherly goodness in a special way. Thus in the presence of God and the congregation I asked my daughters various questions such as:

'Has God provided for us every day all these years, granting us His good gifts?'
'Has the Lord kept His promises concerning Canaan?'
'Has He shown that He is a Father?'

At that my spiritual daughters rose as one body, replying with all their heart, 'yea, amen'. Having witnessed the numerous impossibilities and hardships that had come our way and the crevices that had opened up before us, they were conscious that their reply was a powerful testimony of God's goodness, aid and omnipotence. A mighty anthem of praise and thanksgiving rose up to God in response to His loving-kindness.

The six stone monuments at the main entrance to Canaan near the Herald Chapel were a further tribute of thanksgiving to God. Engraved with the Bible verses we had received over the years for the acquisition of Canaan, they expressed our gratitude for all His miracles and aid, which we had experienced up to the moment that Canaan was ours.

Wherever I turned my eyes that day, I was filled with amazement. What marvellous things the Lord had done! My heart overflowed with praise and adoration. Our God is a God of miracles! A Father of loving-kindness, who not only gives promises, but fulfils them! A God whose name is 'Yea and Amen'!

Yea and Amen Is His Name

Ever since the first years of the Sisterhood, I would often play the organ late in the evening with the door to my room open as I sang to my daughters songs of love for Jesus, of

His suffering, of the Father's goodness and the glory of heaven. My daughters would listen, waiting to hear my favourite songs, which they knew so well. But there was one song in particular that I was moved to sing time and again during the years following the Festival of Thanksgiving to the Father. In a dark hour I had written it down in faith, giving thanks in advance that we have a God who accomplishes all His purposes gloriously.

O Lord, I praise Your holy name,
Yea and Amen for aye the same.
I praise the paths ordained for me;
The darkest night has brought the light
And endless fruit and blessing.

O Lord, I praise Your holy name,
Yea and Amen for aye the same.
To a wondrous goal all paths must lead,
For Your will is but goodness, love ...

This song meant a great deal to me, since in several areas of my life I no longer needed to sing it in faith, after having personally experienced that God fulfils the commissions He imparts. It was as if God's name 'Yea and Amen' had been written beneath many of the promises that He had given me; now I had the privilege of seeing their fulfilment.

The wonderful outcome that God had provided after leading us to Canaan along avenues of faith, fraught with trials and temptations, encouraged many others to make ventures in faith. In passing, missionaries from the Far East related how they received a copy of our book *Realities* at a crucial time – just after their children's barracks had been destroyed by a flood. By faith they then undertook the enterprise of building a proper home for the children, which now stood completed. Another time a minister from Africa wrote, 'I am about to establish a Canaan, a work of faith for native children', and an Anglican minister mentioned, 'I should like to help build such a Canaan in England.' 'I already have a piece of property for a land of Canaan', related a Sister serving in India . . . Everywhere God had inspired souls to walk pathways of faith so that Jesus' dominion would become more visible here on earth.

In addition to those who, inspired by the story of Canaan, adopted this plan of God and applied it in their own countries, God raised people who helped us to carry out Canaan's commission. After leading one along paths of faith and suffering, the Lord does not wait until the next world to pour out His good gifts; He repays one now, a hundredfold, even in the midst of persecution, just as He promised. Thus God gave Canaan spiritual friends, and friends who offered practical assistance. He gave us a doctor, who with great kindness and generosity attended to our needs, a chief city engineer, a mayor and a faithful foreman. He provided us with experts to advise us in almost every field of our many-sided commission – the Herald Plays, the printshop, the radio and tape ministry, the farm and beekeeping, the manufacture of praise plaques and ceramics. He gave us benefactors, who with their gifts and sacrifices over the course of the years helped to build Canaan. And last but not least He gave us Canaan representatives, who, after receiving inspiration on Canaan, became 'ambassadors for Christ' in their own land or district.

In addition, the Lord had continued to fulfil the precious promise of Scripture that I had held up to Him ever since 1945, 'I will walk among you, and will be your God, and you shall be my people' (Leviticus 26:12). In spite of us and our shortcomings, friends and visitors have often told us that they had a foretaste of heaven and paradise on Canaan. Year after year countless numbers of people have encountered God here, and have experienced the spiritual renewal and joy that come from contrition and repentance – just as we had done. From the farthest corners of the earth, people travelled to Canaan. Most of them then returned to their countries filled with joy, since repentance and confession helped them to comprehend more deeply Jesus' forgiveness and to free them from their burden of sin. A greater love for Jesus was kindled in their hearts so that they longed to follow Him and suffer for Him.

There was no end to the stream of visitors to Canaan. It had become a gathering-place for people of every Christian background who love Jesus; many others in these last times, including a great number of young people, have come to a personal faith in Jesus and have become His own. In view of all that happened, I felt constrained to sing time and again:

> O Lord, I praise Your holy name,
> Yea and Amen for aye the same ...

Yet the Lord has not only given us many visitors and guests. Not a single day passes when I do not thank Him for giving me daughters whose lives already show signs that all the spiritual struggles have been worthwhile. Mother Martyria and I had taken many pains for the spiritual development of our daughters, lifting them up in prayer. And then the Lord began to impart divine joy. Sisters who were inclined to be depressed became cheerful; those who were deep in bondage experienced release, and the tense became relaxed. Certainly, they have caused me disappointments and inner conflict, but first and foremost they are a great joy to me. I love them dearly; each one of my daughters is like a gem to me. They have all been redeemed by the precious blood of Jesus, who ransomed and won them to be His bride, the bride of the Lamb – and all the efforts made for their sake have not been in vain.

The close relationship that Mother Martyria and I have had with our spiritual daughters from the very beginning, as a family in Christ, has grown stronger from year to year, for the bond of love that is formed by repeated instances of mutual forgiveness is the strongest bond of all. I had not found it hard to forgive, since I was always conscious of my own shortcomings. How often I had failed to be patient, to remain in humble love and to be kind, thus not making it easy for my daughters. Therefore, I thank them for showing me such affection and love.

The love and spirit of oneness in our large family increased in the same measure that our love for Jesus increased. In earlier years a shadow was often cast upon our fellowship because of indifference towards the Lord's commissions and because of a greater concern for self rather than for the furthering of His kingdom. But now this attitude has largely disappeared and our spiritual daughters share the joys and sorrows of the commissions that God has entrusted to us.

The fellowship we enjoy at mealtimes when all the important matters are discussed is a source of inspiration and a new stimulus for our ministries. Faces light up with joy whenever another victory for the Kingdom of God has been won, when letters containing such news from our Sisters stationed abroad are read aloud or reports reach us from all parts of the world about how the commission is being carried out. Everyone looks forward to our 'morning watch' when we have Bible study and prayer fellowship, and no one wants to miss an evening meeting. When we come together for a battle of prayer and faith concerning our ministry, all the Sisters fervently pray that Jesus' victory might be established in the specific commissions.

The monthly private talks with my spiritual daughters are also a gift for me, since I then have the opportunity of sharing many of the precious things that Jesus has done in their lives. And many a blessed hour has been spent in the company of my spiritual daughters when they come to me in small groups. Just as in our meetings for the whole family there is no set programme. Everything is spontaneous, for when the heart is full to overflowing, it cannot but express itself, and so, for instance, I would tell them about the heavenly glory, which is our goal. Or we would feel led to sing songs praising the Father or extolling the love of Jesus. We come together as a happy family, for we are God's children, having one Father, called to be the bride of the Lamb, guided by the Holy Spirit, united in love, and sharing the glorious expectation of the day when we shall join the heavenly throng in worshipping the Lamb of God.

Ever since I became Mother of the Sisterhood of Mary,

369

this fellowship with my daughters has been a very precious part of my life, and therefore, the Lord has given me opportunities to make sacrifices in this respect over the course of the years. In 1952 it was His call to go into seclusion. A few years later it was the many journeys I was commissioned to undertake in addition to the times I spent alone with the Lord, and after my days of travelling were over, I knew how vital it was to remain faithful to my prayer ministry. Therefore, I felt led to plan each year in advance, dividing it into times alone with Jesus and times in the midst of my spiritual daughters together with all the various commitments. The division was equal, usually on a weekly basis. Yet this 'divided life' did not imply that my daughters would suffer as a result, for the Lord blessed the times I was with them all the more.

How grateful I am to the Lord for letting me experience His 'yea and amen' in the fulfilment of His promises not only for our spiritual daughters on Canaan, but also for those stationed abroad. Love for Jesus made them willing to leave Canaan and their spiritual Mothers and Sisters, in order that the kingdom of heaven might dawn in the countries where they are serving. They are even willing to lay down their lives, and in some cases their dedication is already being tested. The specific commissions that God has entrusted to them for their respective countries have become part of their very lives.

It has always been hard for me to send Sisters abroad in these perilous days; however, the Lord has not only required spiritual daughters from us – to serve in our foreign branches – but He has given us new spiritual daughters. The growth of our Sisterhood is also part of God's 'yea and amen'. During the past few years Mother Martyria and I made a thorough survey of the Mother House, trying to see whether we could arrange for more living space, or whether we had to build another annex, and indeed the latter proved to be necessary. Within a span of six years over fifty new Sisters from ten different countries had joined the Sisterhood – at a time when most young people lead a life devoid of ideals, in the apathy of the affluent society and in the bond-age of sin. Year after year when we hold the *Rufschwestern-feier* *, it is deeply moving for us to hear our new Sisters' personal testimonies of how Jesus came into their lives as the heavenly Bridegroom and called them to the Sisterhood of Mary – even across national borders or the ocean.

The same applies to our Canaan Franciscan Brothers, whose Brotherhood was founded in 1967. During my jour-ney to the United States as I was being driven by a minister in Minneapolis to a speaking engagement, I was suddenly aware of a divine summons. The Lord wished to open the way for Brothers to follow our life of discipleship and to partake in Canaan's ministries. It was an unforgettable moment. As Mother Martyria and I were wondering how this call would materialise, many questions arose; but the call was stronger still. Shortly afterwards the Lord called the first four Brothers – two from the United States and two from our country – and engrafted them into our spiritual commission, making them true Canaan Franciscan Brothers. On the one hand, they are able to develop in healthy inde-pendence as a small Brotherhood, but on the other hand, they are genuine spiritual sons of Canaan. With full dedica-tion they help in all our commissions, whether it be on the farm or in the tape or youth ministry, and their deepest longing is to draw from the same spiritual sources that the Lord has granted us over the course of the years.

Another part of the Canaan family is the Sisters of the Crown of Thorns, who heard Jesus' call to communal life at a more advanced age. As single women or widows they left their homes and careers out of love for Jesus. They have made many hidden sacrifices, faithfully bearing with us the burden and the suffering involved in Canaan's com-mission, often spending their last ounce of strength. At the southern end of Canaan they have their house, 'Jesus' Com-fort', where, as the nucleus of our Sisters of Thorns, they provide a home for the latter, for there are members of Canaan's family who are unable to live permanently on

* Service for the commencement of a new course of Sisters.

Canaan. Ever since the time of the revival there have been women who were Sisters of Mary at heart and longed to join us but could not, usually because they were married. They formed the Sisterhood of Thorns, keeping close spiritual contact with us, in particular through their retreats, which are held twice yearly on Canaan.

As I thank God for fulfilling His promises concerning our Sisters of the Crown of Thorns and our Sisters of Thorns, I thank Him especially for the spiritual renewal that He has granted in recent years. They too have gone through periods of maturing and testing. It is a comfort and a deep joy for me to see how they enter combat and suffer in the Lord's behalf – the Sisters of the Crown of Thorns as prayer warriors and the Sisters of Thorns as soldiers out on the front lines, some of them in the thick of the battle, maintaining their bastions for the Lord Jesus in the midst of this dark world. Both the Sisterhood of the Crown of Thorns and the Sisterhood of Thorns are indispensable to Canaan's commission. In many cases they are the mainstay of Canaan's evangelistic outreach and the backbone of the Canaan Friends' Fellowships. And how I praise God for raising so many faithful Canaan Friends at home and abroad! They too long to spend themselves that Canaan's ministries might be fulfilled; they live for heaven to dawn in their surroundings through contrition and repentance.

In addition, the Lord has given me many others who are spiritually close to me, but whose countries and languages I do not know – friends, readers and listeners. Their responses, which are often so spontaneous and heartwarming, I can only return to the Lord and say, 'All God's promises are yea and amen, for He is faithful to His name.'

Grandparents for Canaan

Not only did the Lord give us friends who were close to us spiritually and friends who offered practical help, as well as various benefactors and representatives, but He had a special present in store for Canaan, and this was a great gift for me personally. He gave my spiritual daughters 'grandparents' – as the Sisters fondly called my parents, and as the latter signed their letters and cards to the Sisters.

Canaan and the Sisterhood of Mary had grown very dear to my parents. They knew each one of their many 'granddaughters'. Canaan and the Sisters – particularly those stationed abroad – had a special place in their hearts and prayers. There was not a single festival on Canaan that my parents did not attend whenever their health permitted it; even when they were in their nineties they continued to come. And though my father's memory began to fail him towards the end of his life owing to the infirmities of old age, the matters concerning Canaan and the Sisterhood were all the more vivid to him. He knew what the specific prayer requests were and brought them to the Lord daily in long prayers.

My parents' affection for Canaan and the Sisterhood was an indication to me that God had been at work, and ever anew I was moved to sing in thanksgiving, 'O Lord, I praise Your holy name, Yea and Amen for aye the same . . . ' This oneness had not been the case at the beginning, during the revival and the founding of the Sisterhood of Mary. Naturally, my parents found it very hard to understand the Lord's leading for me from 1935 onwards, as I began to share Jesus' life of poverty. As a college professor and chancellor of a university for many years, my father was perturbed by my way of life. Although he had given me a university education, shortly after I received my doctorate I refused all offers for posts that would have been 'in accordance with my social position and qualifications'.

In the first years of the Sisterhood, before the Mother House was built, my parents selflessly welcomed our large spiritual family into their house at the cost of peace and quiet and living space. In addition, owing to the circumstances, they could not have much share in the internal life of our Sisterhood, which, on the other hand, fully occupied me. That meant yet another sacrifice for my parents. Certainly, I learnt to make time for my parents so that they too could share the concerns of our young organisation whenever the opportunity arose during those years, but since it was not possible for me to give family life priority over God's commission, disappointments and sorrow were inevitable. Later on, in their old age, my parents feared that they might pass away while I was on one of my journeys. This thought weighed heavily on them, and for their sake I was sorrowful too. Yet Jesus had said, 'He who loves father or mother more than me is not worthy of me' (Matthew 10:37).

Moreover, my family found it hard at first to understand some of the leadings that I was following in obedience to a call of God, and consequently, various difficulties ensued. For instance, the 'paths of faith' that God called me to walk were more appropriate to 'heavenly mathematics' than to the sort my father was accustomed to as a professor of mathematics. For him everything had to be worked out and guaranteed in advance with clear estimates and a plan of financing – and I had inherited this trait. But now my parents were surprised with one 'adventure of faith' after the other. Each time they felt the family honour was at stake. I shall never forget the horror my father expressed when I shared with him the commission God had given me to procure the land of Canaan.

How grateful I was to God for proving His faithfulness during the years of the acquisition and development of Canaan. I was especially thankful for my parents' sake; now they could witness that these commissions were from God, as they saw them materialise. My father's amazement grew from year to year as he heard of the miracles that God performed in the Sisterhood and on Canaan. When we prayed together, his prayers would be overflowing with thanksgiving to the heavenly Father. After having seen how God had answered prayers over the course of the years as we followed pathways of faith, my father praised the 'heavenly mathematics' that had helped to establish Canaan. His face would light up whenever I told him of another answer to prayer and another miracle of God. This was indeed God's doing after various difficulties in the past!

This oneness with my parents, this close relationship of love in the Lord Jesus, which had grown so deep in the last ten years of their life, was another instance of God's faithfulness, His 'yea and amen'. He had granted this fellowship of love as the victorious outcome of times of suffering, battles of prayer and tears of repentance, and in this relationship too the spirit of Canaan shone forth, signifying the dawning of the Kingdom of God, the kingdom of love.

Last Hour for Carrying Out the Commission

God had purposed that through frequent times of seclusion and solitude my life might symbolise His full claim upon us, which is to love Him above all things, according to the first Commandment. He willed that I follow the Bible's exhortation to devote ourselves first and foremost to prayer. Seventeen years had elapsed since those October days in 1952 when I followed His call to seclusion, and now a number of airmail letters arrived from various radio stations abroad even as far away as Africa and Asia. The letters contained requests for radio programmes compiled from my writings. God had caused a world-wide commission to develop from my times spent in seclusion and I could only marvel at His doing.

At a time when the clouds of persecution and catastrophe were already gathering on the horizon, God led us to build the Canaan Radio Studio. Humanly speaking, it was not the moment to begin a radio enterprise. We had neither the funds, the experience, the trained staff nor the equipment, and it did not seem likely that the world situation would permit this work for long. God, however, gave me the conviction that I should undertake this venture, and within a very short space of time the studio stood completed. Our Brothers and Sisters on Canaan received new gifts for this professional enterprise and the Lord led a number of able co-workers to join us. It is overwhelming how donations came in to cover the high expenditures.

Thus we began to produce radio programmes, which were interspersed with singing and instrumental music, and in our own studio I could read scripts for the German programmes.

What seemed impossible in the eyes of the experts was possible for God. Within two years our radio programmes (one, two, five, fifteen and thirty minutes in length) were translated into many different languages and broadcast daily or weekly by a good number of radio stations. Thus millions of people on all five continents could hear the programmes, including our brothers suffering persecution for Jesus' sake. Truly, God's thoughts are higher than ours!

Responses came from the Indonesian jungle, Vietnamese war zones, colleges in India, large cities in America, the primeval forests of Burma, emigrant Jews and remote missionary stations in New Guinea and Malaysia. All this filled me with awe and made me worship the amazing and incomprehensible purposes of God. But the swiftness with which the Lord continued to open doors and pave the way was a confirmation to me that very little time was left.

Accordingly, we felt the urgency of producing a film about Canaan as a modern means of portraying the reality of God to young and old alike at home and abroad. Some years earlier as we were contemplating the idea of undertaking this project, we received the verse of Scripture, 'Therefore, my beloved brethren, be steadfast, immovable, always abounding in the work of the Lord, knowing that in the Lord your labour is not in vain' (1 Corinthians 15:58). During that time we had discovered that the production of such a film is no easy task and that we lacked all the necessary prerequisites, but now in 1972 God's moment had evidently come for the Canaan film to be made.

Since many events coincided, we felt that God was giving

us a confirmation to begin this undertaking. Someone recommended a film company to us, which was technically skilled and had the right approach for such an assignment. God was at work. The dates were settled; the timing was perfect. The Spirit of God enabled us to write the script at record speed, although we had no experience whatsoever in such matters. When the shooting of the film took place, the Father gave us two weeks of glorious weather and arranged that many special events, excellent for filming, 'happened to occur' in this very span of time. He took care that donations arrived to settle all the bills that were due. The enemy, however, seemed to be enraged at the film and tried to destroy parts of it during the development and in later stages. But all his attempts were in vain. The Lord contended for the film and thus we were able to commence with the English version even before the German original was finished.

The impact the film had was an indication of how much God must have wished to use this mass medium to draw countless numbers of people unto Himself, the Source of life. He longed to reach the seeking, the spiritually hungry, the discouraged, the lukewarm and those lost in sin, and to kindle with fresh ardour those who love Him. This film had been one of my heart's desires for a long time. Presently the surface of the earth would be covered with manifestations of evil, for a deluge of sin was flooding the world and the vats of filth and depravity were spilling over. For many years I had entreated the Lord repeatedly that this film might be to His glory, that it might be like a fisherman's net, drawing in a large haul for the Kingdom of God. It was my prayer that the time of grace be extended for more souls to be saved. We are privileged in knowing the almighty and all-loving God, who is our Father, and in daily experiencing how wonderful our Saviour Jesus Christ is and what His Spirit can do, but without a film and radio stations we lacked the ways and means of sufficiently demonstrating the greatness of God to people throughout the world.

To be sure, our 'Canaan fire teams' had been working

faithfully on a small scale for years. They distributed the Canaan bookmarks, leaflets and booklets. They put up hundreds of herald boxes indoors and out of doors, and gained permission to mount herald plaques in the centre of towns and at tourist spots; they provided telephone numbers for our 'Dial a Message' ministry. In addition to many other activities they started poster campaigns, invited groups to their homes to listen to tape recordings, and travelled throughout the country to show the Canaan slide series. Yet in my heart there was a lament, 'What is all this in view of the millions in the world?' If only we could give them tangible proof of the reality and greatness of the living God, who can deal with anything and everything including all sinful bondages. If only people could see with their own eyes the tremendous joy that comes from repentance and forgiveness of sin and from living in reconciliation with God and one another! How wonderful it would be if they could see how God can solve all problems and overcome all fears! If only a vivid picture could be painted of the glory of God, showing how worthy He is of receiving all our love!

Now that the Canaan film had been produced, it was being shown in many cities in our country as well as abroad. In Canada Cable Television showed interest in having both the English and German version when the first news of the film reached them. In the United States dates were set immediately for the film to be shown at large conventions and on television stations, and film libraries undertook to introduce the film throughout the country. On Canaan guests from Australia and New Zealand hearing of the film ordered copies even before the film was finished. Offers came from other television companies abroad, and within a short span of time film versions in other foreign languages were made, and ways were sought to make the film comprehensible for the inhabitants of such countries as India, Taiwan and the Philippines.

With this spontaneous and world-wide growth of our commission the Lord showed me the reason why He had

stopped my foreign travels which had been part of my life
ever since my stay at Mount Sinai. In 1970 the course of
my life took a 180-degree turn. That year I was invited to
Indonesia to speak to the Christians on the island of Timor,
where the revival had broken out, as well as at a faith
conference and a commissioning service for missionaries
in Batu. I had accepted the invitation and all the details of
the journey were arranged when God intervened. I became
very ill and the doctor did not permit me to make the journey to Indonesia. With that, travels to further countries
were made impossible, since most of them would have led
me to tropical regions. According to God's purposes I was
now to carry out the ministry by other means – by the radio
programmes and the film as well as by my writings, which
were published more swiftly than expected in many other
languages and countries. With this new development the
Lord did not only intend to relieve me of the journeys
abroad, which were beyond my strength, but He was waiting
for me to come apart with Him in seclusion where He
would impart a new commission to me.

The Shades of Night Are Falling
1970–1973

'Set your house in order!'

About the same time that I cancelled the journey to Indonesia, someone mentioned to me – quite apart from my illness – that the Lord had shown him that I should withdraw
more into seclusion. There I should prepare to go to my
eternal home, set my house in order, equip our spiritual
daughters for later times and train Mother Martyria's and
my successors for their task. Strangely enough, the doctor

expressed himself similarly, even though such thoughts would not normally have occurred to him. In seclusion I had many matters to attend to, but scarcely had I drawn apart when the Spirit of God came over me, constraining me to write down a great deal for the time after I had departed from this life. It was like an outpouring of grace when God granted me an abundance of spiritual legacies for the Sisterhood of Mary concerning the coming time of disaster, for the various sections of our commission as well as for the Sisters who would later bear the responsibility for the Sisterhood. As I was writing for my daughters in view of later times, I was filled with anguish and trepidation. An excerpt from my diary reads:

> I am suffering torment. The air is pregnant with destruction and this is what awaits them!

I felt the urgency not only of preparing myself for the day the Lord would call me to my eternal home, but of preparing and settling everything for my daughters by that time.

Like an undertone during those weeks a gentle melody was playing in my heart. 'O heavenly home, your radiance beckons to me . . . ' In spite of all my sorrow that the ministry of travelling to other nations had come to an end, a secret feeling of joy welled up in my heart. 'Home! Home! Soon I shall go home to my Lord Jesus!' My fervent longing was to be with Him for ever.

A special atmosphere of holy solemnity rested upon those weeks while I was away from the Mother House in complete seclusion – the solemnity of parting grief, the solemnity of the joy of soon going to my eternal home, mingled with anguish at the thought of all that awaited my daughters, who had to stay behind.

Eternity drew close – the City of God, the pilgrim's destination bathed in light. From that time onwards I began to sing with greater awareness:

> There is a golden city bright,
> Far, far from tears and suffering,

And he who sees this place of light
Will ne'er on earth be satisfied;
He's filled with secret longing.

The nearness of eternity made me face the reality of death quite differently. Up till then I had considered death mainly as the privilege of going home to my Lord, and indeed immeasurable joy flooded my heart at the mere thought of going home soon. One of my favourite Bible verses was, 'To me to live is Christ, and to die is gain' (Philippians 1:21). For many years now I had an experience similar to that of Paul, who wrote, 'I die every day' (1 Corinthians 15:31). Thus I was filled with great expectancy and joy at the thought of going to my eternal home, for the longing for heaven always corresponds to the suffering and spiritual dying beforehand.

But now I came to see Death in a new light, in his formidable aspect. Death could be described as the greatest foe of all, for according to Scripture he is 'the last enemy to be destroyed' (1 Corinthians 15:26). Death, whom various Bible passages refer to as a person, is a terrible and fearsome spectre as I came to realise. At the grave of Lazarus Jesus was 'moved with deep anger' (John 11:38 *The Living Bible*) at the power of Death, and He wept. Death brings immeasurable grief and heartache, turning a living person into a corpse in a single moment, destroying a flourishing life with his icy-cold breath. Great men of God and hymnists of old, having personally suffered deep anguish as they faced the dreadfulness of this reality, composed many songs about the awfulness and grimness of death. And everyone who lives in the light, accepting the truth about himself will be able to repeat wholeheartedly the words they prayed:

When I am in the throes of death
And must draw my final breath,
Lord Jesus, hasten to my side
And help me past the stormy tide.
Shorten the hour of death's agony . . .

I could see the relentlessness with which death ends our lives and all our activities. When death befalls us, it is no longer possible to repent. Our last chance is over. We cannot make any more amends. We shall reap the harvest of that which we have sown. Death exposes our life for what it really is.

With death on the threshold it was not surprising that I too was reminded of all that I had done or failed to do in my life, and of instances when I had not borne in patience and love those who had caused me distress. Above all, I was conscious of having failed the Lord Jesus by not showing Him enough devotion, not bringing Him enough sacrifices in love and thanksgiving for His supreme sacrifice, His forgiveness and His love. Events in my life, my manner, my words and actions in certain situations and with certain people passed before me accusingly. During the following months and years the Lord granted me periods of deep contrition. At the same time, however, I was filled with immeasurable gratitude that in His grace Jesus opens the door to heaven for truly penitent sinners for the sake of His blood that He shed in atonement for our sins. The word 'grace' became the most precious word of all to me, for looking back on my life, I could no longer find anything good in it.

The contrition that the Lord imparted to me in the latter years of my life was deeper and more lasting than I had ever experienced before, giving rise to the heartfelt plea, 'Help me to show love where I have failed to do so! Give me a fervent desire to sacrifice in respects where I have sacrificed too little. Let me prove my dedication to You in the midst of suffering and chastening. For the last years of my life grant me the grace to spend myself more than ever for Your kingdom and the commission You have entrusted to us; accept me in all my weakness.'

Now, as my life was drawing to a close, I was reminded of Jesus' words, which had made such a strong impression upon me during my critical illness in 1958. 'I glorified thee on earth, having accomplished the work which thou gavest me to do' (John 17:4). That was my prayer – to be able to accomplish all that had been entrusted to me. 'Let me fully accomplish the ministry unto my daughters. Help me to fulfil the ministry to the nations by other means now. Grant that in the last years of my life I may continue with the ministry of warning and challenging others, no matter what the cost may be. Help me not to give up this task, even though I find it so hard. Let me carry out these commissions through times of seclusion, by sharing Your suffering and anguish over the apostasy of men and over their sins, which are mounting up to heaven. Lord Jesus, give me the strength to do everything possible for the commission that has been my primary task since 1952 – to help to gather those who love You from all over the world and to prepare them for the day of Your coming. Do not let me grow weary now at the end of my life when the attacks of our adversaries and their libels are increasingly disrupting the fellowship of love among Your own and almost destroying this aim of faith altogether.'

In the face of death and eternity we act differently than before. No doubt this impulse is instilled into the human soul by God so that we take advantage of the short time left and make amends as much as possible while we are still living on earth. Consequently, these years were a time when the greatest contrasts were reconciled for me: I was older and extremely frail; yet I accomplished more than ever and seldom had my working days been so long as now. Time and again when I was in a state of utter exhaustion, I would receive new strength from the Lord, living solely from His miracles. I spent much time apart with Jesus and yet I was able to achieve more than ever for the Sisterhood, the foreign branches, the Sisterhood of Thorns, the retreat guests, as well as for the writing and radio ministries.

Thus I can never thank the Lord enough for this new chapter in my life, which began in the spring of 1970 as I lay ill and eternity drew near with its solemn warning, 'Prepare yourself! Cancel the travels abroad! Set your house in order!' Even if I could not understand why the ministry to the nations seemed to end so abruptly, the truth that God's thoughts and purposes are far more extensive and marvellous than we could imagine applied to this situation in particular. Without my having to travel, this ministry now reached all parts of the world. The commission that had been entrusted to me at Mount Sinai was carried out on a far larger scale than if the journeys had been undertaken. At the same time I was able to set my house in order and equip my spiritual daughters; during my times apart with the Lord the commissions were underlaid with inner suffering ever anew, and thus they developed and branched out. Tears over my shortcomings enabled me to speak with a new and greater emphasis on the holiness of God, His coming judgements over sin, repentance as the only way to deliverance, His beckoning love that seeks us in these last times and the blessed expectation of the coming King.

Accordingly the latest pamphlets in the series dealing with relevant topics were written from the perspective of eternity and death. The practical manual in the battle of faith against sin, *So wird man anders (You Will Never Be the Same)*, which was mentioned earlier, and two other books – one about the realms of angels and demons, and the other about the after-life – were also products of these years.

Our Twenty-fifth Anniversary

Whoever 'sets his house in order' first looks to see whether the house needs a spring-cleaning and whether there are any cracks or holes, for if the house is to remain stable and retain its value, it has to be repaired in time. This was the spiritual burden the Lord laid on my heart for the Sisterhood of Mary.

Our twenty-fifth anniversary lay several months ahead, but I knew that without preparation we could not celebrate this festival or enter the future. To be sure, throughout the years we have held regular times of fellowship in the light and have had private counselling talks with the opportunity for confession, and the Lord was able to accomplish a great deal in each one of us as a result. Yet, without being able to define it properly, I sensed that in spite of everything much indifference, unlovingness, preoccupation with work, and other habitual sins had taken root. Some had lost their 'first love' for Jesus. Thus our house, which was supposed to be a 'temple' for Him, was in urgent need of a spring-cleaning. This prospect was hard for me. Nothing would have given me greater pleasure than to call all my spiritual daughters home from abroad for a 'family reunion' with festivals and times of worship, with inspiring talks about our commission, and with prayer evenings to strengthen their faith and to help them master their fear of the dark times ahead. But I knew that first there had to be a cleansing. Thus I surrendered myself to the will of God and consented to carry out this task even if it should last some days – though I did nurture the hope that joy would soon prevail and we could celebrate the festivals.

Yet it turned out differently from what I had expected. God sanctified those ten days at the end of 1971 with His presence in a special way. We were aware of Jesus' presence in our midst as Lord and Judge. When I no longer held on to my cherished plans of joyous times for my daughters, I myself was filled with the utmost resolution that Jesus might have the time and the right to drive out from our midst everything that displeased Him – even if it took all ten days. He must have the right to cleanse His 'temple', for had He not promised us, 'Here I will dwell, for I have desired it'?

As the Lord worked in our midst, I sensed how concerned He was that each one of us might be steadfast in the future, and accordingly He wished to prepare us now, before it was too late, by leading us through the fire of purification. He was aiming at the continuation of our Sisterhood for the time when we, the founders, were no longer alive, and at bringing us all to the heavenly destination – the Marriage Feast of the Lamb.

The Lord granted grace for our spiritual daughters to accept His light. The spirit of truth pervaded our Hall of Zion. No one refrained from saying that which he had to say to others in the light of God. Fear and false brotherly love, on the whole, found no place; instead true love prevailed, which does not abandon its neighbour to his sin, but assists him in his struggle for release in the name of Jesus. During those days I was conscious of God helping me from hour to hour as I led the times of fellowship in the light with the various groups of Sisters – at the time Mother Martyria happened to be ill. Then on the last day as we came together to worship and praise the Lord, we were overwhelmed by His grace. Never before had we experienced such oneness in Him as now when a song of deep thanksgiving and adoration rose in our hearts. Some of my daughters were changed almost beyond recognition, and later warm letters arrived from our Sisters abroad, expressing their gratitude for this 'cleansing of the temple', which had brought them spiritual renewal. With this event the Lord had begun His preparations for the coming jubilee festival.

As the anniversary festival drew near, one thought filled my heart. This festival must be in honour of Jesus, just as the consecration of Canaan in 1966 was a thanksgiving festival in honour of the Father. It must be a Festival of Love for Jesus where He would receive overflowing love from many souls. During this festival He must be worshipped as Lord and Bridegroom, for we had experienced His great love on Canaan. The glories of Jesus must be proclaimed in every possible way, for none can compare with Him. Jesus must be magnified before the visible and invisible world so as to compensate for all the derision and contempt He suffers today. On this occasion He was to be worshipped by a large gathering. He was to receive love, more love than ever before.

Once again I withdrew for a few days of seclusion. As I was praying about the festival, the Holy Spirit gave me the programme as well as the texts and songs for the various services. Upon the suggestion of one of the Sisters a special path was made on Canaan for the festival. We named it 'Jesus' Pathway' as a lasting memorial to His honour. On one side this path was lined with large plaques bearing inscriptions that proclaim the glories of Jesus' name.

On the first evening of the festival Jesus was to be glorified as the heavenly Bridegroom with the loveliest and most exquisite songs and melodies during a service of worship closing with Holy Communion. My ardent desire was that the songs of adoration might continue during the morning and afternoon services the next day, and that our voices might never grow silent in praising Jesus for who He is, how He led us, how He kept us spiritually alive for twenty-five years. There are no words to describe the treasure hidden in repentance and the joy He bestows upon those who love Him.

Such a festival with the sole purpose of glorifying Jesus in a world approaching midnight hour and in an age when He suffers untold blasphemy calls for a special cleansing and purification, since Satan is highly active when Christians plan to feast the Lord. Thus Mother Martyria and I included in the invitation to our friends the sincere request that during the months preceding the festival they too surrender themselves to the Lord for a new and deeper cleansing.

One cannot celebrate such a festival without proper preparation. Figuratively speaking, the clothes must be washed and ironed, and the house made neat and tidy . . . Thus our friends, some of whom will be coming across the Atlantic Ocean or the English Channel or from the north, are also being called to surrender themselves especially to God's chastenings during these last few weeks before the festival . . . May we unite in the prayer, 'Show me all the stains in my garment beforehand so that I can confess them and the blood of Jesus can wash them away. No matter what it costs, prepare me for this

Festival of Love for Jesus on Canaan.' . . . It is important that we be resolute and make an agreement with the Lord, 'Only on this condition will I go to the festival.' The Lord answers earnest prayer. Then this festal gathering will bring great comfort and joy to the Lord Jesus. The heavenly host will rejoice and the angels will carry through the spheres the songs of adoration proclaiming the glories of Jesus, who is the fairest, the purest, the noblest of all, who alone is worthy of our love – the Lamb of God and the Bridegroom of our souls . . .

But first and foremost the Lord began to speak very earnestly with us, the Sisters of Mary, taking us through a new process of inner preparation. At the festival He wished to demonstrate that He evokes exclusive, bridal love in contrite hearts and that He seeks the love of sinners who weep over their sins. God often chooses to speak through incidents in one's personal life, in tangible and visible terms that everyone can understand, as we experienced on Canaan during the months before the festival. We learnt anew how chastening leads to repentance, repentance to grace and grace to bridal love for Jesus.

As an indication that God was still waiting for deeper contrition among us He gave us no snow or rain that winter and very little rainfall in the spring. The drought, which had reached disastrous proportions throughout the country, was bound to lead to a terrible plague of pernicious insects in the coming months. Since we had abandoned the use of poisonous insecticides, the gardens and fields of Canaan were in grave danger. The harmful effect of the drought was beginning to show in the trees and shrubs; the meadows were parched and a greyish-yellow hue. The heavens remained tightly shut, even though in other parts of the country it had begun to rain. At the end of April we were struck by severe frost, and the roses, which are the symbol of love, froze and later the buds on the fruit trees. Then in June when we needed sunshine to harvest the hay, it poured for days on end. God was forced to vent His wrath upon us and stand against us – and this lasted up to three days before the festival was due to begin.

For those months I had received the following verse from the Lord in prayer, 'In overflowing wrath for a moment I hid my face from you, but with everlasting love I will have compassion on you, says the Lord, your Redeemer' (Isaiah 54:8). Then the second half of this verse was fulfilled as well. Like a stream His grace was poured out upon us. By the time the festival came, the roses had recovered from the frost and were blooming in abundance – a glorious sight. The strawberry plants had begun to bud again and brought forth more fruit than ever before, and some of the trees did yield fruit after all. Owing to the rainfall, which did come in the end, the grass had grown high and dense, and at the last moment the hay could be brought in completely dry. All the arrangements for the festival were completed with God's blessing. We were overwhelmed by His grace.

Over 1,500 guests from seventeen different countries came and everything ran smoothly. There was not one bed too many nor one too few. It seemed as though the plans had been made in heaven. The workmen finished their jobs in time. The loudspeaker system functioned properly. Everywhere an atmosphere of love and unity reigned. The spirit of joy, peace and love for Jesus rested upon the arriving guests. The weather on both days of the festival, we felt, was a special gift of His grace, and during the services of adoration the Lord was in our midst as the guests themselves testified. Later many wrote to say what an experience this festival had been for them – a festival where neverending love and worship was brought to Jesus in word and song, and He Himself was present – a festival that continued to live in their hearts. As one among many an Anglican minister said that the service of Holy Communion was like a foretaste of the Marriage Supper of the Lamb. In unity of heart and soul, we all joined in hours of worshipping and praising the Lord Jesus in the Herald Chapel, united in one fervent plea: 'O Jesus, all our love must be Yours and Yours alone.' At the mealtimes in the festival tent, songs were sung and addresses were given by friends from all over the world. We were knit together in one large family. During the festival one song resounded throughout Canaan:

O none can be loved as is Jesus,
None like Him is found anywhere.
'Tis He whom I love, whom I live for,
For no one with Him can compare.*

How my heart rejoiced! Had not my fervent request been fulfilled? Jesus had received the heartfelt praise and sincere love of many souls on those festive days.

The Emmaus Season – 1973

In the year 1972, with all the developments on the political scene, one could sense how swiftly night was falling upon the world. Thus it was very much on my heart to call all our spiritual daughters home to Canaan the following year for some weeks of spiritual training in view of the coming time of affliction. Accordingly, I sought ways and means of bringing them together once more. I could see storm clouds gathering on the political horizon, while sparks of hatred against Jesus were flaring up throughout the world and developing into a conflagration. It was the signal heralding the time when this hatred would also be directed against the members of His Body. The barometer indicated that a world-wide persecution of Christians was impending; this was the future that faced us.

At the same time iniquity was spreading and the sins of man were crying out to heaven; thus it was evident that God would soon reply by sending His judgements of wrath to destroy 'the destroyers of the earth' (Revelation 11:18). I began to pray and beseech the Lord that by then each one of us might lie before Him, judged and humbled in spirit, without the slightest protest, when He executes judgement

* *O None Can Be Loved like Jesus*, No. 32.

in His holy wrath. By that time each one of us must be so humbled beneath his own sins and so full of grief because of the iniquities of the world that he can say, 'Lord, true and just are Your judgements!' In the time of His wrath God will grant protection to those who have this attitude – provided He has not called them to suffer out of love for Him. As the Lord says in Malachi 3:17, 'They shall be mine . . . my special possession on the day when I act, and I will spare them as a man spares his son who serves him.'

Thus I prayed earnestly that God might grant Mother Martyria and me together with all our daughters a time of spiritual training, which we called the 'Emmaus Season' in memory of the conversation the Lord had with the two disciples on the road to Emmaus when He interpreted the Scriptures for them. I prayed that He who has all power and means would give us friends to take the place of our Sisters in foreign branches temporarily, and that He would cover the travelling expenses so that we could all come together for a family reunion. Mother Martyria and I had long discussions with the Sisters in charge of the various departments, and a plan was drawn up for some of the work to be done in advance or postponed until after the Emmaus Season. And the Lord answered my prayers in a wonderful way.

By the time the Emmaus Season began I had not yet fully recovered from a serious illness and thus had little strength to hold the lessons for my daughters. But every evening the Lord gave me a message that reached their hearts, providing them with an abundance of spiritual food for the times ahead. They received biblical training by studying His prophetic word for these dark times as well as spiritual guidelines and encouragement to remain steadfast in suffering. Watchwords for everyday situations, songs and prayers were added to the spiritual provisions.

Although it was a constant struggle to hold back the tide of work that sought to deluge us every day, most of the Sisters during the Emmaus Season were able to have sufficient time for quiet to digest inwardly all that they had heard. It was startling to see how the preliminary judgements of God noticeably increased from day to day during those weeks as I spoke to the Sisters about the coming time of disaster. The world had seldom faced so many catastrophes within such a short space of time – not only natural catastrophes, but also riots, strikes and acts of violence. No one could deny the fact that God had planned the Emmaus Season to take place within those very weeks, because a world disaster, preceded by Christian persecution, is impending.

At the end of the Emmaus Season we assembled in the Mother House Chapel on the evening before our Sisters serving in the foreign branches were scheduled to depart. It was an unforgettable occasion; never before had we been so conscious of God's holy presence when we were together. While I was praying beforehand, I felt led to speak about Gethsemane. I said to my daughters that Jesus was undergoing a second Gethsemane experience today, but on a world-wide scale, and that as His own we were naturally drawn into this struggle. Thus nothing else could bring them through in the coming times but that which saved Jesus in Gethsemane – His battle in prayer and His act of dedication with the words, 'Yes, Father'.

I had written a prayer for an act of dedication to suffering – an act that each one of us could make that evening. It seemed as if this were the last opportunity God would give us to come together in this manner before the time of affliction, and thus it was a painful moment as we said farewell to each one of our Sisters stationed abroad, especially to those going to Jerusalem. Shortly after our Sisters arrived in Jerusalem, they received a number of anonymous telephone calls and then the first threatening letter demanding that they leave the country within four weeks. As Christians they had come under the attack of an underground terrorist movement.

If any one of us had not known the heart of God the Father before, he certainly came to do so during the Emmaus Season. How good, how gracious, how caring, how loving of Him to grant us this time! During the hours we spent together we learnt what God is like. Against the background of the coming suffering, the nature of God the Father and of the Lord Jesus shone more brightly than ever, like a light illumining the darkness. God is eternal Love. He has pledged Himself to help His own in the time of affliction. He is the Almighty One, who is always able to lend help, who is greater than all terror, greater than hostile forces and satanic powers. And indeed, we were so overwhelmed by this love that even the fearful ones among our daughters radiantly declared that fear could no longer have dominion over them; they had learnt to believe – even in view of the coming suffering – that His heart is love, pure love.

Other Christians hearing of our Emmaus Season were most eager to have some share of our experiences. I myself was consumed with a burning ardour to help to prepare the people of today, especially the Christians, for the hard times that lie ahead, which no one will be able to escape and which will bring death to millions. Thus my constant prayer was that the Lord would grant me a new booklet, which could be widely circulated and even distributed in newspaper form. I yearned that it would serve to alert many, bringing them to repentance and giving them guidelines for preparing to meet the future. God answered my prayer by granting me two booklets simultaneously – one primarily designed for Christians* and the other for the public in general.**

However, with the atheistic extremist movements advancing, the threat of war increasing daily, and the campaign of libel and persecution against our Sisterhood well underway, it was truly a race with time to pass on this message.

* *The Eve of Persecution.*

** *Countdown to World Disaster – Hope and Protection for the Future.*

Becoming Like Him in His Death

To Stand at His Side in Degradation

To love Jesus is our calling. My greatest desire for my spiritual daughters was that they would live up to this vocation. Love for Jesus was the pearl of great price that I had found after a long search, and thus it was especially precious to me. I found complete happiness and fulfilment to my life in this exclusive, bridal love for Jesus, which brought me the solution to all my problems and questions. Ever since His love had wooed me and kindled my heart with love for Him, all my thoughts and emotions have revolved round Him. He is the centre of my life. 'Jesus, Jesus!' His name would ring in my heart. Jesus evoked from me prayers of adoration and songs to His honour. He accomplished that which no person could ever have achieved with his love. No one but Jesus could have induced me to choose a way of life that totally contradicted my nature, by calling me to enter seclusion. Only He could have moved me to carry out my much-disputed ministry of warning, in a world torn by conflicting opinions.

In this love for Jesus I was completely united with Him. His life was my life, and His sufferings were mine as well. That which grieved Him grieved me also. When He was not loved, when He was rejected or even hated, it was natural that my heart was set aflame with greater love and devotion, and that I yearned to offer Him solace and comfort.

During this last period of my life, I was filled with immeasurable grief because of the sufferings of Jesus. With the outbreak of amorality, with the unbridling of all passions and the glorification of sin, the forces of evil had caused a dam to burst and soon the deluge was covering the earth. A new flood followed – once again unleashed by the powers of darkness. Defamation and blasphemy of God, ridicule and degradation of Jesus Christ swept across the countries. Satan himself began to make an appearance. For the first time in the history of Christendom there is an officially registered Church of Satan and a Black Pope in the United States, in addition to thousands of Satanist priests, countless numbers of Satan worshippers, a Satanic Bible, gruesome black masses and satanic cults that require human sacrifices. And all the adherents of Satan thrive on the hatred of Jesus Christ.

All these manifestations of evil were spreading like wildfire, but even so Satan was not content. He intended to pervade all strata of mankind, even the Church, with his blasphemies – and he succeeded. Theatrical productions of unprecedented vileness such as *Hair*, *Superstar* and *Godspell*, concoctions of the infernal regions, hit the stages and took over church halls from the United States across Europe to Australia. In some cities they ran for years, often with several performances a day and the tickets sold out weeks in advance. But when films of these stage productions were made, they began to take the world at large. In these presentations Jesus is dishonoured in the most degrading manner, and the audiences – frequently comprising churchgoers, children's groups, Christian youth groups and students from Christian colleges – applaud as Jesus, the Son of God, is portrayed as a clown and a simpleton. But even more terrible was the prospect of a film about 'the love affairs of Jesus Christ'; the film producer tenaciously clung to his plans for this film, which has been advertised as 'blasphemous, pornographic and sadistic'!

To read and hear of these terrible blasphemies caused me deep anguish, for if we love someone, we cannot bear to see him so degraded. Grief-stricken, I thought of my Lord as I knew Him. Jesus is the fairest, the purest, endowed with divine dignity and love. Jesus, exalted, glorified and majestic, is Ruler and Creator of all worlds and all men. But now an exhibition was being made of Him. He was being held up as an object of scorn and derision before millions of people throughout the world.

My heart was filled with lamentation. Long ago Jesus was

crowned with thorns, blasphemed and ridiculed in only one country, by Romans and Jews, whereas today almost every nation, particularly the 'Christian' ones, participate in the derision and blasphemy of Jesus. Today Christians who know of Jesus as the Lord and Son of God, even committed Christians who profess Jesus as their personal Saviour, applaud this derision.

Before me I saw a picture of Pilate showing Jesus to the clamorous mob. Shamelessly humiliated, disfigured by the blows and flogging, clad in rags, Jesus was degraded beneath the level of a human being. Words of contempt were flung at Him – 'Is that supposed to be the Son of God?' It was the hour of deepest humiliation for our Lord Jesus, Son of the Most High! But now, when Jesus was portrayed surrounded by capering clowns and half-naked women, His authority as Judge of the world derided, His Passion ridiculed, and His farewell discourses parodied, I sometimes felt that my heart could bear it no longer. In spirit I could only fall down weeping at the feet of my Lord, who was so dishonoured, though He is Sovereign of the universe; I could only worship His humility in submitting to such treatment. In order that more souls might be saved, He endures such degradation and continues to wait before venting His wrath. In His immeasurable love He suffers the vilest blasphemies so that His own might be shown the way to glory. His hour of deepest disgrace is the opportunity for them to demonstrate not only their faith in Him, but also their willingness to suffer for His sake out of love and gratitude.

I had but one longing – to stand close by my Lord and Saviour in His deep humiliation. Full of anguish over *Godspell* and *Superstar*, I wrote two pamphlets* against these productions. They were then distributed in various countries, with a circulation running into hundreds of thousands. And it was a privilege to learn that a number of people and groups who had nearly fallen prey to this deception experi-

* An answer to *Godspell*: . . . *but at whose expense?* (British edition); *Jesus Blasphemed Again* (American edition). An answer to *Superstar: Jesus Mocked Today.*

enced a change of heart and then even helped to protect others from this harmful influence. They held prayer meetings and distributed the pamphlets and also prevented further performances.

Yet I felt that all this was not enough, since the tide of blasphemy was steadily advancing. New stage and film productions were cropping up, with even worse examples of perversion and filth being shown in connection with Jesus or God the Father.

How often we had sung the verse:

Jesus, all our love must be Yours,
and Yours alone –
Love and consolation for all Your love outpoured.

Today it meant sharing Jesus' anguish at an even deeper level out of love for Him. Never before in history has anyone been so degraded and ridiculed in the eyes of the whole world as Jesus Christ, to whom all love and honour is due. How could I bring Him love and consolation for all His love outpoured? He knew.

In 1970 I was away once more for a time of seclusion when a Sister arrived from the Mother House; she had come expressly to deliver a serious letter to me. The director of a gospel literature service had sent me a circular letter that he had received. In this letter he was bidden to sever connections with us, not to publicise my writings any more and by no means to distribute them, for otherwise it would be necessary to take action against his organisation also. The letter went on to say that if he continued to pass on my books, he would be endorsing my message – the message of a 'dangerous heretic, inspired by a demonic spirit', and that as a result, he himself would come under the influence of this spirit.

Instantly I realised that this was not an isolated event, for with this letter the Evil One's strategy was disclosed. A systematic attack had been planned against my person and the Sisterhood, in order to destroy our commission. At the time I did not fully realise that the ensuing disgrace was the

Lord's answer to my prayer that I may stand by Him when He is so degraded. Since the letter arrived directly after my birthday, I took it as a sign that Jesus was calling me to descend even further into the vale of humiliation in the coming year.

This circular letter signified the launching of a campaign, and soon arrows from every side were hitting me. In the following weeks letters arrived from other Christian organisations that had received the circular letter. These were well-known and influential organisations in our country, whose words were heeded by committed Christians. They too had been threatened, and now some of them were asking for clarification. Behind it all was a man who had resumed the attack against us, harking back to the above-mentioned book of the evangelist with its serious charges and false assertions about us, which was published in 1965. As the spiritual son of the author, this man had taken over the campaign to destroy our organisation, making it his life's mission after the evangelist's death.

He was so taken up with this task, which he felt bound to carry out for the sake of God, that, as he confessed in a letter, this undertaking was almost beyond his time and energy. He requested many personages in the Christian world – some of whom he visited personally – to supply him with the 'incriminating evidence' that he needed in order to support his campaign against the Sisterhood and my person. He also approached leading men in confessional movements and asked for meetings to be convened where he could put forward his false accusations and distorted accounts so that others would take action against us. Throughout the country he held lectures against us and gathered allies to work hand in glove with him in pursuing his goal, which was the destruction of our organisation. And he succeeded in finding confederates, some of whom were envious of the world-wide radius of our commission.

In actual fact it was well known in the Christian circles concerned that this man readily used lies and that his charges against us were not true. Nevertheless even Christian leaders who had taken a neutral stand passed on the slander or did not hinder it, although they realised the injustice of the matter and the harmful effect this libel had upon Christian bodies within the Church. The poisonous seeds that were now sown had even more devastating effects than those in the first twenty years of our Sisterhood.

One report superseded another during these two years. At a large rally for young committed Christians a well-known minister publicly issued a warning against us. In the invitation to a workshop conference of one of the confessional movements the watchword was given – 'war on two fronts'. It was stated that one had to combat not only liberal theology but also an enthusiastic type of Christianity, that is, religious fanaticism, by which we were chiefly meant. The main stronghold against us was situated in northwest Germany, but there were also bases in the southern region. The above-mentioned man established contact, for instance, with a large Christian organisation in the south, which then formed another main stronghold, since its range of influence covered many pietistic circles.

Thus the organisations and fellowships of committed Christians were systematically contaminated by toxic seeds: 'The Sisterhood of Mary is demonic and occult.' Once again the evangelist's book published in 1965 was cited as the main source of evidence: connections with the Roman Catholic Church, charismatic gifts, Herald Plays, emphasis on leading a life of contrition and repentance . . . In addition, 'evidence' from our life was produced; events were listed that had never taken place. For example, it was claimed that a Sister had died from fasting in Israel and that another Sister had died from appendicitis, since we were too fanatical to let her have an operation. And when some believers simply could not understand why we were considered so dangerous, they were told, 'Don't you know that the devil has broken in upon the Sisterhood of Mary?'

Each new report was like a sword piercing my heart. The 'war on two fronts' had been fanned into flame, but within me a fire was set ablaze – a fire of faith and love. Over twenty years ago I had consecrated my life to God for the healing of the breaches in the torn Body of Christ and for the ending of envy and quarrelling among God's children. Ever since then I had spent myself for this cause – and now such contention flared up because of the Sisterhood and me. True, we had always been the focal point of such controversy, but this time the campaign was brought into the open on a far larger scale, and it continued to spread.

The Lord – so I thought at the time – could only have permitted Satan so much scope in this situation, because He intended this enmity to be overcome by even greater love and faith, and wished to manifest His victorious love. It was my firm belief that God would then grant the world the witness of the true body of believers, who would stand together in the unity of love in this age, when many are departing from the faith.

The Lord granted me a special moment of grace in April 1971. A spirit of faith, which hopes against hope, which was not of myself but of God, came over me as I cried from the depths of my heart, 'God cannot let the lies win in the end! Satan cannot have the final victory and destroy the Body of Christ!' Mother Martyria, who in particular shared this suffering for Jesus' sake, and all my spiritual daughters were drawn into this era of faith. In the evenings we would come together for battles of faith and we would hold special times of prayer for this concern. I had the triumphant assurance that God could not fail to keep His word. Now, as I told myself, it was only a matter of persevering in faith and being patient in order to experience victory in the end when the Body of Christ would no longer be torn and believers would be united to form an oasis for Jesus and a fortress against the arch-enemy in an age when Satan exerts such a strong influence. Promises from the Bible strengthened my faith that the Lord would accomplish His purposes. For instance, 'Is anything too hard for the Lord?' (Genesis 18:14); 'With God nothing will be impossible' (Luke 1:37).

In retrospect I cannot thank the Lord enough for giving me love for my adversaries in the midst of all that happened and moving me to pray much for them. I would spend hours singing songs of faith for them and their ministries, and would ask God to bless their organisations and fellowships. Whenever I did so, claiming the blood of the Lamb for them, I looked forward in faith to the day when Jesus would prove Himself mightier and dispel all the hatred from their hearts.

Shortly afterwards a number of incidents occurred which strengthened our faith. Victory seemed to be at hand. A few Christian brothers decided to take steps; for Jesus' sake they could no longer bear to stand by while havoc was being wreaked. A businessman, who was a Canaan Friend, was moved by the Spirit of God to write an open letter concerning 'the distressing situation among groups of committed Christians and confessional believers'. Well-known Christians signed this circular letter, which was then distributed by the thousand.

A senior district judge, the chairman of the City Mission in our town – who as a local resident was qualified to speak – issued a declaration in support of the Sisterhood, because he was so grieved by the libellous attacks made on us. He stated that owing to his position in the City Mission he had been closely associated with us for over ten years in a ministry in the poorest districts of our town; he testified to 'the God-given unity, the mutual love and respect in accomplishing this task'. Furthermore, he made it clear that the *Starkenburger Gemeinschaftsverband*, which is in charge of our district, and the regional *Gemeinschaftskreise* had established that they had no cause to warn others against us. As a lawyer, he pointed out that the libel printed about us

> . . . would have long since been confiscated by the court, and the making of such assertions would have been prohibited if the Sisters of Mary had taken the appropriate measures and filed a suit. In the world people are far more cautious in this respect than in circles of believers where there is no hesitation to defame other groups. In the world people would tread more carefully

for financial reasons, since they would be liable to incur fines for making untrue and ungrounded assertions . . .

In addition, there were other Christian personages, some of whom previously had had little contact with us, but who out of love for the truth felt called to take steps and tried to clarify matters in talks with members of the boards of various Christian organisations.

God seemed to be answering. At a convention of a confessional movement it was even publicly stated that they had nothing to do with this man who 'has already caused so much harm', and a move was made to exclude him from the organisation. The evangelist's book, which he had widely distributed, was no longer to be recommended, but rather warned against, and the majority of the participants – including a large number of ministers – declared themselves in favour of the Sisterhood of Mary. In addition, a Christian radio station in our country was willing to include our programmes in its schedule, after having received many requests for them.

The joy at all this news was as great as the suffering that had preceded it. One evening in particular I shall never forget. We had just received a further piece of good news. Mother Martyria and I, together with our spiritual daughters, were so happy that after our evening meeting was over we continued to give thanks, even making a procession through the house with songs of praise. At last the love of Jesus had been victorious over contention, slander and hatred – or so it seemed. The 'fellowship of love', the body of true believers, whose distinguishing features are unity and love for one another, was beginning to materialise. Our fervent prayers had been answered.

But then there was a sudden swerve in the opposite direction. The initiator of the wave of persecution was not expelled from that particular organisation, since no one had the courage to take action against him. Thus the scene was completely changed. The circular letters that were intended to establish the truth remained generally ineffective. The

Christian radio station was no longer willing to broadcast our programmes, since it had received many letters from our opponents imploring the company not to include us in the schedule – otherwise they would be forced to withdraw their collaboration and support.

Not even the publication of a pastoral word about our Sisterhood changed the atmosphere. A small group of brothers in the Lord, troubled by the effects of the campaign of slander in Christian circles, had come together and taken the initiative out of their sense of responsibility. They decided to publish *A Pastoral Word about the Evangelical Sisterhood of Mary in Darmstadt-Eberstadt* as the outcome of their personal investigation in order to help the many people who had become confused because of the poisonous seeds that had been sown. For instance, they wrote:

> . . . Speaking from personal observation and experience, we declare that many have found salvation, deliverance from sin, and the joy of Christ as a result of a sound proclamation of the Word. Through the ministry of the Sisters of Mary, above all through their literature, many have come to a living faith in Jesus Christ and have become active members in their churches. Others have been led on spiritually and have grown in the faith as a result of this ministry and have then conveyed these blessings to their churches.
>
> We have ascertained that the message of Holy Scripture in its entirety is the sole foundation and guiding principle of the faith, life and proclamation of the Sisterhood of Mary . . .

The *Pastoral Word*, which these brothers distributed by the thousand in our country, was signed by over a hundred clergy and laymen, including many well-known Christian leaders. However, no considerable effect was evident, since the *Pastoral Word* found little admittance to the circles mainly affected by the slander; an iron blockade had been raised there by our adversaries. In some cases the *Pastoral Word* did help to free Christians of their inner conflicts and make them immune to the poison in the seeds of defamation, but the overall effect was that of greater antagonism on the part of our opponents. The fact that a number of well-known Christians from their own organisations had signed the *Pastoral Word* made them seek new ways of destroying our ministry.

Friends and groups that had been well-disposed towards us became reserved and in the end took sides against us. At various places throughout the country Christian leaders held meetings at which the Sisterhood of Mary was the topic of discussion – even while we were celebrating our twenty-fifth anniversary, the Festival of Love for Jesus. Every time there was a sharp clash of opinion. The fanatical attitude of the adversaries was so great that neither those who were neutral nor those favourably inclined towards us were a match for them.

One day Canaan Friends from a neighbouring country came to me in deep sorrow. For years they had been distributing our literature in their country, receiving many requests for our sound slide series to be shown; furthermore, large numbers of their countrymen attended retreats on Canaan. Their 'retired life' had become 'full-time service' for the Lord and they worked zealously because there was so much spiritual hunger in their country for the message they brought from Canaan – the message that contrition is the pathway to love for Jesus and a joy-filled life. But now everything collapsed. Waves of defamation – inspired by the same spirit – were spreading on the other side of the border with the result that many of the Christians there lost interest. No one wished to have any more dealings with Sisters who – as our opponents maintained and propagated – were 'occult, spiritistic and demonic'.

One of the hardest blows for me, however, was the news that a large evangelical missionary radio station, which had been broadcasting our programmes for some time, suddenly cancelled them – again the cause could be traced back to the same source. I knew how great the demand was for spiritual nourishment. Yet, with this blow, the Evil One had succeeded in causing more devastation; millions of souls were affected, including our brethren behind the Iron Curtain for whom programmes had just been prepared.

All this was a Moriah experience on a large scale, bringing me immeasurable grief. Had the arch-enemy thus succeeded in his plan to destroy our ministry and to disrupt the unity within the Body of Christ? Had the promises of God from Scripture not been fulfilled? Had the earnest entreaties not been answered? Had our faith, then, been in vain? Although I had completely dedicated myself to the incomprehensible will of God, time and again my heart was filled with agony at the question WHY.

This campaign had begun in the same year the Lord had shown me that I was approaching the end of my life. Did this imply that of all the commissions there was one commission that would not be fulfilled, although it had been part of my life the longest – the commission to help to gather those who love Jesus? Was I to end my days, identified by my adversaries as 'a demonically-inspired heretic'? What divine purpose could be behind God's act of raising these fanatical, hate-filled opponents? Why did He send this major onslaught from the Evil One, permitting him to disrupt the unity among believers more vehemently than ever – now, during the last years of my life?

Following the Lamb of God

In the darkness of this night a ray of light came from above. A picture came to mind – similar to that which Master Gruenewald had painted on the Isenheim Altar – the picture of the Lamb, and I was reminded of how Jesus endured the cruel blows, the malice, the lies and slander like a lamb on His way to the cross. The picture of the Lamb never left me. Step by step, clasping His cross firmly, the Lamb resolutely moved forward to meet His death, with blood trickling down from the wounds that malice, ridicule and derision had inflicted on Him along the way to Calvary. Gruenewald's painting shows how the drops of blood are gathered into a chalice from which others would then drink the blessings of salvation and healing and in this way the host of true believers would be edified. It was like a divine summons from Jesus. The Lamb of God led the way for His little lambs, His own, to follow Him step by step, tightly embracing their cross, which like His often consists of disgrace and slander, of injustice and contempt. The Lamb of God, whom Paul Gerhardt, a seventeenth-century hymnist, wrote about, grew more dear to me than all else.

> A Lamb goes uncomplaining forth,
> The guilt of all men bearing...
> Goes patient on, grows weak and faint,
> To slaughter led without complaint...

No longer did I have to ask about justice and about the truth being established. No longer did I have to ask, 'When will the members of the Body of Christ be won over by the truth and knit together? When will all the prayers be answered?' I knew that this was the path to take, for where He goes we must go too. Thus amid the pain and sorrow I encountered along this path, I rejoiced to accompany Him – despised, maligned, derided. Not for all the world would I have given up this privilege of following in His footsteps and of sharing His life.

In this picture of the Lamb I found the answer to my questions about why the truth did not prevail in spite of all my entreaties and faith. In Jesus' earthly life the truth had not been victorious either; instead, His enemies won. All the seeds sown by Jesus were destroyed by the Pharisees. In the end His own people turned on Him and even His disciples deserted Him. Falsehood triumphed, for the contemporary religious world regarded Him as a heretic, an imposter and a criminal. He was said to have a demon and to stir up the people.

I knew that Jesus longs for His own to reflect His image, the image of the Lamb. He seeks followers that do not complain and sigh when burdens are placed on them, but who keep their eyes fixed on the Lamb of God when they suffer disgrace, injustice and slander. He seeks His image in us, longing for us to follow Him step by step in love, and in gratitude for the privilege of sharing His path. Along this path the greatest of all is accomplished. Death is followed by resurrection, not only for our personal lives but also for the body of believers. How I thanked the Lord for those years of practice as He led me along many paths of disgrace, for now my soul was at peace and I could love and bless my enemies. Yet the Lord wished to create even greater love in my heart, reminding me of the words of His prayer, 'They know not what they do'.

Although my sorrow was great, I felt deeply consoled, for is not the fellowship of Jesus' sufferings the highest privilege of all? What can be greater than to bear reproach for His sake and to share the sufferings of Him who loved us so much that He laid down His life for us? He is our one true Love, the Bridegroom of our souls, the King of kings, seated at the right hand of majesty in great splendour, and He will come again in glory. Was it not a mark of election to see the words of Scripture come true for my life, 'The disciple is not above his master' but 'as his master' (Matthew 10:24f. AV)?

Thus I knew that I had to choose the path of my Lord and, by doing so, to choose Jesus first and foremost, the Man of Sorrows. Many years had elapsed since I first made this act of dedication, and Jesus not only let me partake of His sufferings in the hidden life when I drew apart to be with Him alone, but He also let me experience the reality of the fellowship of His sufferings in the practical issues of life.

After all the blows and disappointments, after all the Moriah experiences during the battles of faith and prayer for the victory of love among His own, the Lord had comforted me by turning my gaze to the Lamb of God. But was I now prepared to surrender myself unconditionally to Jesus, the Lord crowned with shame, and adhere to this decision to the very end? Was I prepared to prove my love for Him by submitting myself together with my entire life-work to the hardest blow we had yet encountered and which would have far-reaching consequences?

So far, in spite of all the attacks of the Evil One, Canaan had continued to be 'sought out, a city not forsaken'. Retreats were held for guests from many countries. Crowds flocked to the Herald Plays. Services of worship took place with hundreds coming forward for Holy Communion. Canaan was populated by young people from all parts of the world. The publishing house was flooded with orders. The radio and tape department had high season all year long. The printing press, which had long ceased to meet the demand, was obliged to have many a printing job done elsewhere . . . My heart was filled with anguish at the thought that all this could be destroyed.

Was that how my days were to end, after I had lived all my life for those who love Jesus to be knit together as a fellowship of love, foreshadowing of the Kingdom of God? With my consent and dedication I had to face daily the growing possibility that our commission would lie before me in ruins. That would entail the falling away of our friends, the disruption of the groups that had formed spiritually alive centres in various countries, and the discrediting of the message, which had been spread throughout the world through my writings and through the radio programmes.

In the midst of this inner conflict I asked the Lord for a verse of Scripture and received in prayer 1 Corinthians 4:9, which I was deeply moved to read in one of the English versions of the Bible.

For it seems to me that God has made an exhibit of us apostles, exposing us to view last [of all, like men in a triumphal procession who are] sentenced to death [and displayed at the end of the line]. For we have become a spectacle to the world – a show in the world's amphitheatre – with both men and angels (as spectators).

(*The Amplified Bible*)

The Lord could not have spoken more distinctly or more mercifully. As I read this verse, I was cut to my heart, for is it not our Lord Jesus who is being made a laughingstock before the whole world today? An exhibition is being made of Him in the eyes of all mankind; He is blasphemed and derided in stage and film productions, on television and on records, degraded more than any human being. Like a captive displayed in a triumphal procession, Jesus is made a spectacle to the world. How often I had asked myself in view of such derision, 'What can I possibly do to bring Jesus joy and consolation in His sufferings today?' And now this verse of Scripture had given me a clear answer. 'Accompany Jesus along His path of degradation and share His disgrace. Stand at the side of your Lord and Saviour, who is treated with such dishonour and contempt. In doing so, you will comfort Him, for along this path of sorrows your prayer to help to gather those who love Him and to yield fruit for Him will be fulfilled.'

That the Lord was seeking my total dedication to accompany Him along the path of disgrace was confirmed shortly afterwards by an incident on Ascension Day, 1973. During intermission at a large rally of confessional movements, attended by some 20,000 people from all over the country, a voice suddenly came over the loudspeaker. 'The distribution of literature from the Sisterhood of Mary is forbidden and must stop instantly.' Other pamphlets were also being handed out, but the warning was directed specifically against us. The announcement was repeated several times; in conclusion, the remark was added that they had nothing to do with us. A commotion ensued in the hall and there were many indignant murmurs. What had happened? A minister's wife from Westphalia had asked the leader of the convention beforehand if she and her ladies' group could hand out my latest number in the series of booklets dealing with current matters – as was often the case at such gatherings. He readily gave permission, and most of the participants accepted the booklets gratefully. However, as soon as our adversaries took in the situation, they asked for an

409

announcement to be made over the loudspeaker system. Not only was the distribution of our literature at the rally forbidden, but from that time onwards they spread the rumour that the Sisters of Mary do not even heed prohibitions, and used this statement as a confirmation of their warnings against us.

Yet I knew that this was only a further stage in walking along the path with Jesus. It might even reach the point where my name would be denounced before many thousands throughout the world who had heard our message and knew of me. It is an honour to be persecuted by those who are known to be antagonistic to God and who have no desire to be anything else. It is more of a joy, since one is obviously hated for Jesus' sake. But to be hated and persecuted by those who call Jesus their Saviour cuts to the quick, since they are one's brothers in the Lord. This type of persecution does not bring honour, but rather deepest disgrace in the sight of the Christian world, for one is made to stand outside the camp, expelled from the fellowship of believers.

With increasing clarity the Lord showed me that this was Jesus' pathway. His path led to crucifixion and burial, the ruin of His lifework before it was crowned with victory and resurrection. Thus it is not primarily along the path of faith that Jesus knits together those who love Him – although faith is essential – but rather along the path of disgrace, of unrewarded faith, of destruction, of suffering, along the path of crucifixion. Only then does faith receive true depth, since one must believe in spite of disappointments, destruction and death and endure the agony when God seems to act against Himself and His very word.

'He is wonderful in counsel, and excellent in wisdom'

The marvellous purposes of God unfolded before my eyes. The final outcome would not be the ruin of His commissions and the disruption of the unity among those who love Him,

410

but rather the exact opposite. When there is anguish and when wounds are bleeding, out of the soil of suffering a new shoot will rise – the body of true believers. Only when Jesus' disciples enter death with Him, can those who love Him emerge as one body and come to life. Now I could no longer be surprised when, in our case too, the opponents were victorious, despite the fact that their falsehoods and slander could be proved as such. This was the right way; it would lead to resurrection, and when the Lord's time had come the host of those who love Him would come to full bloom – even if I should not live to see it.

In His grace God granted me faith that stretched beyond the abyss of destruction that lay directly before me. He gave me a glimpse far into the future. He was not concerned about small, momentary victories with a little more concord between members of His Body in one country, but rather about the whole body of believers being sifted, purified and prepared, and the bride of the Lamb being completed in number and attaining maturity. Before me I could see the ultimate goal of God's marvellous purposes, which He accomplishes along pathways of death – 'Behold, I make all things new!' How Jesus rejoices at the prospect of the Marriage Feast of the Lamb when the first fruits come home, having been completed in number and having attained full maturity! What a consolation it will be for Jesus to receive the greatest reward for all His suffering – the bride of the Lamb. Then for all eternity He will have the bride at His side – souls who have been made like Him through the power of His sacrificial atonement, and who bear the traits of the Lamb. To live and suffer for this goal is the deepest fulfilment there can be to one's life.

What greater privilege could Jesus have granted me than to let me offer the suffering I underwent in disgrace as a contribution towards the consummation of the bridal host, in accordance with the words of Paul, 'Therefore I endure everything for the sake of the elect . . . ' 'In my flesh I complete what is lacking in Christ's afflictions' (2 Timothy 2:10; Colossians 1:24)?

How could my personal life still be of importance to me when God's vast and eternal plans were involved? Without exception His thoughts are higher and far more glorious than we could ever imagine. The more futile our pathways seem; the more our prayers, our waiting and suffering appear to be in vain, the more glorious will be the resurrection that we shall experience.

Thus ever since 1973 I had another favourite song, a Bible verse, set to music, which I would sing to the accompaniment of the organ many an evening and sometimes in the middle of the day. At a very dark moment the Lord had given me this verse, which filled me with triumphant faith: He is 'wonderful in counsel, [and] excellent in wisdom and effectual working' (Isaiah 28:29 *The Amplified Bible*).

After that year as I lay seriously ill on the verge of death, my greatest plea to the Lord was, 'Grant me the grace to fulfil the commission You have entrusted to me. Lord, do not call me to my eternal home before that.' And He answered this prayer – differently than I had expected, but far more gloriously. He let me partake of the fellowship of His sufferings, 'becoming like him in his death' to use the words of Paul (Philippians 3:10).

Now as my life draws to a close, I am filled with deep gratitude that He has counted me worthy to share His path, in particular the path of disgrace. In this fellowship with Him I have found the deepest fulfilment of all for my life.

Other Books by Basilea Schlink Which You May Wish to Read:

My All for Him—$1.25
A moving collection of powerful meditations on the demands of God upon Christians, and the happiness which follows obedience.
Original title: *Alles Fuer Einen*, 1969. Foreign translations: Norwegian, 1970; Indonesian, 1970; English, 1971-72; Italian, 1973.

You Will Never Be the Same—$1.45
A highly illuminating series of short chapters describing how to successfully deal with specific sins still clinging to the Christian's life.
Original title: *So Wird Man Anders*, 1971. Foreign translations: English, 1972; Norwegian, 1972; Swedish, 1972; Dutch, 1973; Finnish, 1973.

Hope for Man in a Hopeless World—95¢
An appraisal of the causes of the world's present plight, and a declaration of the "way out" by cooperation with God.
Original title: *Und Keiner Wollte Es Glauben*, 1964. Foreign translations: Danish, 1965; Dutch, 1965; Swedish, 1966; French, 1966; English, 1967-72; Finnish, 1967.

Ruled by the Spirit—$1.25
The power of God available today to dedicated Christians. Plus testimonies from among the Sisterhood which indicate how an invigorating working relationship with the Holy Spirit may be enjoyed.
Original title: *Wo Der Geist Weht*, 1967. Foreign translations: French, 1968; Swedish, 1968; Norwegian, 1968; English, 1970; Dutch, 1970.

Father of Comfort—$1.25
Short devotions for each day of the year, intended to teach how to trust God as Father.
Original title: *Der Niemand Traurig Sehen Kann*, 1965. Foreign translations: Greek, 1968; French, 1970; Indonesian, 1970; Italian, 1971; English, 1971-72; Arabic, 1972; Chinese (Mand.), 1972; Norwegian, 1972.

Behold His Love—$1.45
This book is addressed to those who desire to meditate prayerfully on the passion of Jesus, so that they may be led more and more into the way of the cross and into the unity of love with those who love Him.

A Matter of Life and Death—95¢
The rape of planet earth—what caused it, and what to do to remedy it. Carefully documented treatment of the widely discussed problem of global pollution.
Original title: *Umweltverschmutzung Und Dennoch Hoffnung*, 1972. Foreign translations: Dutch, 1973; Finnish, 1973; Italian, 1973; Swedish, 1973.

World in Revolt (booklet)—25¢
An astute review and analysis of the waves of revolution rolling over the modern world, and a plain statement on what can be done about it.

Praying Our Way Through Life (booklet)—25¢
Counsel on how to react to God during suffering, times of unanswered prayer, temptations, worry, despondency, and fear.
Original title: *Mein Beten*, 1969. Foreign translations: English, 1970-71; Swedish, 1971; Norwegian, 1971; Chinese (Mand.), 1971; Indonesian, 1972; Finnish, 1972; Arabic, 1973.

Never Before in the History of the Church (booklet)—50¢
A startling examination of "the Harlot Church" as it exists today in the world.

Mirror of Conscience (booklet)—25¢
A guidebook to earnest Christians genuinely interested in examining the areas of their lives in which they may need victory.

It Shall Come To Pass (booklet)—25¢
A delightfully sympathetic consideration of the attitude older Christians should have toward the "Jesus People."

Available at your local Christian bookstore, or BETHANY FELLOWSHIP, INC., 6820 Auto Club Rd., Minneapolis, Minnesota 55438.